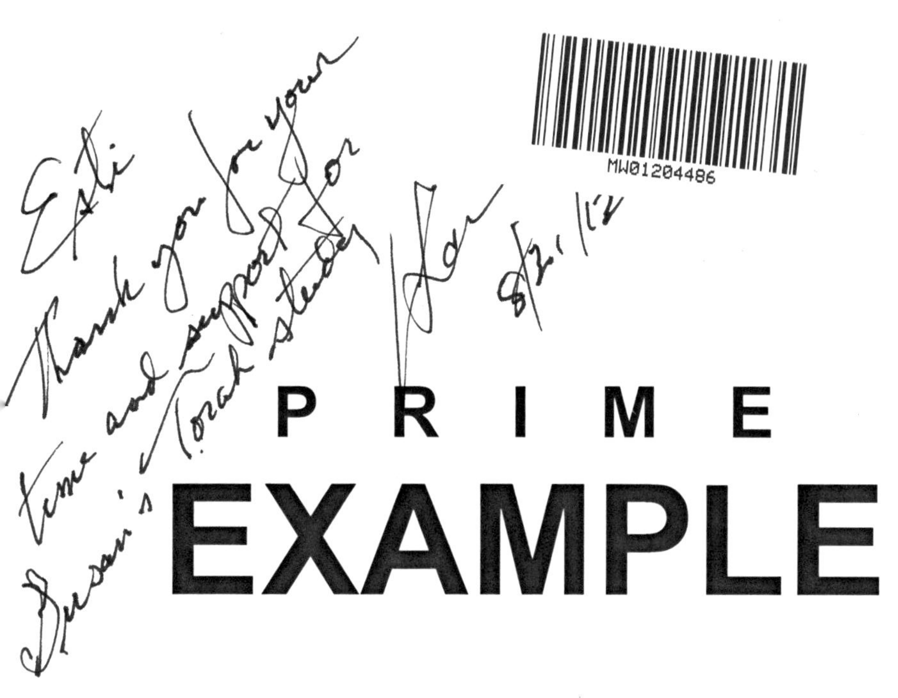

PRIME EXAMPLE

THE TRUE STORY of the Case that Saved ALTERNATIVE MEDICINE in New York State

ROBERT H. HARRIS

NEW YORK

P R I M E EXAMPLE

The True Story of the Case that Saved Alternative Medicine in New York State

by **ROBERT H. HARRIS**

ISBN 978-1-61448-025-9 Paperback
ISBN 978-1-61448-026-6 Ebook
Library of Congress Control Number: 2011927633

Published by:
Morgan James Publishing
The Entrepreneurial Publisher
5 Penn Plaza, 23rd Floor
New York City, New York 10001
(212) 655-5470 Office
(516) 908-4496 Fax
www.MorganJamesPublishing.com

Cover Design by:
Rachel Lopez
rachel@r2cdesign.com

Interior Design by:
Bonnie Bushman
bbushman@bresnan.net

My love to Florina

INTRODUCTION

For thousands of years people who were referred to or called themselves Doctor gained the title by learning whatever was known about medicine in their day from those who came before them.

In the 19th century the practice of medicine became more institutionalized and medical schools proliferated to specifically train people to be physicians.

When students in a medical school completed their training they either did some sort of an internship or went into practice. They did not need a license from anyone. Local medical societies dealt with issues of incompetence, negligence, sexual inappropriateness and a host of other things and they conducted what were often informal gatherings or hearings to determine what, if anything, should be done to deal with their colleague.

In the 20th century one state after another imposed a requirement of licensing for those who wanted to practice medicine. The feeling was that by granting a license they could take it away as a punishment and also require a minimum amount of knowledge to obtain a license in the first place. As time went on states began to use medical licenses as a source of revenue simply because it was a place where they could impose a tax without too much political fallout.

In New York State physicians are licensed under the education law and were, for many years, disciplined by the New York State Education Department.

Sometime around the middle of the 20th century New York State created the office of professional medical conduct under the authority of the Commissioner of Health. The OPMC, as it has come to be known, set up an apparatus for licensing and disciplining physicians.

The system was never created for fairness. It utilizes administrative law judges who serve at the pleasure of the Commissioner of Health. Hearings are conducted by panel members, two of whom are required to be physicians, who are answerable to the Commissioner of Health. The prosecution works with the Atty. Gen. of the State of New York but in truth and in fact is answerable to the Commissioner of Health. If someone wanted to outline the definition of a kangaroo court this would probably be it.

Disciplinary proceedings are not criminal in nature so there is no grand jury to protect the accused. Decisions as to whether or not to prosecute a physician are generally made by investigators (often nurses who don't like nursing) and consulting physicians, all of whom work for the Commissioner of Health.

It was into this grossly unfair, stacked deck, that Warren Levin found himself a part of. No patient had complained to the health department about Dr. Levin. No one else had complained to the health department about Dr. Levin. Only the health department itself had a problem with Dr. Levin.

David Axelrod, a physician and the Commissioner was a brilliant, mean-spirited and depressed individual who unilaterally decided that he wanted to take a prominent alternative doctor and literally prosecute the hell out of him to make an example to other alternative doctors that they better conform to what Axelrod felt was the appropriate practice of medicine.

It should be noted that there have been advances in medicine on an ongoing basis for thousands of years. Those who found new ways to treat patients would, by the Axelrod standard be suppressed and medicine would still be in the dark ages.

Probably the most prominent complementary physician in New York or even in the country was Dr. Robert Atkins. He had authored a book that sold more copies than any other book in world history except the Bible and has been translated into 57 languages. He had a daily radio show that was listened to by huge numbers of people and he was wealthy. It is not surprising that Axelrod picked on Warren Levin who, although he was known as the Dean of complementary physicians by his colleagues did not have the wealth or the public communication and most probably was seen as a much weaker link than Dr. Atkins. It is an interesting fact that Dr. Atkins would testify at Warren Levin's hearing and say that whatever he does in medical practice Warren Levin does better.

This book recounts the horrific abuse of power by the Health Commissioner and those answerable to him to utilize the enormous financial and legal punch of the OPMC for private and political motives rather than for legitimate discipline.

Perhaps the best way to describe Warren Levin's fight is to recall the advertisement, "weebles wobble but they don't fall down."

The bad news is that they started persecuting Warren Levin in 1980 and they didn't stop until the early years of the 1990s. The good news is that Warren Levin has been in practice throughout the entire time and is still in practice today, the end of summer of 2011.

CHAPTER 1

He left his Park Avenue office, umbrella open, for the twelve-block walk to the Metro North station at Grand Central Terminal. A letter, mailed just yesterday had arrived this morning. It came in a plain envelope and was not marked "Personal and Confidential," as it should have been, so it was opened by his receptionist. That was infuriating. His mood matched the weather, chilly. The low temperature and rain were so unusual for the last day of June in Manhattan. He was anxious to get on the train and head home to Connecticut for the weekend. It had been a particularly exhausting week for him, both mentally and physically. He didn't blame his long hours at the office. That was typical for him. His appointments, especially initial ones, tended to be lengthy, and it wasn't his style to rush through his follow-up appointments either. Other stuff was going on, draining him.

He enjoyed his work enormously, got really immersed, and thought of himself as somewhat of a sleuth. Actually, he was a medical doctor. The long hours he spent at the office were the result of his desire to actually *listen* to his patients, and certainly not to talk *down* to them or *at* them, as many in his profession were known to do. The people who sought him out had already been to numerous "conventional" physicians, as he himself once was, who treated their symptoms without probing for the underlying cause of the problem. So their medical conditions were rarely resolved. With invasive, objectionable treatments often the only remaining alternative—the choices were usually *cut, poison,* or *burn* and referred to surgery, chemotherapy, or radiation—patients found their way to his office, saying, "You are my last hope!"

He managed to tuck himself into a corner seat at the end of the rail car. Save for a hum emanating from the distant engine car, it was thankfully quiet when he removed the letter from the envelope. Only the crinkling of the paper broke the relative silence that surrounded him. In spite of its occasionally tainted reputation, the postal service was efficient enough in getting mail delivered within the one-mile radius between the writer's office and the doctor's location. He read it quickly, and his mood darkened even further. His response was immediate. *This guy has got to be kidding! However, I know he's not.* With his emotions fully fired, he pulled out a pad and pen and began to compose a reply.

Dear Mr. Sheehan,

> You have commenced an action against me whose outcome will likely set a major legal precedent, not only in New York State but in the entire country. However, you inform me that I *do not have the right* to select counsel nor to prepare a defense.

He thought about what he had just written and wondered if he needed to have a lawyer review the letter once he completed it and before he sent it. Well, he didn't have a lawyer at the moment, which was part of his problem, and he didn't want to delay in responding to this outrageous letter. He wanted it to go out in the mail immediately. The writer was his adversary, and this was a declared war. *If I win…* or, better yet, *when I win…* Still, he hesitated. Why? Why did he now doubt his ability to win the battle? His hesitation had nothing to do with his practice methods, his treatment of patients, nor his medical ethics. While paranoia was not part of his psychological makeup and didn't color nor infiltrate his thoughts as a rule, he couldn't help but focus on the fact that it was 1989. *I've been dealing with this off and on for nine years now. Nine years.* This nonsense had originally begun in 1980 and then disappeared. Or, he now realized, it had *seemed* to disappear.

He stared at Sheehan's letter and realized that the situation had simply gone into prolonged hibernation. *Now, they're giving me ten days.* In ten days, he was expected to pull up medical charts from 1976, cases that were thirteen years old, and scurry into their offices to meet with them over these former patients. Sure, if he went along with their reasoning that he didn't need a lawyer—since he no longer had one anyway—and there was no need to prepare a defense, July 10 was just fine. The problem was that he didn't agree with their unrealistic view of his serious situation. *What was Sheehan thinking when he wrote this?*

He needed to frame the situation as conservatively as possible in his mind. He struggled to create a conditional mindset. *If I win, it will probably cost me in the vicinity of $100,000 or more in actual expenses, simply for the* privilege *of winning. This, in no way, takes into consideration the wear and tear on my family,* *myself, my patients, or my practice—but, at least, by winning I will still have my license to continue to practice medicine. And that's* if *I win.*

Sheehan was clearly his adversary, but there would be a huge difference in how the end result of the proceedings would affect each of them. When Sheehan completed work on any case of this type, he simply moved on to the next item on his agenda and continued to earn his salary. Terrence Sheehan, the lawyer nominated to drive the effort to capture the doctor's medical license, worked for the New York State Department of Health as a prosecutor; he had a nice, safe job. In fact, Sheehan's position was really cushy, with good hours, a fair salary, plenty of sick days, holidays, good health benefits, and a nice pension at the end of the line. He didn't need to pay rent on an office; put food on the table for the families of employees; or pay salaries to other professionals who worked for him, or to secretaries, assistants and billers—who had to fight insurance companies to collect for services rendered. Everything was handled for Terrence Sheehan who, in addition to prosecuting really *bad* doctors, worked to rid the medical profession of physicians whose philosophy or practice methods differed from mainstream medicine.

Of course, Sheehan had a powerful support system as an employee of the Department of Health. He worked for the State Office of Professional Medical Conduct. What did that really mean: *Professional Medical Conduct? Are they hunting me because my conduct is so professional? The bastards believe that my medical conduct is* unprofessional, *so maybe they need to change the name of the organization. Stop! You're letting your anger throw you off track.*

Tomorrow is the thirtieth anniversary of my graduation from medical school! If I lose this case, they'll take away my license to practice medicine. What will I do to support myself and my family if that happens? I've lost so much sleep over this, and I don't want to alarm Susan any more than necessary.

He remembered how proud he was, how proud his parents had been, the day he received his M.D. degree from Jefferson Medical College in Philadelphia. It was a long time ago, but the implied threat in Sheehan's letter had him thinking back to 1956. He had set up an office as a family doctor, what was then known as a G.P. or general practitioner, before the era where every physician was a specialist in just one disease or body part, during a time when doctors made house calls for six dollars, because an office visit cost only four dollars. Board certification was not even an issue at that time, but when it became the standard, he had diligently prepared himself for the rigorous exams, passed and attained Board certification, then sought recertification in a timely manner. He had put in fifteen years, working very hard, serving a largely blue-collar population across the river from Manhattan, in the borough of Staten Island.

The nature of his practice involved him capably treating the symptoms, infections, and diseases that he diagnosed during office hours or home visits. While he loved his work, enjoyed his interactions with patients, and believed his patients trusted and cared deeply about him in return, he eventually realized that the "typical, mainstream medicine" he was practicing focused on symptom relief, which was the accepted standard of medical treatment. One day, however, one of his own patients, a woman who was not content with symptom relief alone, consulted with another physician, one who added complementary methods to customary medical treatments for what ailed the patient. That unorthodox strategy produced amazing results, and the lady rushed back to her family practitioner to let him know about this other physician. Being an open-minded guy, he decided to visit the other doctor and draw his own conclusions afterwards.

He became a convert after that meeting, excited to learn more about complementary or alternative methods of treating his *own* patients. The deeper he dug, the more he uncovered, and all of it proved beneficial to patients who had long-standing conditions he was now able to actually cure and not just palliate. He began to educate his patients, sharing his discoveries about incorporating strategies that led to a healthy lifestyle, thus making the patients partners in their own care.

In fact, he… He took off his glasses and squeezed his eyes shut for a moment. *Come on, concentrate. Get the letter finished!* He put his glasses back on and grimaced as he realized how huge an effect this whole thing was having on him. He looked at the pad he had balanced on his briefcase. He wanted to let Sheehan know that he understood the inner workings of the OPMC, recalling what he had learned from his former attorney, who had taken him through three rounds of hearings and appeals. She was no longer available to defend him; she had gone on to become a judge. *If these hearings were only structured rationally, I would gladly defend myself* without *benefit of counsel. The way these committees work, however, such a decision would be a serious error of judgment on my part.*

Okay, let's focus on the facts. Larry Storch will play the role of administrative law judge and hear the case. *I'm sounding like a casting director, picking the actors for a play or a movie; that's how unreal this all feels to me and, amazingly,* I *have one of the lead roles.* It was more than possible that Sheehan, the guy whose letter had gotten him all fired up, had simply walked down one floor in the OPMC office and invited Storch to preside over the case, maybe even before asking him if he wanted to go out for a drink after work. That's one issue, he realized, and a really big one. These guys work the cases together, a lot of them socialize together and probably discuss the cases and predetermine the outcome, for goodness' sake. Next, let's cast the part of "the boss." *Whom do the judge and prosecutor work for?* Their boss is the Commissioner of Health, of course, meaning that the very same person who is pulling Sheehan's strings is also seating Storch at the prosecutor's table. What a laugh. As judge, Storch won't be a voting member of the hearing committee, nor will he be a "fact-finder," so his job will be to conduct the hearing and rule on objections. He'll also make decisions on motions, advise on points of law, and handle any adjournment requests. All that sounds fine—in theory. Then, the "whammy": Storch will also "advise" the committee members during the hearing proceedings. How can that be? Storch is appointed by the Commissioner of Health, the one who is chasing after the doctor's medical license. So Sheehan plays the lawyer's role; Storch plays the judge; Axelrod, the commissioner, is the director, who tells the first two guys what to think and do; then Axelrod hires three bit players, called The Committee. *Wow, then* I *walk into the room playing the role of the accused!* Somehow, things were not lining up fairly.

He was getting nowhere on the letter, but the train was moving closer to home by the minute. He needed a mantra, something to get him into the right frame of mind. *I am determined to put aside my misgivings and concerns to focus on the legal battle I am now facing.* He repeated it to himself several times. *That sounds good. Yeah, that sounds right.* As a generally optimistic man, the doctor was doing his best to evoke internal confidence through the thoughts that he was purposefully generating. He glanced down at the sentences he had scratched on the pad in his lap, noticing that the moving train had distorted his handwriting into a quivering rendition that closely matched his inner turmoil, in spite of his attempts at positive thinking and reinforcement.

A time-worn adage suddenly sprang to mind, making good sense: *The deck is stacked against you!* Yeah, it was. He was no dope. The inequalities within the structure of the legal system, as it related to the Department of Health in New York State, were something that doctors only discovered when they were summoned to a hearing. Colleagues who had been through the humiliation of such hearings had expressed confusion and uncertainty when invited into the OPMC offices through a letter or phone call, assured that the brief discussion wouldn't necessitate the inconvenience and expense of retaining a lawyer. He recalled their chagrin and regret when, later, the transcripts of those "discussions" were admitted into evidence in the formal hearing, providing a pre-made noose that was a perfect fit for the medical doctor's neck. He realized that he had everything to lose and that in regaining his peace of mind and holding onto his medical license, if he managed to do that, so much would still be lost. No price tag could ever be attached to the phenomenon of personal anguish, he acknowledged.

I've gone into every one of these meetings with an attorney by my side, and this time won't be any different. Yet, legal assistance posed another dilemma. He followed his thoughts, remembering when the witch hunt first began in 1980, ushered in by his receipt of something called a subpoena *deuces tecum*, ordering him to appear at the Office of Professional Medical Conduct, the OPMC. Just like that! They demanded he bring the charts of three patients he hadn't seen since 1976. The oddest part of this strange subpoena was that these patients had been fully satisfied with services rendered prior to terminating treatment. *So who had complained?* He contacted the OPMC, an innocent enough move, to learn what had launched this unexpected attack against his practice of medicine. The response totally knocked him off his feet. He wouldn't be told *what charges* were levied against him, *who* brought the charges, or *anything* to help him to respond in an appropriate manner. He found himself questioning the allegedly democratic society he believed formed the fabric of the land of his birth. In fact, to further compound his confusion and shock, he was informed that New York State had "inquisitorial powers" *in matters* such as that facing him. *Inquisitorial?* He couldn't believe he had heard correctly; maybe telephone static had muddied the speaker's enunciation. But a repetition of the adjective convinced him that these *matters* were strange and unfamiliar enough to warrant seeking legal help. It took $1,500 and a court appearance with the attorney he hired—he wasn't taking any of the risks some of his colleagues, many of whom were no longer practicing medicine, had taken—to have the subpoena quashed. He wondered whether the *quashing* process would render the subpoena mashed up, useless, broken, unusable, or otherwise ineffective, as that's what the unfamiliar term called up in his imagination; sort of a steamrolling action that drove an unwarranted motion into oblivion. Recalling the competence of his former attorney and regretting that she was no longer able to represent him because of her appointment to a judgeship, which he knew she deserved but which left him, literally, defenseless, he thought about the lawyer he recently retained...then fired.

> The attorney with whom you spoke, and settled on an initial hearing date, is no longer representing me as of last week. Since I am aware that I am entitled to legal representation, I am currently interviewing attorneys in order to make an appropriate choice in a timely manner.

He wondered why everything had to be so complex. The Supreme Court in New York, not to be confused with the revered Supreme Court of the United States, is little more than the local civil court. That's where the doctor and his lawyer ended up on round two, when an identical subpoena, requesting the same three patients' charts, came his way once again. This time, his lawyer wasn't able to get the subpoena quashed. So, they dutifully trotted off to the courthouse. The judge had listened carefully and examined that infamous subpoena, a document that left the defendant clueless as to specific charges, just as it had in round one. The judge wisely decided that New York State hadn't put together enough evidence on this mysterious "crime" to go any further. At that point, the doctor had hoped to hear what they believed he might have done to bring this action crashing down on his head. Instead, another unpleasant surprise: *the judge's decision was appealed!* Still refusing to turn over his patients' charts without sufficient cause, the doctor allowed the case to proceed to the local Appellate Division Appellate Court. The nightmare continued when the tribunal of judges, yes *tribunal*—as the procedural terms became more and more arcane and medieval in nature, matching the "inquisitorial" powers of the state—came through with a split decision. The next move was into New York's highest court, the State Court of Appeals in Albany. His legal bill was $25,000 for that foray into the justice system, and the victory came with a decision that still didn't spell out the charges for the doctor to finally process in his mind. The court stated that, "There must be a minimum threshold showing that the complaint is authentic and it is of sufficient substance to warrant investigation. No such showing was made. It is fitting that before the investigative engines of the governmental agencies are started up against an individual, at least minimal warrant is shown for such intrusion." It was sobering to consider that now, years after this decision was rendered, he could still recall it verbatim. Now he was preparing for yet another mysterious journey into the state's questionable justice system. *I want to address the issue of legal counsel further in my letter, so Sheehan will know I'm not wasting time, but I don't want to sound like I'm whining.*

The next lawyer, a man, had come highly recommended. They met about six weeks ago, discussed the case, and the attorney immediately requested a sizable retainer, which the doctor issued in the form of a check. The lawyer then contacted Sheehan and set a hearing date. Fine. Then the problem occurred. Since most of the doctor's bills were paid either by his office staff or his wife, he didn't realize that he had used a checking account in which a low balance was generally maintained; it was a "petty cash"-type account. The check bounced. The lawyer sent the rubber check to the doctor's office via a FedEx delivery truck. No phone call, as might be expected in a relationship between two professional men, no indication that the lawyer figured he might have been the victim of an honest and easily rectifiable error. He just sent the FedEx guy sailing up to the doctor's twelfth floor office to deliver a cardboard envelope with the bad check enclosed *and included his own bill for sixty-five dollars*—his idea of a penalty for what had been an honest mistake. The doctor was infuriated. That happened last Friday. In the five days since, he had already spoken with *more than nineteen attorneys*, with prolonged consultations of over an hour's duration with eight of them. It had been one of the worst weeks ever, absolutely interminable, as he spent every non-patient hour scheduling phone interviews or personal meetings with attorneys who were recommended by knowledgeable colleagues, many of whom had obviously traveled the same path in the past.

If there was anything he had learned about attorneys, it was that they gave nothing away. Not a minute of their time was off the clock. He recalled from prior bills how every six minutes of a telephone conversation were carefully ticked off and charged at the appropriate fraction of the hourly rate of a senior attorney or a less-expensive associate or paralegal. If papers needed to be copied, both time and supplies were billed. No attorney gave a "free consultation" to a medical doctor, since the two time-honored professions always seemed to be in competition for earning power. Of course, each of the nineteen attorneys had hastened to reassure him that their meeting would be free if the case came to the firm. What a lousy position he was in. He was fighting unknown charges that could result in the loss of his right to practice medicine, so he couldn't allow legal consultation fees to stand in the way of selecting the appropriate representation. He reflected on the fact that Independence Day was looming and saw it as ironic; he hated to think that his *own* independence was now in jeopardy.

What I'd really like to do at this point is to inform Sheehan that I know what I'm up against: that I'm facing the most important legal battle of my life. But I know that the guy doesn't give a damn. He doesn't care if I lose my license. It doesn't matter to him that I need enough time to continue to interview and evaluate lawyers. I need to select the right attorney for this fight, if I stand any chance at all of coming out with only minor battle wounds. There's no way I'm going to pour out my heart to him. He's a flunky for the state. Why should he know how deeply all of this has affected me?

This was a holiday weekend. He had already interviewed every attorney on his list, all to no avail. He wouldn't be able to do a thing until next Tuesday. Even if he and Susan didn't have plans for the weekend it wouldn't have mattered.

Sure, he was entitled to sufficient time to prepare a defense, but lacking legal counsel and not knowing what specific charges the state was alleging, the task seemed impossible. The more he reflected on the injustice of what was happening to him, the more upset he became. He closed his eyes for a long moment, breathing deeply and listening to the progress of the train on the tracks beneath, a familiar and predictable sound, one he heard twice a day during his daily commutes between Connecticut and Manhattan, comforting, soothing. *I've got to finish writing before the train pulls into the station.*

> Once I have retained another attorney, that person will contact you to set a mutually satisfactory hearing date. Meanwhile, please consider this letter my request for an adjournment until *at least* the beginning of September.

He tried very hard to be the gentleman he knew he was, the person behind the three-piece suit he wore to his office daily and to conferences; an individual, mindful and respectful, with startlingly blue eyes that professionally scanned patients' bodies and looked into their souls in a kind, thoughtful way. He admitted to himself privately that he was straining to use non-threatening and only mildly assertive language in this exchange. He would have loved to allow the letter to take on a life of its own, to emerge in a reactionary manner, spitting words out for maximal honesty and effect; but he didn't want to alienate an admitted adversary unnecessarily. It made him think of Philippe Petit, the French *high wire* artist who gained fame for walking between the Twin Towers of the World Trade Center years earlier, in 1974, before all of this malicious nonsense was unleashed on him. The tasks were certainly different, with one man balancing himself carefully on a thin wire, high in a rarified atmosphere, and another man—himself—balancing himself between unknown charges and an unfamiliar justice system and hoping not to fall. One man could die from the plunge from a high altitude; while he, the doctor, would see the death of everything he had worked for, an immediate end to all he had painstakingly labored to garner. His practice would end, his financial security would be gone, his family would suffer, his patients would lose a caring physician, his office staff would have to find employment elsewhere, his prestige would be shattered, his colleagues would witness his embarrassment, and his detractors would believe they had achieved a victory. But who were his detractors? What prize were they fighting for?

The victory in the state court of appeals should have produced a modified subpoena, he recalled, once again reflecting back on his prior experience with the OPMC. He had waited and waited for it to come in the mail, but it never did. Instead, a virtually identical subpoena arrived six months later, requesting the *original three medical charts* that he had refused to produce at the start. But the state had provided no further information. He had gone back to his first attorney—the current judge, who had very capably moved through the legal quagmire with him before—yet he felt upset and confused by the fact that no matter what the ruling, this issue wasn't about to quietly die.

A different judge had presided the second time around, when he and his female lawyer ended up back in the Supreme Court, and that judge informed them that New York State, in its wisdom, had selected a case from a footnote included in the original decision from the Court of Appeals. The footnote referred to an investigation by the New York State Organized Crime Task Force, where the judge decided it was prudent to protect the individual who had filed the complaint that kicked off the case. *A Mafia case, for goodness sake, and they were quoting it to "protect" whoever had filed the complaint against me, and I'm a medical doctor?* How did a ruling on protecting informants in criminal cases come into play? Using this precedent as an excuse to keep from disclosing the party who had filed the complaint against the doctor was, in his mind, totally ridiculous. But as a man who generally had control of his own destiny, the doctor was now powerless and totally unfamiliar with this feeling of impotence. The judge, he recalled, decided to take the complaint into his chambers to read it and make a determination. Although his attorney objected, she was overruled. At least the decision was favorable, once again; the judge decided that there was *no justification* for such a complaint to be made against the doctor. This was his second victory. The first one hadn't lasted.

But it didn't end there, he remembered, because New York State appealed the dismissal of charges. *The Appellate Division had once again reversed itself!* The reversal ushered in round three, calling for yet another appearance in front of New York State's highest court, the Court of Appeals, at the elbow of his female attorney.

Incredibly enough, he remembered, the state was within its rights to play these games with someone's future. He remembered what happened next, and just the thought of it caused the bile to rise into his throat and burn at the same temperature as the anger that festered within him.

His lawyer had decided to have the Supreme Court of the United States weigh in on the matter by requesting a review of the constitutionality of a law that would allow such seemingly disparate actions to occur and reoccur in a democratic nation. The Supreme Court had other, more pressing, matters on the bench at that time and refused to debate the issue. This had knocked the doctor down emotionally; this final punch had taken an awful toll on his determination to remain hopeful and upbeat in the face of such terrible adversity.

This farce had chugged along for six years; cost $50,000 of hard earned cash; and hadn't allowed this articulate, educated professional the opportunity of speaking a word in his own defense. It didn't escape him, however, that—given the chance to hold forth on his innocence, he still hadn't been informed of which crimes they thought him guilty! Now, with round three behind him for several years, he had been "invited" to the OPMC several months ago for a fourth go-round. That's when the business with the latest lawyer occurred. And, now, Sheehan's letter demanding his defenseless appearance in ten days was the proverbial icing on the cake. *I can't believe it. New York State has been chasing after me for so many years. They want my license. It's almost as if it means more to them than it does to me, which is crazy. I wonder if, maybe, I've been chosen as a test case. Get this guy out of the medical field, then it will be really easy to knock down all the other alternative physicians, one by one, and they'll fall like dominos. Was that what this was all about?*

The letter, the letter, read over the letter you just wrote. You're almost home, for goodness' sake. Although he planned to type the letter on his professional stationery, he quickly read his handwritten version, which zigged and zagged in all directions, depending on the trajectory of the train as he wrote each word. Then, with a flourish, he signed his name to the rough draft to signal the completion of the task he had assigned himself on this commute:

Warren M. Levin, M.D.

He slipped the pad into his briefcase, carefully deposited his Montblanc rollerball pen into his jacket pocket, and grabbed his umbrella as the train pulled into the station. Like most people, he had heard stories of how, in the last moments of life, significant events allegedly flashed through one's mind. He could believe it.

In this short train ride, while composing a brief response to yesterday's letter from Terrence Sheehan, Warren Levin had relived the most poignant events of the past six nine years, as they revolved around a subpoena with its mysterious request for specific patients' records, followed by what seemed like a tour of every possible level of the court system.

Now that he had decided to leave his ringside seat and enter the fray with his fists ready for combat, the brief show of confidence that came through in his handwritten letter was rapidly fading. He hated to add yet another burden to those already carried by his wife, Susan, from the events and expenses already associated with this issue. He had no choice. He desperately needed her support.

He walked into the house through the kitchen door. They had bought this house within the past six months and moved into it two short months ago, in April, but he wasn't focused on the pleasure he usually felt upon arriving home. He just stood there, motionless, in the hall. Susan walked over, took one look at his face and was unable to look away.

"Susan, we need to talk," he simply said.

CHAPTER 2

Dr. Levin and his wife, Susan, had decided not to change their plans and to go away for the Fourth of July weekend. They had taken Erika, their three-and-a-half-year-old daughter, along with them, bringing enough books and toys for Erika to entertain herself during the car trip.

"It's a good thing Erika's so young," Levin said. "It seems like this elfin' subpoena is all that we've been talking about lately." Levin was concerned that his language be appropriate. Erika surprised them with her sophisticated use of words when they least expected it, and he didn't want to add unwanted obscenities to his daughter's ever-evolving speech patterns.

Susan looked over at him, her eyes misty. He didn't deserve this, she thought. She knew how hard he worked, how much he cared about his patients, how methodical he was.

"Warren, I'm torn between trying to have some fun this weekend and strategizing the next step in this whole nightmare." Susan's face reflected her lack of sleep as her mind reviewed the same events over and over again, all day, all night.

"We'll try to do both; I promise you," he replied, trying his best to sound convincing. "But Sheehan has even managed to take this weekend away from us. Ten days!" He shook his head in consternation, never taking his eyes from the road. As they had loaded the car early this morning, he hadn't missed the dark shadows under Susan's eyes. As much as he tried not to worry her, as optimistic as he pretended to be when they spoke, she saw through his act. That bothered him more than he wanted to admit to himself. Yet, the facts presented a very bleak picture. He had only ten miserable days to find a lawyer...and that included a long, holiday weekend, no less. If Sheehan didn't grant the adjournment, Levin's new lawyer would have no time at all to get familiar enough with the case to be of any assistance—that is if he even *found* a suitable attorney. "It's crazy, absolutely crazy!" His normally serene countenance was flushed with frustration, and he had a death-grip on the steering wheel. The holiday traffic, with its share of celebrants who had already consumed more than enough liquor to usher in the long weekend, posed an extra threat and required absolute concentration. "We've interviewed a whole stack of lawyers already! Nobody seems right for us. We're not about to find someone this weekend," he said.

"Don't be too sure about that," Susan responded. "I've got a few names with me. One guy was recommended by Alan Pressman, the chiropractor we met when we went to that conference in Albany last year. Remember him?" Levin nodded. "I looked him up and called him earlier this week, because I remembered his story."

"What story?" Levin remembered the name but not the 'story.'

Susan prided herself on her memory for details. "He had been talking to a group during a break between speakers, so I had gone over to listen. You were there, too, Warren," she added, reproachfully. "I didn't hear him explain what charges were leveled against him, but I do remember him saying that he was afraid he would lose his chiropractor's license. He said that the lawyer he used did a great job."

"So what happened with Alan's license?"

"What do you think happened if the lawyer did a great job?"

Levin shrugged, then he chuckled, to show Susan that his sense of humor wasn't completely gone.

"For goodness' sake, Warren, I'm trying to have a serious conversation," she said.

"Okay, please continue," he said, chastened.

"The lawyer Alan used, a man who is known in the chiropractic community since he lectures at the New York Chiropractic College on Long Island, really knew his stuff. He saved Alan's license, so he was raving about him."

"So you called Alan, and..."

"I got the lawyer's name. Listen, Warren, you know how everyone's been telling us that we need to retain a really 'big lawyer'? Well, Alan said that this guy is really *big*, whatever that means."

"Big, small, whatever. If he's the right guy for the job, we'll know it soon enough. I hope we don't run out of money trying to find someone," he said.

He pulled into the parking lot of the resort, cutting the engine, and went in to register. Susan noticed that Erika was asleep in the backseat. Poor kid. She was probably bored stiff with her parents' preoccupation with their crisis. Susan vowed to manufacture enough cheer to make this weekend fun for *all* of them. Warren needed to relax; he had already been through so much aggravation.

For the Levins, just being away from everyone and everything proved therapeutic. They reveled in the leisure time and enjoyed playing with their daughter. For the first two days.

"Are you serious?" Susan asked Levin. "He'll see us on Tuesday? But that's the Fourth of July!" Warren had acted on the referral from Alan Pressman and called the 'big lawyer,' not expecting to even reach him.

"I know. That's what *I* said. But he told me that the office would be quiet and he'd be able to give us his undivided attention. I want to call him back and tell him we'll come, but I need to know you're in agreement," he said.

"Call him. We'll leave for home tomorrow, then. You'll have to let them know at the registration desk. They may charge us for the extra night, even though we're leaving," she said.

"I don't care. If they do, they do. Let me call this guy and tell him we'll be in his office first thing Tuesday morning." Levin sat on the bed and made the call immediately, leaving a message and the phone number of the resort for a callback.

The Levins drove down from Connecticut to Woodmere, one of the fabled Five Towns on Long Island's south shore, arriving precisely at 10:00 a.m., parking behind the law offices of Schneider, Harris & Harris. They were meeting with the firm's managing partner, Robert Harris, the "big lawyer." Hopefully, he would be big enough to take on this confusing case. They climbed the stairs—each of them engrossed in private thoughts, and entered the small waiting room.

"Come on in!" boomed a voice from an inner chamber. Harris stood up to shake hands. The Levins looked at each other, both thinking the same thing. *This guy is certainly big.* Harris must have been about six-feet three inches and at least 450 pounds. Okay…

"Sit down," he instructed them, as he lit a cigar, proffering the humidor toward Dr. Levin, who waved his hand in dismissal. Harris flicked on the air purifier that would keep the Levins from choking on the cigar smoke and asked them to tell him their story.

The lawyer listened intently, all the while absorbing and visually processing extraneous information. Levin was a strikingly good-looking man, and Harris estimated that the doctor was in his mid-fifties. Susan Levin, at about five feet three inches was a bit shorter and a lot younger than her husband, slender, with long, straight, brown hair, and an extremely pretty face. They were a real power couple, he thought, attractive, educated, articulate, and facing a monstrous problem.

"There's something I'd like you to know," Levin added, when he had given the lawyer the basic background of the situation. "I learned from another attorney that the state has the right *not* to disclose the complainant to me. It has something to do with a law that was passed to protect doctors who report *other* doctors to the Office of Professional Medical Conduct."

"So you're saying that another doctor reported you?" Harris asked.

"I'm not saying anything, because I don't know *who* may have reported me, or even *why* this has happened. I've been practicing this way for years," Levin explained. "Why now? Why at all? I'll tell you this much: I'm sick of the whole thing. First they requested the charts of three patients in 1980, and I fought it repeatedly. Finally, I couldn't hold out any longer, so I sent them the damn charts in September of 1986. That should have ended it, right?"

"Well, it didn't," Susan said, addressing Harris, a disgusted look on her face. "They let him *think* it was over. He had complied with their ridiculous request, without them ever supplying a concrete reason for pursuing him, and he didn't hear another word for years!"

Levin continued the story. "She's right. Nothing for nearly three years. Nothing until about six weeks ago, followed by this letter dated June 29, giving me *ten days* to appear. It took them from 1986 to 1989 to review *three charts* that they subpoenaed from me and hounded me for time and again, and they didn't have the courtesy to look them over and contact me in a timely manner. What the hell is going on here?" Levin's level of agitation was growing with the recitation of the facts. His face was red and his breathing labored. Susan reached over and put her hand on his arm in a calming gesture. He patted her hand distractedly and stared at Harris, as though the lawyer had the answers to how the OPMC conducted its affairs.

"Look, I'm still not sure what charges are being brought against you, what you're being accused of," Harris stated.

Levin handed the lawyer the handwritten envelope that had arrived at his office by ordinary mail. As Harris reached for it, Levin glanced at Susan out of the corner of his eye. She looked stricken as she watched Harris take the envelope from her husband. Levin recalled what had happened during their discussion last Friday evening, after he had written Sheehan that letter on the train. When he showed Susan the list of charges, a total of 144, she had run out of the room without even reading them and straight into the bathroom, where she had spent the next hour being sick, returning to the living room looking pale and horrified. He hoped she wouldn't bolt out of the lawyer's office now.

Harris stared at the envelope, the doctor's name and address written in blue ink, no indication of the sensitive material inside, and his brows creased in disapproval. He opened it and saw that it contained two documents, each with multiple pages: a notification of a hearing, and a statement of charges. Harris read rapidly, his eyes covering the page line by line with the rapidity of a grocery scanning beam.

"It looks like just about everything you're doing in your practice is objectionable, if I'm to believe this document," Harris declared, puffing on his cigar and fixing Levin with a stare that cut through both Harris's and Levin's spectacles. "And they're accusing you of negligence and incompetence, too. Actually *gross* negligence and *gross* incompetence. On top of that, they're charging you with *fraud*. So what I'm getting from this is that they think you're a real quack, to use an overused and insulting term. What's going on, doctor?"

"The tests I conduct, the treatments I offer, solve patients' problems on a very deep level," Levin responded, "getting to the root cause and not just palliating the symptoms. I practice good, solid medicine; my work makes a big difference in my patients' lives."

"So why are they after you?" Harris asked pointedly.

"It's a conspiracy, as far as I'm concerned," Levin told him. "The Office of Professional Medical Conduct is looking to rid the medical profession of any doctors who don't practice mainstream medicine: diagnose, medicate, and then rush off to see the next patient in the adjoining examining room."

"Some of the tests and treatments they've got listed here are things I've never even heard about." Harris said. "If what you're doing is so effective, why don't *all* doctors use your methods?"

"Obviously, you're missing the point, Mr. Harris," interjected Susan, a look of annoyance crossing her face.

"And what is the point that I'm missing here, Mrs. Levin?" challenged Harris.

"My husband practices alternative medicine," she responded, distinctly speaking each word. "*That's* the point you're missing."

"Alternative medicine," said Harris, regarding her coolly. "I'm not sure I know exactly what that is." He put his hand up to stop her from interrupting him. "I've heard of a few techniques used by some doctors as an adjunct to their conventional practices, but I can't close my eyes right now and imagine what your husband actually *does* in his office on a daily basis, Mrs. Levin. What I do see in these papers he handed me is that he's being accused of incompetence!"

Susan inhaled sharply through her nose and opened her mouth to respond to Harris's objectionable tone of voice. Levin looked from his wife to the lawyer and decided that he'd better intervene; things were getting a bit edgy already, and there were important issues that he didn't want to see clouded over. "Let me give you an example," Levin began, making every effort to keep his voice even and calm, "a very common example, in fact. I don't know if you know what candidiasis is, but it's a gynecological condition that affects more women than you can imagine." Susan sat back and simply listened, as her husband began to carefully explain this disabling condition to Harris, who seemed quite interested, nodding as he followed the doctor's descriptive narration. "So," Levin said in conclusion, "using Darkfield Microscopy to assist with diagnosis and not prescribing the usual topical creams for these women have made a difference. The dietary changes I suggest and the type of underwear I advocate, plus the large doses of Nystatin, which is a polyene antifungal drug particularly effective with yeast infections like candidiasis, rids these women of the problem and allows them to return to a normal life."

"That's very interesting, Dr. Levin, but I don't think we need to get into all the particulars of your medical practice right now," Harris said.

"The reason I'm here, Mr. Harris," Levin said, leaning toward the attorney, who was comfortably seated behind a massive desk, "is because I'm tired of being hunted and harassed by these people. I want to fight this conspiracy. I want to strike a blow for alternative medicine and my right, and the rights of my fellow alternative practitioners, to practice a form of medicine that makes sense to me and to the patients who seek me out and tell me that I'm their last hope. This is a cause that's bigger than me alone. This case may change the future practice of medicine. It may…"

"Dr. Levin," Harris interrupted forcefully, "I don't want to hear your conspiracy theories or any of this paranoia business. As far as I'm concerned, there is only one issue at stake here that's critical and primary: we have to work to save your medical license!" Harris glared at the doctor, no hint of good humor on his face.

No one spoke, no one breathed, for what seemed like a full minute. Then…

"You're hired, Mr. Harris." This was from Susan Levin. The men blinked in surprise.

She realized that while her husband's cause was noble, nothing really mattered if he was stripped of his license and his right to practice medicine, whether by a witch-hunting organization or a conspiracy by the medical establishment or the laws of the land. Nothing was more important than making sure Warren could continue doing what he loved and did so well: listening carefully to each patient, tirelessly investigating the root causes of their illnesses, helping them change their daily habits and unhealthy ways, suggesting methods of altering lifestyles that were cutting individuals' lives short and making them chronically ill. He had developed relationships with sophisticated medical laboratories, had expensive diagnostic instruments, alliances with other healthcare professionals to supplement his own methods and assist his patients further, and he refused to give up on anyone until he had exhausted every lead. Unless he maintained a license to practice medicine, all of this would be meaningless. It would end. That could not be allowed to happen.

Dr. Levin looked at his wife. He knew her well. She was his main support. She believed in him unquestioningly. But now she had cut through the layers of injustice, anger, frustration, and confusion he was feeling and had gone directly to the nucleus of the issue: his medical license had to be saved. He nodded his agreement to Susan. He nodded his agreement to Harris.

They had just formed a partnership that would result in an unimaginable battle to save the medical license of Warren M. Levin, M.D., family practitioner turned alternative medical doctor.

CHAPTER 3

"Dr. Levin, it's Bob Harris." It was Wednesday evening, and the doctor was already at home. It had been hard to concentrate at work all day long, thinking about yesterday's meeting at the law office and wondering what catastrophe would hit next.

"Mr. Harris, it's good to hear your voice," Levin responded.

"Well, I think I have something to tell you that you'll like even better than the sound of my voice," the lawyer said. "I managed to get the hearing postponed until September."

"That *is* good news. *Very* good news," Levin said, the relief apparent in his voice. "That means we have time to prepare some sort of defense."

"It's going to have to be a very *good* defense. They've got so much stuff in these charges that it's mind-boggling."

"I know," Levin answered simply.

"I didn't want to call you at your office, which is why I waited for you to get home. I'd like to get a bit of information from you right now. Do you have time to talk?"

"I'd like nothing better," Levin told him. "What information would you like?" He could hear the lawyer shuffling papers in the background.

"I see that the state originally asked you for three charts, which you gave them in 1986; and now, they're asking you for four additional ones as well. Talk to me about all these cases, if you will," Harris requested.

"What information do you want?"

"I don't need the patients' names," Harris responded. "What I want from you is this: gender, age, when they first came to see you, what medical issues brought them in, how they found you to begin with, if they had been treated by another doctor for the same problem before seeking you out, what tests you did, what treatments you prescribed, how your relationship was with each patient, how successful the treatment was, when they each terminated treatment, and anything else pertinent to the case. I want to be able to address whatever questions that I'm asked about these patients," Harris concluded.

"Whew!" the doctor said, expelling a long breath. "That's a whole lot of information. Actually, I've made some notes, and I've organized them into a sort of analytical chart. I did that to look for similarities and differences among the patients whose charts had been requisitioned. You know what I'm saying? I'm trying to find common denominators, reasons why these particular patients should be of interest to the OPMC."

Harris cleared his throat noisily, thinking to himself that this doctor sounded like an organized person, unlike so many of the harried physicians he had already defended. "That's probably a good idea," Harris told him. "And what, if anything, did you conclude from your analysis, doctor?"

"Unfortunately, not much. I've used a lot of the same diagnostic tests on these folks, but that's routine in my practice; and I've also put several of the patients on the same treatment regimen. Their presenting complaints were the same, that's why," he said, justifying his decisions. "Anyway, I have this material in my files. Hold on a second so I can find it." Levin put the phone down on the desk and opened the bottom file drawer just as Susan walked into the room. He looked up at her and indicated the telephone receiver in the center of his desk blotter. Susan made eating motions and raised her eyebrows questioningly. Levin retrieved the file and put it on the desktop. He looked at his watch and calculated. It was already 7:30, but sometimes they didn't eat dinner until 9:00. He tapped the face of his Le Coultre and calculated. He held up a finger, indicating that he needed about an hour. She nodded and left his office.

He picked up the phone again. "Sorry for the delay. I have the information in front of me. As far as tests and treatments go, much of it will make little or no sense to you if you're not familiar with alternative medicine."

"I realize that," Harris told him, "but I think that I can learn whatever I need to if we take it step by step. In other words, I'll need you to teach me all about your practice. If you think you can do that, I'm sure I can learn enough to make this alliance work." Harris sounded confident, as though he knew that Levin needed some assurance that he had hired the right lawyer.

"I'm okay with that," Levin said. "We'll just have to find lots and lots of time to do this. Some of it can be explained over the phone, I can spend some time out at your office, but I believe that a piece of it will require you to come into my office, which you should see in any event—to understand that I have a bona-fide medical practice," Levin ended, trying to inject a bit of humor into their serious discussion.

"I expect to spend quite a bit of time at your office, doctor. I want to get an idea about the day-to-day operation, the staff, the patients in the waiting room, your setup, the whole shebang. But, for now, let's get started on the seven patients, the original three and the additional four, whose charts have been requisitioned," Harris told him.

Studying the paper he had unfolded on this desk—which consisted of four sheets of eleven-by-seventeen bond, taped together to form what looked like a map for a treasure hunt, carefully lined and divided, different colors of ink in each of the columns—Levin realized that he had actually begun developing this analysis thirteen years ago, when the very first subpoena was issued. It had been Susan's idea. She thought that maybe they would find a pattern or some type of clue to figure out why the state of New York had selected these three people. On each of the three times he had made the rounds of the court system, he had gone back to this diagram, trying to find a clue. For a doctor whose practice required so much investigative work into patients' backgrounds and disease processes, the state's requisitions had left him embarrassingly clueless; he couldn't find a smidgen of logic, a sensible connection, any reason why these patients were so interesting to the OPMC.

Levin gave his lawyer a brief summary of each of the original three patients, answering questions as Harris asked them. He spoke slowly and clearly to give Harris a chance to take notes.

"Okay, good," Harris told him. "Now, how about the four new cases they tacked onto their agenda?"

"These are four cases from the early 1980's, if you can believe that. And, let me tell you, I recognized the names right away when I saw them," Levin said.

"You recognized the names of patients you saw so long ago? In a practice as busy as yours? I don't understand. What made these particular patients stand out for you?" asked Harris, clearly puzzled.

"There is an organization called the Insurance Committee of Peer Review," Levin began, "which is part of the New York County Medical Society. The insurance companies actually file complaints with this organization, you know."

"No, I didn't know," Harris responded.

"Well, they do," Levin continued. "Anyhow, it has to do with the contracts that the insurance companies have with the individuals whose health insurance coverage they provide. I don't take insurance, for the most part, but my office provides patients with detailed bills that they can submit to their health insurance carriers for reimbursement. The contracts stipulate that the insurance companies will pay for 'routine and necessary services.' Of course, *they* determine what is considered 'routine and necessary,' not us doctors who may feel that a particular test or treatment will benefit our patients."

"Okay," Harris said, "and what was it that they believed was not 'routine and necessary' in whatever you did for these four patients?"

"Things like testing the nutritional state of a patient, using vitamin and mineral tests, for example, was not 'routine and necessary,' as far as they were concerned; and neither was any *treatment* I rendered that used vitamins and nutritional counseling considered to be 'routine and necessary,'" Levin told him.

"So what happened with this Peer Review Committee in these four cases?"

"The first time they investigated me, they sent a physician to my office. A nice guy, actually, very likeable. We talked, and I showed him around. The guy was totally impressed," Levin said. "I explained everything I was doing, how I went about making my diagnoses on these particular patients, and so forth."

"Then what happened?" Harris prompted.

"This doctor reported back to the Review Committee, which did something a bit unusual, which I actually viewed as beneficial to me. They wrote me a letter, and I'm sure I have it somewhere in my records. The letter pretty much said that

I wasn't doing anything that they considered objectionable, but they emphasized that the insurance companies were not obligated to reimburse the patients who paid me out of pocket for tests that didn't fall into the 'routine and necessary' category."

"So it ended there?" Harris asked him.

"Not at all. Some time later, they sent a *different* doctor to my office. While he didn't think I was doing anything wrong either, he really couldn't see the benefit of some of my tests or treatments. I didn't think anything of it. I just figured they had checked me out twice, and since neither doctor had much of an issue with my practice, the committee could now butt out of my business."

"So that was the end of it, then."

Levin snorted. "I was deluding myself when I thought it was over. What happened then was that the Insurance Review Committee changed its guidelines. Once that happened, they sent a *third* doctor out to visit me. This guy gave me a real hard time, questioned everything, wasn't very friendly or very nice about it, either. You'd think he was a cop and I was a hardened criminal. It's a very subjective thing, you know, and he was a real *putz*" Levin told Harris.

"It sounds like it," Harris agreed. "What happened then?"

"I got another letter, but this was not a feel-good letter. They accused me of using unnecessary tests and treatments at that point. They used words like 'objectionable,' 'not customary,' 'useless'; I don't really remember, but it was very upsetting. Three doctors, three different views. Oh, and by the time this third guy, the *putz*, came along, I had a copy of those revised guidelines in my hands. I was infuriated when I realized that they were designed to pick up *everything* alternative physicians like me were doing, *are* doing," he corrected himself.

"So they sent you a warning letter," Harris said.

"Their decision was in favor of the insurance companies, but it didn't end there, either" Levin told him.

"What else happened?"

"The insurance companies suddenly drew some terrible conclusions about me."

"Meaning?"

Levin took a deep breath. It was still hard for him to repeat what had been said about him. "They decided that 'my brand of medicine' was so *dangerous* that I needed to be reported to the Office of Professional Medical Conduct."

"That's pretty serious stuff," Harris echoed.

"You're telling me!" Levin answered. "It really scares me how organizations that are out there to ostensibly 'help the public' can be turned into hunters in the blink of an eye. Protecting the public is one thing, but blatantly *hunting* someone whose life mission is to help the public, as well, by teaching patients to take good care of themselves and assisting them in improving their health and showing them how to contribute to their longevity ..."

Harris interrupted him. "Let's not get sidetracked, doctor. In doing your noble deeds, you are also a money-earning business. Wherever money is involved, and whenever third-party payers are being hit for the money, they're gonna fight. It's just the way it goes."

"Yeah, I guess so," Levin added, resigned. He glanced at his watch. It was 8:30 already. "Do you think we've covered enough this evening for you to work with for the time being?"

They set up another meeting, this time at Levin's office. Both men hung up the phone, each of them reflecting on the evening's conversation and wondering what direction things would take next. Levin looked through the chart once again, wondering if he'd suddenly spot something that he had missed during prior examinations of the various columns, but nothing rose up to meet him, nothing screamed out at him. He carefully folded it along the tape lines and replaced it in his extra-wide file drawer. He sighed. He suddenly wasn't very hungry.

CHAPTER 4

The following week, Bob Harris traveled to the nicely appointed office that Warren Levin maintained on Park Avenue South in Manhattan. As he waited for the doctor to finish with his last patient of the day, he looked around the comfortable and tastefully decorated waiting room. From its appearance alone, the business appeared prosperous but, then, so were many medical practices. Why was the state targeting *this* particular doctor and *this* particular office? He remembered what he had thought of as Levin's "conspiracy theory": since this was not a "typical" medical office focused on medicine as practiced by the "establishment," a word much bandied about during the days of the anti-establishment Hippies, that very characteristic was responsible for the troops to be called out, according to the doctor and his wife. In the days since he had met Levin, Harris had made quite a few phone calls and read a number of articles his staff had culled for him from various journals. Alternative medicine certainly was "different," he acknowledged to himself, and he would begin to learn just how different in more detail today, he suspected.

Levin came out to greet him and escort him back to his office, and Harris couldn't help but make comparisons between the size of his own private space as managing partner of his firm and Levin's area at his solo practice. The doctor's space had a comfy feel, a homey sense, with a large, roll top desk, piles of articles and books everywhere, and pithy little sayings framed and hung on the walls. Patients must feel as though they're stepping back in time, Harris thought, when they walked from the bright, modern waiting room to this dimly-lit, cozy area that exuded warmth and a sense of intimacy. Harris's scan had taken place in the split second before they sat at a small table in two comfortable chairs.

Harris waved away the offer of coffee or a cold drink and opened his notepad, launching into the heart of the issue. "Okay, you told me that for the first patient whose chart they requisitioned you did a number of tests, including a hair analysis, a six-hour glucose tolerance test, a mauve factor test, and blood histamine, spermidine, and spermine tests. The six-hour glucose test I understand, although not your reasons for doing it with this patient. Blood histamine I imagine has to do with allergy testing. Like I told you over the phone last week, I have no idea whatsoever what these other tests are about or your reasons for prescribing them. So we may as well start there."

Levin's narration took on a professorial tone as he patiently and slowly began a thorough explanation of each test while Harris took notes, as though he were in a college lecture class and wanted to do very well on an upcoming exam. In fact, he *had* to do very well on the multiple tests that would follow this instruction. They would be oral exams, conducted in front of a hearing officer whose recommendations might influence the decision as to whether Levin would be allowed to continue to practice medicine...any form of medicine.

"Okay," Harris said. "I follow you. You did a great job explaining all of that stuff. Now, let's get to the treatments. There are eight treatments you told me about. I have a feeling that it's going to take us a couple of hours to talk through this, because I'll have questions and will probably interrupt you a lot. Let's start with this business called 'chelation therapy,' because you told me that this patient received about twenty chelation sessions. What's it all about?"

Levin took a deep breath. Chelation therapy was one of the cornerstones of his treatment regimen for a number of different conditions, coronary artery disease being one of the primary areas triggering such a protocol. He wanted to do a thorough job explaining chelation and making it understandable to Harris, for whom it was unfamiliar.

"Chelation therapy is something I use in combination with other treatments, like drastic dietary changes and nutritional supplements. The important thing to remember here, however, is that I start with a *very* thorough and complete medical workup before I begin suggesting lifestyle changes or *any* treatments. I want to make this very clear!" Levin stared hard into Harris's eyes to determine whether his point had been driven deeply enough.

"Okay, I understand," Harris responded simply.

"With chelation," Levin started, "I'm using a controversial drug. It's called ethylene-diamine-tetra-acetic acid, more commonly referred to as 'EDTA,' so it's called EDTA chelation therapy. This is administered intravenously, two or three times a week, for a total of maybe twenty to forty infusions, or possibly more."

"That sounds a lot like the chemotherapy treatments that cancer patients get," Harris observed.

"Very similar, very similar," Levin agreed. "The main difference is that these treatments are not poisonous to the body, like chemotherapy. Chelation therapy is completely the opposite, although the administration process is the same. In fact, the length of the infusion is much longer with chelation. Each treatment takes about three-and-a-half or four hours."

"How much of this EDTA goes into each treatment. And, by the way, what *is* this stuff?" Harris asked.

"EDTA is a man-made amino acid," Levin told him, "and there are about three grams of EDTA in each infusion. But let me start with the basics. I want to explain the origin of the term, *chelation*, and give you a bit of the history behind EDTA. 'Chelate' comes from the Greek word for 'claw' and refers to EDTA's 'claw-like' structure. This type of treatment ..." Levin stopped for a moment and looked directly at Harris. He certainly didn't want his lawyer to get the impression that he was using something exotic that had no track record within the medical community. "I want to give you a bit of background on this type of treatment to demonstrate that it has a history. It's not something that just came out now that alternative practitioners just jumped on," Levin said. "EDTA has successfully been used in the mainstream for quite a while, by the way, to rid people's bodies of heavy metal poisoning."

"How so?"

"EDTA was first synthesized in the 1930's in Germany, where it was noted that the 'claw' aspect of the amino acid binds divalent and trivalent metallic ions to form a stable ring structure." He broke off and looked at Harris questioningly. "Am I losing you?"

"No, no, go on. Just so you know, I went to The Bronx High School of Science. I remember my chemistry," Harris told him, unable to hide the pride in his voice, both for his *alma mater* and for his impressive memory. If he hadn't just met Levin, he would have made sure the doctor knew just how competitive it was to get into any of New York City's special "magnet schools," and Harris had passed the entrance exams for several of the city's top picks. His reason for choosing Bronx Science, however, was personal: it was co-ed.

Levin assessed Harris a moment and then nodded. "Okay, so with EDTA being water-soluble, it chelates or grabs only metallic ions that are dissolved in water. So at pH 7.4, which is the normal pH of blood, there are various strengths at which EDTA binds dissolved metals, starting with iron—that is ferric ion, plus mercury, copper, aluminum, nickel, lead, cobalt, zinc, and iron—in this case ferrous ion, and cadmium, manganese, magnesium, and calcium," Levin listed. "Since mercury, lead, and cadmium cannot be metabolized by the body ..."

"Then, if the body accumulates these metals, they can be toxic to an individual, and these heavy metals can interfere with various physiological functions," Harris finished.

"Exactly!" Levin said. He was pleased that his lawyer was following his explanation comfortably. "So, with the exception of aluminum, all of the other elements are actually *essential* nutrients that our bodies require for normal metabolic activity. With that understanding, a group of scientists postulated that if EDTA could remove calcium from the walls of the body's arteries, therefore softening hardened arteries, this treatment could make a huge difference in the lives of patients who were suffering from atherosclerosis and in danger of dying from massive heart attacks."

"That makes a lot of sense," Harris told him. "But is there any scientific evidence showing that it actually works that way?"

"I am familiar with a study done by Clarke, Clarke, and Mosher in 1956," Levin responded. "I don't recall all the details, but I know that they used chelation with a group of patients suffering from occlusive peripheral vascular disease. According to the self-report of each patient, these folks claimed that they felt better."

"I'm not sure 'felt better' is scientific enough," Harris told him.

"Well, that's what I recall as an early study, an initial study, in any event. After that, Meltzer and a group of colleagues worked with ten patients in 1960, I think, all of whom had *angina pectoris*; you know," he added, "chest pain." Harris nodded. "Over the next two months," Levin continued, "these people began to report improvements in their symptoms, and that was very encouraging. So someone named Kitchell brought another twenty-eight people into the study, so now there was a total of thirty-eight patients. Unfortunately, the positive effects didn't seem to last; some of the patients expired, and—very honestly, since there was no control group, the conclusion wasn't great. They wrote that EDTA chelation, as used in the study, wasn't clinically useful in treating coronary disease."

"That's unfortunate," Harris said, "because it could have been helpful in your defense."

"I realize that," Levin said, "but it becomes a very expensive proposition for any of us who would like to publish a study proving the effectiveness of some of the treatments that are considered so controversial, because we'd have to recruit experimental and control groups and spend a whole lot of time and money following the patients and writing up the work. The big funding comes from the pharmaceutical industry, and they make those grants available to medical people conducting drug trials on patients, not those of use using non-conventional treatments to *avoid* drugs and surgeries. It's a real shame."

Harris nodded. "By the way, are *you* the person who administers the chelation therapy treatment to each patient?"

"Many times I am, or at least I'll start the infusion. But a staff person will take over from there, check in on the patient periodically and so forth."

"And where are you when all this is happening? Are you in the office or what?" Harris asked.

"I'm *always* in the office during those treatments. I may be seeing other patients, or I may be on the phone talking to a patient or another doctor. I might be writing an article for my newsletter—and I'll have to give you a copy of our latest newsletter before you leave. The main thing is, I'm here," Levin told him.

"That's good," Harris responded. "By the way, as I try to understand the difference between your practice and a more traditional medical practice, how many patients do you tend to see every day?"

"Not very many," Levin told him, "especially when I have a new patient coming in."

"What does 'not very many' mean, doctor?"

"I might see only four, five, or maybe six patients some days."

"That's not typical of most medical practices, where appointments are set fifteen minutes apart and there's a lot of double-booking going on, just in case someone doesn't show up. Most patients expect to wait at least an hour or more when they have an appointment with their doctor," Harris stated.

Levin nodded. "Well, that doesn't happen here. *This* is not that type of medical practice. As I started to tell you at our first meeting, I *listen* to my patients, I really listen. When they come in here for the first time, they've usually been everywhere else first, sometimes to a whole collection of medical doctors and specialists. They've had loads of tests, been prescribed tons of useless medications, and told that nothing further can be done to help them, informed that only more kidney-harming or liver-damaging drugs can potentially be given to them, told that surgery is the only answer—but, even with the surgery, their problem may not disappear. All this, and then they walk through my door."

"And you listen to them complain to you for hours on end?" Harris joked.

"Not 'hours on end,' but I take a lot of time listening to understand them and their experiences, to create a comfortable relationship with them so they feel like they can talk to me. I don't rush them or look at my watch or take phone calls. I stay with them in the moment, take a few notes to remind myself of things I don't want to forget, and write it all up later. My intake form is very long and very thorough, so after an initial appointment, I generally know a whole lot about the patient, the presenting problem, the medical history, prior treatment, and where the patient is at psychologically. You know something," Levin said, his eyes focused on a distant memory, "I can't imagine going back to the type of practice I once had, practicing the kind of medicine you're taught in medical school, the kind practiced by the allopathic, you know, the traditional, guys, where you have to figure everything out in a few minutes, and the patient feels like he's gone through a whirlwind and isn't sure that his doctor's even getting the point."

Harris didn't respond. Levin's words were calling to mind his own experiences in the offices of various medical doctors he had gone to as a patient. He regarded Levin silently. *I'll bet this guy's patients really like him.* He waited for the doctor to resume lecturing him on his brand of medicine's unusual tests and treatments.

Taking Harris's silence as a cue, Levin returned to the topic of chelation therapy, explaining how this treatment had benefited not only the initial patient they discussed but numerous others, whose cases might be pulled into his defense. "Chelation therapy actually fits into my practice in a number of ways," he told the lawyer. "Heavy metal poisoning is a catch-all phrase, and a lot of people think that someone has to have worked in the mines of Pennsylvania for decades, breathing in coal dust, to end up with a condition like that, but it's not true at all."

"Enlighten me," was Harris's response.

Levin smiled. "Sometimes builders will buy land near former hazardous waste sites, and they'll put up a housing development. The people who buy those houses and raise their families there might be breathing high levels of arsenic from the soil and rocks on or near their property every time they are outdoors, gardening, barbequing, playing on the lawn. Over time, well, arsenic can kill you if it isn't removed from your cells. Welders in ore smelting plants have died from cadmium poisoning.

"Here in the city, lead poisoning is a big issue. Kids in old apartment buildings will frequently eat lead-based paint chips that they pick off peeling walls, true. However, lead gets into our bodies in more subtle ways. Listen, every day I walk from the train station to my office and back to the station at the end of my day to commute home. I am very well aware of the lead I'm inhaling from lead paint chips out on the street, from the fumes of leaded gasoline from the cars, trucks, and taxis passing me. We get rid of a lot of that lead when we urinate, but it really builds up dangerously in the kids who grow up around here. I give myself chelation treatments to make sure none of the poisonous substances from the environment cause me any lasting damage. A lot of people who grew up in the city, though, drinking water coming through the lead pipes in their buildings, walking in these streets regularly, and have mouths full of mercury-based amalgam fillings in their teeth often end up here with memory problems, fatigue, and a general feeling of malaise. You can't imagine how helpful chelation treatments are to these folks."

They segued into other tests and treatments, with Levin carefully connecting the dots for Harris, making his diagnostic process and subsequent treatment choices emerge with more and more clarity. It was a lot of new information for Harris to digest, but he knew he was up to the task. Besides, he was beginning to suspect that this case would prove to be a major career challenge, something he was ripe for at this juncture. He had the experience and appetite necessary to tackle the job. Not to be ignored was the fact that he enjoyed a good fight.

He retrieved his car from the parking garage and reviewed the facts in his mind as he drove back out to Long Island. New York State was taking an interest in this doctor's cases, some from thirteen years earlier. Maybe Levin's methods were unusual, but he found that he was impressed with the doctor's knowledge, thoroughness, intelligence, and alleged results in areas that seemed, at first glance, out of his range of expertise. For example, they had talked about how mercury invaded cells in the human body. Harris had never considered the possibility that psychiatric issues could arise from mercury overload, but Levin told him about a patient whose behaviors were very repetitive and perseverative, and a psychiatrist had diagnosed her with OCD, Obsessive-Compulsive Disorder. The medication prescribed for the young woman hadn't made a bit of difference, and the girl's nonstop talking, phone calls to her parents, and constant repetition of the same issues time and time again—one day she had called her parents from her out-of-state college twenty-five times to complain about an upcoming exam!—were taking a toll on the older couple. During the girl's summer vacation, Levin began treating her for the mercury in her system that he suspected was causing these psychological issues. With each dose of chelation, both the girl and her parents had been thrilled and excited by the positive changes in her behavior.

Harris was impressed, and he didn't impress easily. *If this was alternative medicine, why is it the* alternative *and not the standard?* He shook the thought from his mind. Yes, he was hired to defend Levin, but he didn't want to get caught up in alternative medicine just yet. He needed to keep pushing the doctor and pushing him hard. Harris knew that in preparing a solid defense, he had to put himself into the prosecutor's position and make his client prove everything to him, *beyond the shadow of a doubt*, as the old legal adage went. Only then could he, as a judicious lawyer, craft a viable defense. And Harris wanted to create a defensive strategy that was strong enough to fly solo, buzzing threateningly over the heads of Levin's accusers. In fact, his goal was to do just that.

CHAPTER 5

Harris sat at his desk the next morning, reviewing his notes from the previous day's meeting with Levin. He asked his partner, Sandi, to join him. He planned to run some of freshly acquired knowledge by her. She was an appropriately skeptical lawyer, and he wanted to see if she'd buy into his explanation and understanding of alternative medicine. Her reaction would be helpful in judging how the hearing committee might respond to anything he would offer in defense of Warren Levin.

"So who brought charges against him?" Sandi asked.

"It looks as though there are no other complainants, other than the state of New York," Bob responded. "No patient has complained. But the impression I'm getting from all of this is that even if patients knowingly seek unconventional medical treatments, with the understanding that these treatments are not given within mainstream medicine, New York State *still* feels obligated to 'protect them' from the doctor who is offering those treatments, whether they've asked for the state's protection or not."

"Weird," Sandi said in response to Bob's explanation. "Really weird. So if I had a medical problem, and if my doctor's treatment proved to be useless, and someone told me about your Dr. Levin, and I went to his office—knowing that he'd be doing something different from my regular doctor ..."

"Not only from *your* doctor but from *most* doctors," Bob added.

"Okay, from *most* doctors," she continued, "but his treatments didn't harm me, maybe they even helped me, whatever, and I didn't complain about him, New York State might *still* chase after him on *my* behalf? Is that what you're saying?"

Bob nodded affirmatively.

"But that's crazy!" she said.

"Yeah, well, this is what seems to be going on. Anyway, let me give you an idea of some of the stuff he told me. Women having been coming into his practice with greater and greater frequency, and so many of them have this condition called 'candidiasis,' a gynecological problem. There's an infection going on in the vaginal area, so they go to their gynecologist, who prescribes a tube of antifungal cream, and says, 'Come back in and see me in two weeks. Goodbye.'" Bob snorted dismissively.

"I've had vaginal infections," Sandi said without hesitation, "and sometimes the cream takes care of the itching and discomfort just fine. So what am I missing?"

"According to Levin, you're right. But a *fulminating* Candida infection, with malodorous discharge and discomfort, can be downright disabling. Some of these women were missing days and weeks and months of work from this problem. He told me about a couple of cases, in fact showed me the charts, of a few women who were out of circulation for more than a year with this condition. He said that some of these ladies came into his office crying and upset beyond belief."

"What did he end up doing to help them?" Sandi asked.

"His approach was multifaceted and, by God, effective in most cases. Even in the worst cases. He would tell the woman to start wearing cotton panties or no panties at all, but to absolutely avoid nylon and any type of synthetic panties. Since Candida first develops in the digestive tract, he would initially prescribe very large doses of Nystatin, an antifungal drug that isn't absorbed into the bloodstream at all. It moves through the digestive tract and effectively decreases, and sometimes eliminates, Candida growth," Bob told her. "Oh, and a little 'sidebar,'" he said—using a term that the legal profession coined for a quiet little conference between opposing counsel and the judge in front of the bench during a trial. "Levin told me a little tidbit on how Nystatin got its name. It seems as though Nystatin was originally manufactured from a weird mold that was discovered during an excavation somewhere in upstate New York, so the first three letters, N-Y-S, pay tribute to that. You know, New York State."

Sandi sat across from him, listening thoughtfully. "Thanks for the bit of trivia," she said, rolling her eyes. "So far, I still don't hear anything terribly objectionable," she said, getting back to the doctor's situation.

"Okay, so I'll continue on. The doctor would then recommend to the woman that she eat nothing containing yeast and, even more importantly, nothing containing sugar or large amounts of carbohydrates."

"So far, so good," Sandi responded.

"Then he'd prescribe—for lack of a better term, a 'cocktail' of supplements to assist in boosting the immune system."

"Bingo!" said Sandi.

"Bingo what?" Bob asked.

"Bingo, the problem. Outside of suggesting that it's a good idea for a patient to take a multivitamin pill every day, I can't imagine a doctor 'prescribing a cocktail of supplements,'" Sandi responded. "What kind of supplements? And who was paying for these supplements; certainly not the patient's insurance company, I'm sure. I can just imagine the insurance company people laughing over bills submitted for these 'cocktails.'"

"Sandi, according to Levin, these supplements are what assists in boosting the immune system to help the body fight off the infection. To me, this seems to make a heck of a lot of common sense. Anyway, that's beside the point. Do you know what the state actually is charging here?"

"No, what?"

Bob snorted. "*They're charging him with over-prescribing Nystatin*, even though no one can actually state what the harm is in prescribing more than the recommended dosage! You know," he continued, beginning to warm up to the topic, "after talking to Levin, I've come to realize quite a few things I've never thought about before concerning medical practices. It's not that the mainstream gynecologists don't care about their patients as much as Dr. Levin does. They don't do things *his* way because, in medical school, they really didn't learn anything meaningful about environmental contributors to medical problems—aka nylon panties in this case—or the impact of nutrition on breeding and maintaining ill health. No, I take that back," he said. "They learn that Vitamin C prevents scurvy and Vitamin D prevents rickets. But the very idea of giving *vitamins and minerals* to patients in an effort to boost their immune systems is completely foreign to them. Most docs are taught to diagnose, and then sit right down at their desks with a prescription pad. And when the salespeople come to medical offices, they come with samples of creams and pills for the doctors to distribute and prescribe. They don't come in with vitamin and mineral samples, and those things generally don't require a prescription anyway."

"Those pharmaceutical guys…and gals go into doctors' offices with a lot more than just creams and pills," Sandi said, smirking.

Harris was thrown off. "What do you mean?" he asked her.

"I remember being in my doctor's office for a routine checkup. This guy comes in, along with a female assistant or whatever she was, representing one of the bigger drug companies. They were followed by someone from the local deli, who had all kinds of packages in his arms. Delicious-smelling packages," she added, emphatically. "The receptionist ushered them straight into a back room, and when I went past there as I was heading toward the examining room, I saw the most amazing lunch spread I had ever seen. These drug reps cultivate loyalty from the doctors and their staff. They spend money to get themselves in the door. I remember my mother's doctor giving her some prescription pill samples once, and asking her to let him know how they worked for her anxiety. He said that a 'cute drug rep' had dropped off pizzas for the staff and left the samples at his office when he couldn't find time to meet with her. That's ludicrous! So the doctors depend on these drug reps to keep them current on the latest meds…"

"And to feed the staff," he finished.

"And to feed the staff," she agreed.

Bob then told Sandi what he had learned about chelation therapy, referring to his notes on occasion, but generally speaking by memory, secretly pleased that he had already internalized much of the information that he'd need to understand as he developed a defense for Levin. For Sandi, this was as new and unfamiliar as it had been for Bob yesterday, except now *he* was playing the role of professor, carefully watching his "student's" eyes for understanding. Sandi was a bright woman; there was no doubt about that. She was the best attorney to discuss the issues with, because she digested the information quickly then immediately went for the bulls-eye.

"So you're saying that this chelation therapy treatment could lead to kidney damage?" she postulated.

"Only if it's not administered slowly, over a three-and-a-half to four-hour time period," Bob said. "Otherwise there's no significant risk."

"Needles always pose a risk," she countered.

"True," he admitted. "An infection can result when a needle is inserted into the patient's arm, but if this is done properly, with all protocols for appropriate hygiene observed, the risk is eliminated. Actually," he informed her, "I was told that hundreds of physicians have been doing chelation therapy treatments for many years now. They have an association called ACAM, the American College for the Advancement of Medicine, and this group actually trains doctors on all aspects of chelation therapy. They've been around since 1973, when the association was then known as the American Academy of Medical Preventics, so it's no fly-by-night association. The point, here, is that a heck of a lot of physicians, who went to medical school and trained in traditional medicine, just like Levin himself, are now administering chelation therapy to their patients as a complementary treatment to whatever else they do."

"Interesting," she said. "That's new to me."

"To me, too, believe me. Levin gave me some ACAM stuff to read. It looks like a legitimate enough organization, not for profit, and devoted to educating medical doctors and others in the field of health care about whatever is new in complementary, alternative, and integrative medicine. The group is actually devoted to helping physicians improve their skills, expand their knowledge, and sharpen their diagnostic procedures. At least, that's what they claim in their literature," he added, glancing at her. "Anyhow, ACAM prides itself on letting the public connect with its doctors, promoting the whole idea of patients becoming partners in their own medical care, rather than viewing their doctors as unapproachable, god-like figures. I think that's pretty good. I don't know about you. By the way, this group offers board certification in chelation therapy. However…and this is a big thing; this certification, this group even, is *not* recognized by the larger medical establishment."

"How come?"

Here Bob took a deep breath and exhaled it slowly and noisily. "Part of the problem surrounding chelation therapy is to be found in the fact that it's very difficult to corroborate in a scientific way how much, if any, benefit the patient derives from the therapy."

Bob gave Sandi a brief primer on EDTA chelation therapy, relishing the opportunity to teach what he had just learned. "Levin says that this treatment can be effective against a number of medical conditions, including kidney and heart disease, arthritis, Parkinson's disease, emphysema, multiple sclerosis, gangrene, psoriasis, and other serious conditions. I'm not saying that Levin himself is treating serious illnesses like these with chelation therapy, but a number of his colleagues within the alternative field have claimed notable results with a number of these conditions. Levin tends to be more conservative in his approach, which is a good thing, as far as I'm concerned."

"Especially when New York State is after his license," she agreed.

"That's what I mean. What hurts his case in using this treatment is the lack of scientific proof as to its effectiveness. Take blood vessel disease, for example. The only way you can evaluate blood vessel disease, from what Levin tells me, is through an angiogram. Nobody's going to do before-and-after angiograms on a patient to determine the results of chelation therapy, because there's a prohibitive risk associated with an angiogram. So even if Levin notices that so many of his patients are reporting how much better they feel, establishment medicine is absolutely unwilling to judge the effectiveness of this treatment the reported outcomes."

"Has this issue come up anywhere else but in New York?" Sandi asked him.

"Sure," he responded. "From what he tells me, the Florida legislature passed a law *prohibiting* the medical board from prosecuting doctors who used chelation therapy for the treatment of atherosclerotic heart disease."

"That's good!" she responded.

"Yeah, but in the state of New Jersey, the medical board issued a directive that treating atherosclerotic heart disease with chelation therapy is to be considered *professional misconduct* and a basis for the *removal of a doctor's license to practice medicine!*"

"Wow," said Sandi, "so depending on where you practice, you can be governed by completely different laws. This is a thorny case, to say the least."

"Yeah, I know. But let me tell you something," he said reflectively, "I like this guy. I believe him. He's credible. He makes sense. He's bright. Sure, a lot of what he does in his practice is different, but he's convinced that it works. And, from what he's telling me, his patients are glad that they found their way to his office. And something else. . ."

"What else?"

"Irrelevant, maybe, but in the midst of all of this angst, all of this aggravation, this disruption to his practice and his life and his family, he's kept himself very balanced, psychologically, I think. In other words, he's no nut case, no fanatic. He's even maintained a sense of humor. It's hard not to like this guy," Bob told her.

"I know, I know. You'll defend him, because that's what you were hired to do, but if you like the guy as well, that just makes it more appealing to you. I have a feeling you're going to end up becoming a crusader for alternative medicine now!" Sandi said, standing up and stretching. They'd been talking over an hour, and she knew she'd have a pile of phone messages waiting when she went up to the receptionist's desk.

"You never can tell!" Bob said with a smirk, stubbing out his cigar in an unusual ashtray, designed to immediately extinguish the butt and stop the fumes from spewing out. "No, you never can tell," he repeated softly to himself.

CHAPTER 6

Bob Harris picked up the phone and dialed Levin's office. Harris was looking at a letter he had just received from Terrence Sheehan, the prosecuting attorney. He needed to speak with Levin immediately.

"Bob, what's going on?" Levin asked him, sounding a bit breathless. Whenever he got a call from his lawyer, he was worried that the state had found another charge to add to its growing list, another nail for his coffin.

Without preamble, Harris barked, "Who is Victor Herbert?"

"Victor Herbert? Why are you asking me about him? What does *he* have to do with anything that's going on with *us*?" The shock was apparent in Levin's tone, something that didn't escape his attorney's ears.

"I'm holding a letter that Sheehan sent me. He says that Victor Herbert is going to be, and I quote, 'the *state's only witness* in pre-trial discovery.' Who *is* this guy?"

Levin didn't answer, but the rapidity of his breathing increased, as did its volume.

"Warren?" Harris asked, aware that something was going on, something that he himself didn't yet comprehend. He waited.

"Bob...look, can I call you back?" His voice was subdued, deflated.

"You can call me back, but I really need you to talk to me about this man. I assume you know who he is," Harris responded, softening his voice a bit.

"Yeah, I'll talk to you about him, all right. But not right this minute, okay? I've got a patient waiting to see me. I'll call you back. This is a short appointment. Give me about an hour." He closed the phone softly, dazed.

Harris called Sandi into his office. He had been discussing the case with her on a regular basis, so she was familiar with the details and Bob's growing defense packet as well. He told her about the conversation with Levin, but everything they postulated was just conjecture. They had no idea what Levin would say about the state's witness, what the implications would be. Bob tried to keep himself busy returning calls and signing letters he had dictated to his secretary. He watched the clock. Levin was prompt, he had learned; a man of his word.

"Bob, you're not going to believe this," Levin said, when he called back. "Victor Herbert! What a joke. On top of the ridiculous charges the state has brought against me, bringing Victor Herbert in…as the *state's only witness*, no less, has got to be the biggest joke of all!"

"I'm waiting," Harris responded somberly, not getting "the joke."

"I don't even know where to start in trying to explain Victor Herbert. First of all, he's a doctor, an M.D., and he's also a lawyer. He's a pretty smart guy; that much I'll give him. But the guy's got no class, none at all," Levin continued.

"I don't think the state is necessarily looking for a classy guy," Harris told him, "just somebody who can chew you up and spit you out. So he's a smart guy; he's got no class. What else?"

"Wait, I have a dictionary here," Levin told him, grunting as he reached into one of the cubbies in his roll top desk to grab it.

"A dictionary?" Harris asked him.

"Give me a minute," Levin said. Harris could hear him rapidly flipping pages across the phone line.

"'*Quack*:'" Levin began reading, "'an untrained person who pretends to be a physician and dispenses medical advice and treatment; a charlatan.' I read that to you so we'd both be clear on the definition of the noun, 'quack.'"

"Okay, I'm now clear on the definition of the noun, 'quack.' I don't know why I needed to be clear on it, but I assure you, it's crystal clear to me," Harris, said, playing along. "But what does this have to do with …"

"This has *everything* to do with Victor Herbert, Bob, which is why I wanted you to hear that definition. I need you to understand that this guy applies the term, 'quack,' to educated doctors, not uneducated pretenders who are charlatans—as the dictionary states—but to doctors like *me*!" he said, emphasizing the *me*. Levin took a deep breath and began speaking again. "Victor Herbert has proclaimed himself to be a *Quackbuster*, with a capital Q. He's made it part of his life's mission to go after medical doctors...*medical doctors*," he repeated more forcefully, "who happen to practice medicine differently than he does! He's made it such a significant part of his career to pull medical licenses away from doctors who think or act differently than he does, who find value in alternative treatments, in using methods that don't jell with what the mainstream—establishment, allopathic, or whatever adjective you want to use—physicians do and say and how they test patients and what they prescribe and treat and ..." His voice grew more agitated with each word he spoke.

"I see," is all Harris said. "So what does Victor Herbert know about alternative medicine that the state has selected him—and no one else—as their 'expert witness'?"

"Nothing! Nada! Not a damn thing," Levin barked, his agitation re-emerging. "He's no expert on the treatments I use or the things I do! All he wants is my license! This stinks; this really, really stinks."

"Warren, look," Harris said in a reasonable tone of voice, "let me request his *curriculum vitae*. That should give me a better idea of what he's all about. Then we'll review it together and talk more. Okay?"

"What choice do I have? Ever since this nightmare started, it's as though I've lost control of my life! They're calling all the shots, and we're running around like crazy, working insane hours to prepare a defense. In the meantime, my practice is suffering, my family is suffering, I'm not sleeping at night, I'm ..."

"Warren, enough! You're not alone in this. You've got a very supportive wife. Your patients love you, and your colleagues respect you. You're paying me, true, but you've made a believer out of me, which is not an easy thing to do; and that's something that will come across in my defense of you. Take it easy; you'll live longer." Harris pressed the button to end the call then immediately dialed Sheehan's office. He needed to look into this Victor Herbert business, and fast.

They met in the city for dinner, a quiet little restaurant, doctor and lawyer, plus two copies of Victor Herbert's sixty-page *curriculum vitae*, a totally impressive pile of papers.

"Holy smoke!" Levin said, loudly enough for several patrons in the restaurant to glance over at their table. "Whoa!" He lowered his voice, conscious of his lapse in manners.

"What?" Harris asked him.

"Oh, man," he said, shaking his head from side to side and referring him to one of the pages, then motioning Harris to turn the pages even faster. "Look at that; look at that!" Levin insisted, jabbing the page in front of him so hard that the water glasses on the table were threatening to spill over. "I can't believe this; now it all makes sense; it…all…makes…sense!"

"Warren," Bob said in his most patient voice, the kind one would use with an overly tired and cranky child, "help me out here. What makes sense? What are you looking at?"

"Victor Herbert gave a lecture at the 93rd annual meeting of The Association of Life Insurance Medical Directors of America!" Levin blurted, speaking rapidly. "Look at that title, would you? Just look at that title!"

Harris found the place on his own copy and read aloud, "How to Recognize Questionable Diagnostic Tests and Therapies." He looked up at Levin.

"Bob, don't you get it?" He picked up his copy again and waved it. A look of disbelief was on his face. "This…is…collusion!" he stated, spacing out the words for emphasis. "Collusion."

When Harris still didn't react, Levin put the papers down on the table and leaned forward. "Remember when we discussed the additional four patients that the state tacked onto the original three charts they first requisitioned?" Levin asked, speaking slowly and deliberately.

"Sure," Harris responded. "Those four resulted in the insurance companies making a complaint against you to the OPMC, correct? They wouldn't reimburse the patients for your treatments and decided you were dangerous enough to report, right?"

"That's exactly right," Levin said. He sat back, and for a long moment seemed lost in his thoughts. *Wow, just when I thought things couldn't get any worse.* Herbert is the state's only witness, which is bad enough. And Herbert gave a lecture to the health insurance industry, specifically designed to make them suspicious of the tests and treatments used by alternative physicians: "How to Recognize Questionable Diagnostic Tests and Therapies." Levin was irate. Why didn't the jerk just call it, "How to Recognize Doctors Practicing Alternative Medicine?" he wondered. That would make the partnership between Victor Herbert and the insurance industry that much closer and more efficient. That way, alternative physicians would be reported to the OPMC in even greater numbers and could be annihilated even more rapidly. *Herbert* colluded *with the insurance providers, as far as I'm concerned, so they'd help him in his quest to take the medical licenses away from doctors like me*. The state of New York is bringing in an enemy of alternative medicine as an "expert witness." How much more ridiculous can this situation become?

The waiter came to take their order, and Levin snapped out of his reverie. Over a glass of wine, he continued where he had left off. Fixing Harris with a serious look, he said, "Either the insurance companies or the Peer Review Committee that reviewed the complaints reported me. Incidentally, I never saw that report. But look who primed the wheel for this whole thing? Look who listed the tests and therapies he *didn't* use in his own practice and probably called them fraudulent. Look at who is responsible for making the insurance companies reluctant to pay for the kind of work I do. Look, look!" Levin's face was beet red, as he insistently tapped the same spot on Herbert's list of accomplishments.

"I see, I see," Harris responded. "Now the two of you will be coming face to face for the pre-trial discovery. Whew."

"Bob, you don't know the half of it. You really don't. I *know* who Victor Herbert is; I *know* what he's all about. Listen," Levin continued, warming to the topic, a sneer on his face, "this guy was working at the Queens V.A. Hospital, *the V.A. hospital*, for God's sake, and he was asked to leave! What doctor ever gets invited *out* of a V.A. hospital? Especially an American-born and American-educated medical doctor! That *never* happens. But it happened to Victor Herbert. He's just that kind of guy. A lousy, unpleasant person. So he went to work in the Bronx V.A."

"Tell me about his lousy, unpleasant side," Harris asked.

"Oh, that's easy," Levin countered. "I'll give you one unforgettable example to keep in the back of your mind. Herbert gave a lecture once..." Levin began, and then added, "As you can see, Herbert apparently gives *lots* of lectures," he chuckled. "Anyhow, to stick to the topic, Herbert was the invited guest speaker at this particular meeting, and he was up on the stage behind the podium, and this guy—who happened to be the executive director of an organization called People Against Cancer—decided to tape record the speech. No big deal, right? Well, it apparently *was* a big deal for Victor Herbert, for some inexplicable reason. Herbert actually stopped speaking when he noticed the guy had this large cassette recorder on his lap, calling everyone's attention to something few of us could see, since the guy was sitting up close to the front. Herbert demanded that the guy turn off the recorder, but I guess the request didn't make any sense to this guy, so he didn't pay attention; he kept the tape recorder running. When Victor Herbert saw that his 'command' was being ignored, he became infuriated. Now this is happening in front of a group of doctors and allied health professionals, where there should be a certain type of decorum, you know? Anyway, when the guy didn't comply, which immediately became obvious to Herbert, let me tell you what he did. Like a panther, Herbert stepped out from behind the lectern, hunching his shoulders up around his neck, and glaring at the guy in a menacing way…In fact, I was sitting near the back of the hall, I remember, and I think I saw sparks flying out of Herbert's eyes from way back there. There was a sharp intake of breath from the audience as a whole, because this was so out of character for a speaker, literally issuing a warning and making a visual threat, from the stage. Anyhow, before anybody could anticipate it, Herbert jumped off the stage, ran into the audience—and Herbert's a little guy, a little guy with a giant Napoleonic Complex, if you ask me—and pulled the recorder out of the guy's hands; then he physically assaulted this guy!"

"You've got to be kidding!" Harris declared. "This is a joke, right? You've got to be kidding!"

"No, I'm not, and there were plenty of witnesses," Levin said, satisfied that he had a gripping enough tale to relate to his lawyer, amply demonstrating Victor Herbert's "style." "Herbert was arrested and convicted, which I know he denied. People talk, you know. But a lot of us knew he had been convicted. His good luck, though, got the charge overturned on appeal because of some minor technicality. So this is the kind of low-class stuff this guy is prone to, just so you have a clear picture of him," Levin ended.

Now it was Harris's turn to lean back in his chair, regarding Levin thoughtfully. He laced his fingers together and placed his linked hands over his ample midsection. He was smiling.

"I'll offer a small fortune for your thoughts right at this moment," said Levin, curious.

Harris continued smiling wordlessly a moment longer. Then he sat up straight in his chair and rubbed his hands together gleefully. "Let me tell you something, Warren," he said, the smile still on his face, giving him an almost angelic look, "I'm really gonna enjoy making a mess of Victor Herbert, the state's *only* expert witness!"

"As they say, Bob, from your mouth to God's ears!"

"That's exactly what I have in mind," Harris stated with a chuckle. "Let's eat!"

Something had been nagging at the lawyer during the entire meal, while the two men tried to relax and enjoy the evening. Finally, Harris, who obviously hadn't been listening to a story Levin was telling him, said, "Warren, I've got it! I've *got* it!"

Levin, who had been telling Harris about something Erika had done which had him and Susan laughing hysterically, was startled for a moment. "I'm sorry?"

"I've got it, I said."

"I don't have the vaguest idea *what* you're talking about, Bob."

"Not *what*, Warren, *who*," the lawyer said.

"Okay," Levin responded, "then *who*?"

"Victor Herbert, that's who. Who else would I be talking about?"

"I don't know. I was telling you about Erika, and ..."

"And I'm sorry I wasn't paying attention, so you'll have to remember to tell me the story another time. I have an idea about Victor Herbert." Harris leaned back and smiled, looking so self-satisfied that he knew Levin was suddenly intrigued. "We already know about Victor Herbert's medical and law degrees, and we know he's smart. You told me that he's testified against countless complementary physicians." Levin was nodding his assent, curious as to what Harris was leading up to. "You also led me to understand that he's super aggressive in the courtroom, from what your colleagues have told you of their experiences. Have I got that right?"

"Yeah, everything you just said about him is right." Levin wondered where the discussion was leading.

"Okay, here's my idea, and you don't have to tell me I'm brilliant tonight. You can wait until tomorrow. That's okay."

Levin opened his hands in a pleading gesture. "Bob, how long is this foreplay going to continue?" he asked. "Tell me, already!"

Harris laughed. "Okay, now listen carefully, Warren. Here's my plan. Victor Herbert doesn't know who the hell I am, does he?"

"No, I'm sure he doesn't if you've never met in court."

"We haven't, so we agree he doesn't know me."

"Agreed."

"Well, I plan to know him so well before we ever step into that hearing room that if he's about to answer a question, I'll be able to write the script for him if he forgets the words." Levin stared at him, open-mouthed. "Look, here's the master plan," Harris began, rubbing his hands together gleefully, as he tended to do when he was really excited about one of his ideas. "If this guy has done so much testifying, there's going to be a lot of evidence out there."

"Evidence? What do you mean by evidence?" Levin was puzzled.

"Oh, there'll be written depositions, there will probably be audiotapes, there might be videotapes, you know, evidence that he's testified."

Levin started to think about what he was hearing. "Bob, I think you've got something," he said thoughtfully.

"You think?" Harris responded, echoing Levin's tentative tone.

"No, listen," Levin said, his mind racing. "I know so many alternative docs who have been under the gun, and so many of them were Victor Herbert's targets. I'm not sure I can give you any names right this minute, but I can start making some calls tomorrow from my office. I have a feeling, a very strong feeling in fact, that if any of my colleagues have what you're looking for, they'll be more than happy to share it with me. You can't imagine how many of us, over the years, have labeled that guy 'a one-man, search-and-destroy team.' Wow! I've got to give you credit," he said to Harris, his eyes no longer looking tired, even after their after-dinner aperitif.

Harris said to him, "Warren, listen, get on the phone as soon as you can tomorrow. I'm sure one doctor will refer you to another and then another. Tell them to send whatever they have immediately. In fact, give them my name and office address, and let them send stuff directly to me. I'm going to do the same thing!" Harris declared.

"What 'same thing'?" Levin asked.

"I'm going to get on the phone first thing tomorrow morning and start calling medical defense lawyers. I'll bet there are plenty of them who have stuff on Victor Herbert. I figure, as the stuff comes in, I'll read depositions when I can during the day, I'll listen to any cassettes as I'm driving anywhere, and I'll pop the videotapes into my VCR player in the evening and watch Victor Herbert rather than television shows. How's that?" the lawyer queried.

"It couldn't be better, Bob, it just couldn't be better."

Levin's whole demeanor had changed, Harris noted. They had just added an important segment to their defense packet. *Know thy self, know thy enemy. A thousand battles, a thousand victories. He may have been a Chinese general and author who was born in 500 BC, but Sun Tzu's stuff is as relevant to this case today as it was back then; maybe even more so.*

Neither Harris nor Levin delegated the telephone calls to staff members, feeling that they had to generate the inquiries themselves. And both of them hit major jackpots…repeatedly. In fact, the problem, in both cases, was getting the doctors and attorneys they called to hang up the phone! Victor Herbert had made a huge impression on both the legal and the medical community. The doctors wanted to tell Levin how Herbert's testimony had insulted them, the awful names he had called them from the witness stand, his attempts to make them seem like charlatans to the hearing committee. The lawyers regaled Harris with stories of Herbert's attempts to intimidate anyone who asked him a question he either couldn't answer or chose not to respond to, how Herbert didn't hesitate to curse out a defense lawyer who challenged him, how he had defied a judge.

"Send a copy of the audiotape," they told these people, "Send a copy of the deposition," they said, "Either send the original or a copy of the video cassette tape." "Please, send it right away! The license of the doctor who opened the first large alternative medicine center in New York City is on the line. Don't delay! Please help us!"

Materials began to arrive at Harris's office on a daily basis. He read, he listened, he watched, and he learned. At the end of every day, Harris rubbed his hands together in anticipation of the upcoming battle. When he met with Levin, he shared his optimism. Levin was still worried, though. Harris understood. If their roles were reversed, he knew he'd feel the same way.

Harris knew himself well. He had gotten to know his client well. Now, he was studying the enemy with a determination to know *him* even better than he knew himself or his client. He had little doubt about his ability to do just that. He rubbed his hands together again, signaling his satisfaction with his progress. It was midnight, and tomorrow was a work day.

CHAPTER 7

"I really didn't sleep very well last night," Levin admitted to his wife, Susan, as he got ready to leave for his office.

"Neither did I." she responded. "The bed kept shaking, because you were tossing and turning all night." She had thought about starting a conversation with him at about three in the morning, so that they could discuss the things she knew were bothering him, but decided that whatever restless sleep he was able to get was better than none at all.

"Sorry," he said, putting down his briefcase and pulling on a light overcoat.

"No apologies needed," she responded, straightening his coat collar. "I'm just as nervous as you are." She held his face between her hands tenderly and looked deeply into his eyes. "You know how much I love you," she whispered, kissing him warmly. "Please call me as soon as you can."

He took off his glasses and blotted his eyes with a handkerchief. "Don't worry, I will," he said, carefully folding the handkerchief back into its original square shape. He stood in the entry hall for a moment longer, just staring at Susan, seeming to draw strength from her presence.

She noticed a definite twinkle in his blue eyes before he picked up his briefcase and left the house, and that made her happy. The relentless efforts by the state of New York to discredit her normally upbeat spouse had resulted in what she thought of as his *brief moments of dejection*, because that was all he would allow; so it was at those times that she made an extra effort to buoy his spirits. She stood by the front door, watching him leave. She was awed by his resiliency, his strength, his tireless pace, his ability to see the bright side of the darkest issues, even his willingness to fight what he perceived as injustice. She offered a silent prayer. *Please don't let anything happen today to upset him any further.*

The pre-hearing conference was on the agenda first thing this morning. His heart seemed to beat in time with the vibrations of the train's wheels as he thought about it. It was Monday, September 18, nearly three months since he had responded to Sheehan's letter on the train. Peacetime was over. The war was about to begin. The enemy was preparing to strike. *Boy, can you get any more dramatic, Warren?*

Levin already knew who would be present today, and he and his attorney had discussed it over the weekend. Besides the two of them, the prosecuting attorney, Terrence Sheehan, would be there; and the administrative law judge, Larry Storch, would be, as well. In fact, in their weekend discussion a number of issues had come up, further fueling Levin's conspiracy theory. *Point one:* Sheehan worked for the Office of Professional Medical Conduct, which was a division of the New York State Department of Health, and *both* of those units were part of the State Education Department. *Point two:* Storch worked for David Axelrod, M.D., the Commissioner of the Department of Health, who had been appointed at the beginning of the year by the Governor of New York. Axelrod, a diminutive, thin man with gray pallor and chronic depression, had decided to distinguish himself during his administration by ridding New York State of what he considered a scourge on the medical profession: physicians who practiced alternative medicine. In prosecuting Levin, often called the "Dean of Alternative Medicine " in N.Y. by many of his colleagues, Axelrod undoubtedly convinced himself that this would set the proper tone for his administration and allow him to rise to fame in the process. *Point three:* The analysis of points one and two yielded the result that the attorney prosecuting Levin and the judge hearing the case both worked for the same people. Yet the judge was to be an *impartial* hearing officer. Levin and Harris wondered how that was even possible. While it didn't seem necessary to proceed to point four, it added fuel to the conspiracy theory. *Point four:* The hearing panel, *chosen by Axelrod,* was selected for its willingness to *support* the commissioner's point of view; and this entire group was allegedly a *neutral* presence in the hearings! How much more ridiculous could things get? he wondered. He was soon to find out.

Client and attorney met outside of the building on East 40th Street. They walked in together and perfunctorily greeted the others. They sat down at a conference table for a discussion. Levin was composed and impeccably dressed. Harris was businesslike and self-confident. Each thought the other was portraying the proper amount of comfort in the presence of the state's henchmen.

The pre-trial hearing was primarily a venue to review the procedures that the hearing would take. Sheehan told them that the panel would be composed of three individuals: two medical doctors and a chemist. Yet the statement they both remembered and discussed in great detail once the conference ended was one made proudly by Sheehan, who said: "Victor Herbert is the soul of the state's case!"

Sheehan couldn't stop there, however, because he apparently felt a burning need to elaborate about Herbert. "This expert has written extensively," he stated proudly, as though he were Herbert's mentor, "has published books on the question of 'quackery,' so this expert is not someone who has never seen or heard of anything like Dr. Levin and his practices. He knew these practices intimately before we even contacted him!" It seemed to Harris and Levin that the prosecuting attorney was doing his absolute best to set the tone of the coming hearing, complete with a prejudicial slant meant to influence the "neutral" administrative law judge.

An hour later, the meeting was over and they left the building.

"That gives you an idea of what's coming up," Harris said, unnecessarily, as they walked along the street. "The funny thing is that both of them are nice guys, but they have jobs to do, and those jobs are often not very nice."

Levin was quiet, lost in thought, as he walked next to his lawyer, whose taller and heftier frame gave Levin the sense that he was with his bodyguard which, he supposed, was true to some extent. *This is what they call 'Indian summer,' a beautiful time of year in the city and inthe suburbs. Too bad Sheehan had to paint black clouds all over the horizon.*

"I love it," Levin muttered sarcastically, picking up his pace to match his frustration. "Sheehan manages to put the words 'quackery' and 'Dr. Levin' into the same sentence. Quackery!" he repeated with disgust. "Okay, we already knew that the great Victor Herbert was going to be the state's only witness, but then Sheehan goes and says that Victor Herbert is the 'soul' of the state's case against me."

"Yeah, I heard that, too," Harris huffed, struggling to keep pace. "Hey, slow down, Warren."

"Sorry." Levin scaled back. "I almost blurted out what I was thinking!" Levin laughed.

"Which was...?"

"I wanted to ask Sheehan, 'How do you spell it?' Is it 's-o-u-l,' as in the 'heart' of the case, or is it 's-o-l-e,' as in sole witness, or what?" said Levin.

"Frankly," said Harris, not cracking a smile, "I was thinking of this guy Herbert as the s-o-l-e of my *shoe*, since my intention is to step all over him!"

Levin enjoyed the first full, belly laugh that he could recall since receiving Sheehan's order to appear for a meeting in ten days. "I'm going to keep that image in mind, Bob, I really am." He laughed some more, just thinking about it. "You know," he then said, "Susan and I have done a lot of talking about this, as you can well understand, and I've come to a conclusion."

"I can't wait to hear your conclusion," Bob responded.

"While she's still not buying into it, I firmly believe I was 'chosen' to do this job, to go into court, to fight the good fight for the cause of alternative medicine. However, while that may be my overarching goal, I also want two other things: to save my license, and to have you expose Victor Herbert for the jerk I know he is. If we can bring down Victor Herbert, we'll have done a really good turn for the cause of alternative medicine, and for all the colleagues that have suffered and will continue to suffer because of that poor excuse for a doctor…and a lawyer," he added, remembering Herbert's credentials in both areas. Levin stopped in front of a luncheonette. "How about a cup of coffee?"

They slipped into a booth with red vinyl benches, with enough rips in each seat to leave a huge expanse of stained, white cotton padding visible. Each man attempted to position himself on an area of intact vinyl, which left them sitting diagonally across from each other.

"Susan wants me to just concentrate on saving my license, and I agree that we need to make that happen or nothing else will matter too much, but I can't tell you how excited I've become over this whole thing. Okay, I'm worried. I won't deny that. My whole life is at stake here. But alongside the feeling of worry is a sense of genuine excitement."

Levin ordered a bottle of water and a fruit cup. Harris ordered regular coffee and a large, sugary donut.

"I thought you were going to have coffee?"

"I really just wanted to sit and talk for a few minutes. I don't drink caffeinated beverages," Levin added, by way of explanation.

"Yeah, yeah, I know, healthy eating and all that stuff."

Levin chuckled, then turned very serious. "You know, Bob, when someone has committed murder and is caught, there's a good chance he's going to lose his freedom and spend the rest of his life behind bars. Okay, the guy took a human life, and it's only fair that he receives a severe punishment. In my case, I've spent years studying and learning, and continuing to learn, as I practice medicine—to improve lives, to save lives, to help people."

"Your point being?"

"It feels like the state is coming after me vindictively, as though my life's mission has been to *murder* people. They don't agree with my methods of practice, my diagnostic tests, or my treatments. I understand that, or," he corrected himself, "I'm *trying* to understand that. But 'they' aren't my patients. *My* patients are fully aware of what I do and why I do it. They comprehend the fact that I'm an alternative medical practitioner. I don't accept them into my practice unless they receive full disclosure and I have their informed consent. We try to help them get insurance reimbursement, but my patients already *know* that they may not be reimbursed, often aren't; and still they continue to come to my office. In return, I'm being hunted like the worst kind of criminal. And now, they're siccing that dog, Victor Herbert, on me. I'm sure it will give him a great deal of pleasure and a real sense of victory if he can sink his teeth deeply into me and tear off a chunk. What is that Shakespearean quote: 'A pound of flesh' from the 'Merchant of Venice'?"

"Shylock, the Jewish moneylender planned to extract a pound of flesh from the guarantor of a loan when the guy defaulted," Bob added, "but he didn't succeed in getting to cut off the flesh."

"Well, I'm not about to let Victor Herbert succeed, either; I don't want him to get close enough to me to cut me up."

"Don't worry," his lawyer assured him, "to get to you, this guy Herbert's gotta get past me, and it's not gonna be easy, believe me!"

"That's what I'm counting on," Levin said, trying not to catch his clothing on the ripped seat as he extracted himself from the booth.

They walked to the corner and shook hands. Levin had a patient to see, and Harris headed for the parking garage, towing his luggage cart with its file boxes and litigation bags. Victor Herbert occupied the central point of their collective thoughts, and their thoughts about him were far from flattering.

CHAPTER 8

On Wednesday, September 27, Levin and Harris went to the hearing room on Eighth Avenue and 33rd Street, and this time the panel was present as well. Not to be forgotten was the state's "sole" witness, the "soul" of the case against Warren M. Levin, M.D., the notable, self-important Victor Herbert, M.D., J.D., whom Harris had already pegged as "a legend in his own mind."

Doctor and lawyer had done their homework since the pre-hearing conference, and they knew more about the players than they cared to know. The chemist, Robert M. Briber, was chairing the hanging committee. He worked for New York State, which they found more than interesting, and tended to cast his votes in whatever direction the reigning commissioner happened to be leaning. Since they knew that Axelrod had plans to chase every last alternative medical practitioner out of the state of New York, they figured Briber's mind was made up before he stepped into the hearing room. Robert J. O'Connor, M.D. was a retired gynecologist from Staten Island, an Irish guy who took pride in the fact that he had never performed an abortion. The third was Margaret H. McAloon, M.D. She was actually a professor of medicine at The State University at Buffalo.

Ordinarily, when a prosecuting attorney from the New York State Attorney General's Office, such as Terrence Sheehan, introduces an expert like Victor Herbert—the doctor/lawyer with a *curriculum vitae* that appears unassailable on the surface—that witness is accepted without question. Bob Harris had a different strategy in mind, after listening to more and more of Levin's stories about Victor Herbert. Harris requested the opportunity for *voir dire*, the legal process in which a prospective witness is examined by opposing counsel to determine whether his expertise is real and meaningful.

Therefore, prior to the start of the official hearing on September 27, Harris looked forward to interrogating Victor Herbert.

"Dr. Herbert," Harris began, "in your application to medical school, were you completely honest in everything you wrote?"

"Of course, I was," Herbert answered gruffly, without stopping to reflect on the issue.

"The way I understand it," Harris countered, "you lied about your financial situation."

"My finances *were* and *are* my private business, and you have no right to bring up anything concerning that issue in here!" Herbert bluffed.

"Well, that's not true, Dr. Herbert, because as an expert witness, the panel needs to be assured of your ability to be honest and truthful. But it looks to me like you lied on your application to medical school, going into your career as a doctor based on a bald-faced lie!"

Herbert took a breath and made a visible effort to collect himself. "If I couldn't show financial means, they wouldn't have accepted me!"

"Oh, so it looks like lying is okay *when the ends justify the means*, isn't that right, Dr. Herbert?" Herbert didn't take the bait. He remained silent.

"I see that on your original application for a position at the VA Hospital, you claimed expertise in foreign affairs of countries in North Africa and Southeast Asia," Harris said.

"That's right," Herbert responded.

A small smile appeared on Harris's face, making it appear as though he was impressed by Herbert's vast knowledge of Third World areas, many of whose physicians end up staffing the nation's VA hospitals. "Would you," asked Harris, "kindly tell us what kind of currency is used in Cambodia?"

"Cambodia?" Herbert repeated. "Let's see." He thought for a moment, then admitted, "I really don't remember right now."

"Cambodia uses the *riel*, but most Cambodians prefer the U.S. dollar; but that's all right," Harris said. "Perhaps you can inform us what kind of currency is used in Burma."

"I don't recall."

"No problem," said Harris, "it's the *kyat*. How about Malaysia, then, since Southeast Asia is one of your areas of *special* knowledge."

Herbert shook his head no, his lips tight.

"It's the *ringgit*, Dr. Herbert. You might be more comfortable, then, with the North African currencies, so let's try, oh, any one of these three: Algeria, Tunisia, or Libya, it doesn't matter."

Herbert sat silently, glaring at Harris.

"That was an easy one, Dr. Herbert, because all three of those countries use the *dinar*. One final one, a bit harder: Egypt."

"I...don't...recall!" Herbert responded, spacing each word evenly in a snarl between his teeth.

This time Harris's smile was broad as he lectured Herbert. "Egypt uses the Egyptian pound or *geneih*, which is divided into 100 *piaster*." Harris was pleased to see the color creeping up from Herbert's collar. It didn't take long for the attorney to pick up Herbert's style: when he didn't know something, he resorted to intimidation, either with looks or tone of voice. He picked up Herbert's c.v. "Dr. Herbert, you are board-certified by the American Board of Internal Medicine and the American Board of Nutrition, I see."

"That's right," he snapped.

"Okay, please tell us, how does one become board-certified?"

"By completing the requisite training in an accredited institution and by taking and passing the board examination in that subject," Herbert answered confidently.

"I see that you passed the exam for the American Board of Internal Medicine in 1959, and you passed the exam for the American Board of Nutrition in 1967."

"That's correct, Mr. Harris."

"Well, that's interesting, Dr. Herbert, because I have a copy of a letter here, written by Kevin Scrimshaw, which informs you that you have been *waived* in the board certification process by the American Board of Nutrition by general acclaim of the examiners *without* having to take any examination whatsoever!" Harris heard a sharp intake of breath from the area where the panel members were seated. "And, not only that, Dr. Herbert, but on your rather extensive c.v., I was unable to locate *anywhere* that you had any significant specialty training and/or residency in nutrition." Pausing once again for effect, Harris added, "I guess we'll just have to assume, once again, Dr. Herbert, that *lying is acceptable* if the ends justify the means." Harris could see the muscles working overtime in Herbert's jaw.

"Dr. Herbert," Harris began, anxious to press his advantage, "do you have *any* prejudice that you are aware of towards or against Warren Levin?"

"I have no prejudice with relation to Warren Levin," Herbert said, managing to bring an even tone to his delivery.

"I thought you might say that, Dr. Herbert, so I have an editorial you wrote for the *New York State Journal of Medicine* three years ago, in 1986, in which you state: 'I have brought charges of professional misconduct against several egregious offenders engaged in a pattern of fraudulent and incompetent practice. I testified about some of those offenders before U.S. Congressman Claude Pepper's hearing on 'Quackery' in 1984 and before the New York State Assembly Republican Task Force on Health Fraud in the Elderly in 1985. It is no secret that these physicians are still practicing.' And, Dr. Herbert, I have a transcript of the Pepper hearings, and in that transcript, you have read the name of my client," Harris wheeled around to point a finger clearly at Warren Levin, "into the Congressional Record *not once, not twice, but three times*! Not only that, Dr. Herbert," Harris continued relentlessly, "but you also cited my client, *by name*, to the New York State Assembly."

At this point, after handing the exhibits to the judge to be marked, Harris turned to Herbert, who was still stunned from being caught in his latest untruth. "Did you bring charges against Dr. Levin before the Office of Professional Medical Conduct?"

"I object!" Sheehan shouted.

Not deterred, Harris continued, "Because if you did, that makes you the complainant and also the witness. This violates *any* concept of a fair trial!"

Storch, the administrative law judge intervened at this point. "I will not render a decision on this objection until I can research the law as it pertains to this issue," he wisely declared. "The hearing will be suspended at this point. We will reconvene next week."

A week later, Bob Harris listened as the state of New York, in the body of Terrence Sheehan, Esq., presented its case against Warren Levin, reading in a sonorous voice from the charges offered to the court as Exhibit A.

"Your Honor," he began, "in the State of New York, Department of Health, State Board for Professional and Medical Conduct, in the matter of Warren M. Levin, M.D. whose ..."

Sheehan went on to state Levin's medical license number, the date it was granted, and its current active registration dates. "The factual allegations are as follows: Between on or about May 23, 1976 and on or about November 4, 1976, Respondent treated Patient A for numerous complaints at Respondent's office." Levin's office had been in Brooklyn at the time of the charges, which only drove home the point that it had been 13 long years since the doctor had even seen "Patient A." "In the course of his treatment of Patient A, Respondent ordered the following tests which were not medically indicated: hair analysis; six-hour glucose tolerance test; mauve factor test; blood histamine, spermidine and spermine tests. Respondent rendered or prescribed the following treatments for Patient A, which were not medically indicated: approximately 20 sessions of chelation therapy, 'prostate,' which is noted as 'animal prostate gland cells' here, 'RNA,' hydrochloric acid, methionine, 'CMBPR,' adrenal cortical extract, numerous minerals and vitamins."

Sheehan paused, took a sip of water, and began reading again, as though there were 100 people in the room, rather than eight plus the court reporter. "Respondent inappropriately treated Patient A by administering, or ordering the administration of, numerous intravenous and intramuscular injections of unknown substances."

This time Sheehan spun around and fixed Levin with what was supposed to be a significant look. Levin remained impassive. Harris watched Sheehan's theatrics. "Respondent *knew* that the tests he ordered and treatments he prescribed for Patient A were of *no medical value* in the treatment of Patient A," he continued. "The chart maintained by Respondent for Patient A does not contain adequate patient complaints, personal, medical and family histories, examinations, diagnoses, interval notes, treatment plans and rationales for tests ordered and therapies prescribed," he read, turning the page to begin reading about Patient B.

Sheehan informed them about Patient B, an Alzheimer's patient; Patient C's "numerous complaints" of a medical nature; Patient D's numerous diagnoses, including metabolic dysperception, hypomagneseuria, glaucoma, malabsorption syndrome, prostatitis, obsessive compulsive disorder, and first degree heart block—then he proceeded to say that these diagnoses were *not medically substantiated.* He then droned on about Patient E's hypoglycemia, hypothyroidism, candidiasis, and allergies; Patient F's coronary artery disease with coronary insufficiency and malabsorption syndrome—making the same claims for both Patient E and Patient F, that the tests and treatments were not medically indicated. These last patients had been treated at Levin's current Manhattan office. He said a few brief words about patients G & H, then turned and announced, as though he had completed listing accomplishments and was about to present an award, "Respondent is charged with practicing the profession *fraudulently* under New York Education Law Section 6509(2), in that the Petitioner charges..."

Harris and Levin had already read through this document, and they assumed that the panel and judge had done so also. They knew that everything had to be read into the record, and they were quite certain that Victor Herbert was reaping the full benefits of this recitation, as evidenced by the self-satisfied smirk on his face.

Sheehan continued to present charges, including "practicing with *gross negligence*, committing *unprofessional conduct* as defined by the Board of Regents, *professional misconduct,* and engaging in conduct in the practice of medicine which evidences *moral unfitness* to practice medicine. This was literally a "stewpot of charges," as Levin correctly described it when he and Susan first met with Bob Harris nearly three months earlier.

In conclusion, Sheehan made a statement intending to tie his introductory remarks together. However, as far as both Harris and Levin were concerned, there was a ridiculous undertone that caused them to scribble notes to one another. "The standards that Dr. Levin breached," began Sheehan, his voice taking on a self-importance not yet earned in the hearing room, "are the *minimally acceptable standards* for all physicians in the state of New York," he declared. He went on to repeat what he had said in the pre-hearing conference at which the panel members were not present. "Dr. Victor Herbert is the 'soul' of the state's case against Dr. Levin," he claimed, "and there isn't *any other doctor* who is qualified to testify about Dr. Levin's incompetence!"

Levin and Harris had written nearly identical notes to each other, citing the point that if Levin had not lived up to "minimally acceptable standards" for any physician in New York, then *any* physician in New York would be *more than qualified* to testify against him. It made no sense that Victor Herbert, and *only* Victor Herbert should be given this dubious "honor."

Harris rose to his full height, splendidly attired in a tailor-made suit that emphasized his commanding presence, one of the benefits of his ample build. The attorney for the defense would finally get the opportunity to address the court. "Lady and gentlemen," he began, using his best orator's voice, and earning a snicker for his identification of those present in the courtroom, "the true scope of this hearing is not about an individual, bumbling, and incompetent family physician, but rather, it is a test of the right of a physician to practice according to the point of view and philosophy of a minority group of physicians. Patients have rights, also, and they should not be deprived of those rights, among which—and this is a central issue in this trial—is the right to choose what type of medical care they wish to pursue. Dr. Levin is a *pioneer* among physicians in his recognition of how to assist patients in pursuing wellness through *non-drug-oriented therapies*. And for this, he is being persecuted and prosecuted; for this, his personal and professional life have been turned upside down and made to exist in this unnatural position for *years and years* while the state took its sweet time in deciding *whether* to pursue charges and *how* to pursue those charges."

Harris was just warming up, and not a sound could be heard in the room as he paced and spoke, keenly eyeing each panel member in turn. "Think about it, all of you, think about what it would be like if a letter arrived at your professional office years and years ago, asking you about something you had done in your job years and years earlier and asking you to defend your actions. Think about how you would feel if you repeatedly had to spend money for a lawyer to assist you in court: first one level of the court system, then the next, then the third; only for it to begin again years later. And, no, you can't claim 'double jeopardy,' as Dr. Levin once hoped he could when he had to go through a second round of appearances and expenses. Since 'double jeopardy' wasn't an option the second time around, how about when a decision in Dr. Levin's favor was reversed? If he couldn't plead to 'double jeopardy,' he sure wasn't able to have the court system look at 'triple jeopardy,' yet that's exactly what it was. After three complete circuits of three escalating court levels, finally all charges are dismissed. So it's over, and Dr. Levin gets his life back, right? Wrong. It's not over: it only starts once again from the very beginning, but this time in front of a hearing panel. This time in this building, in this room, on this day, with all of you present."

He paused; he wanted to be sure that they digested each image he had presented, images of themselves being relentlessly hunted. "Dr. Levin is in this situation for nine years already. Nine years! How well would any of you have held up for nine years, trying to do your job and earn a living, trying to play your role as a family member, hoping your finances will hold out, hoping that *you'll* hold out psychologically. Imagine yourself sitting down, reading page after page of charges against you that make you sound like the world's worst professional, criticizing everything you do or have ever done, questioning everything you stand for." Harris didn't miss a couple of rapid eye blinks that told him he had driven some of his rhetoric to a deep level in one of the panelists.

"One day you're a well-respected professional," he continued, "and a pioneer in your field, held in high esteem by your clients or patients, revered by your colleagues, essential to the professional groups you belong to and contribute to, to the groups in which you are an officer and leader...and the next day you're fighting to stay alive in your profession, fighting a fight that goes *on and on* for nine years. This is not a simple malpractice trail, lady and gentlemen. This is way, way bigger than that. *And the state has called only one alleged expert to the stand.* So be it. We're ready, Your Honor. The Defense is ready," said Harris.

It was now time for Victor Herbert to take the stand, which he seemed to do with great relish. Watching Herbert walk from the chair against the far wall to the chair in the center of the room, Levin couldn't help but think back to an earlier time, when he and Herbert had been at a meeting together. They had been adversaries then, too. It was 1980, nine years earlier, when Levin was vice-president of the American Society of Bariatric Physicians. At that time Levin had been advocating the importance of nutrition in disease prevention and control in his own practice. As weight-control specialists, bariatricians needed to understand the importance of nutrition to assist them with their work with bariatric patients, many of whom weighed in excess of 300, 400, or even 500 pounds. The organization thought it would be very interesting to sponsor a debate on the subject and brought in Victor Herbert, who was already developing notoriety as a one-man search-and-destroy machine aimed at alternative physicians, whose licenses he was determined to assist New York State in removing. Levin remembered that Herbert stopped at nothing during that debate, resorting to fabrication and lies of all sorts, in an effort to discredit anything that Levin postulated.

Now, nine years later, Victor Herbert was being put "on stage," given a microphone and an audience, and quite reminiscent of the Red Guard's work in Communist China during the Cultural Revolution, where formerly powerless teens suddenly had the authority to point fingers and make accusations against once revered and respected individuals, Victor Herbert was being presented by Sheehan as a god-like figure. *Amazing*, Levin thought, simply amazing.

Once Sheehan had moved past the details of Herbert's extensive *curriculum vitae*, listing honors and publications, positions held, and numerous self-aggrandizing lists of accomplishments, he paused to let the scholarly weight of the man he insisted on referring to as *the state's unassailable witness* fully penetrate the minds of the assembled group.

When Harris was finally invited to question the state's shining star, he decided to get right to the heart of his concern, since it was related to something Sheehan had allowed to slip out in the pre-hearing conference.

He purposefully strode over to Herbert. "Dr. Herbert," he boomed, making the most of his advantage over this much smaller man, who was seated before him, "do you have an opinion as to whether or not Warren Levin is a 'quack'?"

"I would object to that question!" Sheehan rapidly shouted. "It is inflammatory, unnecessary! There is *no* charge in this statement of charges that Dr. Levin is a quack! It is just a question from left field, and I object to it!"

Harris didn't miss the rapidly rising color that moved up Herbert's face, originating at his shirt collar. He had a feeling that, had Sheehan not stopped Herbert from answering that simple question which would have gotten to the heart of Herbert's prejudicial feelings about Levin, he would have scored some major points in the proceedings. Unfortunate!

"All right, Dr. Herbert, maybe you don't have to answer *that* question, but I am going to repeat my question from last week: Did *you* bring charges against my client before the Office of Professional Medical Conduct?"

As he had a week earlier, Sheehan objected loudly, and said that his witness did not have to answer the question. When Harris countered the objection, Sheehan raised his voice, speaking over Harris and citing a particular section of New York State law, after which Harris indicated in an ever-rising voice that the cited law did not pertain to the proceedings underway. This argument continued unabated until the administrative law judge interrupted forcefully.

"All right! I have heard enough from both of you," he said, eyeing the attorneys. "As Mr. Sheehan indicated, we *did* discuss this at another conference on the record, though outside the presence of the Hearing Committee," he added, glancing toward the members of the panel, "and I am going to *allow* the question, and I'll lay out my rationale for it on the record. I will start off first by noting that the section cited by Mr. Sheehan deals with *disclosure*, and that is *not* the situation that we are facing here. The section cited refers to information or material protected from disclosure by statutory or case law. Dr. Herbert is *not* a party to these proceedings. The question will be asked of Dr. Herbert as a *witness*. He is, to the best of my knowledge,' Storch added, glancing sideways at Herbert, "not an employee of the Department of Health; therefore he is not a party to this action.

"The Department has argued that disclosure of the identity of the complainants is barred by the statute. The statutory authority in question, which is Public Health Law Section 230, paragraph 11, subparagraph A," he quoted, "deals with reporting of professional misconduct. It identifies who is *obligated* and who may *disclose* the misconduct. It then provides 'such reports shall remain confidential and shall not be admitted into evidence in any administrative or judicial proceedings.' Both the statute and the regulation address documented statements, referring to either reports or complaints."

Storch paused to be sure everyone who wanted to make notes on what he was saying did so, and he held up his hand to discourage either lawyer from speaking, since the next thing he would say provided the heart of his ruling. "*They are silent on the question of disclosure of the identity of a complainant while testifying,*" he said in a very deliberate manner, glancing around the room to make certain he was understood. "I have concluded that this question to a witness, as to whether or not he made a complaint to OPMC regarding Respondent is *not expressly barred* by either the statute *or* the regulations."

Storch wasn't finished. "The Department has also argued that such a bar should be compelled so as to encourage patients and victims to come forward with their complaints. I find their arguments to *not be applicable to the case at hand*. The witness is *not a patient*, but another physician, an *expert witness* retained by the Department for these proceedings." It was obvious to Bob Harris that Storch did not take the responsibility of presiding over this hearing lightly and had apparently done thorough research on this crucial issue.

"My next level of inquiry is whether the information sought is otherwise admissible into evidence. The basic test that I use for deciding the admissibility of evidence is a three-part test: Is the information *relevant*? What is the *probative* value of the evidence? Does the probative value outweigh any *prejudicial* effect that it might have on the opposing parties' case—in this instance, the case brought by the Department of Health?

"Here the witness, Dr. Herbert, is a *nonparty witness*. He is *supposedly* a neutral," he said with a touch of sarcasm in his voice. "He is *not* a party to the proceedings. But he is, rather, presented as a dispassionate expert. If he is, in fact, both complainant *and* expert, such information would be important to the extent to which any bias he might hold against Respondent impacts on his credibility as a witness.

"My ruling is that the disclosure of information sought by the question posed is *not* barred by the statute or regulation. Its probative value *outweighs* the prejudicial effect that it might have on the Department's case. *I will allow the question and will direct the witness to answer it*. Objection overruled. I am asking you, Dr. Herbert, to answer the question now."

Bob Harris exchanged a quick glance with his client. If they could have done so, they would have loved to join hands and gleefully dance around the hearing room together. Instead, they both pasted serious, dispassionate expressions on their faces. Only the gleaming in Levin's blue eyes and the sparkle in Harris's brown eyes betrayed their inner thoughts ... if anyone was paying attention, which was doubtful. All eyes were fixed on Victor Herbert. He was sitting at center stage... literally and figuratively.

When Sheehan broke the silence following Storch's order, there were startled murmurs around the room.

"*Just one minute!* My superior has told me to inform the witness...to *direct* the witness *not* to answer the question, since it *violates* the statute!" he shouted.

As Levin watched what seemed to be a circus routine of leaping attorneys, his own lawyer spun around to Storch and forcefully said, "I would like to note for the record, Your Honor, that the Attorney General gives further indication of ..."

Sheehan cut him off and also addressed the judge. "I object to legal argument! You have made your ruling. It is now up to the witness…"

"This is *not* legal argument," said Harris.

"This is an objection to my question."

"This is an objection to your objection!" Harris fixed Sheehan with a glare that shut the prosecuting attorney up immediately.

Levin watched in amazement as his hefty defense attorney made a move toward the prosecutor that seemed to render him weightless, as though he were performing an act of levitation. Harris was just warming up, and it was clear that he was outraged.

"The Attorney General is *not* the attorney for this witness, and his direction to a witness not to answer is *incestuous*! It is a further indication of the fact that this witness does *not* come in here simply to tell the facts as he knows them, chips fall as they may. Rather he, in essence—and I only say this in a descriptive rather than a negative term—*is a hired gun for the state*, if his answer is based upon what the state lawyer tells him. *He is not here represented by the state; he is here as a witness for the state!"* Harris was totally caught up in his argument, his footfalls solid and dramatic, punctuating his speech.

Levin was very proud of his lawyer at that moment and thought that his argument was absolutely brilliant. He couldn't help but glance at the panel and was pleased to note what appeared to be nods of assent. Levin had trouble restraining a smirk that threatened to rearrange his serious, courtroom demeanor, so he reached for his glass and swallowed the grin along with a sip of water.

"I have heard enough from both of you!" Storch said severely, glancing from one attorney to the other until both regained their composure. "Sir," he said, turning to Victor Herbert, "a question has been posed to you. I have deemed that question to be proper and lawful, and I have directed you to answer it. Are you going to answer that question?"

Herbert's gaze swept over everyone in the courtroom before settling on Storch, an attempt Levin recognized as an "up yours" power play. He leaned back in his seat, jutted his chin out defiantly and stated, "I am going to follow the direction of the attorney for the state, who has stated the public policy of the state, as I believe it to be correct; and because you, Your Honor, have taken a position which appears to be opposite to the public policy of the state, I will stick to the advice of the counsel for the state."

Before anyone could completely absorb Herbert's blatant defiance of the judge's directive, yet another unexpected outburst followed, almost out of context, by Sheehan, who shouted, *"I would object..."*

"Mr. Sheehan, I am talking to the witness now. You will hold your objection!" Storch retorted.

Sheehan paid no attention to the judge. "I object to your talking to the witness now! You are about to browbeat the witness into complying with your request. I submit it is *improper* for you, in any way, to cross-examine or further question this witness," he added disrespectfully. "He told you he does not choose to answer that question. I submit that that is the end of it. You should not attempt to get him to answer the question or to go behind his response in some way!"

Storch fixed Sheehan with an authoritative glare. "I am *not* browbeating the witness. He is here under oath. A question has been put to him. If he intends to refuse to answer the question, I intend to know the reason why."

"No!" shouted Sheehan. "What *right* do you have to question this witness as to what his sworn testimony is?" His continued lack of respect for the hearing officer was not lost on the panel. As far as Levin and Harris were concerned, this display of anger was to their advantage. "*Mr. Harris* is satisfied with his answer," Sheehan continued, making an assumption without a basis, "so why shouldn't *you* be? *You have no right* to go into his psyche as to why he chooses to believe what is public policy or not."

Go into his psyche, thought Levin. What an odd choice of words. It sounded like Sheehan was attempting to gain the sympathy of the Hearing Panel by evoking an image of mental cruelty. He snapped his attention back to the speaker, who was far from finished.

"This is, I submit, improper," Sheehan lectured the judge. "We laid the groundwork as to what we were going to do today. It has come to pass. I submit that we now agree that he," referring to Victor Herbert, his "sole" witness with a nod of his head, "is going to be disqualified as you said he probably would be. I will accept that!"

No kidding, Levin thought. *You will accept that.* Ha!

Sheehan started up again. "Maybe Mr. Harris and I can agree to waive written briefs on this issue, in the interest, as Mr. Harris previously stated, of having the Commissioner expeditiously review this matter. I would be willing to waive written briefs. I don't know about Mr. Harris," he said, turning to Harris, portraying a business-as-usual demeanor as though he had not just defied the judge and completely ignored everything the judge said.

Harris didn't hesitate to respond to what was beneficial for his client. "I absolutely *will* waive written briefs. I see no reason to reiterate what you have said so well," he added, with sarcasm-tinged grace. Then Harris turned to the judge. "But Mr. Sheehan is in error when he describes me as being satisfied with the witness's answer. *I believe the witness's answers are contemptuous of the court!* I believe that a witness does not, in a civil proceeding, make the decision as to whether he will or will not answer; and I believe that the instruction of the Attorney General to *disregard the instructions of the judge*, because the Attorney General's opinion is that *the judge is not right*, is not law and order: it is *chaos*, and it is an affront to the system!"

Levin regarded Harris admiringly. Since the proceedings had yet to allow Levin to speak a word in his own defense, he felt a real thrill of excitement as he heard Harris say exactly what he himself would have said if given the chance. He nodded his head affirmatively, totally approving of his attorney's inspired presentation and happy to note that Bob was not yet through with Sheehan and Herbert.

"I do *not* agree with the witness's answer, and I do *not* agree that the Attorney General is acting appropriately in instructing a witness not to answer something that a duly constituted court and judge have decided *should* be answered. You couldn't be further from correct in saying that I am in agreement with the answer. I not only *disagree* with the answer, I believe that we have not maintained lawful process here."

Storch took a deep breath. "We are at an impasse," the administration law judge concluded aloud. "The witness has refused to answer the question, despite the fact that, pursuant to Section 230 of the Public Health Law, paragraph 10, subparagraph E, 'The Administrative Officer shall have the authority to rule on all motions, procedures and other legal objections, and shall have the authority to rule on objections to questions posed by either party or the Committee members, within the confines of this hearing,'" he quoted.

"*I* am the sole authority," he declared, eyeing everyone in the courtroom meaningfully, "on what is lawful and what is admissible into evidence, within the confines of this hearing room. I have made a ruling," he continued, turning to face Victor Herbert, "and if *you* do not answer the question, I will discharge you from testifying under my general authority," he said, quoting the pertinent law, "which provides that 'The Hearing Officer shall have the power to do *all* acts and take *all measures necessary* but not otherwise prohibited by this part for the maintenance of order and the efficient conduct of the hearing.'"

With a tone of anger creeping into his voice, Storch said, "It is not the province of either the prosecuting attorney *or* the witness to decide which questions will be answered. To borrow a quote from another attorney in a somewhat different context, 'I am not a potted plant; I am here for a reason!' If the Department believes itself to be aggrieved by any rulings made by the Administrative Officer, there is a mechanism established for challenging those rulings," he said, his attention on both lawyers. "Following the issuance of the Hearing Committee's report, the parties may file exceptions to the rulings and the Commissioner may, if he finds those rulings incorrect, he may remand the case with a directive for further proceedings. *That* is the appropriate method. I would, of course, be bound by the Commissioner's ruling, whatever that might be," Storch told them.

Levin couldn't help but think, *Of course, you'll be bound by the Commissioner's rulings, Mr. Storch; just as the Hearing Committee is here to do the Commissioner's dirty work; and Sheehan is answering to the Attorney General—both of whom are pulling Victor Herbert's strings. This amazing conspiracy is united in its task: get Levin's license at all costs, even if you have no foundation on which to build your case.* Levin forced himself to pay attention, because Storch still had more to say to Victor Herbert.

"...but I cannot allow the prosecution or the witness to ignore my rulings and then carry on with business as usual. That would make a mockery of these proceedings and send us down the road to anarchy. *If you are not going to answer the question, sir, I will now discharge you from your obligation to testify as a witness.*" Sheehan waited for Storch to take a breath, so his interruption would not be as rude as his prior ones. "We would object to that ruling as well," he began. "We submit that you *have no authority to ever disqualify a witness* or strike testimony from the record!"

"I am not *striking* testimony. I am *preventing* testimony!"

"It is analogous to striking."

"It is not!"

Geez, thought Levin, they sound like school kids arguing on the playground!

Storch wasn't through yet. "I am going to repeat what I just said a few moments ago, Mr. Sheehan. The regulation clearly says unless it is prohibited, I may 'take all measures necessary for maintenance of order and the efficient conduct of the hearing.' That is what the regulation says."

"Nowhere does the regulation say that you can disqualify a witness!" responded Sheehan, warming up for another round. "You seem to give yourself powers that aren't listed. There is a seeming contradiction."

At this point, the judge looked like he trying very hard to contain his fury at the tone being used to address him and the blatant disrespect the prosecuting attorney was showing him in front of the state's witness, the Hearing Committee, the defense attorney, and the Respondent. He was determined not to let it continue any further. "I see no contradiction," Storch stated firmly. "Your objection is noted. *The witness is dismissed!*"

Sheehan turned to Victor Herbert apologetically. "Would you wait outside?" he asked.

Harris sensed an opening and grabbed the opportunity. "Your Honor," he began smoothly, "although this is a beautiful and clear discussion, nonetheless, there is a very large cloud which looms over Dr. Levin and, at the beginning of these proceedings, I noted that the Department chose a three-year delay from its receipt of his charts until the point at which it proposed charges. Since the long-term effects of this on Dr. Levin, both psychologically and professionally, are awful, I would ask that anything that can be done to get this matter in the hands of the reviewing authorities be done; so that if the charges are to be dismissed, they are dismissed; and if the charges are to be litigated, they are litigated; and that this not be an opportunity for the State to enjoy another three-year delay."

"Your point is well taken, Mr. Harris," said Storch, as he adjourned proceedings for the day.

CHAPTER 9

Even with Victor Herbert out of the picture, Harris knew he had to continue working on his arsenal of defense materials. Their next step would be to do further research on certain legal points and for Levin to prepare Harris to respond to and counter medical questions with sufficient knowledge and comfort. Levin had been taking copious notes, Harris realized, so they would be able to develop an exhaustive outline at their next strategic meeting.

Levin's practice was too busy for him to be able to meet with his attorney during the week, so he was pleased that Bob Harris was amenable to weekend meetings that often turned into medical marathons. As they sat in the conference room at Schneider, Harris & Harris on Saturday morning, the mail arrived. Harris sorted through, tossing aside envelopes with checks, solicitations, and bills. He selected only one nine-by-twelve envelope and slit it open.

"Let me make a copy of this, Warren," he said, exiting the conference room briskly.

Levin reached across the wide table and retrieved the envelope, noting the return address: State of New York, Department of Health, State Board for Professional Medical Conduct. He inhaled sharply, the time-worn axiom, "No news is good news" running through his mind uninvited.

They sat across from one another reading the report of the Hearing Committee intently. Their breathing, the faint ticking of the wall clock, the rattle of a turned page the only sounds in the otherwise still room. The report, dated November 30, was addressed to The Honorable David Axelrod, M.D., Commissioner of Health, State of New York. It listed the committee members and the Administrative Officer of the Hearing Committee by name, giving June 20, 1989 as the "date of Notice of Hearing and Statement of Charges against Respondent." Then it listed all of the significant dates throughout the remainder of the year: September 18, Pre-Hearing Conference; September 27, Intra-Hearing Conference, which was the *voir dire* session, where Harris capably began his task of discrediting the state's "sole witness"; September 27, Hearing; November 6, Intra-Hearing Conference; November 13, Hearing and Final Deliberations.

They finished reading everything at nearly the same moment and simply stared at one another, both dressed casually for this Saturday meeting, glad of the relative silence that surrounded them, allowing for private reflection. Harris was the first to break the silence.

"Warren, if you don't mind," he said, "I'd like to read portions of this aloud. Sometimes it helps to hear it, as well as to see it."

"Be my guest," Levin responded, fairly subdued.

"I'll start with a statement of the case, since the stuff before that is only names and dates. 'The Department has charged Respondent with practicing the profession of medicine *fraudulently*, with *gross negligence*," Harris read in what he considered a "lawyerly" voice, strongly emphasizing the most painful terms, just as the prosecuting attorney tended to do, "'and with *negligence* on *more than one* occasion, with regard to six patients. Additionally, the Department has charged Respondent with the *failure to comply* with a subpoena *duces tecum*, as well as the failure to provide a copy of another patient's medical record, upon receipt of a written request from the patient.' Are we both clear on all of this stuff?" he asked his client.

"Crystal clear."

"Fine. Let me continue. Now I'll move on to the conclusions of the 'august panel' which appeared at the hearing," he intoned sarcastically. He suddenly jumped up from his seat and shouted, "First and foremost, we did it!" He pounded his meaty fist on the table for emphasis, causing Levin's heart to skip a few beats in surprise. "We damn well did it, Warren!" Noticing Levin's demeanor, he asked, "Why the glum look?" The attorney suddenly seemed deflated and sank back into his chair.

Levin regarded him with a patient and weary smile. He was tired and not sleeping very well at all, and it was affecting him. "Bob, I've been involved in this…this…"

"Crap?" Harris suggested helpfully.

"Yeah, 'crap,' with the state of New York for nine years, nine long years, as you so capably brought out during the hearing. My experience is that they give with one hand and take with the other. So forgive me if I don't share your enthusiasm. Sure, it looks good for us today; I'm worried about tomorrow. You can't possibly go through two rounds of three court levels as I did, where I'm cleared and everything is alright; then suddenly I'm 'guilty' or whatever, and I have to come back and repeat the same thing all over again on round three and not become somewhat skeptical. Don't forget, for me these pre-hearings, intra-hearings, hearings and whatever other names they gave them, for me, was like a multi-level round four. I'll try to feel a bit happy for the moment, though," he promised with a laugh, "I really will."

"Fine!" Harris said, turning back to the material in his hand. "The Hearing Committee's Conclusion reads as follows." Now he was into his courtroom orator's voice. "'The Department's witness,'" he proclaimed, "'Dr. Herbert,' the asshole," he added the descriptor to get a laugh out of Levin, "'*was discharged*,' I repeat, *discharged,* 'by the Administrative Officer upon his failure to answer a question during *voir dire* examination.' Wahoo!"

"I don't see 'wahoo' in there," Levin said lightly, his mood picking up a bit.

"You don't?" said Harris, with a puzzled look on his face. "I sure do! Anyhow, it says, 'The witness did not give *any* substantive testimony relative to the charges. The Department then rested without putting in any proof relative to the charges. Given the lack of proof, the Hearing Committee was *unable* to make any factual findings. Therefore, the Hearing Committee can only conclude that *the Department has failed to sustain its burden of proof.*' You hear that, Warren? '…*failed to sustain its burden of proof.* The Committee notes that this turn of events resulted from the discharge of the Department's witness upon his failure to answer a question, upon an order of the Administrative Officer directing a response.'"

"So what I'm picking up from this," Levin told him, "is that you did such a great job discrediting the 'soul' of the case—the state's 'sole' witness, that the state's whole case simply fell apart. Don't get me wrong, Bob, I'm thrilled. I just don't believe it. Maybe they sent another envelope to us taking it all back. You want to look through your mail again, just in case?"

Harris noted that Levin was speaking with a bit of levity, sounding a lot like the person he must be when he wasn't stretched to the breaking point. "There's nothing more from them in the mail. May I continue?"

Levin signaled his assent with a palms-up, floating gesture.

"'The Hearing Committee wishes to express its *frustration* at its inability to reach the substantive subject matter of this proceeding. The Committee is of the opinion that the Commissioner of Health should review the Administrative Officer's rulings in this matter...'"

"There you go, Bob! That's exactly what I'm talking about!" Levin said, his tone serious and concerned. "'It's all over, Dr. Levin,'" he began, putting his own words into the Committee's mouth. "'There's nothing more to worry about. We're dismissing Victor Herbert, the jerk. The state failed to prove its case. It's over. Go back to your life. Enjoy your family.' Yeah, right! 'Oh, but Dr. Levin, we'd like the Commissioner—who's the one who *really* wants to get rid of guys like you in medicine to clean up New York State, so only guys like Victor Herbert can see patients anymore—we'd like the *Commissioner* to look over the decision of Storch, *one* of his hired guns who made the mistake of taking the "soul" out of our case against you. Even though the Commissioner gives *us* our marching orders, we'd look like jerks if we did this any other way, so please, dear Commissioner, find a way to "remand the case for further proceedings."'" Levin was breathless and flushed when he completed his paraphrased rant.

"Go home, Warren. It's Saturday. Spend the day with your family. They need you. You need them. We don't have to do anything more today. I mean it," said Harris, prepared to walk Levin to the door.

Levin nodded wordlessly, collected his papers, including his copy of the Committee's decision and left.

"Warren," Susan said as they sat in their comfortable living room, the pages held between them, having read through the Committee's words together, Erika playing with a doll on the carpet near their feet. "I can't believe this! This is wonderful!" She looked deeply into his eyes, thinking for the hundredth time what she would give for eyes so brilliantly blue, puzzled by the despair she saw there that was simply not a normal part of his psychological makeup.

"Sweetheart," he said, his left hand covering her right hand, in which the Committee's papers were clutched, "I'd like to celebrate this as a victory, but…"

"But you don't think it's going to end here, I know." She reached over and patted his left hand. "Let me play lawyer, now," she teased. "I want to read the Committee's recommendations as though I were announcing them in front of a packed courthouse," she said.

"Sure, why not," said Levin with a smile. He was so lucky to have Susan, and he knew it. She had been through so much in the past nine years, and she had done absolutely nothing to deserve it—*except for marrying me*. She loved him unconditionally, and that was apparent to him. She was such a tremendous ally in everything he was going through. These legal bills had hurt them financially, but she carefully budgeted their money, even though she liked nice things. Helping her husband keep his license was paramount in her mind, and if it wasn't against the law, she'd love to scratch the eyes out of anyone who spoke against him, even though violence was not a part of her profile. She just wished she could hurt the people who were trying to hurt him; that's all. She never forgot an injustice, she never forgot a slight, and he knew that the people who had made his professional and personal life so miserable for so many years—the words and actions of these people—would be permanently engraved in Susan's brain until her dying day. Flattering to him, but damaging to her, he feared.

She began to read in a clear, cool tone, different enough from her normal speaking voice to alert Erika, who looked up inquiringly from tending her little baby doll. "'Recommendations,'" she began. "'The Hearing Committee herein recommends the following: Number one: That the charges against Respondent, Warren M. Levin, M.D., be DISMISSED,' and, Warren, I'd like to call your attention to the fact that the word, 'dismissed' is both capitalized and underlined!" she added, "'based upon the lack of proof,' and I really wish they had capitalized and underlined 'lack of proof,' because that's *really* important in my mind, 'put forward by the Department;' and number two: "That the Commissioner of Health review the evidentiary rulings made by the Administrative Officer, with a remand for further proceedings, *if appropriate*.'"

Her energy spent, she sat back down next to him, and they continued to read what the committee had put into Appendix A, all of which was labeled, "Introduction."

At least the committee had considered the circumstances fairly, Susan felt. While she had not been present at the proceedings, in their limited time together Warren had given her a blow-by-blow play of every event in which he was a participant.

The committee indicated that it became obvious to them that the state's only witness, who was presented to them as an "expert," was shown during *voir dire* examination to have had prior contact with Levin and/or certain professional organizations in which Levin was associated. Therefore, they must have decided that Victor Herbert *did* have a prejudicial attitude toward the respondent, the couple deduced.

It was obvious to Susan, after everything Warren had told her, that the lawyer she had chosen to save her husband's license had made some excellent arguments that the committee apparently paid attention to. At least that was the impression their findings indicated. She didn't blame Warren for being skeptical. If she let herself go into her own pit of skepticism, she was afraid she'd end up dragging him down with her. She wasn't about to do that. This was a victory...at least for the moment. She was determined to enjoy it.

"Let's dress up and go somewhere tonight!" she proposed gaily. "I'll call a sitter for Erika."

"Hey, why not," Warren responded. She deserved to go out somewhere for an evening of fun, he thought. And so did he.

CHAPTER 10

Not surprisingly, Warren and Susan Levin's evening out led to a discussion that neither one of them anticipated. Susan was worried about money, but so was Warren. Pre-hearings, intra-hearings, hearings, post-hearings—whatever they were called—had resulted in hours lost from the office for him. The time it took him to do research and organize material to assist his attorney in preparing a solid defense also took time away from his practice. The hours he spent at Bob's office or on the telephone, going over medical information bit into his time even further. Often, he worked very late, fitting in patients he wasn't available to see earlier in the day, since there were periods when hearings occurred twice and three times in a single week. The expenses for his legal defense also ate into their income. The financial hit the family was experiencing was terrific and painful, but for Levin, the time away from his family was the most excruciating aspect of the case. He had always worked hard and never minded it, mainly because he had a loving wife and darling daughter to come home to. Well, they were still there, but he wasn't. Erika was usually sleeping when he got home; many times so was Susan. As he reflected on the events of the past few years, as the legal hold on him intensified to a painful degree, he realized that the strategy they had just developed couldn't hurt their circumstances; it could only help...if it worked.

In the morning, Susan was typing in a driven, rhythmic pattern at her husband's office, having made arrangements for another mother to take Erika home to play with her daughter after pre-school. In all capital letters, Susan had written an article in the quarterly newsletter that Levin's medical office sent to its patients. On the front page, in 36-point, bold, capital letters, the headline, "DR. LEVIN CHARGED WITH PROFESSIONAL MISCONDUCT!!! NEW YORK STATE MOVES TO REVOKE HIS LICENSE!!! <u>YOUR RIGHT TO CHOOSE YOUR PHYSICIAN IS IN PERIL!!! A NEW ERA OF MEDICAL INQUISITION IS UPON US.</u> While the last two sub-titles were in smaller print, Susan stuck with the caps and decided to underline each word separately. She then proceeded to write the entire article in capital letters, desperate to draw the readers' attention to it from beginning to end. She wrote in the first person, as though her husband was speaking directly to his readers. They had discussed the content of the article last night over dinner and developed their approach, so she was comfortable addressing their readers from his vantage point, since she totally shared his sentiments on the topic.

Susan took the readers through the saga, in a condensed form, starting from the very beginning, with the state's request for the original three medical charts and Warren's refusal to release them without knowing what he was being accused of and by whom. She then mentioned the six years of court appearances, broken into three rounds, each ending with trips to Albany's Court of Appeals. She followed that with the relinquishing of the charts, three years of judicial silence, and a sudden reappearance of unthinkable charges against him. She spoke of one patient complaint by a young woman who did not receive medical records requested because the records were unfortunately lost, the result of a human error by a staff member. She added in the four new cases, where insurance companies' refusal to reimburse had resulted in a peer review committee complaint to the state.

"Clearly," she wrote in capital letters, "this is a thinly veiled attack on the kind of medicine that has come to be known by several different names: alternative, holistic, wholistic, nutritional, preventive, orthomolecular, and complementary are a few of the designations that have been applied. It is this small but steadily growing group of practitioners that has the industrial complex frightened over their potential loss of income!" She gave a few examples to illustrate her point, then continued, adding that "...individual doctors all over the country have been brought up on charges and have been forced—under threat of loss of license—to discontinue a particular kind of alternative practice, whether test or treatment." She indicated that many of these physicians had simply stopped using methods they knew to be "different" yet effective for their patients, making the point that if Warren lost *his* license for the tests and treatments he was using, as a representative of alternative medicine, "...then they will be able to rapidly eliminate every treatment approach to medical care except for drugs, surgery and radiation." She wanted people to focus their attention on the worst possible alternatives for deadly diseases where no definitive therapies were guarantees of a cure or a good quality of life, diseases where conventional medical treatment generally offered three options: cut, burn, or poison. Anyone who wasn't willing to undergo surgery, radiation, or chemotherapy would have no recourse if alternative medicine was forced to discontinue its practice of strengthening the body to improve its self-healing abilities. The worst part of the whole fiasco was the implication that patients would lose their right to select physicians and treatments of choice and be subject to legislative, pharmaceutical, and medical society controls, with their dogmatic pronouncements and heavy-handed techniques.

Susan planned to include a petition in this newsletter, to collect the signatures of Warren's supporters. She'd also slip in a form that would guide patients who wished to write a testimonial outlining their care at Warren's medical office. Then she added a final appeal to the readers: *"Please consider a donation to the Warren M. Levin, M.D. Legal Defense Fund. Every bit helps! Thank you!!"*

Along with informative articles Levin himself had written for his patients and other readers, this issue also contained explanations, in his own words, of what he had endured over the years from the likes of the medical establishment. However, he also wrote of cases he had taken on of patients coming from doctors in that very establishment who had exhausted their traditional forms of treatment for these patients yet failed to effect a long-lasting cure of the problem at the root of the symptoms their treatments were designed to relieve. Levin explained the usefulness of tests he had performed in detecting root causes and treatment strategies that proved effective, much to the relief of chronically ill and suffering patients who had already been to countless specialists to no avail.

Levin launched his own appeal in the very same explanatory article. "I need patients who had significant memory impairment who can testify to major improvement after treatment at World Health Medical Group," as his practice was known, "so-called 'hypochondriacs' who magically recovered from these 'imaginary' complaints, patients with chronic digestive problems who experienced dramatic relief of symptoms, 'walking time bombs' with only 'months to live' without radical surgery or therapy whose condition improved without those invasive treatments.

"I am putting out a call for people to testify. If you are unable or unwilling to testify, it would still be very important if you could write a letter in which you detail your positive medical experience with my practice for me to present in my defense to the board," he wrote. "We would like to deluge Governor Cuomo's office with letters objecting to the infringement of an individual's right to choose alternative medical treatments. We think that now is the time to write letters to legislators and newspapers."

He remembered reading over what he had written, knowing that this had *never*, to his knowledge, been done before by any other physician under attack. Considering that, as an alternative practitioner for years, he had known from private conversations with his colleagues when another doctor was being investigated for a practice the medical establishment considered "dubious" or "unwarranted," but this information was kept closely guarded within the ranks and certainly not broadcast. Of course, after his and Bob's series of phone calls to countless medical doctors and numerous lawyers, they now had an arsenal of cases at their disposal, and Levin was flabbergasted to discover how many of his colleagues had actually been hunted in the past by the state. Some of them were no longer in practice, he learned, some were in "supervised practice"—a watchdog approach invented by the OPMC for remediation purposes, where another doctor and/or the state is always looking over your shoulder until you complete the terms of your 'probation'—and others had been assigned to take numerous courses to correct their "incompetencies." Once this newsletter went out, he was certain that the shock value alone would elicit valuable responses and additional assistance, hopefully of the monetary sort.

Susan put the finishing touches on her article that literally screamed off the page to be noticed, and she also felt that this unprecedented honesty by a practicing physician living under a thick, dark, dismal legal cloud for so many years, all at the whim of New York State and its incredibly misdirected Department of Health, would undoubtedly elicit visceral reactions from the readership. She was hopeful that an outpouring of supportive responses would be the outcome of her husband's brave decision to totally expose himself to patients who viewed him as an authority figure with a beautiful wife and child and a completely perfect life. She hoped that his effectiveness in their medical care would not be compromised. She left the finished copy on his desk and let the receptionist know she was leaving.

Levin sat to read what Susan had written as soon as he could break away from work for a moment. *She nailed it*, he thought, deciding that the "headline story" of the issue was a perfect complement to the material he had prepared. Now for part two of their plan.

He picked up the phone. He needed to inform his lawyer about what they were about to do from his side of the defense table and what he hoped his lawyer could do to assist.

"Since you're suggesting it, Warren, I'm willing to get onto radio programs and discuss your situation, if you're comfortable with it," Harris told him. "I'll make some phone calls of my own. I don't know whether you're aware of this or not, but I've already spoken on Atkins' radio show a number of times. In fact, he told me that every time I appeared, his ratings went up!" Harris boasted. He was referring to Robert C. Atkins, M.D., internist and cardiologist, who wrote *Dr. Atkins' Diet Revolution* in 1972, a book that sold millions of copies with its unusual approach to nutrition. Atkins counseled controlling carbohydrate intake and emphasized consumption of protein and fat, including saturated fat, along with leafy vegetables and dietary supplements.Atkins had opened the Atkins Center for Complementary Medicine in Manhattan, making him a kindred spirit in this fight, as far as Harris was concerned.

"If you can land another gig with Atkins, that would be great!" Levin enthused. "I'll see what I can get you from my end. We may as well let the whole world know what's going on here. It can't make things any worse, I figure, and it just might marshal some support for me. Frankly, I'll be curious to see what comes of it."

"Fine," Harris said. "We'll talk." He hung up.

CHAPTER 11

Bob Harris sat at his desk puffing angrily on his cigar. He looked at his associate. "Sandi, I can't believe this crap! The court reporter is trying to extort us!"

"What's the problem?" she asked calmly. She was used to the managing partner's histrionics when he thought something unfair was happening.

"Three dollars and twenty-five cents is the problem," he snorted, his ample chin quivering with indignation. "That woman expects us to pay three twenty-five a page for the damn transcripts of the hearing!"

"That'll cost a fortune, if this hearing is forced to continue!" she exclaimed.

"It's a monopoly, designed for these court reporters to make extra money. They're putting the screws to Warren on this one, and he sure can't afford it. The problem is that I won't be able to launch a suitable defense on his behalf if I don't have those pages. That idiot just stared at us when we asked her for transcript copies. I want that stuff in my files, no matter what, win or lose. And, trust me, we're going to lose."

"Didn't you tell me that the charges didn't stick?" she asked.

"Let me tell you something, and I told my client the same thing. In fact, if you've heard any of my radio broadcasts lately, you know exactly what I'm talking about."

"You're the medical defense guy in this office, Bob, and I know you think the system isn't fair; that much I know."

"That's an understatement, Sandi. This system is corrupt! A guy goes to medical school for four years after undergrad school, then an Internship—Warren did his at the US Naval Hospital in Newport, R.I.—then he did General Practice in the Navy, after which he obtained his license to practice in N.Y. State. He takes the required Continuing Medical Education courses to maintain his license. There was no Board of Family Practice in 1959, but he joined the American Academy of Family Practice, and was an officer of the local chapter on Staten Island. In 1973, the American Board of Family Practice was recognized and Warren was "Grandfathered in". The FP Board was the first one to require recertification in the US. Warren passed the exams multiple times at the required 7-year intervals, after CME courses over the years to maintain his board certification. Doctors literally build their *lives* around their work," he said, his voice rising along with his color.

"Yeah, Bob, I know. So do lawyers," she said. "So do a lot of professionals."

"My concern is my client!"

"Obviously," she said, a smile tugging at the corner of her mouth. She knew he regarded her legal expertise highly and, often, from the intensity of his lobs—which she likened to a vigorous, exhausting game of racquetball—came an approach or a possible solution. She functioned as a player who gently returned the ball for his next aggressive smack.

"Do you know that I've been losing sleep over this?" he growled.

"I'm sure you have."

"I'm going to get those transcripts; nothing will stop me."

"I believe you."

"Hey," he said, suddenly looking up.

She followed his gaze but saw nothing remarkable.

"Hey," he repeated, putting down his cigar.

"Hey, what?" she asked.

"I think I've got it!" He was rubbing his hands together with pleasure.

"Isn't that a line from a movie or a musical?" she asked, playfully.

"I think I've got it!" he sang, matching her mood and smiling.

"I can't wait to hear it, Bob. Your schemes are famous...are legend," she amended, "at least around this office."

"And this one may be my best!" he said, playing along.

"Actually, I was very impressed by your *latest* one. In fact, we *all* were," she added, sweeping her arm toward his closed office door, beyond where the reception desk, waiting room, and other associates' offices were located.

"Which one was that?" he asked, momentarily thrown off track.

"You know," she prompted, "the one where you figured out how to get all of those transcripts and tapes and ..."

He started to laugh. "Ah, the famous 'Know Thy Enemy' plan, you mean. That really was brilliant, wasn't it?" he asked her, puffing up importantly.

"I almost hate to admit it, Bob, but I might never have thought up anything quite that 'creative.'" She looked up at him under lowered brows. "You know what I think?"

"As always, Sandi, I'm waiting with bated breath."

"You need to have a really *devious* mind to come up with these types of plans. *That's* what I think." Her comment was made with a touch of humor.

"Enough said. I'm a lawyer. What do you expect? If I can't outthink the opposition in advance, the case is lost. Anyway, let me tell you about my next 'devious plan.'"

"Sure."

"I'm thinking that this is a New York State hearing, right?"

"Yeah."

"So I'm thinking about FOIL. They must have a FOIL officer on top of this stuff." Harris was referring to the Freedom of Information Law.

"You have a point," she conceded, "but confidentiality might play a role in all of this."

"What confidentiality? It's Warren's hearing, for God's sake. He's there. I'm his lawyer. No, no, no. Confidentiality be damned. I've got to find out who the FOIL officer is. There's a meeting tomorrow that we've got to be at, so I'm going to push my way through this."

The intercom announced a call for Sandi.

"I can't wait to hear what happens," she said, heading for her office to take the call.

"I wanted to get here early today," Harris said to Levin, as they walked into the hearing room. They were meeting with the judge and prosecutor only, presumably to tie up all the loose ends.

"Mr. Storch," Harris said, walking up to the judge's table.

The room had a wall of windows overlooking Eighth Avenue, with a counter below the windows. The judge and the committee members, when they were present, sat at a long table with their backs to the windows. The defense table, where Levin was now seated and where Harris would shortly join him, was on the left as one entered the room. The prosecutor's table was across from the defense table, forming an inverted U. The part that Harris liked best was the witness chair, which was placed smack in the center of the U. That had put the witness, the infamous Victor Herbert, who was no longer a part of their problem, in the role of "Monkey in the Middle." Just the thought of how Herbert had sat there as he peppered him with questions that he couldn't or wouldn't answer brought a smile to the defense attorney's face. From what he had noticed about Herbert in the videotapes he had studied, *the guy probably had wanted to leap out of his chair and grab my throat. Well, he was too short to have reached my throat, but he would have tried to grab onto* some *part of me, I'm sure. At least, it's* one *of the few humorous things about this case.*

"Mr. Storch," Harris repeated, for emphasis, "I have a question."

"Ask away, Mr. Harris."

"Who is the FOIL officer for this hearing?"

"The FOIL officer? I really don't know," Storch responded.

"I am," responded Sheehan, rising from the prosecutor's table, where he had busily been sorting a stack of papers.

"Good," responded Harris, relishing the moment. "I have something for you." Harris extended an envelope to him.

Sheehan opened the envelope. He was as tall as Harris and as thin as Harris was heavy. His eyebrows creased over his blue eyes. "What's this about?" he asked.

"That, Mr. Sheehan, is a *continuing* FOIL request, which will allow us to get copies of the transcripts produced here for twenty-five cents a page." Levin could see how much his attorney was relishing every moment of the exchange.

Sheehan attempted to return the loose page and the envelope, but Harris didn't extend his hand to receive it. Sheehan held onto it reluctantly and explained, "We don't honor these for transcripts. You've got to pay the court reporter."

Harris took in a deep breath to prepare for his retort. "No, Mr. Sheehan," he responded, "you *didn't* honor these for transcripts *until now!* As of today, that's changed. Warren Levin doesn't have the money to spend three dollars and twenty-five cents a page for this, and without it I can't defend him properly. So either you're going to make it possible for us to have the transcripts on a timely basis at twenty-five cents a page, or I'm going to the Supreme Court. As you know," Harris continued, fixing Sheehan with a meaningful look, "you're the FOIL officer, so your refusal to honor a request carries with it *very* significant fines!"

Sheehan looked down at the paper in his hand and compressed his lips tightly. "I'll have to get back to you on this, Mr. Harris," Sheehan said, tucking the sheet back into the envelope and inserting it into the inner pocket of his suit jacket. He stepped out of the room briefly, returning in time for the scheduled meeting with the judge and defense counsel.

Once the proceedings broke for lunch, Sheehan pulled Harris aside. "I'm going to give you my transcript, Mr. Harris. If you're willing to reproduce it on our machine during lunch time, you can have it for nothing. If I have to copy it for you myself, as the FOIL officer, it's going to cost you twenty-five cents a page." Obviously, it would save Sheehan the time and effort required if Harris agreed to do the work himself.

"Well, Cardinal," Harris said, beaming, the "Cardinal" being a reference to how well Sheehan's name fit into a pontifical title, specifically *Terrence Cardinal Sheehan*, "I thank you. Seeing as you can use a good lunch," Harris said, enviously eyeing Sheehan's slim silhouette, "whereas I," he said self-deprecatingly, patting his ample midsection, "will not fade away if I don't eat right now. I'll head out to make the copies! Thank you, again."

"You're welcome, Mr. Harris," Sheehan responded stiffly, his decision resulting from some heated conversational exchanges with his superiors in Albany.

During the lunch break, Harris and Levin went to the administrative office, where a copy machine some twenty feet in length instantly produced not one, but two copies—one for each of them, with the mere push of the button numbered "two." They were now in possession of transcripts of all prior proceedings since the hearings had begun. Harris and Levin shared a high-five gesture and a genuine smile of merriment.

"Okay, Bob, I'll admit it, it was brilliant!" Sandy conceded. "A bit ballsy, but brilliant."

"My sentiments exactly," Harris said. "Now I think I'll be ready when the shoe drops."

"What makes you think it's gonna drop?"

"This flawed, lousy system they have for hunting doctors who…"

"Oh, no," Sandi said, getting up and moving rapidly toward the door. "I'm not going to listen to any more of this. Sorry, I'm working overtime on a horribly contentious divorce case, and I need to get back to it."

"Fine, abandon me," he called after her.

He lit a cigar. He'd be speaking tonight on Dr. Serafina Corsello's radio show. She was a brilliant alternative physician. The timing was good, he knew, as she had a healthy practice and a solid listening audience. He wanted to make his presentation extra strong.

He began to think about the fact that such a disparity existed from state to state in its professional disciplinary process for physicians. He had once defended a doctor in New Mexico, and he recalled that breakfast had been provided for the prosecutor, the judge and for himself. They sat together and chatted, and Harris had found it to be a completely collegial experience, where the judge didn't want extraneous testimony given for the sole purpose of making the doctor look bad. If the doctor had truly done something wrong, that judge insisted that the focus be on the act itself, with the thought of taking action only when necessary. Proceedings there were conducted fairly. Physicians were given the opportunity to right their wrongs and seek rehabilitation or some retraining. While New York authorities could also recommend rehabilitation and retraining, those penalties were more often imposed upon conventional physicians; while with complementary and alternative doctors license revocation was the preferred outcome. The disciplinary process was ostensibly in place to protect patients, true, but not to strip them of basic freedoms, like the right to choose a physician who provided a safe, alternative treatment for a condition others had failed to cure.

While Harris's practice was based in New York State, he had a breadth of experience in medical defense and other litigation, having tried cases in a total of forty-four states thus far. In New York, he characterized the physicians' disciplinary experience as "us versus them," where he and his clients were fighting not only the OPMC but, more significantly, a powerful lobbying body made up of legislators, who united with traditional medical practitioners and were supported by funds from the pharmaceutical and insurance industries. He had plenty to talk about in the radio broadcast this evening, and he wasn't planning on making his presentation very palatable to any of "them."

"Thank you for inviting me this evening, Dr. Corsello. You can't imagine how *much* I've been looking forward to discussing some of the gross injustices that physicians like you, who practice an alternative form of medicine, are subject to on an ongoing basis." Bob Harris regarded Serafina Corsello with admiration. She was bright; there was no doubt about that. Following a rigorous education in her native Italy, she was the first foreign-born female accepted into the psychiatric residency program at St. Vincent's Hospital in Manhattan. She formulated her own theories, connecting mind and body with wellness and illness, leading her into a medical practice that integrated mainstream medicine with complementary and alternative treatments. She was an attractive, glamorous woman with large eyes, high cheekbones, short blonde hair, and an ample chest, Bob noted.

"It's a pleasure to have you on my program, Mr. Harris," she responded in her melodious, lightly accented speech. "You have a reputation as a friend to those of us who believe that the body is able to fight illness and disease in a natural, healthy way, without harmful and unnecessary medications with terrible side effects."

"Well, I'm proud to say that I've been successful in saving the medical licenses of a number of unjustly accused and persecuted physicians who are willing to try new ways to treat chronic problems that people have not been able to get help for with doctors who practice traditional medicine," Harris said, aware that his words were being broadcast as he spoke.

"Yes," she said. "I often tell my patients that I see life as a dance of balance between positives and negatives."

"I'm so glad you said that," said Harris, "because I'd like to make your listeners aware of a very big *negative* that may impact their ability to choose physicians who offer treatments that are not sanctioned by the so-called 'establishment,' as dictated by legislators, insurance companies, and paralyzed medical societies."

"When we spoke before this broadcast began, you referred to something that sounded suspiciously like the 'Spanish Inquisition' for New York doctors!" she said dramatically.

"That's *exactly* what it is, Dr. Corsello," Harris said, matching her dramatic tone. "I'm currently defending a fine alternative physician who has been pursued by the Office of Professional Medical Conduct for the past nine years. *Nine years!* For your listening audience, I'd like to explain a few things in detail," he added.

"Please do. I'm sure they'll be interested in what you have to say. Mr. Harris is a good speaker and an interesting storyteller," she said into her microphone. "The story he will tell you is a true one, so please listen carefully."

Harris went on to explain how the state pursued Levin, invoking "inquisitorial powers" when asked for an explanation of why they were requesting three patient charts. He took them through the conference which occurred *in camera*, in the judge's chambers, where a mafia case was cited as the reason why Levin's accuser could not be identified. He then warmed to the topic even further, as he explained the disciplinary structure for doctors in New York State.

"So we get to the part where the governor appoints the Commissioner of Health, and we've now got a beauty of a commissioner who wants to pull all physicians who don't practice medicine in a conventional way out of the game completely," Harris said. "So I walk into the hearing room with my client, a fine doctor, a pioneer in alternative medicine, a well-respected, dignified gentleman, and we find out that the deck is totally stacked against us."

"And how did that come about?" encouraged Corsello.

"By the commissioner appointing the judge who's hearing the case, by the commissioner appointing the hearing panel—making sure the panel is made up of individuals who have a reputation for pulling licenses from alternative physicians, and by the state selecting a witness—only *one* witness," he emphasized, "a doctor who calls all alternative medical practitioners *'quacks,'* and who is a self-appointed *'quackbuster'!* Oh, before I forget to mention it, on top of all this, the state's attorney was instructed—probably by the same commissioner—to play the role of the *witness's lawyer*, advising the witness what questions to answer and what not to answer. How does *that* sound to you, Dr. Corsello?"

"It sounds to me, Mr. Harris, like your work is really cut out for you, does it not?"

"I'm a big guy, Dr. Corsello, as you can see," he chuckled, "and I think I'm big enough to handle it, no matter how tough they're trying to make it for us."

With Corsello's earlier agreement, Harris then gave the appropriate information to any listeners who might be inclined to contribute to Levin's Legal Defense Fund. Then he sat back admiring Serafina Corsello as she added to the topic and smoothly closed her program with a short meditation for the audience. They stood and kissed goodbye, Italian-style, on both cheeks.

Harris had put in a good day and would sleep well tonight.

CHAPTER 12

Susan usually entertained for the holidays, at least 20 people would come, and she was a fabulous hostess. Since the hearings had totally ruined Rosh Hashanah for them in the fall and had continued to hang over them until the acquittal in early December, Susan realized that anticipating a peaceful and quiet family celebration would help to restore balance and usher in the Festival of Lights in a meaningful way. While Chanukah didn't start until December 23 this year, it seemed more fitting to avoid having company and simply spend time quietly with Erika, who had to have been affected by the underlying tension that ruled her parents' deceptively calm exteriors at home.

Levin left his office at 2:00 P.M. on Friday to get home well before sundown, which signaled the official start of the holiday. He and Susan planned to introduce Erika, who would be four in April, to the traditions of the Jewish faith. She was a bright little girl, and they wanted this holiday to be special for her.

Susan met him at the door with a smile and a kiss. He put his briefcase down to pick Erika up and fly her all the way up toward the ceiling. She looked down at her father with a sweet smile and said, "Daddy, hurry up. It's gonna be dark soon. We have to light the menorah!" He blinked to hide a rush of emotion. He kissed her and put her down, sharing a meaningful look with Susan, who was as devoted to their little charmer as he was. She smiled and motioned him with her head to go get ready.

"Erika, let me tell you the story of Chanukah," her father said, when he returned to the dining room.

"Daddy, I *know* the story!" she announced unexpectedly. "A long time ago when the Jews...that's us," she added, pointing to herself and her parents, "got attacked by an army, their menorah got stolen away. It was a lamp, and it always had bright light, but the fire went out. The bad soldiers dumped all the special oil on the floor, and that was the oil the Jews used to light the menorah. And the bad soldiers brought pigs into the temple…like we go to our temple, but there are no pigs there. And the soldiers were making noises they were not supposed to be making in there, because it's not right," she added, glancing at her parents for approval. "Then, some of the Jews started to fight the soldiers, and they kept on fighting with them for two years!" she said, her eyebrows raised. "Two years must be a long time," she said, thoughtfully, "because I'm gonna be almost six years old in two years, and I'll be big then." Her parents chuckled at how serious Erika had become upon drawing that conclusion. The little girl continued. "The Jews were the winners of the fight, and they cleaned up the mess in the temple and put back the menorah. But then there was a problem," she said sadly.

"What was the problem, honey?" Susan asked her.

"They didn't have enough oil for the menorah was the problem."

"They only had enough for one day, Erika," said her father.

"Only one day," she repeated.

"So what happened?" her mother asked.

"Well," said the little girl, counting on her fingers, "there was oil to light it for one day, but it was still lighted up the next day, and the next, and the next, and…" She held up eight fingers. "The menorah kept on being light for eight whole days!" she concluded.

Her parents laughed with pride and pleasure. She had probably learned the whole Chanukah story in her nursery school class. They had been so preoccupied with their legal problems that they hadn't realized how much Erika had matured in her understanding of concepts. Susan and Warren hugged each other warmly, then gathered their daughter into their embrace.

Susan picked Erika up while Warren lit a taper and put it into the little girl's hand. Susan carefully guided the lit taper toward the *Shammos*, also known as the servant light, which was in the middle of the menorah and set at a higher level. Warren took the taper and blew it out, while Susan and Erika used the *Shammos* to light the first candle on the right, according to custom. Then Warren carried the menorah to the bay window at the front of the house and placed it on the sill, thus giving the miracle of Chanukah a prominent position in their home, all of which they explained to Erika, who nodded seriously as she listened.

During dinner, which included the traditional *latkes*, fried potato pancakes, Erika asked a lot of questions about Chanukah, genuinely showing both understanding and interest in the topic for one so young. Her parents hadn't felt as relaxed or as close to their religion and culture for a lot longer than they cared to admit. The memories of the hearing and the distress of the past six months faded into the background, at least on this one evening.

After dinner, Warren pulled from his pocket a wooden *dreidel* he had kept from his childhood home and sat on the living room carpet with Erika, showing her the Hebrew letters, one on each of the spinning top's four sides. He explained that each of the letters stood for a Hebrew word, and the translation of the phrase, *Nes gadol hayah sham* was "A great miracle happened there." Erika was quick to clarify the miracle for him, in case he didn't realize that one day's worth of oil created eight days worth of light, and he smiled with pleasure as they spun the top.

Susan joined them after cleaning up in the kitchen, bringing Chanukah *gelt* for each of them in the form of a chocolate coin wrapped in gold foil. Their gift to Erika on this first night of Chanukah was a game called Simon, which came with a slogan: "*Simon's a computer, Simon has a brain, you either do what Simon says or else go down the drain.*" The game had been around for twelve years already and, although she wasn't even four yet, they thought Erika would enjoy it. Susan had already loaded it with batteries, so Warren pressed a button, and Simon played a musical, three-tone sequence, each tone lighting one of the four light bars—yellow, blue, green, or red—on the circular game. The objective was to have the player carefully listen and observe, then touch the light bars in the correct order to reproduce the sequence. The musical tunes increased in number of sounds and difficulty as the game advanced. They kept playing at a beginner's level, though, laughing at their mistakes as each took a turn, until Erika's yawns alerted them to the fact that her bedtime was approaching.

Warren realized that he felt as free as the Jews had so long ago, when they had fought so valiantly and emerged victorious. Susan looked so happy this evening, as well. It had been a wise choice to celebrate the first night of Chanukah this way. He sighed with pleasure. Deep in his mind, though, lived a nugget of doubt: would this freedom last or would it come to a crashing end?

Back at his medical office on Monday, Levin decided to bring the day's mail back into his own office and open it himself. He was horrified at what he was seeing. He didn't know what to make of it. It seemed like every envelope contained the same thing, only from a different company. What was going on? What was happening? His mouth open with disbelief, he examined the pile he had stacked on his desk: "Due to nonpayment, your life insurance policy is hereby cancelled," "Due to nonpayment, your lifetime disability policy is hereby cancelled," "Due to nonpayment, your family health insurance policy is now cancelled," "Due to nonpayment, the employee group health insurance policy is now cancelled."

Without wasting a moment, Levin tore into his controller's office. He had hired Peter Rosen last year to complete his staff and remove the responsibility and annoyance of bill-paying chores from his own to-do list. He had signed countless checks for Peter to make the bill-paying process as smooth as possible. *Insurance companies normally sent warning letters to clients if their bills weren't paid on time. Had Peter received warning letters?* The companies generally sent reminder notices repeatedly, and then a clearly marked final notice—Levin knew that from a previous time, before Peter came on staff, when a bill had been misplaced and not paid on time. And where was his insurance agent in this whole thing, the guy who handled all of his policies? Had he called Peter? Had he called anyone?

Peter looked up from his desk, startled, as Levin burst through the door, his face twisted in anger, a pile of papers clutched in his fist haphazardly. "Dr. Levin..." he ventured tentatively, "uh..."

"What the hell is going on here?" Levin demanded, slamming his fist on the controller's desk, pushing the fistful of papers toward the man's chest. "What have you done to me? Or what *haven't* you done, might be more to the point?" Levin was breathing heavily, his upper body bent over the center of the desk toward Peter.

Peter tried to explain himself; Levin had to give him that. But nothing made any sense, and the controller knew it.

"Get out of this office before I call the cops!" Levin demanded. "Just get the hell out of my sight. I trusted you! How could you do this to me? To my family? To the entire staff? All of the insurance coverage I have...we *all* have," he said, gesturing toward the reception area, "gone! Cancelled! I've had some of these policies for decades? Did you *get* the bills? Where are they? Did my insurance agent call you? What did you tell him? Did the companies call?"

Levin's questions were fast and furious, and he wasn't waiting for answers, wasn't interested in any excuses.

The controller looked frightened. He had never seen Levin this way. Like the rest of the staff, Peter knew that Levin had been facing a lot of professional difficulties and legal battles, but he couldn't recall ever seeing the doctor so out of control with anger. He backed up in his chair slowly, preparing to pack his briefcase.

"Just get out now!" Levin shouted, and his receptionist came to the door, concerned. Levin waved her away when she called out to him.

The controller was stuffing papers into his briefcase.

"Leave everything here, Peter, or I *will* call the cops!" Levin warned.

"My st-stuff," the controller stuttered, "I'm just…"

"Listen to what I'm telling you! Just get out. We're going to comb through every item in this office after you're gone. If something's yours, you'll get it back. We'll send it to you. And that's more of a courtesy than you deserve. More of a courtesy than you gave *me*! I should sue the life out of you. That's what you deserve!"

Levin could see he had really scared the guy. *Good*, he thought. He *should* be scared. Peter edged around Levin, sticking close to the walls as though he feared the doctor would lash out at him physically, just as he had done verbally. He grabbed his coat and hurriedly left the office. Levin shut the controller's door firmly, whispering a quick apology to the staff members who had heard all or part of the exchange and went into his own office.

So much for peaceful holidays, he thought, trying to recapture the warm feelings of the first evening of Chanukah only three days earlier. The more he thought about it, the more upset he became. He hadn't wanted to listen to Peter's excuses, and he certainly didn't want to hear any of Ben's. Even though Ben Kaplan had been his insurance agent and close friend for years, this event was inexcusable, as far as Levin was concerned. Now, he'd have to get Susan involved in calling the companies to get the policies reinstated. That was the first step.

"Susan, listen, I'm staying late at the office tonight to meet with a couple of guys who have been chasing after my insurance account for a long time," he told her on the phone. It was January second, and Susan had succeeded in convincing the insurance companies to be reasonable and not to allow coverage to lapse on any of the policies, especially when she and several of the support staff had cleaned out Peter's office and discovered piles of signed checks *in the ceiling panel directly above his desk*. As incredulous as the story was, and whether or not the customer service reps or their managers believed it, they explained the circumstances to these people and had most of the policies reinstated. In fact, Levin himself had taken a check down to the Blue Cross/Blue Shield office in person, fearing that the staff or his family's coverage would lapse in the time the postal service would take to deliver his check down the block. The most painful blow came when Levin's lifetime disability policy, one that he had been paying very reasonable premiums for, since he had taken it in his twenties, fresh out of medical school, was *not* reinstated. The company was willing to offer coverage only until Levin became 65 years of age, no longer for the entire span of his life, should he become disabled. That was an unfortunate loss but one that apparently could not be rectified.

The insurance agents walked into the office right on time, as soon as the staff had left for the day. Levin sat with them, explaining the circumstances that had led to the meeting in painful detail. They nodded in sympathy. "So now I have a new life insurance policy," Levin told them, "but it doesn't matter. I'm willing to give it up if what you've got to tell me sounds good."

Levin completed the necessary paperwork, answering questions and making copies of whatever documents the agents requested, and then one of the men opened his briefcase and removed a blood pressure cuff. "I've got one here in my office," Levin said. "After all, this is a medical office, you know," he added with a smile.

"Oh, that's okay, Dr. Levin," the shorter of the two men responded. "I'm used to using my own equipment. I guess I'm just more comfortable that way."

Levin nodded and removed his jacket. He loosened his tie and unbuttoned his shirt to offer his upper arm. *Wow, this is like being a patient in my own office.* He smiled at the thought.

"One-fifteen over seventy, Dr. Levin. You're in great shape," the man said.

"I have to be," Levin told him, "since I now only have disability coverage until I turn sixty-five." Although that was an unfortunate truth, they all laughed lightly, since he had made his statement in such an offhanded way.

After putting himself back together, Levin went into the men's room to produce a urine sample, and he followed the same routine he generally did, testing the urine in the cup. He walked back into his office, his face pale and somber. "I don't think we can go any further, gentlemen," he told them.

Both agents sat there, unsure how to respond. The taller of the two spoke. "Did we do or say something wrong, Dr. Levin?"

"No, no, it's not about you. It's about me. I have trace amounts of blood in my urine. I just checked my urine sample. I don't know what's going on, because this never happened to me before, and I always check. I'll have to call you and let you know where this is all going, but there's nothing we can do right now."

When they had left the office, Levin picked up the phone and contacted Dr. Michael Gribetz, a urologist Susan had been using for decades and, as a professional courtesy, Gribetz agreed to see him immediately. Levin had to make another call before he left the office.

"I've got a lot of work to do, Susan," he said into the phone, "so I'll sleep here tonight and see you tomorrow." He knew Susan would never object, because she preferred that he not bring work home.

"Okay, Warren," Gribetz told him, "there are only so many tests I can perform here at my office. But what I'm seeing, and you can see it clearly yourself," he said, pointing to the x-ray on the light box, "appears to be a huge bubble. Probably a cyst. It's only on the one kidney, though. The other one's clean. I'll make sure to get you into the hospital for tests first thing tomorrow morning."

By the time Levin left Mt. Sinai Hospital the next day, he had the results of the tests that were taken and a definitive diagnosis. Three tests had been done, and the results were conclusive. There was the IVP, an intravenous pyelogram, that involved him laying on a cold x-ray table and having contrast material injected into a vein in his arm, which traveled through his blood stream and collected in his kidneys and urinary tract, turning those areas bright white for the x-ray. It took about an hour, he recalled, because the kidneys had to process the contrast solution, while a serious of x-rays recorded the exact size of the kidneys, capturing the urinary tract in action as it began to empty. A sonogram and CT scan were also done. Again, a professional courtesy was extended to him, and the radiologist immediately read all of the films and met with Levin and his urologist to discuss the results.

Levin returned to his office during the latter part of the day, his manner subdued. He was a bit less chatty and jovial with his patients, who cited his friendly manner as one of the highlights of their visits to his office. Unlike many physicians, he never hesitated to warm up the atmosphere with a story or a joke. Today his behavior had been noticeably different.

Usually, Levin hated being alone with his thoughts on the train whenever he was coming home with news he was loath to share. This trip was different. He found a seat, closed his eyes and—in spite of the noise and the lurching—entered into a meditative state. He commanded his Consciousness to "…turn off the Blood Supply to my right kidney." The trip seemed remarkably short. He entered through the kitchen door and just stood there, immediately keying in to the look of apprehension on his wife's face. "Susan, we have to talk," he told her.

Over dinner, she asked the question that was on her mind since he had walked in. "What's going on, Warren?"

"I went to see Michael Gribetz."

"Michael? Why?"

"Susan, I…I have a tumor." His face was impassive. He didn't want her t o panic.

"A tumor? A tumor where?" She was beginning to breathe faster.

"My kidney."

"Your kidney. I see," she said, swallowing, not wanting to ask the next question but needing to, as Warren wasn't volunteering any information. "Is it benign or malignant?" she asked just above a whisper, although no one was around to hear.

"It's malignant," he responded, looking down at his folded hands.

"Malignant," she repeated, feeling numb. "How big is it, Warren?" she asked, taking the chair next to his, putting both of her warm hands atop his cold ones, as tears ran down her cheeks.

"Big," he responded, turning to her, tears in his eyes as well. "It's about the size of a grapefruit. It's got to come out. I need to have surgery."

"Oh, my God!" Susan exclaimed, "oh, my God." She took a napkin from the napkin holder in the center of the table, wiped her eyes, blew her nose, then got up and left the room, walking down the hall.

"Susan," Warren called after her, his emotional state a bit fragile at the moment, "where are you going?"

"To my office," she responded, heading directly to the room she had designated as her own private office at the far opposite end of the house. "I'm going to call Michael Gribetz," she told him.

"Why?"

"Because he's the doctor, and you're the patient. That's why."

Levin walked into her office and sat near her desk. None of this had a humorous twist, he acknowledged, but he laughed softly to himself. Susan was moving into what he always thought of as her "Crisis Control Mode." She was asking his doctor how long the surgery could be postponed, so that she could get the medical office set up for her husband's absence and find a way of doing "damage control" with the staff. He heard her tell his doctor that she didn't want anyone to know that he'd be operated on for cancer. When she hung up, her face was set with determination. He looked at her with admiration, thinking, *she's some woman!*

"Warren," she told him, "Michael was very reassuring, and I think three weeks will be enough to do what we have to. I'm calling our lawyer and our accountant in the morning. We don't know what the outcome of this will be, but we need to know that everything's in place." She looked at him questioningly. "Are you all right with this?"

"Susan," he responded, "you're right on top of everything…as usual."

She smiled at the compliment. "I don't want you to worry about anything but getting yourself as strong as possible for the surgery. You can leave the rest to me."

"I know," he said, and he really meant it.

With her parents' reluctant agreement ringing in her ears, the Levins put their daughter, Erika, and their new housekeeper on a plane to Florida, where they would remain for several weeks. If the surgery went according to plan, with no complications, they planned to join Erika at her grandparents' home, they told the little girl, "while daddy rests." The couple then drove directly to Mt. Sinai Hospital.

It was Sunday, the 21st of January. In the three weeks that had elapsed since Warren had come home with his frightening diagnosis, Susan had watched him prepare for the surgery in a relentless manner. He was always careful about the foods he put into his body, so that remained the same, with him avoiding processed foods, fatty meats, caffeine, sweets, and enjoying healthy salads, whole-grain breads and cereals, fruits, vegetables. However, he increased his supplements, taking gargantuan daily doses of vitamins and minerals. Prior to the surgery, he managed to donate blood twice, in the event he required a transfusion; he wanted to make certain that he was given his own blood and not the blood of an unknown donor. Susan believed that her husband was in the very best shape possible. While he was preparing his body for the process, Susan prepared the medical office for temporary changes. The staff was informed that Warren would be having prostate surgery, which required six weeks of recuperation, so the couple would go to Florida for part of that time, she explained. The staff was put on staggered shifts and given some vacation time. Temporarily, everyone was informed, the office would be open three days a week instead of five.

The Levins parked in the hospital garage and entered the building from the basement, where the patient registration office was located. They waited in the lobby for the remainder of their "entourage" to arrive. In minutes, both their accountant and their attorney appeared beside them, briefcases in hand and matching looks of worry on their faces.

"Relax," Levin told them. "We'll cover all the bases before I go under the knife tomorrow." Neither man responded but both seemed uncomfortable being with their doctor client, who was about to become a patient himself in a hospital.

The patient registrar was appropriately solicitous, since the incoming patient was a physician. Still, she couldn't help but glance repeatedly at the men in long, dark, winter coats, hats, and briefcases, who she thought looked like FBI or Secret Service, flanking the Levins. Since Levin's paperwork had been completed in advance of his surgery, they were ready to show him to his hospital room.

"What's all that stuff?" the registrar asked, indicating suitcases and packages that seemed more appropriate for a two-week cruise rather than a brief hospital stay.

"Don't worry about it," Susan told the woman impatiently. "It's what he needs while he's here, and I'm staying over for the first three nights, so I have my stuff, too."

"Yeah, well, it's a good thing you have a private room," she said, rolling her eyes, and asking two of the maintenance people to load everything onto two extra-wide wheelchairs, the kind used for extremely obese patients.

The group left for the elevator, the two staff members pushing the wheelchairs. Levin had requested a private room in the old wing of the hospital overlooking Fifth Avenue. He knew that the new wing would be beautiful but was worried that environmentally unhealthy materials might have been used in its construction.

When the elevator arrived at their floor, a nurse, alerted by the patient registrar, met the group to escort them to the room. Susan walked in first, scanned the room thoroughly, her eyes missing nothing, and very aware that this private room was costing them $500 extra per day. "I don't know about you," she said to her husband, "but I'm not staying here!"

Levin looked at her, puzzled. "What's wrong with the room?"

"Warren, look at it," she said, gesturing broadly with her arm. "The blinds are broken, the room is filthy dirty, the walls are cracked, it's dark, it's dingy, it's gloomy, and it's absolutely disgusting! Since you're going to be unconscious," she added, looking his way, "and I'm going to be conscious the entire time, I refuse to stay here! It's that simple." She did a smart about-face and walked right out of the room, followed by Levin, the lawyer, the accountant, the nurse, and the two staff members with the wide wheelchairs piled sky-high with their luggage and other items.

Levin shrugged helplessly, an apologetic smile on his face. "I guess we're not staying here," he told the nurse.

"You'll have to go back downstairs to Patient Registration, then, and let them know," the nurse replied.

"Can't you just call them?" Susan asked.

"No, I'm sorry, I can't do that. You have to go back downstairs." She turned away and walked back to the central nurses' station.

The six of them, along with the stacked wheelchairs, headed back down to the basement, walking directly over to the desk of the obese black woman who had checked them in.

"What's the matter?" she asked, eyeing the group suspiciously once again, wondering if the "Secret Service guys" had seen something they didn't like, and she was curious enough to want to know.

"The room was horrible!" Susan told her. "He can't stay there," indicating Levin. "*We* can't stay there."

The registrar wondered if the two guys in the black coats were armed. They were silent observers, she noted, watching their eyes scan the area as they hovered over their "charge." She consulted the bed-board chart, made a quick call, and told them, "We have a beautiful room up in the new wing, in the VIP area. How does that sound?"

"We'll have to see it first," Susan said, not giving an inch.

"Fine," the registrar said, wondering who the patient really was. He must be pretty famous, she thought, only she couldn't place him. She told the staffers the room number, and watched the group move off toward the bank of elevators once again.

As before, a nurse met them when the elevator opened to a spacious area, windows illuminating a sparkling, clean floor, the walls painted in muted earth tones, the upholstered chairs new, and the table piled with newspapers and current magazines. She led them down a wide corridor to a private room.

Wow, thought Susan, *this is more like it*. Two comfortable chairs were in the bright room, a small refrigerator, a laminated mahogany bureau and wardrobe, patterned sheets on the bed, a quilted comforter folded at the foot of the bed. The entire group appeared impressed.

"Just one minute," Levin said. "I have to check something."

"Check what, Dr. Levin?" the nurse asked, a tone of annoyance creeping into her voice. Apparently, her colleague from the prior floor in the old wing had alerted her about this strange group.

"Check the inside of the closet," he said. The nurse walked over to the closet with him, curious. He opened the doors and peered into the closet, which was constructed of particleboard, laminated on the outside only with mahogany veneer. "No good," he pronounced. "I can't stay here!"

The entire group looked at him in surprise. Susan appeared mortified.

"What's wrong now?" asked the nurse, who may have also been called by the patient registrar as the group rode the elevator.

"The inside of this closet has exposed particleboard, which contains Formaldehyde, a toxic substance. The particleboard should have been covered with wood or Formica to make it safe. I can't stay in this room."

The nurse took a deep breath without taking her eyes off Levin. Susan was sure the nurse had decided she was dealing with a real nut-job. Finally, the woman spoke. "I've got *one more room*, Dr. Levin, and that's it!" She stomped off in a no-nonsense manner, and the group tiptoed after her. Arriving at their final room offer, an equally bright, new, and spotless place, Levin immediately inspected the closet. Noting that the interior was lined with Formica, he nodded his assent.

The staff members pushing the wheelchairs seemed relieved to get away from the group, but Susan asked them politely to move the two chairs from the adjoining room into her husband's room temporarily. The Levins needed to sit down with their advisors and discuss the legal and accounting matters that had to be settled prior to the surgery scheduled for the following morning.

The discussion was organized and moved quickly; appropriate papers were amended and signed. Both men were notaries and able to witness and notarize one another's documents. Once everything was complete, the lawyer and accountant took it upon themselves to move the two borrowed chairs back where they came from, shook hands with Levin and Susan, and wished the doctor good luck and a speedy recovery.

Alone in the room, Susan unpacked the suitcases, putting everything into the closet and bureau. She took out the VCR they had brought, along with the educational videos Warren had requested, his reading materials, articles and magazines, and even an air purifier. She had located a health food store nearby, as well, and had arranged for the store to juice vegetables and deliver them to Warren immediately, as the vitamins and enzymes contained in the fresh juice would lose potency if not ingested within thirty minutes. A private nurse would be on duty for the first three nights. Susan would also spend those same nights in the room then stay locally with friends in Manhattan for the duration of Warren's hospitalization. She put the suitcase full of vitamins into the closet unopened. She knew she'd have problems with the medical staff if they had any idea of what the Levins had brought with them.

It was difficult for Susan to concentrate on anything she tried to watch on television or read while Warren was having his operation. Anesthesia and surgery always came with risks. He was in his fifties, which complicated matters even further, she knew; because older people didn't bounce back as quickly as younger ones. The thought that she had been trying to push away for weeks, ever since he had come home with the horrible news was what if he *didn't* make it? The thought of living without him was one she was unable to even consider. She loved him too much, and she knew how much he loved her. Their meeting with the lawyer and accountant, yesterday, however, had forced her to think about unimaginable possibilities. What if the cancer had spread and he needed chemotherapy and radiation? What if his tumor was inoperable? What if he never completely recovered and lived out the rest of his life disabled? What if he died? What if…?

Her thoughts were suddenly interrupted by the loud ringing of the telephone in the hospital room. It took her a moment to collect her thoughts. She darted across the room and grabbed the receiver. She listened as the surgeon spoke to her, not interrupting even once.

"Thank you," she said softly, "thank you so much."

The stress of the prior weeks and her worries about Warren's health came out then in huge, heaving sobs. The floor nurse, passing the room, came in and put her arm around Susan, who was still standing by the nightstand with the telephone.

"What's wrong? Is it bad news?" the young woman asked with concern.

Susan was unable to respond. She shook her head and reached for the tiny box of tissues next to the phone. She wiped her eyes, blew her nose, and tried to compose herself. The young woman continued to hold her. Finally, she took a deep breath, cleared her throat, and said, "No, it's not bad news. It's *good* news," and started crying again.

The surgery had gone well. They removed Levin's left kidney and adrenal gland. The cancer had not spread. Neither chemotherapy nor radiation was indicated. He was encouraged to get up and walk the day after the surgery to prevent adhesions. Susan was by his side. They'd be leaving the hospital for home in a few days, and then they'd head down to Florida, where the winter sun would be warming and relaxing. Levin knew he couldn't take a full six weeks to recover. They'd be bankrupt if he did that.

Susan picked up the phone next to Warren's bed. "Hello, Bob," she said, her heart skipping a beat at the sound of the lawyer's voice. "I hope you called to ask how Warren is doing."

"Of course, I did," boomed Harris. "Is he in a position to speak to me now? It's important"

"Can it wait?" she asked.

"I don't think so," he responded.

Wordlessly, she handed the phone to her husband. After exchanging pleasantries with Harris, she watched his face drop. He didn't say anything more. Finally, she heard him mumble, "Bye," and he handed the receiver to her, and she hung it up.

"Warren?"

"The Commissioner of Health, Axelrod, remanded my case back to the hearing panel," he told her. "I can't think about this now. I don't *want* to think about this now." He lay back on his pillow, closed his eyes and started to take slow, deep breaths in what Susan recognized as his "meditation mode."

Somehow, they managed to get through the next few days at the hospital, followed by several days at home prior to heading for Florida, without ever discussing the hearing. He had simply put it out of his mind. He needed his concentration focused on healing his body, not on tearing himself apart with worry. Susan decided that this was not the time to force him to speak about it. She would follow his lead on the issue. Once they got back home and he felt well enough to return to work, she knew that they'd get to the issue soon enough.

CHAPTER 13

"Warren, what in the world are you *doing*, when you're supposed to be resting?" Susan asked, standing at the door to his home office. "*Warren*, I'm talking to you!"

Levin blinked a few times, his concentration broken. "I'm…writing a letter."

"It's *Sunday*, for goodness' sake, and you just got out of the hospital yesterday. *What* could be so important?"

"Come on in and take a look," he responded, pulling the sheets out of the computer's printer and handing them to her.

"You're writing to the *Disciplinary Committee on Grievances*? Who are they? What's this about?"

"I'm filing a complaint against Victor Herbert with the Appellate Division. I've been writing this letter in my mind for months, ever since the judge dismissed him from testifying as an expert witness," Levin told her. He had put together a three-page letter and believed he had documented every last thing that had so upset him when Herbert was railing against complementary and alternative medicine, its practitioners, and everything Levin stood for.

Susan remained standing and started reading. "Interesting," she said. "You've pinpointed a 'documented lack of integrity' and say that 'he's unfit for continued service as an attorney.' Does he even practice law? I thought he has some exalted position in a VA hospital."

"I don't know if he practices law or not, but the guy has a law degree, and he's a liar! He has lied and lied and lied whenever it suited him. Bob did a *great* job exposing him for the liar he is, true, but what he did to me deserves consequences!"

She laughed. "I've got to hand it to you, Warren. Even when you're angry and want to see someone punished, you still show class!"

"What? Where?"

She read from the letter: "'There are very few men with the necessary intelligence and intensity to acquire both a medical and a law degree in today's world.' Nice touch," she commented. "Then you give him the zinger. 'Such an individual must be held accountable to even *higher standards* of integrity by virtue of the *implied brilliance*. Unfortunately, Dr. Herbert has used his position for demagogic purposes for many years.' Oh, so you're taking it beyond the hearing room where he attacked you."

Levin nodded. "Sure! This guy's been after my colleagues for so long. He's, in essence, been after *me* for years! You can't imagine how many alternative practitioners lost their licenses while Victor Herbert sat in a chair and lied about every imaginable thing, doing his best to make them look like the 'quacks' he insists on calling all of us. Susan," he said, his tone measured and reasonable, "this guy's evil. He's really just a *horrible* individual. He's not acting like a doctor, and he's not acting like a lawyer. He's a demagogue, intent on pursuing his own agenda and, frankly, he doesn't give a damn how many lives or careers he destroys in the process. If this was the Old West, I can imagine Herbert riding into town on a pinto pony with a whole bunch of warriors around him, a loincloth and a bunch of scalps hanging from his belt! That's how I've begun to view him. You had to be there to watch that smug little prick with the Napoleonic complex get his dander up every time Bob questioned him. Anyway, why don't you just keep on reading? I've told you everything that happened in that hearing room, from beginning to end, so you should be able to pick up on anything I might have left out."

Susan cleared her throat dramatically and continued. "'He has railed against those who dare to disagree with his opinions; he implies that his opinions are facts and has frequently misapplied statistics in his speaking and writing, while at the same time objecting to statistics used by others,'" she read. She scanned the next paragraph silently. "Oh, Warren, you're going to tell them that you've been brought up on charges?" she asked, her face showing alarm.

"Sure, why not? I've been cleared. That makes my letter even stronger, I think."

She regarded him for a moment, the doubt plain on her face. She read silently for awhile, then summarized. "So you've outlined the charges they leveled against you, included pages from the hearing transcript to support your points, talked about Herbert's lies on his med school application, his lies about his expertise in foreign affairs, the dubious credentials you saw in his 60-page c.v., and his lie about having been an officer in a Special Forces unit. Then you went ahead and mentioned stuff he said to you years ago! Why would you do that?"

"Just as you said before, *to support my point*. I'm probably saying this for the hundredth time, but this guy has had it in for me—for everyone like me who practices medicine differently from what he learned in medical school—for a *very* long time, and this hearing gave him the opportunity he was looking for. I want to make it very obvious that he planned to stop at nothing. Then the judge threw him out. The judge saw him for the jerk he was."

"Okay, I see," she said, hesitantly, not really seeing at all. "The issue about him not answering whether or not he brought the charges against you I can understand. For goodness' sake, if he was your accuser, and it certainly seems like it, and then he was called as the state's only witness against you…I guess the point is, you'd think, as an ethical lawyer, he would recuse himself from being a witness at your hearing. Is that the right word?"

"Yeah, Bob said exactly that, in fact. That it's one thing to bring charges, unfounded ones at that, but to refuse to answer the question as to whether he brought the charges, and then he's sitting there… You know, Susan, Bob and I have been talking a lot about this. The Medical Board of the OPMC has about 150 members, give or take. The people that Commissioner Axelrod tends to select on a regular basis to sit on hearing panels—especially when alternative physicians are being brought up on charges, usually trumped-up charges or charges that are nonspecific," he added, "are from a small group, maybe twenty-five or so—the ones he's *certain* are going to vote his way. *Get the non-establishment doctor out of the profession!* I assume that's the battle cry for this group."

"So you're saying that these three panel members, the ones who were at your hearing, are from a 'select' group that the commissioner counted on to vote against you?" Susan asked.

"According to Bob, whose primary focus as an attorney is physician defense work, he's seen them time and again at hearings and can always predict what direction they'll take; and the direction is usually against, not for, the doctor on trial."

"Great," she muttered sarcastically, "just great. On the other hand, they voted in *your* favor."

"Bob said it would all hit the fan once Axelrod got wind of what they did, and I guess that's exactly what must have happened," he said, his voice tinged with resignation.

"But, at least, they won't have Victor Herbert."

"True. Look, I've got to be realistic. I had hoped the case would *not* be remanded back to the hearing room. No such luck. Bob says we've *got* to go back in. Well, you heard my side of the conversation in the hospital," he said, looking at her as she stood beside his desk. "I didn't even *ask* him whether 'remanding' means the same panel members, the same judge, the witness they threw out. All I know is that without Victor Herbert and with a different panel, maybe a different judge, too, at least I might get a fair hearing. It couldn't possibly be worse than it was. Think about it. Three panel members, commissioner's pick. They've got Storch, who works for the commissioner. They've got the prosecutor, Sheehan, who works for the commissioner. What a crock! Bob's infuriated, because the legal system is being bastardized here. Where is 'innocent until proven guilty'? Where is 'a fair trial' with an impartial panel or with 'a jury of my peers'? Where is the 'impartial judge'? Where is the witness who really is 'an expert' in my type of work? Where," he added with a laugh, "is the witness who doesn't have the District Attorney jumping all over with objections and advising him whether to answer a question or not...who is not even embarrassed to say in front of everybody that *his superiors* have instructed him on how to *counsel* the witness?"

Levin sighed deeply. "You know, Susan, according to Bob, Storch showed a lot of courage, a lot of guts when he threw Victor Herbert out as a witness. On the other hand, Bob thinks he's really gonna get reamed over that. Who knows? Maybe he already has gotten his head handed to him. I admire Storch for keeping his cool, I've gotta tell you. Sheehan was downright insulting to him over what he 'was allowed' to do and what he 'shouldn't' be doing. It was almost as though he were warning him: 'Wait till I tell the Commissioner on you! Then you're *really* gonna get it!'" Levin had a bemused expression on his face. He had never imagined there could be such a flagrant disrespect for authority in a courtroom...well, true, it wasn't really a 'courtroom,' with a high judge's bench, which alone serves to convey a sense of distance and authority between the lawyers and judges. But Storch was a judge, albeit an administrative law judge, so the entire fiasco had struck Levin as rather odd. He looked at Susan.

"Oh, boy," she said, sighing deeply. "Here I am thinking about how we started out with such a fabulous holiday," she said, remembering the first night of Chanukah. "It finally felt like nothing was hanging over our heads. People had even begun sending in donations to help with your defense. It's very gratifying to realize you have so many supporters." She saw him nod in agreement. "So, when 1989 finally came to a close, I figured things would really begin to change for the better. Oh, no, not for us. First, we had to deal with that unbelievable insurance mess at your office. Just as we solve as much of the problem as we can and reinstate most of our coverage, the next catastrophe hits. Cancer, of all things! Is it possible that there's a black cloud following us around everywhere? Is it... Warren?"

"Yes?"

She had a half-smile on her face. "Remember that Li'l Abner cartoon in the funny papers?" she asked.

"Sure, I used to read it all the time. I loved it."

Susan laughed, remembering something. "Warren, do you remember that character...um," she said, biting her upper lip, fishing in her mind for the name, "um, Joe, Joe Bif...Bisp. . . Bip—I don't know, something like that? He was called 'the world's worst jinx,' and he had this black rain cloud over his head at all times."

"Where did you pull that memory from?" he asked laughing. He winced. "Ouch," he said. "As they say, 'It hurts when I laugh.'"

"Oh, Warren," she said, reaching toward him with concern.

"I'm fine, I'm fine, don't worry. I sure do remember Joe," he told her. "He was a well-meaning, friendly guy, but he was very lonely. People didn't want to be around him because they got hit with the bad luck that was always hanging over his head. You know, I saw an interview on television with the cartoonist, Al Capp. It was a really long time ago. The guy's been dead more than ten or twelve years now, if I remember correctly. Anyway, he said that he gave this character, Joe, an unpronounceable last name, and the only way you could say his name was by blowing a 'raspberry,' you know, a 'Bronx cheer,' which I will not attempt to do at this moment, as much as I'd like to, because it will be painful, I'm afraid."

"So I'll do it for you," said Susan, spraying him with a series of 'raspberries,' until she collapsed into a chair in hysterics. He laughed softly, holding his abdomen, enjoying the moment and glad to see Susan in such a playful mood.

When the moment had passed, she tried to pick up the thread from their earlier conversation. "Well, frankly, I was hoping we had seen the last of that black cloud that chased us for the last six months of last year. Now, as I really pay attention to this stuff you're saying about the people involved in the hearing, you're really scaring me."

"I'm scaring myself, too," he admitted, with a sigh. "Maybe that's why I'm trying to take some kind of action, gain back a little control, since I've been feeling like they've taken all my power away from me. Anyway, read the rest of the letter."

"Hmm, interesting," she remarked. "'. . . therefore the state's attorney general had *no right* to instruct him as a witness. The validity of that interpretation was *not questioned by anyone* at the hearing or since.' That's what you were alluding to before, when Sheehan told Herbert not to answer Bob's question, after the judge ordered him to answer, isn't it?"

"Yes."

"So, now the closing. 'I believe that perjury and refusal to obey the direct order of the judge represent egregious examples of failure of an attorney to live up to the minimum standards of conduct of the legal profession, and I request a formal review with appropriate sanctions.' Nice," she said approvingly. "It's almost funny. Here, they brought Herbert in to get you. Now, you're going after Herbert! He deserves it."

Levin nodded, a yawn escaping at the same time. "Let's go to sleep."

CHAPTER 14

"Bob, did you get a copy of this?" Levin asked, holding the telephone receiver so tightly that his nail beds were white. Levin was breathing rapidly, and his voice was thick with anxiety. He wanted to pound his roll top desk with the phone until the wooden slats shattered and the wires broke through the phone's cracked plastic casing, but he restrained himself. He realized that, in spite of his attorney's admonishments over the weeks that had elapsed since he was declared innocent, Bob's insistence on continuing to meet over medical issues in anticipation of a possible callback had been all too realistic. Even with the attorney's call to his hospital room, Levin had steadfastly refused to focus on the fact that his case had, indeed, been remanded for additional proceedings. During his brief recuperative period in Florida, he also blotted the thought from his mind. His goal at the time had been to rest and instruct his body to heal, so that he could get back to work as soon as possible. His strategy was apparently solid, since he managed the impossible after having major surgery by returning to work after three short weeks. *And now this!*

He was holding a thick manila envelope that had come into the office with the day's mail. That meant that while he and Susan were doing their best to avoid focusing on the fact that he'd be back in court shortly, the state of New York probably had the packet prepared. He hadn't even sat down to read the thing yet. Just the sight of it had punctured his mood so badly. The one thing he *had* done was to check the final page for the date. The oversized envelope appeared identical to the one he had received last June. He wanted to be certain that some clerk hadn't simply stuck the old paperwork into an envelope and sent it out to him again, even though his hearing was over and done with. When he saw the handwritten date on page 15, at the end of all the typewritten charges, he realized that this was not the result of a clerical error. It was clearly a document prepared in February of this year and mailed out at the end of last week. His heart was pounding. For some reason, when he received the panel's decision exonerating him, even though he *knew* the case was subject to review and remand by Axelrod, he didn't think that he'd be "on trial" for another fifteen pages of charges, just as he was the first time. Didn't that other hearing have *any* significance at all? Okay, he could understand them asking him to come in and, perhaps, speak on behalf of the benefits of some of his treatments that fall under the rubric of 'alternative medicine,' but a packet this thick meant nothing but trouble. Big trouble. Again. He and Susan had studiously avoided the topic since Bob's call prior to their leaving the hospital. It only came up once, when he was writing the complaint letter against Victor Herbert before they left for Florida and briefly the next morning when he told her what he believed this reappearance would entail; and he was wrong, wrong, wrong!

"Warren, don't let it get to you," Bob said. I need you to stay as calm as possible. Do you have patients to see this afternoon or can you get away?"

"Not now! I can't get away now at all. I'm very busy. It's Thursday. It's my late night. And I'm upset, Bob, very upset. I can't imagine what this is going to do to Susan!" he said, apprehension about his wife's response overshadowing his own distress.

Harris wasn't concerned about the doctor's wife. He had to move his client into crisis mode, work with him to develop a viable action plan. There was no opportunity for sympathy or histrionics. "I'll make time for you this weekend. If you've got plans, I suggest you cancel them," he stated authoritatively. "In fact, I'd like to come to *your* office," his lawyer told him. "There are a number of things I'd like to get a better understanding of anyway, so it's time for you to start playing professor again, and this time you've got to get me all the way through medical school. I'm gonna need all the knowledge I can stuff into my head. And I'm serious, Warren, dead serious."

"Let me talk to Susan first. I'll get back to you."

"Warren, listen …"

But Levin wouldn't let him continue. "Not now, Bob, not now!" He cut the call off and buzzed his receptionist, telling her to hold any calls and to tell his next patient he was running late, something that he rarely allowed to occur. He wasn't about to call Susan now. He had to get himself under control. He certainly didn't want to allow a setback in his recuperation. Only three weeks post-operative, he felt unbelievably fine, but he didn't want to push his endurance by allowing all of this emotional pollution to build up. He switched on his desk lamp, locked the door and darkened the room. He sat behind his desk, pushed the roll top all the way up, and glanced at the sign on the wall nearby: "*Rule number one* is, *don't sweat the small stuff*. *Rule* number two is, it's *all* small *stuff*." He often gestured toward this framed quote when patients started listing their worries in a never-ending litany and he got the sense that their recitation had taken over their typical conversational style. Now he wanted to apply the adage to himself, but what he was facing wasn't "small stuff" at all; it was the re-emergence of a nightmare he had already lived through, first with his repeated triple rounds with the court system, then with the incredulous and ridiculous antics in the hearing room.

He started to review it all again, in spite of his decision to shut it out of his mind. Since *when* did a state-employed prosecutor forbid an expert witness from answering a question? Since when did that very same prosecutor inform a hearing panel that "his superiors had *instructed* him not to allow the witness to answer the question"? These images were slamming his brain from one end of his skull to the other. At least that's how it felt. First one image then another. All of the images neatly fitting into the phrase, "kangaroo court," which a colleague had suggested to him after a recitation of a day's worth of events in the hearing room. While he had heard the term before and assumed he had a surface understanding of it, he had been curious enough at the time to look it up, and it turned out to be a perfect description of what he was going through.

The colloquial phrase, he learned, refers to a sham legal proceeding. *Check.* It describes judicial proceedings that deny due process. *Check.* Within due process, much was assumed within the American court system. For example, an accused is entitled to witnesses summoned on his behalf, but that wasn't happening. *Check.* One has the ability to control his own defense, yet he had no control over anything that was happening. *Check.* He was supposed to have the right to cross-examine someone brought in to testify against him, and Bob had gotten nowhere with a key question to the state's sole witness. *Check.* He had the right not to incriminate himself; yet he was certain if they could push him into incriminating himself, they would, which is probably why they originally told him to come in without an attorney. *Check.* He should have the right to exclude evidence that is improperly obtained, irrelevant, or inherently inadmissible; and most of what Victor Herbert said was totally irrelevant. *Check.* How about his right to exclude judges or jurors on the grounds of partiality or conflict of interest? *Double check there.* He was supposed to have the right of appeal, but he wasn't about to appeal the panel's original finding of innocence, and he didn't think he could appeal the state's decision to remand the case. *Check.* Finally, he was entitled not to be tried on secret evidence, yet that was *exactly* what was happening. *Check.*

When considering how successful his hearing had been in stripping him of all of the sacred and inalienable rights he thought he was entitled to as an American citizen, it really scared the life out of him. Where were his democratic rights under due process? he wondered. Now, with this decision to remand the hearing, the chill that took hold of him was very real, for the outcome of a trial by a kangaroo court was usually determined *in advance, usually to convict.* This was a *devastating* thought.

Bob was a good lawyer, an experienced lawyer—experienced in medical defense, so Levin knew that he and Susan had chosen well. Bob had shared a number of facts during their meetings that Levin almost didn't want to know. He remembered the attorney telling him, "Warren, listen, this guy Briber, who's on the panel is a guy who really *loves* being the public member. I've come across him in this setting at least four or five times in the past, and *never once, not one single time*, did he ever vote in favor of a doctor!" With the case remanded for hearing, Briber would be sitting in judgment on him once again. Bob's characterization of the guy wasn't terribly flattering, and he trusted Bob's take on these panel members.

Suddenly, Levin's mouth fell open as the memory he had been reaching for and trying to recover for months suddenly came into focus like a speeding car about to strike him. Briber! How could he have forgotten? Why hadn't he been able to remember this sooner? *I have to tell Bob this weekend.* Maybe this would make a difference. But that was only *one* panel member out of three.

There was the OB/GYN guy, Robert J. O'Connor, M.D., nice enough, grandfatherly in appearance, but as Bob so eloquently stated, "Warren, this guy's over the hill! He's unable to even *entertain* a discussion of something that's as unfamiliar to him as alternative medicine. That's probably why he has such trouble staying awake during the hearings. I'm just waiting for his head to fall backward on his chair and for a loud snore to erupt." So there was no comfort for Levin from this panelist either. The overweight Dr. McAloon, according to Bob, "was brilliant, wanted to be liked, but is so darned conservative that if she didn't learn it in med school, she sure as heck wasn't teaching it to her medical students at

SUNY Buffalo, and therefore it didn't exist." In this case, the "it" referred to the foundation of Levin's entire practice!

He remembered how the judge, Storch, in an effort to do the right thing, the just thing, had instructed Victor Herbert to answer Bob's question as to whether or not he had filed the charges against him. He remembered the panel, for goodness' sake, taking a vote and *instructing* Victor Herbert to answer. He recalled Sheehan jumping in, playing lawyer to the witness, instructing him *not* to answer, at which point Storch dismissed Herbert then asked Sheehan whether he had *other* witnesses to present. "No, I don't," Sheehan had responded. "Dr. Victor Herbert was the heart and soul of the state's case against Dr. Levin. We have no other witnesses." *Heart and soul*, he had thought at the time. *Just* when *did Victor Herbert graduate from being just the soul of the case to also becoming its heart?* "Very well, Mr. Sheehan," Storch had said, "I'll now ask the panel to deliberate," and deliberate they did, resulting in the glorious missive which stated that the hearing committee had found *no reason to convict. No relevant testimony* had been presented to substantiate any of the huge collection of charges the state had brought against him. *Innocent! Charges dismissed! Not guilty*, and all that good stuff.

In fact, he and Susan viewed that decision as the *one fair event* that had occurred throughout the kangaroo proceedings, proving that justice does triumph. Or so they had thought for this very brief period.

He took several deep, cleansing breaths, snapped off his desk light and leaned back in his chair. Meditation was helpful for everyone, not only his patients, and he was rather expert at blocking out extraneous sounds and thoughts and putting himself into a state of relaxation within minutes. If he was going to make it through the day, if he had to break this horrible news to Susan, if he needed to cancel any weekend plans to meet with Bob, if he …"

The tiny alarm clock on his desk twittered its soft alert, and he snapped his eyes open and let his fingers search for the lamp's switch. He felt as though he had slept for hours but noted that only 30 minutes had elapsed. He had restored his equilibrium and knew he would manage the rest of his lengthy day without focusing on anything extraneous to his medical responsibilities.

He'd sleep at the office tonight. The bad news could wait until tomorrow.

CHAPTER 15

It was a little after two o'clock when Harris arrived at Levin's office on Saturday. A thought or two had occurred to him on the drive into the city, so he took a seat in the waiting room and spent a few minutes jotting down a couple of sentences to keep the ideas fresh in his memory.

In the meantime, Levin had finished up his work, unaware that Harris had arrived, and was seated at his desk eating a salad, reflecting on what had happened last evening. He had gotten home later than he planned, using his commuting time to review the contents of the envelope that had arrived on Thursday, upsetting him so much. He also spent a few moments considering how he might ease into the topic of the pending crisis with Susan and decided there was no easy way. He remembered that she had gotten physically sick after seeing the original list of charges last year. At the time, although she knew there were 144 of them, to this day she had never read through them, promising herself and him that one day she would do so. How would she cope with knowing that they hadn't thrown *any* of them out but had simply jammed in a whole lot more? *How would he tell her?* No, there was no simple way, he told himself again.

She had been in the kitchen when he arrived, walking in through the back door and just standing in the hall. Susan had tentatively moved toward him, wiping her hands on a dish towel, her face taut with what he recognized as worry. "What is it?" she had asked him. "What's wrong?" It would have been useless to have asked her *why* she thought something was wrong. They weren't into playing games with each other, especially when they had been through at least four rounds of pure hell together while keeping their marriage intact. His main observation of his wife's emotional state was that Susan seemed to be at her breaking point, like she couldn't possibly cope with or survive another cycle of hearings, the next obstacle under the omnipresent black cloud of his future.

"Susan," he had said, "let me read Erika a bedtime story first, and then I'll have a quick bite." "Then?" she had prompted. "Then we have to talk," he had told her. "That's what I was afraid of," she had said, her eyes filling with tears, as she quickly turned away and returned to the kitchen, where Erika was calling her.

He had changed his clothes and washed up, while Susan quickly bathed Erika, all the while recalling what he had read on his train ride home. It hadn't taken him long to scan the entire fifteen pages, a total replay from last June, along with additional charges for his use of vitamins with patients; but the documents demanded that he keep flipping pages back and forth, just to make things more uncomfortable, he figured. The page bearing the title "Charges on Remand" was divided into three columns, *Specifications, Paragraphs, and Subparagraphs*, in which were numbers and letters, requiring one to repeatedly reference the original charges in detail. The document itself consisted of what the state referred to as *Factual Allegations* and *Specification of Charges*. This was all too familiar to Levin, who had practically memorized the contents of last year's indictments. As his train had pulled into the station and Levin had hurriedly tried to jam the stapled packet back into the envelope, it was then that he discovered an *additional* two pages, which he somehow hadn't seen, either when he had slit open the envelope in his office or when he replaced the thick report after the call to his attorney. He jiggled the envelope to make room, slipped the packet on top the contents within, snapped the envelope into his briefcase, and walked out of the train.

At home, when he and Susan sat down to have "the talk" she dreaded, he emptied the envelope onto the cushions of the living room couch and pulled out the two-page set he had noticed earlier, and they read it over together. It stated, "COMMISSIONER'S ORDER" at the top right of the first page in capital letters and was addressed to Larry Storch, Administrative Officer; Terrence Sheehan, Esq.; and Robert H. Harris, Esq. *Nice of them to send a copy out to me*, he thought. *I'm glad they remembered that it's* my *professional life on the line.* The document, signed by David Axelrod, M.D., Commissioner of Health, State of New York, summarized the proceedings and mentioned that the Hearing Committee had recommended that charges against Levin be dropped.

"NOW," the next paragraph began, with NOW in capital letters,

...on reading the transcript of the hearing, the exhibits and other evidence, and the findings, conclusions and recommendation of the Committee, I hereby *reverse* the order of the Administrative Officer directing the discharge of Victor Herbert, M.D., J.D. as a witness, direct that testimony eliciting whether Dr. Herbert complained about Respondent's practice or competence to the Office of Professional Medical Conduct should *not* be allowed, and *remand* the case to the Hearing Committee in order to complete the taking of testimony.

The Public Health Law *prevents* the disclosure of the identity of a complainant in a professional medical conduct proceeding.

At that point, he and Susan had paused in their reading and just looked at each other. Words were not needed. The remainder of the paragraph justified its opening sentence, at least in the eyes of the Commissioner, they postulated. While Axelrod had closed by saying that "respondents *may challenge* the credibility and objectivity of an *expert witness*," it almost seemed a direct contradiction of everything that had already occurred in the hearing. Axelrod then closed with,

I take *no* position with regard to Dr. Herbert's expertise or credibility or with regard to the merits of the charges against Dr. Levin.

They had each read that final sentence aloud to hear it resonate and try to determine its meaning, as it seemed too hypocritical a statement for Axelrod to have made deliberately. So *Victor Herbert was in again*, they realized. They'd *never* find out if he was the complainant or not. And *all* the original players were reinstated to their prior positions in deciding the outcome of Levin's professional life. Incredible. It was as though Axelrod, himself, was playing into the joke that the hearing had already become. The problem was that it was a very *bad* joke with extremely dire consequences as it moved, like an avalanche down a mountainside, toward inexperienced climbers who were about to be buried alive or knocked into a bottomless void. The avalanche was moving toward Levin with increasing support and power, courtesy of New York State, the couple realized.

Their discussion had kept them up past one in the morning. They dropped into bed beyond exhausted.

Harris knocked on Levin's office door then turned the handle and let himself in before Levin could break away from his thoughts enough to respond. Harris wasted no time. "Come on, finish your salad," he said, his eyes taking in a healthy meal in a Tupperware container that obviously was prepared at home. He knew Levin lived the lifestyle he preached to his patients: clean living, vitamins, minerals, and healthy food. Harris patted his ample belly and decided that he'd starve to death if he had to follow Levin's dietary restrictions.

"Bob, wait," Levin said, noticing that Harris was heading out of the office. "Sit for a minute. I remembered something important the other day, and it might have some bearing on my case." Harris sank into a chair, one eyebrow raised in curiosity. "It's about Briber, the 'hired gun' on the hearing panel."

"He's some *rude* S.O.B." Harris volunteered. "I'm planning to put him in his place when we have the next hearing. What did you want to say about Briber?"

"I *knew* there was something familiar about him, but I never said anything to you before because I couldn't place him. Well, let me tell you: I've apparently got a 'history' with the guy!"

"How so?" Harris was interested.

"There was a doctor who was practicing alternative medicine in upstate New York a number of years ago. The Office of Professional Medical Conduct hauled him up on a bunch of trumped-up charges. I knew the guy from various meetings we had both attended, but I didn't know him all that well. I was thought of as a 'pioneer,' and some of my colleagues even referred to me as the 'Dean of Alternative/Complementary Medicine' on the east coast because I opened the first holistic health center in New York City. So, the point I'm making is that more doctors knew and recognized *my* name than I did theirs. Anyway, this fellow asked me to testify on his behalf. He was using one of the treatment protocols I recommend and use in my practice all the time, and..."

"Warren, this sounds like it must be an interesting story, but we've got to..."

Levin held up his salad fork like a flag. "Please, let me finish. There's a point to this story." He put a forkful of salad into his mouth and chewed and swallowed quickly, as though he was afraid his lawyer wouldn't give him much more time to eat. "I gave extensive, and I mean *really extensive*, and lengthy testimony on behalf of this doctor. I'm afraid my assistance wasn't successful in helping him retain his medical license," he added regretfully. "Well, one of the charges *I'm* facing in my *own* hearing is the *same one* I testified about. And guess who was on the hearing panel that pulled that physician's license?" He looked at Harris meaningfully.

"You've got to be kidding!" the attorney shouted indignantly. "Briber? Briber was on the panel and heard you testify about a treatment you're now using in your practice? Why the hell didn't he recuse himself? I don't understand!"

Levin shook his head. "I thought the same thing the other day when it came to mind, but maybe he didn't make the connection. Remember, I didn't connect any dots when I first saw *him*."

"Okay, I've got an idea, Warren. Interestingly enough, it's something that occurred to me as I was driving here. With what you're telling me now, my plan is even *more* relevant. I'm going to request an examination of the panel. I'm going to ask the judge to let me conduct a *voir dire* with them, just I did with Victor Herbert. Who knows? Maybe we can get rid of Briber." He thought for a moment and said, "With all honesty, though, the way things have gone so far, we'd better not count on the state doing anything remotely reasonable. Herbert's back in the game, and I'm sure they're not about to let us remove Briber, who's another one of their key players, but we can always try. Come on, let's get started." Harris hefted himself out of the chair and Levin, looking regretfully at his unfinished lunch, snapped the lid on the Tupperware container and tossed it into his small refrigerator.

He followed Harris out of the office, suggesting they head to the lab. "Bob, there's a test I use, which of course they are charging has no value or medical necessity, but one that I've found very useful in my practice. When they challenge its validity, I want you to fully understand it in order to defend its use," the doctor told him.

Walking to the lab, Levin looked around him with pride, noting the interesting layout, which made it possible for thirty-eight part-time and full-time employees to navigate the area comfortably while they went about their business. When Levin had leased the space, he envisioned creating his own "Camelot" within 6500 square feet on Park Avenue. They had gutted the existing office when they took over, and Susan had worked with the architects, wearing a hard hat during the construction process, to design something that fit with the architectural adage, "Form follows function," and in this office, that certainly held true. There was a circular reception area, a corridor surrounding it, and examination and treatment rooms off the curved corridor. There were separate bathrooms for males and females, a billing area, a back office, a laboratory, and Levin's private office. Staff members included other physicians, chiropractors, naturopaths, an allergy technician, a nutritionist, a person who provided colonic therapy, nurses, physicians' assistants, a lab tech, a file clerk, and a full-time secretary who assisted with the quarterly newsletter and with other correspondence. Then, there *had been* a full-time bookkeeper, the one who had nearly landed them in the poorhouse, which still might be Levin's final destination if things didn't begin to go his way, he realized.

Harris looked around Levin's well-equipped lab, marveling at the variety of instruments he observed on the clean, neatly arranged counters. "Boy, Warren," he remarked, "this stuff must have set you back a small fortune. What are you doing here, cloning your patients?"

"I'd probably be in a lot less trouble if I were," Levin said, wryly. "The instrument I'd like to introduce you to is called the Darkfield Microscope, and that little critter cost me $14,000, so yeah, this stuff is expensive, but I really think it's worth it. My lab tech had never worked with one of these before coming here, now he brags to friends of his about how amazing dark field work really is."

Levin took a sharp from container of sharps, pricked his finger, and squeezed a bead of blood onto a slide which he then placed on the stage of the microscope. He set the focus and invited Harris to take his place on the stool.

Harris had always loved science and recalled his lab days from high school and college fondly. He was surprisingly excited to be seated at a laboratory bench once again and eagerly took off his eyeglasses and leaned into the microscope's lens to fine-tune the focus wheel. "Hey, Warren, I see things moving around in here, these circles on a black background, and they sure look like lousy drivers: they keep bumping into each other," he laughed, thinking of the bumper cars at the Coney Island amusement park he had loved as a child. "Oh, wow! These circles slip around, move along, bump into these big guys. This is great!"

Levin chucked at Harris's child-like enjoyment of the sophisticated microscope that was one of the instruments casting a large shadow over the integrity of his practice. "Okay," he told Harris, "you can play with it again later. Let me tell you a few things about what you're seeing and how this analysis is beneficial to my patients."

"Yeah, sure," Harris told him, "but I'd like to see what happens if I add *my* blood to yours; if they start a fight or what."

Levin shook his head in wonderment. *Bob was nothing but a big kid at heart, a big, big kid!*

"Down, boy, we've got work to do," Levin told him, "right now!"

"Okay, okay, I'm coming." Harris slid himself off the stool, and they returned to Levin's office for their "lesson."

"I'll speak slowly, in case you want to take some notes," Levin told him after they were seated, as that was how they normally proceeded when Levin instructed Harris on medical issues.

"Fine," Harris said. He was back in lawyer mode and very serious.

"Believe it or not," Levin began, "you can tell an *enormous* amount about a person's life and health energies by viewing their live blood. We look at the shapes of the blood cells and other properties, as well. When blood cells are stained for normal microscopic study, you know, those cells are dead; but we still get a lot of information from them. However, the *live* blood cells, like what I just showed you, can tell us an even larger part of the story. On the other hand," he cautioned, "this is really *not* a diagnostic procedure in and of itself. I find it valuable in many ways, and it often sends me down a trail of tests that can lead me to the causes of a patient's illness. It can dramatically show evidence of oxidative damage to cell membranes. Another thing I look for with Darkfield Microscopy are the nutritional aspects of blood morphology, which help me determine whether a person's body is producing nutrients in sufficient quantity or whether they require nutritional supplementation."

Harris stopped writing and looked up at him. "You mean you can tell all of that from one measly drop of blood?" he asked.

Levin nodded.

"So it seems to me that when you're prescribing your healthy 'cocktails' of vitamins and minerals for patients, your prescriptions are based on scientific evidence, wouldn't you agree?"

"Absolutely! This is one of the main points we need to make in my defense. You've got a guy like Victor Herbert sitting there and calling everything I do 'quackery' with 'no scientific basis.' A well-equipped lab in a medical office is as scientific as you can get! I doubt that Victor Herbert has ever put his eye to a microscope like the one you just tried. Most doctors haven't. They never learned how to use them, they couldn't afford to buy them, they've heard others knock their value, whatever. I was hooked the first time I actually saw a sample of live blood and understood how it could assist me. You may be interested to know that even a doubtful patient, who needs to corroborate what I'm telling him in order to follow the protocol I set out for him, has a complete change in attitude once I have my lab tech bring him in here and show him how I drew some of my conclusions."

"Okay. You're doing a good job convincing me. Keep it up, so I can do a good job convincing *them*," Harris said.

Levin went on, tutoring Harris further about "reading live blood"—calling it *the play of life at the cellular level.* He explained the difference between Darkfield Microscopy and phase contrast. He instructed Harris about bright field microscopy. Levin spoke of healthy and abnormal red blood cells and white blood cells, and ended where they started: with the bead of his own blood that he had placed on the slide in the lab for Harris to study.

"Blood is supposed to form a bead when you prick the finger, but that doesn't always happen," he told the lawyer.

"It always happens when someone pricks my finger!" the lawyer told him.

Levin nodded his approval. "That's good, Bob. But when it doesn't happen, and for some patients whose blood I take it doesn't, I'm looking for a number of things. It might be indicative of low protein, simply because their diet doesn't include sufficient amounts of protein; it could be a lack of digestive enzymes, which might indicate something as serious as pancreatic cancer, believe it or not ..."

"My dad died of pancreatic cancer," Harris interjected. "It's a lousy disease."

"I know. Sometimes the lack of beading can point to kidney problems or anemia, as well. Sure, we need to go a lot further with any of these things I'm telling you about, but I think you can see where I'm leading with the dark field testing. Think about it," Levin told him. "Think about whether you've ever had one of your doctors actually prick your finger to take a drop of blood, where he would actually *notice* whether or not the blood beaded up. And that's *before* the blood is ever examined under the microscope!"

"Never. I've never had a *doctor* prick my finger to take a drop of blood, as a matter of fact. I've punctured my finger once or twice on a sliver of glass, so that's how I noticed that it beaded up, but I never thought of it that way until you mentioned it before. When I think of someone taking a sharp to a fingertip," Harris told him, "I think of a diabetic person testing his blood sugar. I think about how that person's fingertips must ache and pinch and be extra sensitive and sore. But having a *doctor* look at a dot of blood and then analyze it in front of me? Never."

"My point exactly," Levin responded. "I rest my case!"

Harris laughed. "Hey, you're the doctor! I'm the lawyer!"

CHAPTER 16

Warren Levin sat down to collect his thoughts. He and his attorney had spent a great deal of time together yesterday, and Levin was particularly pleased with how eagerly the lawyer took to the medical information he taught him. Harris understood the doctor's explanations and aptly demonstrated an uncanny ability to present complex and accurate responses to the questions Levin fired at him as they practiced for anticipated volleys in the hearing room. Levin chuckled to himself. *After all, Bob's got a pretty good teacher, if I do say so myself.* He appreciated the fact that Harris seemed to take a real interest in the case, so money was not the driving force behind the lawyer's expenditure of hours. In fact, as Bob laid out his newest defense strategy, Levin had been impressed, both by Bob's plan and his willingness to execute it without keeping an hourly log. The attorney proposed that the doctor allow him to spontaneously visit the medical office and approach patients in the waiting room to speak with those who might be willing to voluntarily discuss their medical care under Levin. Unusual, sure, but the doctor was confident enough in his patient base to allow Bob to follow this creative approach.

Now it was Levin's turn to expand their defense portfolio. He felt he could reach more people by sending a letter, knowing that his name on the return envelope would surely be enough to prompt the recipients to open it, if only to satisfy their own curiosity. He planned to have the letter copied and mailed tomorrow morning by his staff, so he dated it February 19, 1990, hoping that nine was a lucky number for him, and addressed it broadly to *Colleagues, Patients, and Friends*.

As with the earlier appeal he and Susan had collaborated on in the practice's quarterly newsletter, Levin decided not to hold back. Once again, a plea was going out for written testimonials, individuals willing to testify in person, and—uncomfortably—money. He offered a synopsis of the proceedings thus far and appealed for advice, informing them that New York State would be putting him back "on trial" in May. In the midst of it all, he allowed them to see that his sense of humor was intact by including a reference to April Fools' Day. While Levin was totally open about his situation, he decided to write in the third person, as though he were a journalist reporting on a doctor under fire by the authorities or as though he were part of the legal team representing an unfortunate physician. He told them that Robert Harris was the twentieth attorney interviewed in the selection process, designed to locate the best-qualified litigator to take on this major, ground-breaking, medical defense case. He even introduced the group to Victor Herbert, explaining that the state's sole witness had perjured himself, under oath, regarding his prejudice against the hapless doctor, going as far as Herbert's disqualification as a witness. He then outlined the entire method by which New York State grants medical licenses and reviews its physicians. Licensure comes from the Board of Regents, he explained, while complaints against physicians are heard by members of the State Medical Board, who then report to the Commissioner of Health, before turning everything in to the full Board of Regents, whose Chairman issues the final determination for action: dismissal, revocation of license, censure, suspension, or public service.

Although he and Susan had decided to keep the matter of his cancer private up to this point, Levin decided that the recipients of this letter needed to know exactly what types of challenges he had been facing in order to understand the severity of what lay before him at this critical juncture. He switched to a first person narration, deciding that he could no longer pretend to be on the outside looking in, because this part was way too personal, forcing him to take ownership. He was amused by how he internalized his frightening medical diagnosis when he received it, telling himself "*...while I was waiting for the Commissioner to decide on what he was going to do, God gave me something to keep me from being bored!*" He made a point of referring to the strategies he had advised so many of his patients to follow and how they had assisted him with his own medical situation. "*Why shouldn't they know how meditation helped me? My own doctors were shocked by the results, for goodness' sake. I meditated once prior to surgery, after informing my surgeon in advance that my intention was to shut off the blood supply to my tennis-ball-sized tumor. The radiologist reported a renal artery angiogram as showing an "avascular" tumor, [although kidney cancers are notoriously very vascular], the pathologist reported seeing almost entirely necrotic tissue, and the surgeon was mystified by the absence of blood supply to that tumor. Since the literature now* *confirms that I fall into a 90%, ten-year cure rate, I can assume that the cancer is completely gone.*

At fifty-seven years of age, Levin truly believed alternative medical techniques were the key reason for his ability to return to a full-time work schedule so rapidly. Considering the fact that his convalescence period and Axelrod's decision had coincided—had somehow come together to occupy the same space in his universe—his quick recovery in the face of so much potential internal turmoil had to be credited to his coping style, which was informed by his medical philosophy.

Levin was both pleased and proud to have already amassed a group of fine physicians who had agreed to testify on his behalf, if the need ever arose—and it certainly had arisen, much like the Loch Ness Monster, in fact. He let his readers know that these individuals included a department chief of nutrition at a university medical school, a former health commissioner in another state, a chief of cardiology, a vascular surgeon, an expert in allergy and pathology, and someone he never could have imagined would have honored him so: Linus Pauling, Ph.D., a two-time Nobel Prize recipient who held 48 honorary doctoral degrees and was truly an icon in the scientific community. Dr. Pauling had agreed to speak on Levin's behalf ... *free of charge*.

He wanted his colleagues, patients, and friends to know that this situation was one he had been enduring for the past ten years, yet he had not been allowed to give any testimony on his own behalf in all of that time. And, while he was well-known and well-regarded, he realized that few knew the extent to which he represented alternative medicine outside of his private office and how much time and effort he had expended on its behalf, so he wondered how he might let his readers understand his philosophy of "giving back" in the form of professional participation.

He consulted his *curriculum vitae*, which he always kept current, because it was occasionally requisitioned when he agreed to testify on behalf of a persecuted colleague or when he was joining a new professional organization and/or accepting a nomination for an office within one of the associations he belonged to. He wanted to allude to the fact that he had contributed a great deal of time to worthy groups, rather than simply devoting himself to the endless pursuit of the almighty dollar. *After all, I have served either on the Board of Directors or as Governor or Trustee of The International Academy of Preventive Medicine, The International College of Applied Nutrition, The International Academy of Metabology, The American Society of Bariatric Physicians, where I was also vice-president, The American*

College of Advancement in Medicine, The American Board of Chelation therapy, and several other smaller organizations. Plus, I have taken the time and effort to become board certified in four areas: Family Practice, Chelation therapy, Environmental Medicine and Bariatric Medicine. Surely all of this must count for something! But I'm not about to start listing my professional memberships. I don't want to appear pompous. I'll simply allude to my involvement in an offhand way.

He was a man who had worked hard to create a balanced lifestyle. Plus he knew that his voluntary efforts, which offered interesting professional relationships and gratifying social opportunities, also kept him on the cutting edge of his chosen profession. He was a frequent guest speaker or panelist at numerous meetings, and he accepted the honor of running for office whenever his name was proposed, as it often was. He had done all of these things for so many years for all the right reasons, so why not make a point of informing the people he needed assistance from? He acknowledged the internal battle going on in his mind over this issue and came to a decision. He first agonized over the wording of what he would write, and then he simply took his chances.

Levin had made up his mind that he had been chosen to be, for better or worse, a test case, "THE PRIME EXAMPLE" nominated by the State of New York to represent *all* alternative and complementary physicians. He wanted supporters to realize that weeks after a surgical procedure that could have yielded a horrifying prognosis, he was now anticipating an even *bigger* battle. *I am primed for this fight. I've been in training for 20 years! I've retained a terrific litigation attorney, who knows and understands Victor Herbert and the issues. By emerging victorious, we will have a precedent on which to challenge the AMA and the insurance companies.*

He started writing again. It was humiliating for him to expose himself this way. He caught his lower lip between his teeth and thought about it. He and Susan had pooled their efforts for a financial appeal earlier, when they believed they had won their case and needed some assistance to settle the debt they had amassed. Now, he was returning to the ring to fight until one of the opponents was severely beaten. He viewed himself as the boxer the audience identifies as the underdog, a lightweight meeting a heavily muscled opponent with a killer instinct. In the movie theaters, the patrons usually let out a spontaneous cheer when the underdog gained some ground, while the spectators in the actual film gasped in disbelief that the favorite whom they had bet on might actually lose. If the little guy won, audiences left the movie house smiling, thinking of themselves and their issues, wondering if the film would inspire them sufficiently to confidently confront the bully in their lives.

Levin sighed deeply. *I hate to appeal to a group of friends and colleagues for financial assistance.* Once again, an internal skirmish was occurring. As objectionable as he found the request to friends and colleagues, however, asking patients for money was abominable, and he needed to justify the strategy to himself first. *Why should I turn to my patients for help? They have already paid my fees—many times without the full reimbursement of the health insurance companies which had received their premiums for years. Strangely enough, these same companies would probably have paid for the* same *tests in another doctor's office. The cost in terms of personal and family stress has been beyond estimate for me. I have already incurred about $100,000 in legal fees, and there is no insurance coverage for that. I have lost income from time out of work while my overhead continues. If I lose this fight, which I am both proud and excited to have been chosen to "compete in," we* all *lose—because my patients will no longer have the right to choose the type of physician and the type of medicine they want for themselves and their families. I* must *make this broad appeal for funds, because I will be unable to continue the fight without financial assistance.*

Levin continued to write until he had said everything he believed his supporters and contributors had a right to know. He exhaled. This letter had been the hardest one he ever had to write, he acknowledged to himself. He knew that without adequate financial support, bankruptcy was a certainty.

This case had made a freedom fighter out of Warren Levin. On the other hand, the medical establishment had always been enmeshed in controversy. He knew there had been huge differences of opinion over estrogen replacement therapy in menopause at one time, anticoagulant therapy in coronary disease had come under fire, the debate over lumpectomy versus mastectomy in breast cancer was an ongoing debate, and those were only three examples. Yet physicians used these treatments on living patients: sometimes the treatment was successful, and other times the method was an abject failure. New drug therapies gained favor when studies were funded by the immense wealth of the pharmaceutical industry. As far as alternative physicians went, money was not forthcoming from outside sources, as he and his fellow practitioners used fewer drugs and, instead, helped patients understand the mechanics of their own bodies and how to fortify them for disease prevention. Trying to pry research dollars out of wealthy industries for his purposes was similar to trying to convince the citizens of a country at peace to allot huge defense budgets to fortify against enemy attacks that were not imminent. But if a country was an intermittent target of surrounding lands, then peacetime was the *ideal* time to build defenses. The human body, a constant target of environmental conditions and the temptations of processed and fatty foods—combined with tobacco use, quantities of liquor, and illegal drugs—was a land constantly under siege yet perceived by its inhabitants to be existing in a state of peace unless ravaged by disease. Therefore, most people had little awareness of how their choices affected their health. While mainstream medicine might not support his recommendations, Levin's patients knew better than most others about the value of a healthy body. He hadn't gone into detail about the unusual treatments that accelerated his own rapid post-surgical recovery, yet he was certain that the coffee enemas and megadoses of vitamins he had prescribed for himself had made all the difference.

Levin read over everything he had written. It ran for six pages, single-spaced, but he believed that nothing was extraneous. If people were to open their minds, hearts, and pocketbooks to him, he owed them complete honesty in return.

He walked down the hall to Susan's office. He valued her input. With Susan in his corner of the ring, it was possible to anticipate fighting harder than ever before in his life. Always a positive thinker, he saw the striped-shirted referee holding his gloved hand up in victory, as Victor Herbert's battered form lay unconscious at his feet. Levin smirked. *For a peaceful man, Warren, you sure have a vivid imagination!*

CHAPTER 17

Bob Harris had a small but effective law firm on Long Island. With six attorneys, each with a particular area of concentration, things tended to run smoothly. Sandi was a great divorce attorney, Mel was a superb litigator and training one of the newer associates to shortly take over for him, Norman liked the grunt work of research and preparation of briefs, Paul enjoyed corporate law, and Randy worked as a criminal attorney "of counsel," meaning he wasn't really part of the firm per se but rented an office on premises and was available to them for criminal law. Bob handled medical defense and had done so for over twenty years. Nevertheless, when the attorneys met in the conference room over lunch, case discussions prevailed, and the collegial atmosphere was invaluable to all of them, as they readily offered strategies and assistance to one another.

Interestingly, only Bob Harris relished the opportunity to speak in front of an audience. He had a wealth of information, was a superb storyteller, and had created numerous opportunities for himself as a "performer," whether in the classroom, on the radio, at meetings, when entertaining socially, or when fired up about a topic. At the time he took on Warren Levin's case, Harris was a lecturer on medical ethics and forensics at the New York University School of Dentistry, the Nassau County Medical Center, and the Queens County Dental Society. He was also a faculty member at the University of Michigan School of Law; a former lecturer of business law at Queens College, City University of New York; a professor of jurisprudence at New York Chiropractic College; and an occasional lecturer on forensic medicine and medical ethics at North Shore University Hospital. He used all of these venues to both teach and to learn from others. He had a good memory and recollected information well, was an international traveler who had extensive knowledge of other cultures and legal systems, and—most important for a litigator—could think well on his feet. Good legal defense work required an attorney to be articulate, to have an imposing courtroom presence, to have done and internalized a great deal of research, and to have the ability to recall facts as they pertained to the case.

Harris always believed that his size was a plus, not a minus, in the courtroom. He would caution his classes of chiropractic students, "Make sure you take good, clear x-rays, because a muddy x-ray will hurt your case in a courtroom. And something else. Go out to the waiting room, greet your patients, and as you lead them back to the examining room, 'accidentally' drop a sheet of paper. You're a doctor, so their instinct will be to bend down and pick it up. If a guy is coming to you with back problems and wants to go out on disability, and he effortlessly bends down and retrieves that paper for you, well, doctor, you're going to have a problem, a *big* problem, if this guy cheats the system and gets on disability. And, believe me, you don't want to face a guy like *me* in a courtroom," he'd emphatically state, drawing himself up to his full height and puffing out his chest with importance. Although his forte was medical defense, the budding chiropractors got the message, he realized, as they nodded somberly and scribbled notes.

Harris left the conference room at his office, satisfied that the firm could do without him for the week. He left for Levin's office to meet with some of his patients, since all of them had received the letters that the doctor's staff had sent out the previous week. Still, the receptionist had put a stack of letters out on the counter, knowing that people who came early often read whatever was available. Harris and Levin believed it was a good strategic move to have as many patients as possible meet the lawyer handling their doctor's defense. The patients' interest would be piqued by this intimate glimpse into their physician's private arena, which could definitely work to the defense lawyer's benefit. Harris wanted to get a sense of who came to Levin and why, which individuals believed enough in what the doctor was doing to often pay out of pocket with little hope for insurance reimbursement. Harris also wanted to learn more about the treatments offered, but from the patients' point of view. He would make it clear to each of them that they didn't have any obligation to speak with him; it was purely voluntary.

Harris parked in a garage on Park Avenue and walked to Levin's building, dragging his ever-present luggage rack piled high with bulging litigation bags, and taking the elevator to the twelfth floor. Peggy, the receptionist, knew he was coming and informed him that the doctor's private office was available to him for patient interviews. He thanked her and sat next to a woman in the waiting room who was actually engrossed in Levin's letter, shaking her head from side to side in amazement as she read about the travesty of justice that Levin had outlined.

"Hello," said Harris, who had put his coat and briefcase into the doctor's office and come out dressed in a business suit. "I'm Robert Harris, Dr. Levin's attorney."

The woman, who appeared to be in her late fifties looked up at Harris in shock. "I ...I was just reading about you in here ... in Dr. Levin's letter!" she exclaimed.

"Well, isn't that interesting," Harris countered. "I've leapt right off the page and materialized right in the midst of the waiting room," he said in his usual half-joking manner.

The woman just sat there, staring at him, wondering about this unexpected development. "Are you one of Dr. Levin's patients?" he asked her.

"Yes ... yes, I am," she responded, still staring.

"Dr. Levin has given me permission to speak to any of his patients who might be willing to talk to me."

"Talk? About what?"

"Anything," Harris said. "How long you've been coming here. How you found out about Dr. Levin and the work he does. Why you came here. What keeps you coming back? Anything you want to say. It's completely voluntary," he told her. "But the more I learn, the better I can defend Dr. Levin." The woman sat there, her mouth open, regarding Harris for another moment, as though to ascertain whether or not to entertain his request. She took a long breath and expelled it noisily, having come to a decision.

"Mr. Harris, I'd be glad to help," she said with determination.

"Fine, then follow me back to Dr. Levin's office, and we can talk for a few minutes."

The woman got up. "Peggy," she said to the receptionist, "when he's ready for me," referring to the doctor, "will you please let me know?"

"I certainly will," replied the secretary, glad to see that Harris had made a good start. Peggy liked her boss. She liked his wife, as well. Susan came into the office a lot, assisting in whatever way she could and helping with letters that had to be written and also the quarterly newsletter. She often brought Erika, who was adorable. Peggy would give the little girl paper and crayons, and Erika would quietly sit and draw, very comfortable in her father's office. They were nice people. Doctor Levin was a good doctor. *This shouldn't be happening to him*, Peggy thought.

"Feel free to call me Bob," said Harris, determined to establish a comfortable enough atmosphere for the woman to be as forthcoming as possible.

"I'm Lisa Golden, and you can call me Lisa."

"Great. Lisa, instead of me questioning you and making you uncomfortable, I'd rather that you told me whatever you'd like me to know." Harris figured he'd evaluate her as she spoke. She might eventually be willing to testify, if the state allowed Levin to call patients to the stand; she possibly could prepare a history and testimonial to be admitted into evidence on Levin's behalf; or she could just be a source of additional useful information.

"Okay. I've been seeing Dr. Levin for about six months now," she began. "I don't know how familiar you are with …uh, women's medical issues … Mr. Harris … uh, Bob," she corrected herself, "but … uh, I had this terrible …uh, this awful … "

"Candidiasis?" Harris said, finishing her hesitant sentence.

She nodded. "Okay, I guess you've heard the term."

"Actually," he told her, "your doctor has been very good about teaching me a whole lot about candidiasis, so I am familiar with how … uncomfortable …" he paused, hoping she'd pick up the thread.

"Uncomfortable is an *understatement*, Bob. It was absolutely horrible for me, horrible! I'm a professional. I've been teaching for twenty-five years in the New York City School System, and I recently became chairperson of the English Department in my high school. Well, last September," she corrected. "I had had yeast infections and urinary tract infections in the past, but after I came back from a trip to Mexico last summer, whatever it was, the beach, the food, whatever, I developed an infection that just wouldn't quit. This is so embarrassing," she said, turning her face away from him.

"I know, Lisa, I've spoken to a few other women about it, and I couldn't believe what they told me," he lied, hoping to get her to continue.

She swallowed and blinked a few times. Looking toward the wall to her left rather than at Harris, who was sitting across the table from her, she said, "The smell! The constant discharge! The itching! The pain! I had never experienced anything quite like it before. When I came back from my trip, since I was still on summer vacation, I'd make plans to meet a friend for lunch once in awhile. So I would shower and dress to go out. By the time I was ready to leave my apartment, I was drenched …you know, down there."

"Very common with candidiasis," he murmured comfortingly.

"It was terrible. I wore pads; I tried internal protection to control this awful, constant secretion and smell. With enough planning, I could make it through the day, but I was still on vacation. What would I do when school began and I would take on my new position? What would happen then? And, not only that," she added, "but I found that I was exhausted all the time! I never used to get tired like that. This wasn't normal for me."

"What did you do then?" he prompted.

"I went to my gynecologist. He prescribed the usual creams and salves. Nothing different than any other time. When they didn't work, I got very worried, but he said that was all that was available for my problem. 'Your problem.' That's exactly what he called it: *'your problem.'* I had been going to this guy for years; I trusted him." She shook her head regretfully. "I left his office and called my sister in Arizona. She admitted that she had been through the same thing the previous year, which I had never known. She told me she had gone to someone who practiced 'alternative medicine.' 'What's that?' I asked her. She said, 'This guy is a regular doctor, but he uses complementary methods … extra, different strategies besides the things other doctors do. He made a number of suggestions that worked for me,' and she told me a few things. I didn't want to do anything just on her say-so, so I asked a few people if they knew anybody practicing this kind of medicine, and Dr. Levin's name came up three times. I figured he must be pretty good if so many people knew his name, so I came here."

She went on to explain that Levin and his staff provided a great deal of education about causative factors, taught her about proper diet—emphasizing the role of sugar, yeast products, and carbohydrates in maintaining this infection, and conducted "unusual tests" she hadn't heard of before and illustrated their value. Levin told her to wear cotton panties or no panties at all, but she explained that the latter wasn't an option for her; she wouldn't be comfortable going into a high school building that way. She said that when the doctor prescribed Nystatin for her and put her on a large dose of the medication, he had made certain to explain to her that the drug passed directly through the intestinal tract without entering the bloodstream, so it wouldn't create toxicity in her vital organs, which made her comfortable enough to fill the prescription and begin taking regular doses. He also recommended a steady regimen of physical exercise and a vitamin cocktail to increase the body's immune response and assist her body in fighting off the horrid fungal infection that was torturing her. She never wavered from Levin's plan for her recovery and credited him with teaching her how to be a good partner in her own health care. Her tone was actually worshipful, Harris noted, as the woman spoke to him. Then she added, "But I've got to get my friend Lois to talk to you."

"What's Lois's story?" Harris asked.

"I'm sure she'll tell you herself, but she teaches in another high school in the city. She hadn't been feeling well for months but never wanted to talk about the problem. When I shared my story with her back in November, because I was so happy to be rid of that embarrassing problem, that's when I learned that she had taken a leave of absence from her school in September, a medical leave, because she couldn't bear to embarrass herself and just didn't feel too well. That's when I told her about Dr. Levin, and she couldn't wait to see him. She's back at school now, too. Let me speak to her first. Can I have her call you?"

"By all means," Harris said, thinking that, as teachers, these women would be able to write good case histories and testimonials if they didn't want to come forth and speak about their "female problems."

Peggy tapped on the door. The doctor was ready to see Lisa. She had taken a personal day today and planned to see a show right after her appointment, so she took Harris's card and left the office, promising to speak to her friend Lois in the evening.

A man was in the waiting room when Harris walked in. The guy was reading Levin's letter also, he noticed. Harris made his pitch and the man seemed eager to speak with him, but he suggested waiting until he finished with his doctor's appointment. "It'll be a brief one," he promised.

It wasn't long before Peggy escorted the gentleman to Levin's office, where Harris awaited him. No prompting was necessary. The patient began speaking before he even sat down.

"My name is Dick Spokes, and I'm 60 years old. I've been Dr. Levin's patient for the past three years, and I'll probably keep coming here for the rest of my life," he announced. "I'm a lawyer, and I was a deputy mayor in the Lindsay Administration. Let me tell you something, Bob," he leaned in toward Harris, as though ready to share a secret, "I'm no fool. I've had Type I diabetes, insulin dependent, for most of my life. I know what that does to a person: heart problems, kidney problems, visual problems. But I've kept a pretty tight control all this time and hoped I would avoid the typical complications."

Harris noted that the attorney was articulate, trim, well-dressed, and self-confident. *A great witness.*

"Then one day I began to notice that my vision wasn't as sharp as it used to be. Okay, I wear bifocals, fine, but the sharpness wasn't there. I figured I needed a new prescription. But I also wanted to make sure that my eyes were as healthy as I thought they were, so I made an appointment to see Dr. Lance Vadnais, the head of Ophthalmology at Lenox Hill Hospital."

"Nothing like going all the way to the top," Harris echoed.

"My sentiments, exactly. So what did he tell me? 'You have diabetic retinopathy, Mr. Spokes. We can help you.' 'What kind of help can you give me?' I asked. 'We can treat the retina with a laser, and that will help you; it'll clarify your vision…for a while.' What's 'a while'? I asked him. 'It depends.' 'On what?' 'On your eyes. With some people, it can be six months or more before we do another treatment.' 'Okay,' I told him. 'What's the down side?' I'm a lawyer," he said to Bob, "so I need to look at an issue from all angles."

"Understood. I'm the same way."

"Which is what I figured," Spokes chuckled. "Anyhow, the doctor says, 'Each treatment will reduce your total vision a bit more.' So I asked him, 'Doctor, are you describing laser treatments as putting me into an inexorable downward spiral towards blindness?' Just like that, blunt as could be. You know what he answered? At least I have to give him credit for being honest, for not trying to snow me. 'I'm afraid so, Mr. Spokes. Depending on how well you tolerate the laser treatments, you'll eventually lose *all* of your vision.' I shook his hand and thanked him for the consultation. I paid my bill and left the office. I made an appointment with Dr. Levin."

"How did you hear of Dr. Levin?" Harris asked.

"I was already his patient. I don't remember who originally told me about him, but I had been coming here for general medical care. So I told Dr. Levin what had happened at Lenox Hill and asked him if he thought chelation therapy might be of any value in treating diabetic retinopathy. He was honest," Spokes said, nodding, "he was really honest. He told me that he had been doing chelation therapy on patients for years but had never heard of using it for that reason. He said, 'Look, Dick, chelation therapy won't hurt you; it's got no down side. The only thing you'll lose is the time it takes for the treatments and the money it'll cost you, because insurance usually only reimburses for chelation in the case of heavy metal toxicity, which is not your situation.' 'When can I start treatment?' I asked him, and he laughed. So I worked out my schedule and came in three times a week for weeks and weeks. In the meantime, I made an appointment at Lenox Hill for the laser treatment. You're gonna love this, Bob!"

Spokes then related the events of his repeat visit to the ophthalmologist, who began the visit by examining Spokes's eyes once again. The doctor was absolutely incredulous, Spokes told Harris, because he was unable to find *any* trace of diabetic retinopathy in *either eye*!"

While there was no medical research or published studies to support this finding, the fact remained that the *only* change in Spokes's routine between the two visits to Lenox Hill was *chelation therapy*. Spokes offered to arrange a meeting between the two doctors to discuss these unbelievable results, but the ophthalmologist flatly refused, saying that he'd probably lose his chairmanship if he were "to embrace such an outlandish treatment."

Harris sat in the ensuing silence, letting the narrative sink in. Unfortunately, Warren Levin's professional life was in such a state of chaos that he didn't have the time to write up this spectacular case for publication if, indeed, he were able to convince the editors of one of the more prestigious medical journals—like the *Journal of the American Medical Association* or the *New England Journal of Medicine*—to consider accepting such an article that flew in the face of established medicine.

By the time Harris left Levin's office, he could hardly wait to return the following day. Levin was well-liked by his patients, he saw, who were well-treated and well-educated by their doctor and his staff. Patients understood their medical issues, what tests were being done and why, what their role was in the treatment of their ailments, and they didn't hesitate to recommend their practitioner of complementary medicine to their families, friends, and relatives. At least that was the impression Harris got from his first day of patient interviews.

By Friday afternoon, when Harris invited Sandi into his office to share the details of his meetings with Levin's patients, she was clearly impressed with what he had accomplished. While his strategy had been a bit over the top, in her earlier estimation, Bob's "inventive ways," as she thought of them, often yielded unexpected results that bolstered the defense of his cases admirably.

"So, Bob, you got back in touch with these patients and they agreed to come in or write their case histories as testimonials?" she asked.

"They did," he replied proudly, leaning back in his chair and drawing deeply on his cigar. "But I haven't told you about one of my prize finds yet." He waited for her to prompt him.

"So tell me already," she said. Sandi was always matter-of-fact and not given to the same dramatic cues as favored by the firm's managing partner. Harris always thought that her demeanor was one of the reasons why she did so well for her clients, who often screamed and fought their way through divorce hearings while Sandi sat back waiting for them to run out of steam before she presented her demands as calmly as though she were ordering a take-out meal by phone. *Okay,* she'd say, *so we're asking for the house on Long Island, the condo in Florida, custody of the kids, and $650 a week in alimony and child support so we won't let the judge know how violent your client has acted toward my client since she requested this divorce.* Harris had sat in on these meetings several times to watch Sandi in action. When the opposing client opened his mouth and started ranting again, the guy's attorney—because Sandi generally represented the women in divorce proceedings—would put his hand on his client's arm to silence him, whisper into his ear; then the red-faced husband would clench his jaw and shut his mouth, and the attorney would try to bargain the impassive Sandi down somewhat. She generally didn't budge and didn't show a bit of emotion throughout these highly charged meetings. Sandi's client usually wiped the floor with her soon-to-be-ex husband. It was an unparalleled performance on Sandi's part, and her blood pressure never rose in response to the atmosphere in the room.

Harris was very different in his style, but his success rate in his area of specialization, medical defense, matched Sandi's in the divorce arena. "This other guy came in at the end of the week, the real *piece-de-resistance*," he added. "He's a retired court reporter named Harry. It's really spooky, in a way, because for all of his years in the courtroom listening to testimony and preparing the transcripts, you'll never guess what types of trials he was involved in."

Without a hint of emotion, Sandi stated, "I'll bet it was medical malpractice."

"Wow, you got it! Medical malpractice is right. So the guy had amassed quite a bit of knowledge about the medical profession and various treatments and such by virtue of his job. Anyhow, he gets this pain in his chest one day and goes to see his cardiologist, telling him that the pain comes and goes, but anytime he exerts himself that's when he feels it. Okay, so the guy's over seventy, and the cardiologist certainly doesn't want a lawsuit on his hands, so he says to him, 'Harry, look, I'm calling a taxi for you. I want to send you right to the hospital to have an angiogram. They're gonna pass a wire through the groin and go looking around inside, and if you need an angioplasty to clean out your pipes, they'll do it right then. If they think you need emergency open-heart surgery to bypass some of your clogs, they'll take you to the O.R. and crack your chest open.' You know, the full *megillah*," Harris added.

"I'm sure that made Harry really happy," Sandi remarked dryly.

"Wait'll you hear this! Harry said, 'No, thanks, doc,' and he walks out of the office, leaving the doctor holding the telephone receiver in his hands; he was about to call the hospital to tell them to expect Harry. So Harry goes down to theNY County MedicalSociety library on Fifth Avenue, starts researching treatments for angina, you know, chest pain," he explained, looking at Sandi, who nodded that she understood the term. "Somehow he comes across Warren Levin's name. So Harry gets a taxi and heads straight for Levin's office and ends up starting chelation therapy that same day!"

"No kidding?" Sandi said, favoring Bob with raised eyebrows.

"No kidding. I gotta tell you. It's been years, and he's still going for regular chelation treatments. He's in great shape; looks like he's in his fifties!" Harris told her. "So, after he retired from his job at the New York Supreme Court, he bought himself a condo in one of those old converted hotels on the boardwalk in Long Beach. Anyhow, he rides his bike every morning, rain or shine, snow or sleet, on the boardwalk for a good hour or more. He's never had an angiogram or any invasive cardiac treatment to this day. His chest pain is nonexistent. And you wanna know the best part of the story?"

"Why not?" Sandi responded. "I've heard all the other parts of the story."

Harris sniffed. "His girlfriend moved in with him, and she and Harry have a *real active* sex life!"

Sandi laughed. "Bob, I've got to hand it to you. People tell you the darndest things. So is Harry willing to testify on Warren's behalf?"

"He can't wait!"

CHAPTER 18

Throughout the balance of the winter and into the spring, the doctor and lawyer collaborated, analyzing transcripts from their earlier hearings, with Levin continuing to instruct Harris in medical issues and Harris appearing at the doctor's office whenever possible to continue interviewing patients. Contributions for the embattled physician's defense fund, deftly managed by Susan Levin—who handled the business end of the medical practice exclusively after the fiasco with the controller—continued to roll in. The impetus for the unprecedented support, Levin believed, came out of his willingness to do battle with the ruthless Victor Herbert and Levin's reluctance to slink away from the skirmish and simply surrender the medical license he so valued.

On May 14, Levin was in good spirits as he and Harris entered the room for the resumption of the OPMC or Office of Professional Medical Conduct hearings. Since Harris's request for a *voir dire* examination of Victor Herbert had been granted, the morning began with Herbert seated in the center of the U-shaped formation. Sheehan had led the doctor/lawyer through his paces as though six months had not passed since the last time they had all been together. Considering that Dr. Herbert had been *ejected* as the state's witness, it was far more than six months since he had appeared before the panel as a witness.

Harris had outdone himself once the proceedings were underway, using the reinstatement of Herbert as an excuse for objections, interruptions, and lengthy rebuttals. As Herbert became more and more irritated, and his annoyance spilled over onto the prosecuting attorney, the hearing officer—in an attempt to contain the building emotion and prevent chaos from erupting—called a one-hour recess, instructing the witness to leave the room. The judge had decided to hold an impromptu Intra-Hearing Conference.

The panel members were seated at their table. Larry Storch, the administrative officer hearing the case, immediately went on the record regarding Harris's remarks about Herbert, the "heart and soul" of the case against Levin, who had been dismissed then reinstated as an expert witness.

"Mr. Harris, I am trying to think of the right way to state this," the judge began, in an attempt to soften the impact of the words that would follow. "I am finding your conduct in the hearing to be most objectionable. To *continually* attack, in the course of argument, on questions, and to make broad-brush statements challenging the honesty, credibility, truthfulness, whatever, of the witness is going beyond the pale. If this is the kind of conduct you intend to exhibit during the course of the hearing, I will *remove* you from these proceedings, and we will continue without you."

Harris knew that if the administrative law judge made good on his threat, Levin's case would be totally lost. He glanced at his client and immediately noticed that the impact of the statement had been strongly felt at the defense table. Harris had to word his reply carefully.

"Judge, I am sorry that you are nonplussed by what you describe as my *conduct* and *behavior* and also by the conclusions you have drawn regarding that behavior. The fact of the matter is that in previous *voir dire*, it was established that this 'gentleman,'" he said, referring to Victor Herbert, "who is now testifying as an *expert* was, in fact, asked to leave; and I have the documentary evidence to show that. For him to come in and state as a basis for his expertise his tenure in places where he was *not permitted to remain* is a kind of *ad hominem* argument." Harris used this legal expression, which covered more ground than an entire paragraph, since—in addition to its definition of attacking someone's reputation—it also referred to the dirty politics of a smear campaign, which so described the state's relentless interest in ruining Warren Levin. "We will soon get to the point that it will be *impossible* for Your Honor and the panel to distinguish facts from fantasy!"

Harris wasn't finished yet. "While I am sorry that you find my behavior objectionable, the state has indicated that it has *one witness* and they are using this witness, despite the fact that his 'sterling career' has been checkered by innumerable incidents which seem, in so many ways, to demonstrate his extremism." Harris wanted to call attention to Herbert's over-the-top behaviors outside, as well as inside, the hearing room. "It is *not* appropriate for me to sit back in the defense of Dr. Levin and allow this man to state that his expertise comes from his tenure, for instance, at theQueens VA, when he was *marched out* of theQueens VA based upon the documents that we have subpoenaed and obtained under Freedom of Information."

"Mr. Harris," Storch said, his tone reasonable, "if you wish to bring out that type of information, the *place* to do it is on cross-examination."

Levin watched his lawyer tensely. *Knowing Bob, he won't back down.*

"Your Honor, the *last* hearing in this case was six months ago. These unfair delays, which are endemic in the Office of Professional Medical Conduct hearings, make it incumbent upon defense counsel to *remind* the panel of facts which have been testified to in the past, due to the lack of continuity in these cases." Harris looked at the panel members, assessing whether he had their full attention before continuing. "To have *these* panel members walk away for another month or two with the feeling that Dr. Herbert is an *expert* and, based upon that expertise, has testified to a lack of competence—or whatever it is that he's trying to say about Dr. Levin—is simply not fair." Harris chuckled, in a mock attempt to find humor in his own behavior. "I understand my *enthusiasm* may be a bit upsetting to the Court, which is not my intention, since I have a great deal of personal and professional respect for the Court. It is truly not my intention to play a game or undermine your authority."

Storch nodded solemnly, appearing mollified by the lawyer's response. The panel members seemed to take the comment at face value, as well.

Harris pressed his advantage, returning to his original criticism of Herbert, as though the prior exchange had never occurred. "I have a serious concern that this is a *very* dangerous situation in which a witness comes in after six months and presents himself as having expertise based upon a *jaded background*. Having said all of that, I am prepared to deal with any further objections in cross-examination in the normal way," he concluded.

Storch looked at the lawyer, wondering whether further admonishment was called for based on the additional slur Harris had slipped in about Herbert. His mind made up, Storch sighed audibly and said, "You are *most* kind, Mr. Harris, and I am very glad to hear that you are 'willing' to allow the testimony to go forward." The touch of sarcasm in his voice was slight enough to leave the listeners wondering whether their minds had supplied the extra coloring to the canvas before them. As an afterthought, "I am instructing, however, that if you exhibit this kind of behavior again, I *will* entertain a motion to have you excluded from the hearing room."

The moment of truce had passed quickly. Harris got back on his feet, his eyebrows lowered, and addressed the judge. "Exactly what *kind* of behavior are you talking about?" he challenged. "Defending my client?"

"This *zealous* defense of your client is what I'm talking about, Mr. Harris. Going over the line."

From his position next to the judge at the prosecution table, Terrence Sheehan, the prosecuting attorney murmured, "Mr. Harris is a litigation attorney, Your Honor. He has done this for many years. He *knows* he can't do that." Realizing that he had the undivided attention of the panel, Sheehan decided to enact his own drama. He stood up and walked into the center of the U-shaped setup, now that Harris was standing behind the defense table near his client. He decided to dissect Harris's "behavior" for those present, since it had become the topic of discussion this morning. "Number one, Mr. Harris wants to show off for his client. Number two, he wants to see how far he can drive Dr. Herbert into aggravation, hoping he'll decide not to come back." He watched Harris sink heavily into his chair reluctantly. "This is a calculated, intentional attempt to incur a little bit of your wrath, but who cares, if he achieves the overall purpose of destroying Dr. Herbert's willingness to be involved in this case." Sheehan suddenly raised his eyebrows, as though a fresh idea had occurred to him. "I request an order," he said, facing Storch, "*barring* Mr. Harris from making these objections, which are *not* objections but just testimony. And if he does it again, I request an order that he be excluded, *on his own motion*, so to speak, by his insistence on following this patently, obviously egregiously improper conduct."

It was clear to Harris that Sheehan's "bright idea" was born from Storch's earlier admonishment of the defense attorney. Harris was furious.

Sheehan wasn't about to let his currently advantageous position in the disagreement pass without an even more valiant push. "He knows it is *totally* out of bounds and totally impossible to act like that at a hearing, but unless he is reined in, I submit and I predict *he is going to continue to do it* for the next fifteen to twenty hearing days. So, again, I am requesting an order acknowledging that if he does it again, it is obviously intentional, and he has to be *thrown out of the hearing* on the grounds that he is attempting to destroy the hearing!"

Harris didn't want to listen to any more from theprosecuting attorney and would have liked to engage in all-out verbal warfare, but he decided to play it safe. He remained seated at the defense table and, paying no attention to Sheehan but addressing his response to the judge, deliberately spoke softly, in contrast to Sheehan's vocal crescendo. "I don't believe that it requires any more than a simple denial. Antagonizing Dr. Herbert and you is not my point. And the notion of me showing off for my client is ludicrous. With regard to your issuing an order on 'what if' in the future, my suggestion is that such an action only be taken at the point at which counsel thinks this prosecution is being negatively affected."

As he had hoped, by ignoring Sheehan, he succeeded in further irritating the prosecutor, causing Sheehan to appear unreasonable. "Right now," Sheehan retorted, "you are *deliberately* trying to destroy the decorum in the courtroom so everything can be ruined. *Your only hope is to cause chaos and get Herbert and the Panel fed up!*" A muscle was twitching in Sheehan's left eye, an outward sign of his current state. "I request an order stating, number one, what you have done already; and number two, putting you on notice. If you do it again, you are going to be *excluded* from the hearing room, and Dr. Levin is going to have to get *another* attorney or defend himself!"

Harris heard Levin inhale sharply. He wanted to reassure his client but didn't want to lose focus. Sheehan wasn't through with him yet.

"There is *no way* one of these hearings can be conducted with an individual bent on terrorizing the entire room, which is what you have been doing so far."

Again, maintaining a reasoned tone, Harris responded, this time directly to Sheehan. "I don't know what 'terrorizing the room' is, Mr. Sheehan. I don't know if a Hearing Officer has the right, since he doesn't have the power of contempt, to *exclude* a lawyer. The right to choose an attorney is solely within my client, who is *not* here as a volunteer. We can deal with the other issue at such time as it *becomes* an issue, Mr. Sheehan. So, until it *is* an issue, I don't have anything to say about it."

The judge had heard enough. His lips were compressed from frustration. "*I* will say two things at this point. One is that I am *not* going to issue such an order right now. The other is that I am putting you on notice, Mr. Harris, that if the conduct you have exhibited to date continues in such an egregious fashion, I *will* entertain a motion to have you excluded. While I do not have contempt power, under the Department's regulations," Storch continued, citing chapter and verse of the law, "I *do* have the power to take all measures necessary for the efficient conduct of this hearing, as I have done earlier in the proceedings. To the extent that your conduct makes it impossible to conduct our hearings in an efficient and fair manner," he warned, making his statement general, "I *can* and I *will* exclude *any* person from the hearing room who is creating such a disruption."

"Judge Storch," Harris began, rising and standing behind the defense table, "I would like to suggest, then, that this Hearing Panel be *disbanded*, because your warning to me has now created what I believe is a substantial and an unfair, chilling effect on my defense of Dr. Levin."

Hearing this sent Levin's heart racing. Harris was literally defying the judge in making this statement. Would he be removed as a defense attorney? Or, less likely, was Harris casting enough aspersions on the Panel for the judge to consider a radical move?

Harris then fixed Storch with a withering look. "If I have to be worried that a spirited defense of a doctor's license is going to incur the contempt of the Hearing Officer enough to *expel* me, then I am forced to comport myself in a way which is *unnatural* and may not be in the best interests of my client. Therefore, I believe that Mr. Sheehan's request and your warning to me are *both* inappropriate."

Stop, Bob, Stop! You're only making things worse. I like a good fight as much as you do, but this is going too far. What will happen if the judge makes good on his threat and tosses you out of here? What am I going to do then? Start all over with another attorney, start teaching him about alternative medicine from the very... Oh, God, Bob's not through yet!

"I believe that if I have done something that requires expulsion, you ought to expel me and let the higher courts decide whether you have the *right* to do it. On the other hand, the kind of warning that you have just given me prevents my client from getting a fair hearing." Harris sat down.

When Storch didn't respond, Sheehan stepped in, trying to sound reasonable. "No client has the right to have his attorney behave in an *illegal* fashion."

"I don't know what *illegal* ..."

"Giving testimony in the middle of *my* direct examination," Sheehan clarified. "You didn't say, 'Asked and answered'; you didn't say, 'Irrelevant.' You got up and said, 'This is the way the testimony *really* is.' That is crazy, and you *can't* do that!"

Harris, still seated, turned his attention back to Storch. "I am dealing with what I believe is becoming an increasingly apparent case of *prosecutorial misconduct*."

Sheehan walked over to the defense table and looked directly down at Harris. "*Why* do you have to engage in these insane outbursts?" he demanded, angrily.

Harris matched Sheehan inch for inch in height and had more than double Sheehan's body weight, which he considered an advantage. Therefore, he once again stood, the defense table between him and the prosecutor, and stared at Sheehan, eyeball to eyeball. "When the witness is asked to draw a conclusion while the entire room is looking at data in front of them which *clearly* indicates that there are *other* things which are not being dealt with, I believe that there is *bad faith* on the part of the prosecution, and if my blood boils a little in the presence of that, you are absolutely right, because it is offensive to the entire system of justice for a prosecutor to do that. I am not here in a game." Harris began to tick off his points on the fingers of his left hand. "I am defending a doctor's medical license, and I am not prepared to sit back. I am not prepared to have my behavior chilled. But I am prepared, in the face of *appropriate* prosecution," he said, emphasizing the "appropriate" in point three, "to present a proper defense."

Harris then walked around the table, leaving Sheehan staring at an empty space for a moment, and walked back over to face the judge. "So, if you are giving warnings to *anyone*, then I would respectfully suggest, Your Honor, that a warning be given as well to the prosecution. If he finds me incitable, he should know that the provocation is secondary to bad faith on *his* part in asking questions which are *calculated* to mislead."

Storch took off his glasses and laid them on the table. He brought his thumb and forefinger together over his eyes. "Mr. Harris," he began, using a tone of voice more suited to addressing a recalcitrant adolescent, "the way to deal with questions that you believe are intended to mislead is to object to the question at the time it is posed. It is *not* appropriate to wait until the question is answered, then get up to make a speech. That is what direct examination and cross-examination are for. Look," he continued, deliberately softening his delivery, "this is not a trial in Supreme Court. We are not bound by the strict rules of that system; we are somewhat looser here. However, there are some elements of proper procedure which are maintained in our hearings and that includes direct examination, cross-examination, and the proper techniques governing both."

Harris had a thought. "Can we go off the record for a moment, Your Honor?"

When Storch agreed, the court reporter sat back, enjoying the opportunity for a brief pause and flexing her fingers. The Panel members sat back in their seats, as well, as they had been pressed forward the entire time, attentive to the energy in the room. Levin took his glasses off as well and briefly closed his eyes to block out the bright light of a sunny morning. All too soon, the sidebar ended, and the spectators returned to their previous postures.

Storch, putting his glasses back on, addressed the hearing room. "As I said, I am *not* going to issue an order at this time, but I *am* putting Mr. Harris on notice. With all that said, we have taken *enough* time. Let's close the record on this Intra-Hearing Conference and get back to the official hearing."

CHAPTER 19

It was the middle of August, and no significant progress had been made with regard to the hearings, Harris thought. Victor Herbert had continued to occupy the "monkey-in-the-middle chair," pontificating as he went along, answering Sheehan's questions, which were obviously designed to extract damaging testimony against Levin's style of medical care. He thought back to the last session which had been held in May, recalling his efforts to goad Victor Herbert into theincendiary style he had employed in the past, the act that had come perilously close to having Harris ejected from the hearings.

The giant machine of New York State's Office of Professional Medical Conduct was clearly inefficient, he thought, in spite of Storch's words regarding "efficiency in the hearing room." In fact, the wheels of state justice were so rusty that Harris had a concern regarding potential witnesses for the defense: elderly patients who, nearly a year earlier, had relished the thought of testifying on behalf of the doctor they trusted and cared about. Harris hoped they were still alive when and *if* the time came.

He had battled with Victor Herbert in May, counting on the knowledge he had gained from the medical instruction provided by Levin, supplemented by copies of numerous articles and excerpts from reference books that were highlighted in yellow and starred in red ink to catch his eye. The tests and treatments presented in the indictment were numerous, and Sheehan was using Herbert to prove that *everything* Levin did was extraneous, useless, and even harmful to patients, while also casting doubt on Levin's ability to accurately assess and diagnose the patients named.

In his *voir dire* session with Victor Herbert, Harris had decided to approach the issue of intravenous megadoses of Vitamin C, quoting an eminent scientist who supported this viewpoint. Herbert responded that the scientist, who was *not* a medical doctor, *only a chemist*, tended to recommend megadoses of *oral* Vitamin C, and then hurried to add that such doses were harmful and induced acute diarrhea. Then he somewhat amended his statement, offering that the scientist's latest book referred to a "correct dose…that produces a nice healthy diarrhea." Herbert had given a snort of derision, saying, "There *is* no such thing as *healthy diarrhea*." Harris had immediately come back with questions on Vitamin C deficiency, as the topic continued, with the ball quickly moving between them at lightening speed during cross-examination.

From there, Sheehan introduced the chelation therapy treatment that Levin had provided to a patient fourteen years earlier, in 1976, calling it objectionable. When Harris had objected to the characterization, Sheehan had countered with, "If you do something that is experimental but turns out to be the *right* thing to do, you are much less at fault than if you do something experimental which is *never* subsequently found to be effective. So from that point of view, I believe the State should be allowed to prove that chelation for a patient such as Patient A in 1976 was not only *experimental* and *wrong* at that time, but it has *never* been proven to be any good. I believe it is our burden to show that this procedure was wrong *then,* and it has *remained* wrong right up until this date." To this, Harris had responded, "My objection is that what is acceptable medical treatment is *not* determined by missives from the Department of Health and Human Services. It is *not* determined by the FDA." Reading aloud a quote he had found and thought pertinent, Harris had intoned, "The *best* clinical judgment of the individual practitioner is consultation with his *patient.*" On a roll, Harris had then ventured that, "Having a bureaucrat pontificate about what *is* or *isn't* permissible medical treatment, based on a couple of other guys he might have spoken with, is not the standard by which one measures unprofessional conduct." Pressing the issue of bureaucratic foolishness, he had added: "The government, with absolutely *nothing* to substantiate its view, simply states, *'This treatment is no good!'*"

The debate about the efficacy of ChelationTherapy continued for several hundred more pages of transcript, with Herbert postulating that it was a toxic treatment, especially for a patient with kidney disease; then he went on to deny its effectiveness in arteriosclerosis. But toward the end of Herbert's testimony, Harris was able to score a point for the defense by getting Herbert—the proponent of double-blind, peer-reviewed studies—to admit that they *weren't* necessarily required to prove efficacy of treatment in ChelationTherapy.

Sheehan's questioning had then moved toward Levin's use of vitamin therapy for his patients, with Sheehan attempting to have the words 'a vitamin injection' changed to simply read 'vitamin,' after claiming to have *proven* that Levin had committed a wrongful act. Harris had objected, claiming surprise and charging prosecutorial bad faith once again, since an accusation of wrongdoing had been leveled against Levin *without* the prosecutor elucidating what "wrong" he was claiming to have proven! Harris had continued his protest saying, *If he is accused of having given intramuscular doses of vitamins, and that is inappropriate, and he is so charged, fine. If he is accused of prescribing oral vitamins, and they are inappropriate, fine. The testimony is virtually* concluded, *and counsel wants to create a* wider *range of accusations after* failing *to prove specifically what this man did wrong.*

Harris had been appalled with Sheehan's next move. The prosecutor had agreed, saying, *He is right. I want to make a broad charge that* all vitamins *were not indicated. I don't care whether they were injected, oral, or applied to the skin. I agree that this is an amendment made late in the case, but I don't think that is too much of a surprise or too prejudicial.*

Just as Harris was about to unleash an indignant response, the judge cut in. *I am going to overrule your objection, counsel,* he told Harris. *Counsel for Respondent has had the records and knows what information is in the chart. I don't find any undue surprise, and I will allow the amendment.* Harris was outraged but helpless to counter the judge's decision without subjecting himself to censure, he feared. At that point, Harris had briefly tuned out on the proceedings. He later read in the court transcript that Victor Herbert had concluded this portion of the hearing by stating categorically that Levin had *ignored* the medical problems of the specific patient under discussion, following up with a spiteful statement that the patient's treatment was *far below* the minimally acceptable standards of medical practice. Belatedly, Harris had thought, *Score one for their side. A* big *one*...for the moment.

At a point in his testimony Herbert had testified that taking maga-doses of Vitamin C caused "metastatic oxylosis." When Harris questioned him about this "terrible disease" Herbert said that it was described in , "hundreds if not thousands of journal articles."

The next hearing day Harris brought in a Medline search and asked Herbert if he agreed with the parameters of the search. He did. It show exactly one article published anywhere in the world on the subject. The author:Victor Herbert, M.D., J.D..

Harris had gotten Lisa Golden, the teacher turned high school English Department Chairperson, who was the first patient he had interviewed in Levin's office, to come in as a witness for the defense. One of the panel members, Dr. O'Connor—whose background as a gynecologist was well behind him in retirement—focused on the infection that had brought this woman in her late fifties to see a physician practicing alternative medicine. *Prior to seeing Dr. Levin, what did other physicians tell you about your condition?* O'Connor had asked. *About the same thing,* Lisa had initially responded. Then charging ahead without the embarrassment and hesitation she had initially exhibited when Harris first approached her, she said, *"I had a heavy discharge, itchiness, so I was told I had vaginitis.* O'Connor then asked, *"Did anyone ever tell you prior to Dr. Levin that you had a Candida condition?* Lisa had simply said no. Since O'Connor had referred to the Darkfield test at this point as one of Levin's diagnostic tools, Sheehan asked Victor Herbert, *What is a Darkfield Microscopy examination?* Instead of responding directly to the question, Herbert instead passed judgment, which infuriated the defense. *Darkfield Microscopy, as reported here, has* no *legitimate basis for being done in this patient.*

As the transcription tape churned out of the stenographer's machine at a steady rate, the topics Herbert testified about under questioning from the prosecuting attorney covered a number of different areas: adrenal cortical insufficiency, first-degree heart block and the formation of an oxalate, corticotropin and its role in regulating the rate of secretion of the glucocorticoids, and Cortisol and hydrocortisone in ACE injections. Harris smiled to himself, remembering how he had cross-examined Herbert, in an effort to get the doctor to admit that Cortisol and hydrocortisone were identical steroidal hormones. Levin had instructed Harris carefully on this topic, so the lawyer understood that hydrocortisone, a hormone also known as Cortisol and secreted by the adrenal cortex, controlled the body's use of fats, proteins, and carbohydrates. He privately acknowledged that he had enjoyed "badgering the witness," as the popular expression used on television courtroom dramas went. In fact, there were repeated times when Sheehan jumped up agitatedly to say, *Objection, objection, objection to instructions by Mr. Harris.* Then Sheehan would turn to Storch and, pointing an index finger, say, *"It's your job to give the witness instructions!"* Harris had relished giving orders to Herbert. Asking him to read a portion from a reference text by Goodman and Gilman's *The Pharmacological Basis of Therapeutics*, then immediately having him switch to the Sixth Edition of the AMA's *Drug Evaluations,* published in 1987, stopping Herbert midway and referring him to another section of the page, then instructing him to begin reading where he had originally left off in the first book, then back to the other tome, then back again.

Harris had then summed it up for Herbert nicely. *When I point out to you that Cortisol and hydrocortisone are synonymous, and you tell me that Cortisol is a trade name for hydrocortisone, I have to ask you this, Dr. Herbert: In what way do you and I disagree?* Harris laughed aloud thinking of Herbert's answer: *"Because you are talking about Cortisol and Cortisone as being the same thing!"* he had barked. Harris had regarded him for a long moment, allowing Herbert's response to ring out and be remembered by those present, before he softly retorted, *"No, Dr. Herbert, not Cortisol and Cortisone; Cortisol and* Hydro*cortisone."* That was a fine moment for the defense attorney, scoring him a good-sized win.

In true Victor Herbert-style, the doctor/lawyer had blown his cool a number of times that day, Harris happily recalled. After Herbert had screamed out to Harris more than once during the long day of testimony, "*You're a liar!*" Harris had tried to score some extra points with the judge. Storch excused Herbert from the room several times following these outbursts to discuss the situation, so on one of these occasions Harris had reminded the judge of his ruling after the first personal attack earlier in the day. He was hoping Storch would penalize or eject Herbert for his lack of decorum in the courtroom or reprimand the state's attorney for not taking action. He had hoped in vain.

By the end of that long, tedious day, Harris felt that the score was fairly even, although he hated to acknowledge that the prosecutor had been successful in using Victor Herbert to gain so many points in the fight against his client. *Enough reminiscing. That's all in the past. What matters is the present, and I'm really looking forward to this evening.*

Bob Harris left his car with the valet at the Four Seasons Hotel on East 57th Street and Lexington Avenue and walked to the hotel's famed dining room, where he was shown to his reserved table. He immediately noticed his dinner companion walking toward him and respectfully stood, as the maitre'd escorted the elderly gentleman to where Harris waited.

There was very little that impressed Harris these days. But the man who warmly shook his hand before removing the signature black beret from his shock of curly white hair, while regarding the lawyer through lively and curious blue eyes, rendered Harris speechless for the moment. They sat across from one another at one of the twenty-six tables under the forty-foot ceiling in the softly lit dining room, the tall, wide windows framing the glow of early evening in Manhattan's late summer.

"Excuse me for staring, Dr. Pauling," the lawyer said, trying not to appear as awestruck as he felt. Linus Pauling—the only individual to be awarded two undivided Nobel Prizes, holder of forty-eight honorary Doctor of Philosophy degrees, author of numerous books and articles for the general public on the diverse topics of science, peace, and health—had walked the seven blocks from the venerable Benjamin Hotel, where he was staying to attend a conference in Manhattan, to meet Bob Harris at the Four Seasons for dinner. Pauling had been contacted by Levin and had agreed to this evening's meeting with the doctor's attorney. Pauling's pioneering work in brain-fluid chemistry and the therapeutic efficacy of vitamins in cancer had led the scientist to broaden the concept and develop the field of Orthomolecular Medicine, which laid the foundation for Warren Levin's medical practice, as well as those of his fellow complementary and alternative physicians. The term, meaning "right molecules in the right concentration," delineated the approach to the prevention and treatment of disease and attainment of optimum health, based on the physiological and enzymatic actions of specific nutrients, such as vitamins, minerals, and amino acids present in the body. Upon receiving the phone call from Levin requesting the meeting, the scientist stated that he would be "absolutely delighted" to do so, and Levin suspected that the sentiment was genuine. Harris, thrilled by the prospect, was determined to select a location that was convenient to Pauling's hotel in Manhattan, as well as deserving of the man's august presence. Thus, the choice of the Four Seasons, with its ambiance and reputation for unparalleled cuisine.

"Mr. Harris, stare away!" Pauling responded, as good-humored as his reputation purported him to be.

The waiter came, and the men ordered. Harris, who rarely touched liquor, nevertheless made a recommendation for a fine wine, and Pauling cheerfully agreed. They began to discuss Warren Levin's case before their salads even arrived. Pauling and Levin had met several times when the eminent scientist had lectured to meetings of A.C.A.M. [the leading organization in educating Physicians in Complementary Medicine.] In addition Pauling had been the featured speaker on an educational cruise, in which their cordial relationship had been established. That association was further strengthened at the Second International Symposium on Stress, held in Monte Carlo, and sponsored by Dr. Hans Selye. Pauling had been one of four Nobel Prize Winners at this prestigious meeting, and Levin had also presented a paper and was honored by serving as a moderator of one of the daily sessions. So Pauling knew of Levin's work and was aware of his ongoing battle to retain his medical license in order to continue that work. Levin's courage in the face of adversity sparked Pauling's interest.

"Let me tell you something, Mr. Harris," he began.

"You can tell me anything you want, Dr. Pauling, if you call me Bob."

The older man laughed appreciatively. "Okay, Bob, let me tell you something. During World War II, I offered the U.S. government the use of my laboratory and my services as a research consultant. I made a number of contributions, in fact, for which President Truman presented me with the Presidential Medal for Merit." He shook his head at the memory, which had been a particularly proud moment in his life. "A few years later, when McCarthy-ism hit us, I was treated almost like a traitor!"

"I wasn't aware of that," Harris said.

"Oh, *I* was!" They both laughed. "Anyway, my patriotism, my stand against the abuse of nuclear arms, all forgotten. I was denied a passport and couldn't even travel abroad to attend scientific conferences, if you can believe it."

"On what grounds," asked Harris, ever the lawyer.

"The State Department said that my leaving the country was 'Not in the best interests of the United States,' whatever that meant."

"How long did that go on?" Harris was genuinely curious.

"Until 1954, when they finally decided I wasn't a dangerous individual, a communist, a subversive, or whatever they thought I might have been, so they reinstated my unrestricted passport."

"Why 1954 exactly?"

"Because that was the year I was awarded the Nobel Prize in Chemistry. So the State Department had a bit of egg on their face." Pauling laughed at the recollection.

Remembering what he had read about the man prior to their dinner date this evening, Harris told him, "They must have had a *few dozen eggs* on their faces a few years later when you got the Nobel Prize for Peace."

"I hope so, I really do. They made my life rather...difficult for awhile. The point I'm trying to make here, Bob, is that I *know* what it's like to have people watching you, restricting you, coming after you, examining everything you do. I know from experience. And, while all of that happened to me nearly forty years ago, the one thing I took from it was how awful it is to have our freedoms curtailed. We live in the greatest country in the world, and freedom is the shining nucleus at its core. If we're deprived of our freedom, any of our freedoms," he amended, "for even the *smallest* amount of time...it leaves an indelible impression." The man was pensive, his thoughts momentarily obscuring the light in his eyes.

Harris nodded. No comment was necessary.

Their food arrived, the wine was poured, and Harris tried to find a gentle way to ask Pauling a question. He had noticed that the scientist had a Parkinsonian-type tremor and, while he had managed to eat his salad quite comfortably, Harris wanted to find a way to help.

"Dr. Pauling," he ventured, tentatively, "I wonder if I might cut your food up into manageable, bite-sized pieces for you."

Pauling looked at Harris, his blue eyes regarding him with appreciation. "I thank you for your kind offer, Bob, I really do. However, I've devised a fine strategy to handle this 'little problem' of mine. Watch, and I'll show you." Pauling picked up his knife and fork, placed his wrists on the table's edge to steady his tremulous hands, and demonstrated to the lawyer's amazement his ability to cut his veal chop, not effortlessly, because the maneuver required both concentration and some degree of effort, but adequately enough for the elderly man to continue to converse while enjoying his meal.

Pauling, at age eighty-nine, was an interesting and captivating dinner companion. His mind was agile, his memory flawless, and his speech measured and clear. He encouraged Harris to fill him in on all the details of Levin's case, since he only had knowledge of the bare outline, and he reiterated the commitment he had made to Levin when the doctor had contacted him.

Linus Pauling was thrilled to be asked to testify on behalf of Warren Levin. It almost seemed to Harris that the man was yearning for the opportunity to relive his past as a professor, an activist, and a well-informed individual with a strong belief system.

"Just write down the address for me, Bob," he said at the end of the evening, "and I'll meet you both at the hearing room first thing tomorrow morning!"

CHAPTER 20

Harris woke up very early the following morning. He was still glowing from his three-hour dinner with one of the most important scientists of the century. Pauling had asked Harris to talk to him about his own life, so the lawyer told a few courtroom stories and a couple of personal anecdotes. The scientist picked up on the amount of airline travel Harris had done over the years then unabashedly shared his own discomfort about flying. *"So once,"* Pauling began, *"one of our government's agencies—I won't say which one,"* he smiled, *"invited me to Washington D.C. I wasn't even fond of short trips by plane, and here I was out in California. So I took a train to our nation's capital. They handed me a top-secret list, and pretty much said to me, 'We need these things, but they don't exist. We'd like you to invent them for us.'"*

Just like that? Harris had asked.

"It's the government we're talking about, Bob, so yes, 'just like that.' I catch my train back to the West Coast, my mind already filling up with ideas. By the time I get back to California, I already have the workings of three new inventions in my mind." In response to Harris's incredulous look, he elaborated. *"I see you're wondering what those things might have been,"* the older man chuckled. *"Well, since they're no longer top secret, I'll tell you about the one I was most pleased with: a valve that allows pilots to breathe oxygen at high altitudes. It was good for the pilots, sure, but what really makes me happy is that it was later adapted for use on incubators for newborn babies."*

Harris had been stunned, listening to the man whose work he had quoted about a point so divergent from breathing life-sustaining air. Just yesterday, Harris had quoted from Pauling's work on Vitamin C, truly an "apples and oranges" situation, when one considered how far removed from one another these topics were. He recalled darkly how Victor Herbert had dismissed the information out-of-hand, since the source was *only a Ph.D., not an M.D.*, and *only a chemist. Only a chemist, my ass,* Harris thought. Linus Pauling was the *real thing*: a true genius. Certainly nothing like Victor Herbert. So Harris wondered if Pauling knew who Victor Herbert was.

"Yes, unfortunately I do know of Victor Herbert," the man had responded, sounding genuinely regretful to be saying anything negative, *"and I can sum the man up by saying it's a pity that such a good mind has to go to waste for such stupidity."* The comment had pleased Harris enormously, putting them in the same corner of the ring in more ways than one.

Although it was Pauling's intention to get to the hearing room on his own the next morning, Harris had driven the man back to his hotel and decided on a change of plans at the last moment. *Can I pick you up tomorrow morning and take you to breakfast?* he had asked. *"I'll have coffee in my room in the morning, Bob, but I would be delighted if you'd pick me up."*

As they were driving to the hearing office on East 40th Street, Pauling said, "I really want to thank you for the delicious meal last night and the even more wonderful wine you selected. I assure you I slept very well."

"The pleasure was all mine, believe me, Dr. Pauling," said the attorney, thinking that—as far as an evening at a restaurant with a companion was concerned, that dinner would be written into his memoirs as one of the high points of his life. "And I'm sure glad you're well rested, because I suspect this is going to be a long, long day."

"Yes, well, that may be so. Hopefully, I can be of assistance to Warren." At a stop light, the two men turned to face one another, and Pauling unexpectedly said, "Bob, Warren is certainly *lucky* to have you for his attorney."

Harris felt a rush of warmth envelop him, and his eyes stung as he moved forward on the green light. "Thank you," he told Pauling. "You'll never know how much that means to me."

The Panel knew from yesterday that Linus Pauling was due to testify this morning, and everyone was already seated. When Pauling entered the room, everyone immediately sprang up, honoring the legendary scientist and Nobel Prize winner. Harris was gratified at the appropriate welcome given the eminent scientist, especially since he feared that things might become less than respectful as the day progressed and Sheehan led the inquiry.

While Dr. McAloon was unable to be present for the hearing, she had indicated that she would review the transcript before the next meeting. Dr. Pauling was sworn in, told that the proceeding would be videotaped, and asked if he had any objections, which he did not. Prior to the commencement of taping, however, Harris had a brief disagreement with both the panel chairman and Sheehan over Harris's insistence on reading Pauling's four-page biography into the record. Harris prevailed and began, in a sonorous voice: "Linus Pauling was born in Portland, Oregon on the twenty-eighth of February 1901 and was educated in Oregon, receiving a BS in Chemical Engineering from Oregon Agricultural College in 1922 and a Ph.D. from the California Institute of Technology in 1925—and 47 others after that!" Harris continued for the next fifteen minutes, outlining the scientist's professorships at Cal Tech and other California universities, and his visiting professorships at a number of prestigious institutions outside of the state and the country. He then presented Pauling's research accomplishments and publications, as well as his more recent application of chemistry to biological and medical problems. Harris informed the group about the awards, medals, and Nobel Prizes that the elderly man had garnered over his distinguished life, and the lectures that had since been instituted in his honor at various institutions of higher learning. He covered the scientist's publications—over one thousand, mentioning the title of his latest book, published three years earlier, *How to Live Longer and Feel Better*. Harris even read aloud the fact that he had lost his wife in 1987, after 64 years of marriage, four children, fifteen grandchildren, and eight great-grandchildren. When Harris finished reading, he checked the facts with Pauling, who added that he and Abram Hoffer had just completed a manuscript due for publication in 1991, tentatively titled *How to Control Cancer with Vitamins*.

Harris launched into his direct examination. "Dr. Pauling, are you being *paid* to come here today?"

"No, I am not being paid at all."

"Are you under subpoena to come here today?"

"No."

"Why are you here?"

The scientist smiled. "Well, I am very much interested in nutrition, the health of people, and control of disease—especially by improving people's health through the optimum intake of substances normally present in the human body. I named these substances Orthomolecular substances back in 1968," he added. "At first, my interest in all of this was a result of the fact that I had been working on mental diseases for about thirteen years, calling it Orthomolecular Psychiatry, which is the use of vitamins in large doses to control acute schizophrenia." He continued in this vein, mentioning his book, *Vitamin C and the Common Cold*, which led to his research into combining Vitamins C and A to benefit cancer patients.

"I was involved with several physicians in setting up the Orthomolecular Medical Society, and since its inception, I have been the honorary president and on the editorial board of the *Journal of Orthomolecular Medicine*." Pauling also mentioned some groundbreaking research and the formation of international symposia that resulted from his research with cancer.

Harris then asked, "Have you ever testified for a doctor in a license hearing before? Anywhere in the world?"

Pauling took a moment to consider the question. "I have testified, I think, for only *one* physician in the past."

"How did you decide to testify as a witness for Dr. Levin?"

"He wrote to me and asked if I were interested in his case. I *am* interested because I believe that physicians who emphasize *nutrition* and *preventive medicine*, especially with the use of orthomolecular substances, are beginning to practice the medicine of the future, perhaps the medicine of *ten years* in the future. This means that organized medicine will recognize that this is a very valuable way of changing the present, customary methods of treatment of disease that will lead to improvement in health of human beings. So I am eager to do what I can to prevent efforts to *suppress* the development of this contribution to medical practice."

Harris was ecstatic with Pauling's response, and he had briefly glanced at the impassive faces of the panelists and prosecution after noting the pleased glint in his client's eyes. "Dr. Pauling, have you seen the charges against Dr. Levin in this case?"

"I read a list of perhaps a dozen pages of charges, yes."

"You know that he is charged with fraud, gross negligence, gross incompetence, misconduct, and unprofessional conduct. You are aware of that?"

"I read that, yes."

"Doctor, are you familiar with Dr. Victor Herbert?"

"Yes, I have known him for about twenty-one years now."

The attorney was so anxious to ask the next question he hoped that he wouldn't stumble on the words and lose the impact. "Do you have an opinion of Dr. Herbert as a scientist and physician?"

Pauling took a deep breath before answering. "I don't think that he *is* a scientist. It seems to me that he has little understanding of science and little ability in that field. I am not in a position to judge his ability as a physician, however."

"Have you had personal dealings with him as a scientist?"

"Yes, I have met him several times, and I can tell you what happened."

Harris couldn't wait to hear the stories. He literally felt as though he could jump out of his skin in anticipation of Pauling's response.

"I was asked to be one of the three or four speakers at the dedication of a new medical school in New York City," Pauling began, "Mount Sinai Medical School, where Dr. Herbert was at the time, Professor of Medicine. I wanted to speak on a medical subject. This was before I had gotten interested in cancer. So I talked about Vitamin C and the common cold and said that the evidence that we have now indicates that if people were to increase their intake of Vitamin C to quite a large amount at the first signs or symptoms of the common cold, they could prevent its development; they could stop the cold in its tracks. While I didn't meet Dr. Herbert at the meeting, I received a letter from him, a *vituperative* letter, which began a correspondence between us."

"What did the correspondence concern?" asked Harris.

Pauling told him that Herbert had requested proof of Pauling's claims, which Pauling provided and Herbert rejected time and again. "Victor Herbert, you know," Pauling said to Harris, "is *not* a scientist. He doesn't *know* how to assess evidence. I don't think he knows much about biostatistics. He just *refuses* to look at evidence." Pauling then spoke of being on a radio program with a biochemist from Hoffman LaRoche—the pharmaceutical company, and Victor Herbert. "Of course," he admitted, "there were two of us 'ganging up' on Victor Herbert, and there is no doubt that his beliefs aren't based upon the evidence; they're based upon some sort of *bias*."

"I see," Harris responded, really, really seeing that Victor Herbert was who Levin had made him out to be.

Pauling started speaking once again. "I see in magazines and in newspapers Victor Herbert stating that vitamins greater than the Recommended Dietary Allowance have *no* value for any persons in health or disease."

"Is that true, Dr. Pauling?"

"No, it is perfectly, completely *false*," Pauling answered, without hesitation. "I can't understand this fellow. I certainly wouldn't want him to be *my* physician!" Several people in the hearing room chuckled, then cleared their throats uncomfortably.

Harris proceeded to have Pauling talk about the value of randomized, double-blind, controlled trials, and was informed that while the first of them had been carried out fifty years earlier, a lot of important medical discoveries had been recently made *without* the trials. He then referred to the efficacy of both Vitamin C in cancer and aspirin for headache as *not* having been introduced into medicine via such trials.

Harris then moved into a significant issue in Levin's practice. "Doctor, are you familiar with disodium EDTA chelation?"

"Yes."

"Doctor, we heard testimony here from one of the state's witnesses," *who is the* soul *of the case,* he added, privately, "that Chelation Therapy is a fraudulent therapy for anyone other than those with high levels of lead in their blood."

Pauling turned his palms up and shrugged his shoulders. "The reading that I have done and discussions that I have had with physicians who use EDTA Chelation Therapy for cardiovascular problems have caused me to form the opinion that it has *much* value in a cardiovascular case. In fact, I included Chelation therapy in my book, *How to Live Longer and Feel Better*, in the discussion of heart disease.

I am considering having it myself sometime in the future, but I first want to wait until I get *old*."

The hearing room broke out in spontaneous laughter when the eighty-nine-year old scientist made that statement. When the room came to order again, Harris asked his next question. "Doctor, are you familiar with the use of hair as a body component for use in hair analysis, vitamins, heavy metals, and various constituents of the body?"

"Yes, I have checked up on hair analysis."

"It was described by one of the state's witnesses as a fraudulent test. Do you wish to comment on that?"

Sheehan was on his feet instantly. "*Objection!* The question misstates the evidence. The evidence was that the test had no value in the treatment and diagnosis of human *mental* illness." When Harris rephrased the question to focus on the validity of hair analysis in diagnosing mental illness, Sheehan objected again. "Dr. Pauling is a scientist, not a physician, and he is now being asked to give a medical opinion about a medical treatment."

"I am going to overrule the objection," the judge stated. "You may answer the question."

Pauling nodded. "If the tests are reliable, then I would think they might well provide some significant evidence about the pathological state of the person."

Harris was satisfied. "I would like to turn now to a six-hour glucose tolerance test. First, Dr. Pauling, are you familiar with such a test?" Receiving an affirmative answer, Harris then asked, "Do you agree with the State's witness that it is a fraudulent test?"

"Same objection," stated Sheehan, and again was overruled.

Pauling looked at the judge. "I don't see how a knowledgeable person could describe it as a fraudulent test."

Harris decided to make a broad grouping at this point. "Doctor, I would like to go over some of the specific tests that Dr. Levin used, and without asking you about their efficacy with regard to a particular patient, I would simply like to know whether or not you agree with the state's witness, who claimed from the outset that these tests were fraudulent."

"Again, I have to object to the question!" Sheehan elaborated at this point, indicating, that "the testimony related to patients. The witness did not in every instance state that the test itself did not show what it claimed to show. His main point was that these tests were *not indicated for these patients*, and they had *no value* in the diagnosis and treatment of human beings. I submit that the purpose of this hearing is the relevance of these tests to medicine and Dr. Levin's right to charge people for them. *That's* the issue."

Harris spun around to face Sheehan, who was seated at the prosecution table with the judge. "Twenty-six times the state's witness used the phrase, 'fraudulent test'! I believe that if cross-examination and rebuttal have any meaning at all, that it is appropriate for me to ask someone who is coming here with knowledge to testify whether he agrees that a test is fraudulent." Taking on a conciliatory tone, Harris further elaborated: "If the state's witness had merely said this test or that is not indicated for this particular patient, I would *not* ask this witness to debate that because he is, in fact, a scientist and not a physician. But once the State's witness went beyond that point himself and called a test *fraudulent*, it purports that the test is not indicated for *any* human being *at any time*. I think my question is certainly fair in view of the zeal with which the state's witness testified." Harris had deliberately used the word 'zeal' to describe Herbert's testimony for two reasons: the first reason was that Storch had reprimanded him for his *own* zeal in defending Levin, and the second reason was that one of the responsibilities of any lawyer defending any client is to defend that client *zealously*, in case the judge had forgotten that directive taught in law school.

"Objection is overruled. Let's proceed."

"Doctor, are you familiar with the mauve factor test?"

"Yes."

"Can you tell us what that test in general is used for?"

"The mauve factor was discovered, as I recall, nearly thirty years ago by Hoffer and Osmond in schizophrenic patients, in their urine. As a patient recovered from acute schizophrenia, the amount of the mauve factor decreased. These researchers and others also reported that the mauve factor shows up in some cancer patients and other seriously ill patients. The mauve factor is a *significant* test that can be added to other information that a physician obtains about a patient with respect to the state of health or disease of that patient. You know," he added as an afterthought, "I sympathize with physicians, since they are required to make decisions about treatment of a patient with only a *small* amount of information about that patient. My observation is that physicians do the best they can to make a proper treatment decision and often must resort to administering one drug after another in an effort to find one that is effective for that particular patient." He laughed softly. "If I were a physician myself, I would want to carry out as many tests as I could on the patient in order to gather enough information on which to base *my* diagnosis and treatment."

Harris was elated. *Score a huge point for us!*

After a moment of thought, Pauling spoke again. "I like orthomolecular substances. I like vitamins."

Following that, Harris asked a series of questions about tests used to determine vitamin concentrations in a patient's body. While Pauling admitted to familiarity with many of the tests named, he was completely honest about stating that drawing conclusions as to the efficacy of said tests was out of his field of expertise. At that point, Harris decided to change direction and get to the heart of the issue at hand.

"Dr. Pauling, the state's attorney has indicated that Dr. Levin's practice is inconsistent with the *minimally accepted standards* of the practice of medicine. Can you comment on that, sir?"

Sheehan jumped in with, "I don't know *how* he can! I object to the question! It's logically impossible, having just looked at the charges. You are asking him to determine whether or not Dr. Levin is *guilty* of the charges."

"Mr. Harris?" asked the judge.

"Dr. Levin is *not* charged with failing to practice up to the minimum standards, Your Honor. That was merely an assertion of the state's attorney. I would like Dr. Pauling, if he wishes to and can do so, to comment on that. This is a question on an approach to medical practice."

"I object to this!"

Harris regarded Sheehan with what he hoped was a neutral look. "It is difficult to frame a question in *specific* terms when the issue, in fact, is more *general*."

Storch realized it was up to him to decide. "With all due deference to Dr. Pauling as an expert in his field, he is *not* a medical doctor. To ask him to comment on the validity of the Department's charges or the issue of whether or not the Respondent has failed to meet minimally accepted standards of medical practice is *beyond* his expertise. The objection is sustained."

Harris repeated the question with regard to Levin's laboratory tests and was met with the same objections, which were also upheld. Once again, Harris switched his focus of questioning.

"Dr. Pauling, are you familiar with the general term, 'Orthomolecular Medical Practice'?"

"I *invented* the adjective 'orthomolecular' when I realized twenty-three years ago that there was a remarkable difference between certain substances used in health care and others. Drugs are usually toxic!"

"*I object!* 'Orthomolecular is *not* in the charges, since it's not alleged that Dr. Levin is an orthomolecular doctor!"

"Mr. Harris?"

"He *is* an orthomolecular physician! He testified to that," Harris told the judge.

Sheehan responded. "It's not in the charges!"

Harris was annoyed, and snapped at Sheehan. "I am entitled to manners! Dr. Levin's practice is *nutritionally based* and has been referred to by the state's witness as 'hogwash,' 'fraud,' and everything else! I want to establish the difference between orthomolecular practice and orthodox conventional practice. I think those are fair questions. In the event the difference is revealed, I am then going to ask Dr. Pauling whether or not he believes that orthomolecular medicine is a *valid approach to the diagnosis and treatment of human illness*." Harris paused a moment and slowly turned around, making eye contact with every one of the people in the hearing room before stating in a clear, paced voice: "That is really the philosophical question of this whole hearing!" He had their undivided attention now. "That is the reason that *he*," Harris pointed to Levin, "is *sitting* in this room, and that he is *paying* me."

Storch decided to reply. "The expression 'Orthomolecular Medicine' has not even come up yet in this hearing. I submit that it is *irrelevant* to get into this big, theoretical discussion."

Harris believed he had an advantage and was determined to press forward. "The *definition* of 'orthomolecular,' as defined by Dr. Linus Pauling, is, gentlemen. . ." Here Harris paused for effect, slowly turning to point to his client, "none other than my client, Dr. Warren Levin!" The lawyer wasn't about to let the state get away with avoiding the issue, especially when they referred to Levin's practice as "nutritionally based" and using all of the techniques involved in the definition of "orthomolecular." Harris was pleased that the judge overruled Sheehan, instructing the witness to answer.

Pauling took a deep breath, realizing that the significance of what he had to say next might bear heavily on the outcome of Levin's trial. "I recognize that vitamins in general have very low toxicity. They are powerful substances, in that a little pinch every day is enough to prevent a person from dying of the corresponding deficiency's disease. But they are so lacking in toxicity, that for most vitamins, one could take one thousand or even *ten thousand* times the daily dose without suffering from any serious toxic manifestation. I thought that this difference was enough to justify my introducing a new word: orthomolecular. The substances usually are effective in improving the general health of a person and potentiating the natural methods of preventing and controlling diseases. This is essentially through improved nutrition, not necessarily just eating foods, since the optimum nutritional intake may require making use of vitamin tablets or purified substances.

"My feeling is that a proper part of the *duty* of a physician in attempting to provide for a patient, for maximal well-being and health, is not only to prescribe conventional treatment but also to advise about nutrition—the proper use of orthomolecular substances to improve the general health of the patient. It seems quite improper for the medical authorities to say that a physician *cannot* prescribe vitamins in whatever doses he considers appropriate in an effort to improve the health of the patient.

"It is the *duty* of a physician to use his knowledge of the functioning of the human body to advise the patient about his diet, *including* dietary supplements, and that it is wise to carry out whatever tests of enzyme activity or vitamin concentration necessary to advise about nutrition."

Boy, he has sure nailed every aspect of Warren's practice. Perfect! All I need now is a specific endorsement of Warren himself.

As though reading the defense lawyer's mind, Pauling fixed his alert eyes directly on Warren Levin and spoke. "I consider Dr. Levin to be a *good* model of the changing practice of medicine to the extent that I have knowledge about him and from what I have read, and also from my brief acquaintance with him as a physician of the future who is interested not just in treating catastrophic illness with powerful drugs or other therapies, but also in doing what he can to improve the *general* health of the patient and to make use of this great discovery that made available vitamin supplements to us to increase the length of life, decrease the events of illness, and to control diseases that the patient has got."

Wow, that's got to be the longest sentence in courtroom history. I hope the stenographer got it all, because I'm dying to read it once the transcript comes out. It's a good thing Pauling isn't speaking from notes because, for sure, they would all think I had written this resounding endorsement of my client and his medical practice.

Pauling also underscored a patient's right to select a physician of his choice. Harris hoped the testimony wouldn't be diluted by the fact that, other than a conference in Europe five years earlier and another meeting they had both attended numerous years before that, Pauling had only known Levin for eighteen short hours.

Following recess, the hearing reconvened, with Sheehan subjecting Pauling to cross-examination. He asked specific questions about the one other time Pauling had testified at a physician's hearing. However, Pauling recalled little of the testimony he had given and was unable to answer to Sheehan's satisfaction, for the most part. Sheehan submitted into evidence a document alleging that Pauling had recommended coffee enemas in the past. He handed the document to the scientist.

Sheehan said, "I would like to ask you whether reading that paragraph refreshes your recollection as to whether or not you, under oath in the past, have stated that *coffee enemas* are probably beneficial to the health, several times a day, to clean out the lower bowel."

Harris promptly objected, and Storch inquired as to the basis of the objection;

"I move for a mistrial!" Harris bellowed.

"Let me hear, Mr. Harris," said Storch, patiently.

"The question that was put to this witness as to whether or not, in the past, he has advocated the use of several coffee enemas a day as a way for people to maintain their general health is a means of using a *dishonest, non-existent reference* to something that is *not here* in order to trick this man. This ought not to be permitted. *I move for a mistrial!*"

Since the issue had come up in the California hearing Pauling had testified at so long ago, Harris offered two pages from that transcript into evidence, whereupon Sheehan, retorted, "I have no objection to the *entire transcript* of this witness's testimony before the California Board going into evidence."

Harris countered, "There is no evidentiary basis for this transcript going in."

"You just offered it."

"I offered *two pages*, and mister, don't be making reference to something I *didn't* do and asserting that I *did* it! Don't even *think* of incorporating that in the presence of this man," Harris stated, indignantly. "You *misquoted* Dr. Pauling, and I think we have a basis for mistrial!"

"Motion for mistrial is denied!"

Harris was angry, having witnessed what he considered an affront to Pauling, but he fought to keep himself under control. "If we can get back to *some* sense of probative value instead of gamesmanship," he began, addressing Sheehan directly, "there is no basis for admitting the transcript of another hearing without showing that in *each* of its parts it has relevancee to something going on in *this* hearing."

"You're two steps ahead of the game here, at minimum, Mr. Harris," said the judge.

"This is not a game!" Harris shouted.

The judge wasn't having it. "Stop raising your voice. I can hear you just fine from where I am sitting. Shouting is not necessary to make a point, Mr. Harris."

"When you refer to this as a 'game,' you cause me to have a surge of adrenaline which I think is *entirely* appropriate. Your *colleague* here believes it's a game!" Harris responded, looking over at Sheehan.

Harris swallowed his anger and allowed the proceedings to continue, along with the questions on the coffee enemas, which were apparently a significant issue at the hearing in California. Sheehan then attempted to extract from Pauling an opinion about the *validity* of the decision that the California Board had reached on the accused physician. Eventually Sheehan got to the point: He wanted to discover what differences existed, in Pauling's opinion, between the two hearings at which he testified. Pauling deftly answered, saying that the basic difference was that, in California, he was *not* shown the charges against the doctor while, in the current hearing room, he had read them *all*. Sheehan then received an affirmative answer when he asked Pauling whether patients should be allowed to seek *unproven* medical treatments for their illnesses, if they so desired. When Sheehan pressed the issue further, fireworks again erupted.

"Dr. Pauling, if the California Board stated that physicians should *not* undertake courses of unproven treatments..."

"Objection!" Harris said.

"Can I complete the question?"

"*No!* You have already said *enough* to what I believe is a sustained objection. I don't *have* to wait for you to pollute the atmosphere more to object."

Sheehan said, "I object!"

Storch spoke. "I want to hear a complete question before I hear an objection," allowing Sheehan to repeat his question before Harris's next objection, followed once again by another motion for a mistrial.

"Mistrial denied. Objection overruled."

Harris and the judge then engaged in a discussion over Harris's allegations that Sheehan's conduct was irreparably *tainting* the Hearing Panel. Once the storm had once again passed, Sheehan changed his line of questioning.

"Dr. Pauling, I believe you testified that, in your opinion, Dr. Victor Herbert was *not* a scientist. Didn't you use those exact words?"

"Yes, I did."

"I believe you stated that *one* of the reasons you think he isn't a scientist is because he says false things about vitamins. Is that true?"

"No, I don't remember having said that. We could read back my testimony," Pauling added, "because I just don't remember. A scientist is a person who seeks the *truth*, and it's clear that this *doesn't* characterize Dr. Herbert."

"At the California hearing, you said that the AMA states that you *don't* need any vitamins beyond the balanced diet, and you said that's pure nonsense. Correct?

"Yes."

Sheehan pressed on. "The AMA *and* Dr. Herbert utter pure nonsense on that topic, correct?"

"That's right." Pauling didn't hesitate one bit. "I think it's contrary to the present state of knowledge."

"When you testified earlier, you mentioned a little radio encounter with Dr. Herbert and a biochemist from Hoffman LaRoche. Do you remember?"

"Yes."

"I believe you stated half-jokingly that you and the biochemist 'ganged up' on Dr. Herbert. Is that correct?"

"That's right. Our opinions were essentially the same."

"Let me ask you this: How much does Hoffman LaRoche contribute to the institute you head in California? How many hundreds of thousands of dollars do they contribute?"

"I think that they have given the institute either fifty thousand or one-hundred thousand dollars a year, which amounts to about one to three percent of our annual budget," Pauling answered.

Sheehan felt he had a decent advantage and moved on it. "Doctor, do you think it is proper for an institute which is the *primary* advocate of megadoses of Vitamin C to accept one-hundred thousand dollars a year from the company that virtually *monopolizes* the sale of that vitamin in the United States?"

"Objection!" Harris said.

"What is the basis?" asked the judge.

"Mr. Sheehan has incorporated within his question the amount of one-hundred thousand dollars, which is *not* what the witness said."

"Sustained."

After showing Pauling a document that stated Hoffman LaRoche, in actuality, had contributed one-hundred thousand dollars *five years ago*, Sheehan asked him to acknowledge it.

"So far as my knowledge extends, yes. But the vice-president has told me that they have had trouble getting more than fifty-thousand dollars from Hoffman LaRoche. *I* think they ought to give us a million dollars or five-million dollars a year, myself!" The hearing room exploded in laughter.

Sheehan didn't join in the laughter and merely waited for the noise to abate. "Doctor, you testified that you were a speaker at the inauguration of Mount Sinai Medical School. Correct?"

"Yes."

"Would you agree, Dr. Pauling, that the reason why Dr. Herbert wrote that letter to you after you spoke is because your speech alluded to the benefits of Vitamin C for the common cold, which was *embarrassing* to various members of orthodox medicine who participated in this inauguration?"

"Objection!"

"Basis?"

"First of all, he is asking for the *state of mind* of the writer of a letter. Second of all, I presume Dr. Pauling hoped that his speech *would* embarrass them into action and learning. But whether it did or not, to ask him what Dr. Herbert *thought,* which then caused him to write a letter is to ask too much of any witness."

Sheehan sneered. "If he knows, he knows, if he doesn't, he doesn't."

Harris went over to Pauling at this point. "Dr. Pauling, do you *know* what Victor's state of mind was?"

"Excuse me, Mr. Harris!" said the administration officer.

"I don't want to sit here and have nothing happen," Harris told him.

"Mr. Harris, you *will* sit! It is not redirect examination. You have made your objection, and I am considering my ruling." Storch looked down at the notes he had made. "The objection is overruled. The witness can answer, if he knows."

Pauling shook his head. "It's *impossible* for me to surmise reasons for Herbert's actions."

Sheehan then moved in a new and interesting direction, trying to establish a prior relationship of some significance between Pauling and Herbert. Harris wondered where it was heading but decided to clip it at its root.

"*Objection!* Irrelevant. The issue of Dr. Pauling's relationship with Victor Herbert is a collateral issue and not part of this hearing. The issue asked on direct was his opinion of Victor Herbert as a *scientist*. They clearly knew one another, but it's irrelevant."

"Mr. Sheehan?" the judge inquired.

Sheehan wasn't about to give up. "Mr. Harris went to the trouble on direct examination of trying to impeach Dr. Herbert through Dr. Pauling. He asked a number of questions all designed to impeach Dr. Herbert. I want to show that they have hardly been enemies. In fact, there is voluminous correspondence on metal toxicity and on social issues with this witness." Sheehan regarded Pauling with a suspicious look. "I don't know if this witness 'forgets' all that, conveniently or otherwise, but I submit I am entitled to bring it out if *they* bring out something on direct examination. If it's irrelevant, Mr. Harris should not have brought it out on direct examination."

Harris went in for the kill. "I don't think it's irrelevant. I think that all it could possibly show is that *whatever* relationship they had in the past, Dr. Pauling is nevertheless willing to testify that Victor Herbert is a *loser* as a scientist."

"Objection to the word, 'loser'!"

"Your objection is noted."

"Dr. Pauling, isn't it true that you've had *extensive* correspondence with Dr. Herbert on medical and scientific matters?"

Pauling regarded Sheehan with a tolerant smile. "I write two hundred letters a week," he said, reasonably. "I remember the correspondence with Dr. Herbert over the common cold. I don't remember others."

Sheehan then produced photographs of letters that Pauling had ostensibly written to Victor Herbert and asked the scientist to look at the photographs to determine if, indeed, his signature was on the letters. In each case, Pauling responded one of two ways.

"No, it doesn't have my signature. My secretary signed it."

"No, it doesn't have my signature. It's on my letterhead."

Having gained no relevant ground on Pauling's earlier dealings with Victor Herbert, Sheehan then decided to further explore the scientist's relationship with the Respondent, Warren Levin.

"Dr. Pauling, you indicated that you have known Dr. Levin for *eighteen hours*. Is that right?"

"I said I met him seventeen years ago, possibly some time in between. I meet so many people that I can't remember all of them. *They* tend to remember *me* better."

"You are more famous than others, so they remember you," Sheehan acknowledged. "However, your current knowledge about Dr. Levin is based primarily, wouldn't you say, on your discussions with him over the last day and a half or so. Is that true?"

"Actually, several months ago he sent me some material which I then examined."

"Would you agree, Dr. Pauling, that your testimony concerning Dr. Levin is based primarily on what *he* told you about his medical practice, the *way* he practices, and what his beliefs are?"

"No, I don't think so. My testimony was largely about orthomolecular medicine and specific comments on the basis of my reading the charges against Dr. Levin and getting other information—hardly at all from conversations with him yesterday."

Sheehan put a puzzled expression on his face, meant to strike doubt in the members of the panel. "Based on the fact that he has been charged with *many* counts of gross negligence, in what way does that lead you to believe he is a good physician? How does that work?"

Pauling didn't hesitate for a second. "Based on the statement of the charges, based on my understanding of the tests that he carried out, and the treatments that he prescribed, I formed an opinion that he is a good, sound orthomolecular physician."

"So it wasn't necessary for you to review the patient charts that are referred to in those charges in order to form that conclusion, right?"

"No, I don't think so," Pauling responded.

After asking a series of questions about the work being done and published by the Linus Pauling Institute of Science and Medicine, Sheehan said, "Thank you very much, Dr. Pauling. I have no further questions."

Storch asked, "Any questions from the committee?"

"The committee has no questions," the chairperson replied.

Bob Harris then began his redirect examination of the witness.

"Dr. Pauling, you have been taking megadoses of Vitamin C for how long, sir?"

"For twenty-five years."

"Is there significant evidence that Vitamin C in megadoses acts as an arterio-chelating agent?"

Pauling thought for a moment. "Vitamin C has *some* chelating power for heavy metals. However, it is not *nearly* as good as EDTA. This was studied in our institute."

"Is the fact that you have taken megadoses of Vitamin C for years a consideration in *your* not having Chelation therapy with intravenous EDTA?"

Pauling nodded. "Indirectly," he responded. "I attribute my good health at my present age of 89 to my having taken megadoses of Vitamin C and other vitamins. I don't have chelation treatments because I don't see any reason at the present time why I should."

Since Sheehan had alluded to Pauling's salary but had not specifically questioned it, Harris decided to pursue the issue, if only to eradicate doubts in the minds of the prosecution and the committee that Pauling's efforts in science were profit-driven.

"Dr. Pauling, would you mind telling us what your salary is with the Pauling Institute?"

"Not at all," he said, "because I think I should get *more*." When the laughter died down, he answered specifically, saying, "I get eighty-five thousand dollars a year—about *half* of what professors of medicine at Stanford Medical School get, on the average."

"Dr. Pauling, in your lifetime, have you *ever* issued, written, or spoken an opinion regarding the efficacies of *any* substance in order to promote the economic gains of a manufacturer or a class of manufacturers?" Harris had listened to Sheehan's line of questioning regarding the pharmaceutical giant Hoffman LaRoche and believed that the prosecutor was attempting to expose a questionable partnership between that company and Pauling's institute.

"I would say no. However, from 1976 on, I included the name of another drug company as a good source of vitamins at a *lower* cost by mail order, so that people wouldn't waste their money buying high-priced vitamins. So *that* company may have benefited. I will tell you that we receive only five-thousand dollars a year from that particular firm."

Harris then pursued a line of questioning regarding the possibility of strings being attached to pharmaceutical contributions to Pauling's institute, of which there were none. Harris knew they were nearing the end of Pauling's testimony, and he wanted to leave the committee with the eminent scientist's take on the entire case against his client.

"Dr. Pauling, do you have *any* reason to believe that Warren Levin presents any past or present danger to any patient who comes within his charge?"

"No more than other doctors," he responded, to a smattering of titters from those present.

"I will stop there," Harris declared, emphatically.

The judge spoke. "If there is nothing further…?" Storch smiled kindly at the scientist and said, "Dr. Pauling, thank you very much for your contribution today."

Pauling appeared puzzled and addressed the committee directly. "Aren't members of the panel going to ask me any questions?"

The chairperson responded. "We're satisfied that the two opposing counsel covered the important issues. We're grateful to you for your patience and your contribution."

Pauling smiled indulgently. "It was a pleasure for me to be here and to talk with you, and I am glad to have had the opportunity."

After five-and-a-half hours of testimony, broken up only by a recess for lunch, the entire group respectfully stood as the octogenarian rose from the witness chair he had occupied all day long. Pauling had spoken eloquently and thoroughly, answering all questions, unless he genuinely did not recall something. Harris postulated that the committee members, themselves up in years, were wondering how well they would have held up under the same circumstances. Most impressively, no matter what the question, the veiled accusation or threat, Pauling never once showed a hint of impatience, anger, or hostility. Certainly, Harris thought, the judge and the panel members would make comparisons between Levin's prominent witness and the irascible Victor Herbert. In any event, Harris was quite sure that everyone present, including himself, would remember spending such a huge amount of time in the presence of genius, in the same room as one of the greatest Nobel laureates the world had ever known. *What a day!*

CHAPTER 21

At the end of each afternoon of testimony, it was incumbent upon the administrative law judge to set several future hearing dates. Storch always attempted to gain consensus from the committee members who, naturally, had other obligations. There were times that it was inconvenient for one of the attorneys to be present, so their schedules were also taken into account. However, neither the judge, nor the committee, nor the prosecutor ever asked or cared whether a date was convenient for the accused; so Warren Levin constantly worked around everyone else's plans. In the meantime, he struggled to keep both his medical practice and his family life viable.

Since the memorable day that Linus Pauling testified, there had been other conferences and days of testimony that involved Harris and Levin's presence at the OPMC hearings. Today was such a day. Harris was engaged in another *voir dire* session with Victor Herbert and currently having a disagreement with Terrence Sheehan. Herbert had, once again, attacked Levin, offering into evidence an article to support his viewpoint; but Harris was determined not to let the flimsy attempt succeed. The publication Herbert was pushing was simply not on *the list*.

Harris addressed Sheehan. "The opinion of the American College of Physicians is clearly promulgated as the position of a subcommittee of their board. *The Harvard Medical School Health Letter* is attributed to *no one*."

"That is a lie, counselor!" shouted Victor Herbert, shooting up from the witness chair. "It is attributed to Harvard Medical School!"

"Dr. Herbert, please," said Storch, holding a palm out toward the witness. The judge was all too familiar with how quickly emotional escalation in this hearing tended to move toward chaos.

Herbert sat back down, his breathing audible, his fists clenched. Harris continued his former argument, addressing the committee. "The fact of the matter is that, while *some* of the things that come from Harvard Medical School are worthwhile, some of those things are *wrong*. We have a witness here," he said, pointing disdainfully at Herbert, "who says, *'I have expertise! I am going to speak my mind!'"* Levin wondered if his lawyer would be reprimanded for his mocking tone and was relieved when the moment passed. "The difference is that *legitimate* journals *cite* the research upon which opinion is based. Whether they are right or wrong is irrelevant."

"Mr. Sheehan?" asked Storch.

Sheehan nodded at the judge. "If it turns out to be wrong, as Mr. Harris said, he is entitled to produce the evidence, which will be introduced for the panel's review." Sheehan then asked the Court's permission to ask the witness a question.

"Go ahead."

"Dr. Herbert, could you tell us whether the *Harvard Medical School Health Letter* is or is not peer-reviewed? Mr. Harris says it isn't."

"Yes, it *is* peer-reviewed." Herbert snapped.

"How is it done?"

"The editor, Bill Bennett, who is a *colleague and friend*," he added, fixing Harris with a withering look, "sends each assigned article out for peer review by experts in the area of the article, and those experts correct any errors and cite the literature to the person who has the final responsibility for completing the article. The experts also make a determination and inform the editor about the article's scientific soundness."

Sheehan continued his direct examination. "Is it or is it not the same procedure that is followed in peer-reviewed journals?"

"It is peer-reviewed!"

"Doctor, let me complete my question," responded Sheehan, proceeding to repeat the identical question and eliciting an identical answer. "Therefore, Dr. Herbert, the only reason that this publication is not listed in the book of peer-review journals is what?"

"It is *not* a journal," Herbert told him, in a mocking, sing-song voice.

"Fine," Sheehan said. "I would offer this into evidence."

Harris stood before Storch. "Judge, the list that I have is a list prepared by the U.S. Department of Commerce's National Technical Information Service. It is entitled, 'List of Serials,' and it *does* contain a number of medical letters as being peer-reviewed. There is *no listing* for the *Harvard Medical School Health Letter*; and this list, put out by the government as comprehensive, covers *every* peer-reviewed serial, *not journal*, in the *entire world*. While I wouldn't want the U.S. government to contradict this witness," he said, sarcastically, indicating Herbert with a gesture of his right thumb over his shoulder, "the fact is that they *do*."

Storch nodded. "Very well." The judge noticed that Victor Herbert got up, walked over to Sheehan, and was engaged in a discussion with the prosecutor. "Dr. Herbert, please *sit down*. Do *not* confer with counsel for the Department in the midst of your testimony. *Do not do it!*"

Herbert stood still and glared at Storch. *"Defense counsel is deceiving the Court!"* he shouted, angrily. Then he walked back to the witness chair and sat down.

Sheehan stepped in, attempting to maintain decorum. "I conferred with Dr. Herbert a second ago, and he...he may have misled me..."

"Stay put in that chair!" Storch interrupted, his attention once again diverted by Herbert's attempt to rise. "*Don't* get up. You are in the middle of testifying. *Don't* ask questions of counsel. Sit *quietly* until I make a ruling."

Harris glanced at Levin, who had deliberately lowered his face over the papers in front of him to hide his smile. Neither of them had heard the judge raise his voice to quite that level before. His admonishments tended to be briefer, as well. *Beautiful, beautiful, keep it up, Victor!*

Herbert thought better of continuing what he had started. "All right," he muttered, his manner deceptively compliant.

Storch made his ruling. "While I am a little concerned about the fact that there is *no* direct author identified for the piece," he said, "I will let the article in for what it is worth. It becomes a question of the weight that will be attributed to it by the Hearing Committee."

Sheehan then moved to admit into evidence three peer-review articles Herbert had handed to him, asking Harris's permission to do so. Harris agreed on the first two but argued the third.

"This witness, as a part of his testimony, is offering an article which *describes* two cases," the defense lawyer stated, "and that is being presented as an *authoritative* article...the authority being the very thing that the state's witness has said is *worthless*, again and again."

"That can be done on cross," said Sheehan. "But I don't hear an objection as to its admissibility."

"Let me hear him out, Mr. Sheehan," the judge said.

Harris decided to point out the obvious to the panel members. "I guess, in the sense that this witness is now *changing his point of view* by offering this, I have no problem with it. We have no problem with accepting two *anecdotal* indications as *proof* of a proposition." Harris figured that this statement would serve his client in good stead later in the hearings.

"I take that as a lack of an objection," Storch clarified.

"It *is* a lack of an objection. In fact, it is an *endorsement* of the general proposition."

"Fifty, fifty-one, and fifty-two are all received in evidence," Storch intoned.

Sheehan returned to his direct examination of the witness, doing his best to discredit Levin's use of a number of diagnostic tests performed on the patient under discussion.

"One other thing, Dr. Herbert, before we proceed to the next patient. Could you tell us whether or not the *cytotoxic test* is or is not permitted to be performed by laboratories licensed by the state of New York?"

"It is prohibited."

"Could you tell us whether or not the *hair analysis test* is or is not permitted to be performed by laboratories licensed by the state of New York?"

"It is prohibited."

"Does New York State *prohibit* out-of-state labs to perform those *same* tests on specimens forwarded from patients residing in New York State?"

"Yes."

Harris was back on his feet. *"Objection!"*

"Wait," the judge instructed Sheehan. Turning to Harris, he asked, "Do you want to put your objection on the record?"

Harris didn't bother responding to the judge's question. "He has to be qualified as an expert on conflicts of law and constitutional law before he can testify as to the efficacy of a pronouncement from New York State regarding what laboratories in a sister state can do," Harris told him, referring to Victor Herbert.

Sheehan answered Harris. "That would be true if the witness was only basing his testimony on his *legal* knowledge," he began. "If he is basing his testimony on a *fact* that he is aware of, namely a state action by New York State against a lab in another state, he is then just giving *factual* information to the panel."

"He didn't *ask* that question," Harris told the judge.

"Why don't we find that out?" was the judge's suggestion.

Sheehan resumed, addressing Herbert. "Are you *aware* of an instance, to your knowledge, where the state of New York obtained an *injunction* against a laboratory located in a state *other* than New York from performing chelation or hair analysis tests on specimens forwarded to that out-of-state lab from patients residing in New York State?"

"Objection!"

Sheehan appeared puzzled. "That was the question the Hearing Officer said I could ask."

The chairperson of the committee intervened, clarifying the issue for Sheehan. "I think there is a problem with your language: 'performing chelation,' you said."

Sheehan acknowledged his error, which Harris was quite certain was a deliberate "slip of the tongue" in an effort to slide in a reference to Chelation therapy, a procedure the Office of Professional Medical Conduct found so objectionable.

Sheehan then rephrased the question for the witness, who referred in his answer to a laboratory in Chicago.

Harris sniffed. "We concede at one time the state of New York beat a laboratory in Chicago into the ground economically, thus establishing a decision which has been applied nowhere else in the country. But to ask this witness to draw the *legal* conclusion that New York is able to promulgate a regulation which binds the behavior of laboratories *all across this country?* That's an exercise in fantasy!"

The issue died right then and there, and Sheehan decided to examine the case of the next patient on the list, asking for the questionnaire that Levin had introduced regarding that patient at a prior hearing.

Harris broke in. "In the interest of the conservation of time ..."

"I object!" Sheehan interrupted. "Mr. Harris is, once again, going to state, *'I will concede that Dr. Herbert says everything negative about my client's case.'* He has done that every day, and he has been told *not* to do it."

"*No one* told me not to do it," Harris countered. "There is no question that Dr. Herbert has shown time and again that *every single thing* that Dr. Levin did in terms of intake, analysis, charting, diagnosis, and treatment is negative and worthless. Let's accept it as his testimony and send him home," he added, flippantly.

Sheehan sniffed at the remark but was not deterred. "First of all, Doctor, this is a questionnaire that you did *not* see before. If you could please take a look at it briefly, especially the complaints on the first page, I would appreciate it."

Sheehan gave Herbert a few moments.

"Doctor, you were not here when this patient testified. Assuming that the patient complained of many years of severe diarrhea, from which he felt debilitated and nervous and anxious and irritable, was the glucose tolerance test that was done for this patient, in your professional opinion, medically indicated?"

"It was *not* indicated for this patient," was Herbert's immediate response.

"Briefly, could you tell us the reason *why* it wasn't?"

"The questionnaire here, which Dr. Levin gave to the patient, is a good questionnaire and it asks a lot of appropriate questions, including family history. But there is *no* family history of diabetes or low blood sugar—except for diabetes in a grandparent, so a routine fasting blood sugar would have been sufficient. Doing a glucose tolerance test would be an exercise in futility. It would be *useless*." Herbert's countenance was fixed in a smug look, one he seemed to favor every time he fired a shot at the Respondent.

"My next question concerns the cytotoxic test. Was it medically indicated?"

"It is *never* indicated. It is a *worthless* test," Herbert spat.

Sheehan continued. "Darkfield Microscopic exam. Indicated for this patient?"

"No! *No!*"

"Dr. Herbert, the RAST test is a legitimate allergy test, isn't it?"

"Yes."

"It was, in your opinion, indicated for this patient on this date, correct?"

"Correct. And it was logically ordered because Dr. Levin's questionnaire has in its allergy section: 'Do any foods cause frequent soft stools or diarrhea,' and the patient checked 'yes.' Also, the patient says at the beginning that one of his complaints is irritable bowel, so it was a perfectly appropriate test in accordance with the information Dr. Levin elicited from the patient."

"The next subject is the gastric analysis using the Heidelberg capsule. My question to you is: Would that test be medically indicated for this patient?"

"Absolutely not!"

Harris recalled how fascinated he had been when Levin had given him a tutorial on the interesting state-of-the-art diagnostic tool designed to measure the pH levels in a patient's digestive tract. The patient merely had to swallow the vitamin-sized capsule to deliver an accurate result to a doctor from this non-invasive test, rather than suffering the traumatizing and invasive insertion of a nasal-gastric tube or endoscope. One single grain of salt within the capsule is the electrolyte that "powers" it once the capsule is activated, and a graph on a monitor visually displays the pH levels and the re-acidification time of the stomach's parietal cells.

"Dr. Herbert," said Sheehan, "you have previously testified about that test in your testimony, and your testimony is the same?"

"Yes."

"With respect to the current patient, was the hair analysis ordered by the Respondent indicated?

"There was *no* basis whatsoever for it in the questionnaire or anywhere."

"Doctor, let's assume that the patient testified that the Respondent diagnosed him with *candida albicans*. Do you find any basis for that diagnosis?"

"There is *no* basis whatsoever in the answers to these questions in the questionnaire for making such a diagnosis. In the 'Allergy' section, the patient checked off 'yes' to the question: 'Do any foods cause fatigue, sleepiness, and rapid pulse?' Now, proponents of this generally *fraudulent* diagnosis take that as diagnostic for this syndrome when, in fact, it is usually diagnostic of a *psychiatric* condition, which in the vast majority of cases turns out to be depression."

"Doctor, the drug Nystatin was prescribed for this condition. Was that drug indicated, in your opinion?"

"No, it was *contraindicated*. Nystatin is a very dangerous drug and should not be given to anybody unless they have a true yeast infection, with pathology from the yeast, with the yeast doing harm, as I testified previously."

"I would like to show you a page from the Petitioner's exhibit and direct your attention to the portion of that page that lists a number of supplements. Were those supplements indicated in the treatment of this patient?"

"*Not one* was indicated. All this stuff is basically *junk* and would do the patient no good, and some of it could have done harm."

Harris would cross-examine the witness after the lunch break, Levin knew. He hoped that his lawyer was successful in undoing whatever harm Herbert's testimony may have done during the morning session. He and Harris conferred over lunch and returned to the hearing room refreshed and ready.

Harris approached the witness. "Dr. Herbert, you testified this morning about Evening Primrose Oil. You said it was worthless therapy, is that correct?"

"*No*. Why don't you play back my testimony, Mr. Harris, instead of *lying* about it?"

The judge didn't want things to escalate again. "Dr. Herbert, we can't just *play back* the testimony. And *without* your characterization of him, Mr. Harris is attempting to recant your line of testimony. You want to repeat the question, Mr. Harris?"

"All right, Judge. Dr. Herbert, is Evening Primrose Oil an essential fatty acid?"

"Evening Primrose Oil is *not* an essential fatty acid. However, a content of it, called linoleic acid may be, although there is some question about it."

Levin began writing on his pad. *Evening Primrose Oil contains substantial amounts of* gamma-*linolenic acid—one of the polyunsaturated omega-6 fatty acids, that are one group of the essential fatty acids (EFAs) which are needed by the body to regulate a number of activities, including insulin utilization, heart function, and mood. Since the body cannot produce EFAs, they must be ingested through proper diet or supplementation.*

Harris asked for a moment to confer with his client, stepped over to the defense table to read what Levin had written, and immediately went back to work on Victor Herbert. This was how the defense team of Harris and Levin had been operating up to now, and the results had often been worth it. However much Herbert would say to discredit the doctor fighting valiantly to save his license was how much harder the defense would fight to attack Herbert's credibility, using proven medical knowledge and solid information during cross-examination.

By the end of the day, the page count from the testimony of the hearings that had begun last year would be up to twenty-five hundred. And the proceedings weren't even half over.

CHAPTER 22

With Victor Herbert's testimony firmly entrenched in Levin's gut, he and Susan had talked far into the night. The doctor had an idea and wanted to share it with his wife. The plan had a two-fold purpose: to allow Levin to truly be heard—to tell the entire story of his saga, his painful odyssey; and to accelerate their fund-raising efforts as the proceedings continued and their coffers were slowly emptied.

The next morning, when one of his patients called in to cancel an appointment due to illness, Levin immediately got on the phone. "Greg, this is Dr. Warren Levin, one of your best customers!" he said with a laugh. Greg owned InstaTape, the company that created the audiocassette tapes Levin made for his patients. The doctor found that these tapes were useful in reinforcing the principles of good health his practice espoused and strengthening the doctor-patient collaborative bond that was so essential for promoting general wellness. Joe's firm also taped the lectures given at the alternative medical meetings Levin attended, and the doctor always bought the tapes if he missed a meeting.

"I need to make a tape, Joe, different from *anything* I've done before." Levin proceeded to explain that he was planning to do something unheard of within the medical world, something more outrageous than the soul-bearing newsletter, followed by the lengthy letter, he had already sent to colleagues, friends, and patients. He now wanted to create an audiotape that would literally open the doors, figuratively speaking, to the very hearing room where his detractors lay in waiting, armed with weapons of destruction, to strip him of his dignity and medical license. Levin had decided to compile a compelling saga, fortified with selected pages from the court transcripts that now occupied over eighteen inches of shelf space in the bookcase of his home office.

Greg sounded appropriately shocked. While he knew Levin was under fire, he hadn't realized how persistent the efforts had been to drum him out of the profession. "Dr. Levin, I'm really sorry to hear about this," Greg said, sincerely, "This is really important." Greg added. Just send me a Master Copy—and GO FOR IT!

When Levin hung up the phone, he updated the journal he had been keeping throughout the grueling process, something he had done from the moment he decided to fight New York State. So he spent these precious free moments bringing everything up to date. After that, he carefully arranged the copies he had made of select pages from the monstrous collection created by the court stenographer.

He picked up his Montblanc pen to begin writing again, noting it's perfectly ground nib. He looked at the finely-crafted white star on its cap. He recalled his father, a graduate of the same medical school Levin had attended, giving him this pen as a gift the day Levin graduated, so that the first time he signed his name, with the designation M.D. following, he would do so with this fine writing instrument. Staring at the star, Levin remembered his father telling him, "You know, Warren, there's a story that's been going around—we don't really know if it's true or not—that a Jew designed this pen for Adolph Hitler so that, without ever knowing it, Hitler was carrying around the Jewish Star of David in his pocket." As Levin reminisced, his eyes misted over, and he wondered what his father would think if he knew how the type of medicine his son had embraced long after graduation would bring him to the forefront of a battle for its continued existence in New York State and, perhaps, elsewhere in the country.

He began to write the paragraphs that would connect one page of testimony to the next. He was determined to make that recording immediately. Joe was expecting him at the studio tomorrow afternoon.

"Hi," he began in a clear, precise voice, "I'm Doctor Warren Levin, and this cassette is a 'Call to Arms' to everyone listening who cares about the rights of patients to choose the kind of medical care they want for themselves and their loved ones. I hope to convince you that this *is* the time for an offensive against the drug-oriented, pharmaceutically funded medical establishment, because we have created a major beachhead, and we can't let the PANIC in American medicine go unexploited." Levin thought of Greg who, like him, would soon be wearing headphones. Greg would be spinning dials furiously on his console, working to get just the right, interference-free clarity and depth of vocal register that would lend additional weight to this serious tape. Levin smiled in anticipation."PANIC is an acronym," Levin stated, reading from the script he had prepared. "P is for Perfidy. A is for Arrogance. N is for Nepotism. I is for Ignorance. And C is for Collusion. Those are serious charges, and this tape provides the evidence.

"The reason that I'm issuing this call is that 18 months ago, I had what seems to be the dubious honor of being selected as the test case in New York for medical policy across the nation. The Office of Professional Medical Conduct culminated a ten-year-old investigation by bringing me up on charges of *fraud* because of my orthomolecular, nutritional, ecological approach to the practice of medicine. Now, after a year and a half of hearings, I *know* that I am privileged to be representing this minority approach, and I want to share with you my excitement about our opportunity to stake out, once and for all, a territory of our own in American medical care, based on solid science, which is now finally being admitted into evidence, thanks to the serious miscalculations of the powers that be in New York!" he said with a flourish.

Levin continued to present the case and its history in great detail. Not to be lost on Greg was Levin's announcement, for the first time anywhere, of the formation of a Medical *Offense*, not *Defense*, Fund, having the objective of collecting the necessary monies to continue to fight all the way to victory, no matter how painful or long the battle.

"Dr. Levin," Greg told him, after completing the time-consuming job and in sympathy for all he had just heard, "I will make as many tapes as you need and keep making more as you run out of them. And, not only that...not only that," Greg restated, his voice breaking, "I'm not going to charge you a penny." Before Levin could open his mouth to protest, Greg stopped him. "I've known you for years, Dr. Levin, and I've recorded your tapes and a lot of your speeches, so I think I know what you're all about. You're a decent guy. This shouldn't be happening to you. Maybe I can't contribute the kind of money to your fund that would make a difference, but what I *can* do," he said, nodding with resolve, "is make the tapes, keep making the tapes, and send them out—at *my* expense—to all of the doctors on the mailing lists of the organizations I service...and to anyone else, patients, family members, friends, colleagues, neighbors, whoever you want, once you give me their names and addresses."

"Greg, I don't know what to say," Levin responded, hardly expecting this outcome. "I'm really touched...and very, very appreciative. I'm honored that you feel that way about me, and I'll gladly accept your offer. Thank you, Greg. Thank you very much."

When Bob Harris received his copy of the tape, he brought it to the conference room, where a cassette tape player had been set up. The firm's lawyers listened, with interest, as the doctor spoke.

> *You see, MY case is unique in the following three ways: No other practitioner has ever been charged with SO many allegations in a single case. Virtually everything I do which differentiates my practice from the establishment's medical approach was placed on the block as a specific charge with both diagnostic and treatment protocols being interpreted as not medically indicated, unnecessary, and therefore fraudulent.*
>
> *In choosing me, the state had assumed that I was just another individual practition with no support system. I feel that I was fortunate in having accumulated, over many years of this kind of practice, a unique history—being elected to the boards of more alternative medical societies than almost anybody else in the country. I can therefore justifiably claim to be a spokesperson for that significant minority.*
>
> *There was a most extraordinary error on the part of the state which was to bring only ONE witness to testify in this case, and that was Victor Herbert—who is not only an M.D. and an attorney but happens to be a "rabble-rousing demagogue" who constantly speaks about the importance of science and double-blind studies when he is criticizing holistic medicine and then spouts meaningless and fancifully fabricated statistics as he attacks.*

Harris stopped the tape in response to one of the associate's frantic hand motions. "Can he say that?" the young lawyer asked.

"Can he say what?" Harris asked.

"You know that stuff about Victor Herbert."

Harris shrugged. "He just did!" was Harris's response. He knew what the guy meant, of course. What legal ramifications could the distribution of such a tape, making slanderous comments about a sue-happy doctor/lawyer have for Warren

Levin? That could be another bridge in the endless series of bridges to be crossed in the future, Harris reckoned.

After dinner, Levin and his wife went into his comfortable office. Without further ado, he pressed the "play" button on the machine, and they sat back listening to his words.

> *About a year ago, I had asked for help for the Warren M. Levin Legal Defense Fund so that I could expose the ignorance and the perfidy of Dr. Herbert, a man who is unaccountably held in the highest esteem by the medical establishment. I also said that we would be guaranteed, at last, an opportunity to present OUR side of the issues in a forum where we would ultimately be heard.*
>
> *My message today is that I believe I have fully succeeded in the initial phase of that quest. Namely, I have been able to get Victor Herbert's sworn testimony on record, and it is just as I had predicted: full of ignorance and full of lies!*
>
> *That's why this case has become so important to all of us and why I think, instead of having a Warren M. Levin Legal Defense Fund, it is time to put our united weight behind the "Legal Offense Fund." It is not a new notion that the best defense is a good offense, but as I am dictating this, my hearings—after 15 months—have proceeded through a very circuitous course to the point at which the state has just rested its case, and we are finally ready to get into defending all of the charges brought against me.*
>
> *So, the state has fired all its ammunition, through their BIGGEST hired gun, and he has backfired! Because of his overblown ego, Victor Herbert's testimony has burst like bubble gum over the face of the witness and splattered the faces of the state's attorney and the medical orthodoxy they represent.*

Susan's face took on a look of worry, and her concern was the same as the neophyte lawyer's had been. Would there be repercussions from her husband's recorded words vilifying Victor Herbert?

Dr. Serafina Corsello's staff had already left the office for the day. She placed the glass mug of steaming green tea on the low table in front of the couch in her private sanctuary, sinking comfortably into the plush cushions. She started her cassette tape player.

> *You know, it really is an accomplishment to obtain degrees in both medicine and law. But Herbert's* curriculum vitae *go far beyond that. It is an awesome document to the uninitiated. It is over sixty typed pages and lists two specialty certifications, membership in twenty-two professional societies, nine editorial boards, and fourteen consultancies, with over six-hundred scientific publications. And Herbert, in his sworn testimony, states that all of his scientific publications are either in books or peer-reviewed journals. That quote can be found on page 108 of the official transcript of my hearing, which is the source of all future references to page numbers. Unfortunately, perusal of his document shows that this is not the case, unless MS. MAGAZINE and WOMEN'S WORLD have recently been added to the Index Medicus! It is one of many fabrications that Herbert creates during his testimony as an expert witness, sworn to tell the truth, sworn to speak of science, and to differentiate fact from opinion.*
>
> *In addition, by virtue of his active appointment to the New York Bar, he is performing, in the witness stand, as an Officer of the Court—and he must accept the increased level of responsibility for integrity that goes with the honor of multiple post-graduate degrees. It is a travesty, therefore, that he tarnishes those achievements by his inability to control his personal agenda, his vindictive pursuit of anyone painted by his broad brush as using what he euphemistically calls "questionable practices."*
>
> *So, you're going to hear what the official transcript of the hearings thus far has to show for the state's case and what it also shows about the level of PANIC in the American establishment of medicine as personified by Victor Herbert. He is the epitome of everything bad in American medical politics today, and he has demonstrated so many times, in the seven days of his testimony against me, that there isn't a credible scientist from any field in—or related to—medicine who could stand up before a tribunal of judges with any kind of integrity and defend the horrendous allegations that he has made under oath. Besides, as my attorney has repeatedly pointed*

out, he should be testifying to the truth and not against me. And, if I'm wrong about it, and if they do find someone else who is willing to support the perfidious nature of his testimony, well, it just further compounds the guilt of the system in power, and it will come out.

Having had her own troubles with both Victor Herbert and the OPMC, Dr. Corsello sank deeper into the cushions, a smile of satisfaction on her face, and continued to sip her tea. She wanted to shake Warren Levin's hand. Dr. Robert Atkins had just signed off his radio program and was about to leave the station when he remembered the cassette tape in his pocket. He went into the first empty office that had a cassette tape player and closed the door. The station would be open and broadcasting for a few hours more, he knew, so he had time. He heard Warren Levin's voice, which he recognized from the numerous meetings they had attended together and from the many presentations he had heard the doctor make in the past.

At the end of this tape, I will read verbatim some, only some, of the unbelievable and, in my opinion, indefensible statements of America's self-anointed, self-appointed QUACKBUSTER, Victor Herbert, M.D., J.D., made under oath. You will hear Herbert's ignorance about subjects ranging from adrenal function and corticosteroid therapy to RNA, through an incredible confabulation about the FDA's reports on adverse effects of drugs, in which he actually says that a single case report of a complication is PROOF that a drug is dangerous. He lies about cytotoxic testing and about his not being paid to testify when, in fact, he was. He misrepresents a basic electrocardiograph interpretation. You will hear enough, I assure you, to understand what perfidy means and why we should stalk our wounded quarry and spread his naked ignorance in full view, so that once and for all the establishment will have to repudiate its chief standard-bearer or share his shame.

As I'm dictating this, I have already spent more than two days on the stand, and I feel my presentation is open to debate, because I have spoken fairly, as if it is indeed debatable; whereas the state's witness has demonstrated his willingness innumerable times to state his beliefs as though they were scientific facts, as immutable and unarguable. And that aspect of his testimony, repeated over and over again, clearly creates an indefensible position for a sworn witness to scientific truth.

However, for the full and proper establishment of an unimpeachable record, it is necessary for me to produce other expert witnesses, who will testify from their credentialed positions, that most of Herbert's dogma is debatable, and much of his so-called factual information is downright erroneous. And I have a stellar array of colleagues, with outstanding academic credentials, who have already agreed to support me in exposing the ignorance and perfidy of Dr. Herbert. To name just a few: Dr. James Carter, Chief of the Department of Nutrition at Tulane and author of a double-blind, placebo-controlled study of chelation therapy; Neil Solomon, who was Commissioner of the Department of Health of the state of Maryland for ten years; Emmanuel Cheraskin, M.D., D.M.D., an emeritus professor from Alabama Medical School; Jeff Bland, Ph.D., President of HealthCom; Abe Hoffer, M.D., who carried out the first double-blind, placebo-controlled study of megavitamin therapy in schizophrenia over 25 years ago; H. Richard Casdorph, M.D., Ph.D., past president of ACAM, and Chief of Cardiology in his community hospital; Russell Jaffee, M.D., Ph.D., Director of the Princeton Brain Bio-Center; Ralph Lev, M.D., a board-certified vascular surgeon and member of the Board of Examiners of the state of New Jersey and the Board of ACAM; Majid Ali, M.D., whose credentials in Allergy and Pathology are impeccable; and Linus Pauling, Ph.D., the two-time Nobel Prize recipient. And, if that's not enough for them, we have many more that are happy to testify. That's what I mean by unimpeachable defense.

Atkins was impressed with the fine group of supporters that Levin had been able to assemble in his defense. He laughed softly to himself, considering how his colleague hadn't minced words one bit in his characterization of Victor Herbert.

Peggy, Levin's receptionist had taken a copy of the tape home with her at her employer's urging. She stayed up well past her bedtime listening to it. While she was more familiar with the details than most of the other staff members, having assisted with letters and newsletter preparation and mailing, she realized that the scope of the doctor's situation was more far-reaching than she had ever imagined.

Then comes the offense. The entire story, with all its twists and turns, must be disseminated, first to the great American public and then, also, to our legislators. Now the issue of funding for the experts and for the enormous cost of the public relations and lobbying campaigns creates an urgent demand for contributions from anyone affected: patients who would be deprived of their right of choice; physicians, restricted in their right to practice; vitamin manufacturers and distributors whose businesses are in jeopardy; and anyone who believes in freedom in America.

Peggy listened, open-mouthed, as the doctor reviewed the entire case, going all the way back to 1980, when he received the first subpoena. His office was in Brooklyn at that time, and she hadn't been the office receptionist, so she was hearing much of the background for the first time. While she was the one who had met Robert Harris when the attorney first came into the office to interview patients, she now heard details of the vital role he was playing in Levin's defense. She listened to the details of the initial *voir dire* session Harris had conducted with Victor Herbert, she learned about Herbert's ejection from the hearing room for not obeying the judge's order to answer a critical question put to him, she learned that the famed Linus Pauling had testified on behalf of her employer—and was then treated to actual quotes from the transcripts. Peggy now understood why, so many times over the past year and a half, Levin had walked into the office, his cheerful personality muted. She knew that he had come straight from the hearing room on those days but little else. Now, she understood the depth of issue at hand.

Abram Hoffer's good friend, a cardiologist, was in town for a conference. Hoffer asked him to stop by his psychiatric office at noon. "Jim," Hoffer said, "do you remember that doctor I flew into New York to testify for a few months ago?"

"Wasn't he an alternative practitioner?" his friend inquired.

"Yes…and he still *is*," Hoffer responded, laughing. "Anyhow, the reason I asked you to join me for lunch at my office was because I have something I wanted you to hear. You might find it entertaining." They opened the wrappers on their sandwiches and put straws into their drinks. Hoffer popped Levin's tape into the player.

So that's where we are as I dictate this tape, and with that background, turn up the volume so you don't miss a word as I quote chapter and verse from Victor Herbert's sworn testimony. Talk about ignorance, listen to this! I've been accused of prescribing RNA: fraudulent. The prosecutor says, "Dr. Herbert, do you know what that is?" He says, "Yes." "Would you tell the panel, please?" He says, "It is ribonucleic acid pills." "What is that?" "Ribonucleic acid is represented by proponents of 'nutrition nonsense' as a cure for defects in the human blueprint."

And then he goes on to talk about the difference between RNA and DNA, saying, "Now the RNA that the proponents of 'nutrition nonsense' give their patients is usually sardine RNA." At that point, Mr. Harris says, "Objection! It is inappropriate for a witness to characterize practices as 'nonsense' or any of that type of editorial verbiage. This man is ostensibly here to inform the panel as to medical efficacy and medical inappropriateness, and the editorializing is certainly not helpful and may be damaging to my client by setting a constant and continuous tone at a time when he is not able to speak up to defend himself."

Well, the prosecutor argues about it, but the judge says, "I agree with Mr. Harris. I am going to instruct the witness again," (It's a lot of times he's been instructed.) "to leave out the editorial analysis. Dr. Herbert, you are here to answer questions and to render your expert opinion but without unnecessarily editorializing and characterizing either the respondent or the types of medicine that are at issue." Sheehan argues again that he should be able to give editorials, and the judge says, "There is a difference between editorializing and offering expert opinion."

On page 350, in the effort to prove that the sardine RNA or non-human RNA administered by mouth has no value to human beings, Herbert answers, "It is worthless, because as soon as RNA, any RNA, from any animal or any fish, hits the upper small bowel, it is digested by a pancreatic enzyme called pancreatic ribonuclease. It is completely broken down. It is the breakdown product that is the individual amino acids and the individual bases that are then absorbed." Well, as Linus Pauling later testified, any school child today knows that there are no amino acids in RNA!

We gave Dr. Herbert a chance to correct that error, just in case he had misspoken. Mr. Harris asked him what the amino acids were in RNA, and he couldn't correct himself. He still maintained that there are amino acid residues after the digestion of RNA. This is a world-class nutritionist, ladies and gentlemen. As Mr. Harris says, "He's a legend in his own mind!" I think it's a great line.

Herbert is on direct testimony, being questioned by the state's attorney, page 771. Mr. Sheehan: "Can you interpret that EKG, and tell us if it is suggestive of a heart block?" Now, I must tell you that the state has already accused me of making an erroneous diagnosis without having the chart. They trumped up the charge. All they had were insurance forms. I don't know how in the world they could have decided, without looking at the EKG, that the diagnosis was in error, but that was one of their specific charges.

Now, Herbert has to come and support that, because when we began the hearings, we did turn over the charts to the state, and they did not withdraw or amend the charges in the ensuing eight months. Herbert's answer is, "It is a low-voltage EKG. The voltage is sufficiently low that I can't tell whether or not there is a heart block." Well, let me tell you, I freaked out because, first of all, I don't agree that it's a low voltage EKG, but that's certainly open to some sort of interpretation. However, the voltage on an EKG has absolutely nothing to do with whether you can make the diagnosis of a heart block, when you can measure a particular time interval, the PR interval, which was very clear on this EKG in Lead Two, which is the best lead to make the diagnosis from in most cases and which was not low voltage.

Now, you must remember Mr. Harris is not a doctor. And when he first saw the charges against me, and I said to him, "Bob, this guy had a first-degree heart block! How can they say he didn't when they don't even have the chart?" He wasn't sure that I knew what I was talking about. We had just met, and at that time I was just another client that he was hired to protect, so I gave him a fifteen-minute dissertation on the EKG, and that fifteen-minute dissertation was enough for him to show Herbert's ignorance when he got him on cross-examination. Listen to these interchanges. I am now reading from page 811, just after that whole business with the fee for Herbert's testimony.

***Harris:* "*Doctor, I am going to ask you, because I'm not a doctor. Low voltage: that refers to the voltage emanating from the patient's heart. Is that correct?"*

Herbert: *"Not necessarily. It relates to the current applied across the leads, so that the person doing the EKG should have simply jacked up the current on the instrument that was making the recording. But, you know, it is an acceptable recording."*

Harris: *"These EKG amplitudes are standardized, are they not, before the test is done?"*

Herbert: *"Yes."*

Harris: *"If you take a look at Lead One before the beginning of the tracing, isn't there a standard? Aren't the first three indications of amplitude an indication of standards?"*

Herbert: *"No, that's the end of the standardization recording. It has been cut off, as you can see. All of that is nonsense."*

Harris: *"You say that 'low voltage' refers to the amount of current applied to the leads?"*

Herbert: *"It is the combination of the machine and the patient's heart together."*

Harris: *"Doctor, how much current is normally applied to EKG leads?"*

Herbert: *"Uh, very little."*

Harris: *"Is it zero?"*

Herbert: *"It is not zero. No."*

Harris: *"How much is it?"*

Herbert: *"I couldn't tell you."*

Ladies and gentlemen, the one thing that we are often called on to reassure our patients about is that the electrocardiogram does NOT apply any current to leads, that all of the current is coming from the patient's heart, and it's merely being recorded by the machine. It is possible to increase the sensitivity, but no current is applied to the leads.

Harris: *"Doctor, once again, the same question: Is it fair to say a low voltage EKG refers to the amount of electricity emanating from the patient's heart?"*

Herbert: *"In part, is the answer."*

Harris: *"Uh, is it fair to say that the lower the voltage emanating from the patient's heart, the lower will be the amplitude on the EKG tracing?"*

Herbert: *"Of course."*

Harris: *"But that phenomenon which would affect amplitude, is it your point of view that it has any effect on timing?"*

Herbert: *"No, it doesn't."*

Harris: *"Doctor, would you please define for me what 'first-degree heart block' is?"*

Herbert: *"It is defined as voltage not getting, uh, voltage not getting through because of some block in the transmission of the current, and you can see that here. But the question is..."*

Harris: *"Just answer my question as I asked it, all right?"*

Herbert: *"Yes."*

Harris: *"Electrocardiographically, how is 'first-degree heart block' defined?"*

Herbert: *"It is defined as 'a change in an interval, a change in the PR interval.'"*

Harris: *"The word 'interval' means 'time.' 'PR interval' is the 'time between the P and the R sensations of the heart.'"*

Herbert: *"Correct."*

Harris: *"What effect, then, would low voltage have on the measurement of the PR interval?"*

Herbert: *"When you have low amplitude, you can't see where it starts. You have low amplitude, but you can see a prolonged PR interval."*

Harris: *"Doctor, is there any evidence of low voltage in Lead Two?"*

Herbert: *"No, Lead Two is pretty good. There is low voltage in Lead Three."*

There is, then, a little altercation with the attorneys and so forth; and then Herbert continues.

Herbert: *"The problem with Lead Two is that after the heart block is shown...see, if you look at the record, you will see that you have the block here and you have an identification of amplitude here, but you don't have an indication of amplitude at the end. It was probably cut off. If I had an indication of the amplitude at the end, I would know whether it was first-degree heart block or low voltage."*

Harris: *"Is it fair to say that there is nothing in this tracing in Lead Two which causes any problem whatsoever in the diagnosis of first-degree heart block?"*

Herbert: *"Yes, that would be fair."*

Harris: *"Then why did you say in your previous testimony that you couldn't be certain? Because there was a low voltage tracing, and you weren't sure whether or not there was first-degree heart block. What was the point of testifying that way?"*

Herbert: *"If I said it that way, I misstated." (And then he goes on, and he says –) "What I meant to say was that this could be a run of low voltage rather than first-degree heart block."*

Harris: *"I see! But, in fact, it couldn't be, because we now agree that low voltage does not affect the PR interval?"*

Herbert: *"There is no PR interval in the [run] of block; the P is wiped out, which is what low voltage does also."*

At which point Harris gives up, and so do I.

Hoffer looked at Jim, who had been a cardiologist as long as Hoffer had been a psychiatrist. His friend was shaking his head in amazement. "On the basis of this type of testimony, they're trying to take Levin's license away?" Jim asked in amazement.

Hoffer just looked at him, not responding. No response was needed.

CHAPTER 23

"If I go into areas where I am not adequately trained, if I assume responsibility of care for patients where I don't have adequate knowledge, then indeed I am not in my integrity. And I go to great lengths to avoid that kind of conflict," Levin said, eyeing the members of the Hearing Panel, as he sat in the witness chair, responding to his defense attorney's question. The weeks and months were rolling by rapidly, and the hearings continued. At least, after every one-thousand pages or more of testimony, the doctor was given an opportunity to be heard by those who would pass judgment.

During redirect examination, Harris wondered aloud how Levin had changed his practice parameters over the years to reflect his ethical position.

"Let me explain something," Levin said, attempting to answer his attorney's question. "In my training, in the Navy, I read eighty-five thousand chest x-rays, so when a 76-year-old man would come into my private office, I believed a chest x-ray was an appropriate thing to do. However, I found that, too often, I was doing routine chest x-rays because I had to keep the machine occupied," he admitted, honestly. "I had to cover my costs. But I didn't *like* the feeling. See, when I left the Navy, the appropriate practice was to do a chest x-ray once a year on every officer and only every six years on the enlisted men. So, in my private practice, my objective was to treat my *patients* as though they were *officers*."

The panel members were aware of his early background from his *curriculum vitae*, which had been submitted into evidence early on in the hearing. After graduating from medical school, Levin had gone into internship at the U.S. Naval Hospital in Newport, Rhode Island, which is what he was referring to, taking a course in Photofluorographic Interpretation at the National Naval Medical Center in Bethesda, Maryland, the following year. He then served as the base radiologist in the United States Marine Corps at Camp Lejeune, North Carolina, prior to opening his private practice as a family physician in Staten Island, New York. He wanted them to understand how his initial experience had informed his early practice methodologies.

"Then," he continued, "I eliminated that lucrative income because I didn't want to be dealing with the problem it caused my integrity. In fact, the cancer screening test that I performed on the patient we've been discussing, due to his weight loss, was something I did fourteen years ago, in 1976. I had taken a weekend course to learn how to properly interpret that test, and I did it. However, I stopped using *that* test because I felt that the information I was getting didn't justify the cost to the patient and the alarm such a test sometimes created. He paused for a moment, thinking. "Medicine is a state-of-the-art profession. I continue to try to practice it the best I can."

Levin looked at the medical school professor seated at the committee's table. "Dr. McAloon, you asked me why I had performed the tests I did on this particular patient if I was planning to do Chelation therapy anyway. I'd like to answer that. The patient came in *requesting* Chelation therapy. When patients go to plastic surgeons and ask to have their breasts enlarged or reduced or their nose bobbed, it isn't *immoral* or *unethical* for that plastic surgeon to grant the request and do the procedure," he said, reasonably. "I strive to provide informed consent. In fact, I think I do that *more* than most practitioners I know. Over the years I have prepared papers for patients, explaining procedures, then discarding them as new and better procedures became available. It's been an enormous task but a labor of love. More doctors should be doing that."

Levin took a deep breath. He wanted to address the issue of Chelation therapy, and he saw that he still had everyone's attention. "As the *first* chelation physician in the state of New York, I happened to be involved in the politics surrounding it when we were struggling to create a protocol. In other words, we who believed in this treatment wanted this valuable treatment to be regulated, so as to avoid the problem of the unscrupulous profiteer who is just going to drip stuff into people's veins without caring for them properly. So I flew all over the country, spending days and days working over the protocol and the constitution and bylaws of our organization, which was then known as the American Academy of Medical Preventics but is now the American College for the Advancement of Medicine. I did all of that so that what we would offer the patient would be something meaningful. After all of that, how could I, in good conscience, *not* follow that protocol?"

Harris followed with, "What *is* that protocol, Dr. Levin?"

"It is included in one of the exhibits."

"Tell us what it says."

"It says that there is a basic workup that is important to evaluate the *status* of the patient. You need basic chemistries; you need to make sure the person is not anemic. Unfortunately, at times, I am forced to do things that I wouldn't consider really optimum in terms of cost-effectiveness to cover me against charges of not being thorough and complete and an adequate physician, and to also protect me from the possibility of malpractice that occurs if I *don't* get a good result. I don't think there is a doctor in this country who doesn't agonize over that kind of decision."

Harris probed further. "Are you saying that the testing you did was to *rule out* contraindications rather than to *rule in* indications for chelation?"

"*Objection!* Leading."

Storch said, "It *is* a leading question, Mr. Harris. However, *this* one I will allow. But let's try *not* to lead."

Levin knew that his answer needed to be as complete and thorough as possible. "I think if a patient comes in and asks for Chelation therapy, I have an obligation to check that person out to make sure that there is no contraindication. If, in the process, I find something *indicating* the treatment—something that the person's health insurance company will recognize, such as heavy metal poisoning—the patient benefits by the thoroughness of the evaluation. So there are economic factors involved in *all* of these decisions. It becomes a Catch-22, however, when the state accuses me of *fraud*, since fraud is a state of mind that *can't* be examined scientifically. As I looked at the panel's questions and knew that I had heard the same ones from Mr. Sheehan, who is trying to show my fraudulent intent, I thought, 'If I *am* a con man, then I am conning you.'"

"*I object!* I object and move to strike the Respondent's tautological critique of the motivation behind the panel's questioning. The witnesses are here to give *factual* testimony, not to engage in psychoanalysis of *why* people ask questions and give sworn testimony about that. That is *totally* improper testimony, I submit." Sheehan was really fuming.

"Would you like to say something, Mr. Harris?"

"I agree with him," Harris unexpectedly responded, lifting his chin toward the angry prosecutor.

The judge was surprised. "Wonderful! I will sustain the objection. I can't strike testimony, as you are well aware, Mr. Sheehan. Once it is in the record, it is in the record." He turned to caution Harris. "This is the problem that you encounter when you use such an open, narrative format in your questioning, Mr. Harris. If you would ask more *questions*, we might get a more *focused* record."

Harris nodded his assent. "Dr. Levin, at one point you talked about a huge circle around the state's witness—Victor Herbert, and the lectures he has given—the testimony in here, and the panel's conclusions. Can you elaborate about that circle, please?"

Levin took the cue from his lawyer. "Sure. I believe we have in evidence a copy of the state's witness's lecture to the medical directors of the Life Insurance Companies of America, in which he outlines all the 'questionable practices' that he thought were quackery and should not be covered by the insurance companies. So the insurance companies, acting on that kind of information, questioned *my bills* to their insureds by bringing them to the attention of the Insurance Subcommittee of Peer Review of the Medical Society. Following that, the Medical Society reviewed those cases and said to the insurance companies, 'Well, this isn't what *everybody* does, so you *don't* have to pay for it.' I had already warned my patients that might be something they would have to deal with," he added. "But then the Medical Society said, 'This amounts to *deviation* from practice' and proceeded to report me as being *deviant* to the Office of Professional Medical Conduct." Levin wasn't through yet. He needed to close the circle around all of the players. "The Office of Professional Medical Conduct contacted the medical *expert* for his opinion as to whether what I am doing is, indeed, deviant. And, of course, the medical expert, Victor Herbert, is the *same man* who gave the lecture to the insurance companies. And he said, 'Yes, this is deviant.'"

Levin sat in the witness chair, making eye contact with each of the panel members, in turn, who were seated at the table across from him. "'It is *so* deviant,' this *expert* says, 'that I went and spoke to the Congress of the United States and the New York Assembly about the deviousness of this. Oh, and I even mentioned Dr. Warren Levin by name. And, in my editorial, I speak of how I have *reported* individuals to the Office of Professional Medical Conduct for this type of devious behavior.'"

He took a deep breath and decided to take a ride to the end of the line. "*Then* he is brought in as the *expert witness* against me, but when asked, 'Isn't it true that you *reported* Dr. Levin?' he says, 'I don't have to answer that, because this is *confidential* information." Levin's testimony was coming from the very depth of his soul, and he hoped that nobody in the room missed that. "I went through six years of the court system over all of this. I told the courts, 'I am being deprived of a basic, fundamental right as an individual in the United States to confront my accuser, and as of this time, that is *still* the situation. I think this is a flagrant violation of my rights." Levin was appreciative of the fact that he had been allowed to finally say to the proper authorities something that had been on his mind and had weighed heavily on his soul for over a decade.

Harris knew that Levin had been waiting months, years, for the right question to be asked, providing the ideal opening to tell his story, to be heard. He had wanted the panel to be aware of the "circle theory," as Harris thought of it, which Levin had related to his defense lawyer so very many times. Harris was delighted that Levin recognized the opportunity when it presented itself. Then, with that information in the panel members' faces, the doctor managed to follow it with most of the remainder of his tale. For what it was worth, Levin had spoken his piece and the testimony was contained in the record, something that could prove valuable later on, Harris calculated.

When Sheehan had cross-examined Levin earlier in the day, Harris had been pleased that his client had handled himself so well under fire. Now, Harris had turned his client over to Sheehan for recross, fully aware that Levin had much, much more to say to those assembled in the hearing room. He wondered if he'd find an avenue open with Sheehan leading the round. Sheehan had launched into his carefully structured inquisition and referred to "one of the significant *alleged* deficiencies in your method of practice, Dr. Levin," but Harris didn't object because of Sheehan's judicious insertion of the word, "alleged."

"I didn't see that allegation in the list," Levin told Sheehan.

"You don't see that as the *underlying theme* running through these charges?" Sheehan asked incredulously.

Levin shook his head no and fixed Sheehan with a totally serious, no-nonsense look. "You have worked *very* hard to prevent me from changing the allegations, as stipulated by *my* perception of what the true nature of this hearing is." Harris could hear Levin working up to the opportunity he needed. "Do you want me to tell you about the *true nature* of this hearing? I will be *glad* to do it, because I don't know if my attorney will do it. Shall I?" he asked no-one in particular.

Harris decided to respond. "By all means!" he exclaimed.

Sheehan regarded the witness. "If this is in answer to my question, you can answer it in any way you like."

The Administrative Officer echoed the sentiment. "Go ahead, Doctor."

Levin smiled. "This is Alice in Wonderland," he began, as though auditioning for a play. "I perceive myself proudly as a representative of a minority group of physicians, most of whom I know very well to be men and women of integrity, and concerned and caring physicians who believe that there are *tests* and *treatments* that are glossed over by the pharmaceutically oriented medical establishment. The state of New York saw Warren Levin as being an early protagonist of this type of practice, but one without much of a forum," he said, letting his voice drop off dramatically at the end of the sentence.

"There are *other* physicians in this city who do what I do. They have radio shows, they write newspaper columns, and they write books. And I have *never* done those things. So rather than take on one of the physicians with a *constituency*, they chose to take *me* on because I am the 'little guy,' and they drew up a list of charges that covered virtually *everything* that I do that I believe to be important in differentiating this kind of practice from a pharmaceutically oriented practice."

Go, Warren, go! Don't stop now, thought Harris.

Levin chuckled. "Because it is a *minority* opinion, a test or procedure done is, by definition, *not routine and customary* and, therefore, they say it is *medically unnecessary*. And on the basis of the fact that I am doing something *different*, my *license* is in jeopardy." He looked at them pleadingly. He started softly and built to a crescendo, saying, "But different is not dishonest. Different is not incompetent. Different is not greedy." He shrugged. "I wish I *had* the profit attributed to me by the state's witness," he said, honestly. "I am not here claiming penury, but when I went into the hospital a year ago to have my kidney removed, I hired a *bankruptcy attorney* because three weeks out of the office was close enough to putting me over the edge of bankruptcy!"

Harris watched the panel members at this point. He saw a few rapid blinks and heard some self-conscious throat clearing.

"It is, I think, a tribute to my industriousness and integrity that I *didn't* choose to go bankrupt. I could have done that. But I am struggling to get out of my financial mess. Admittedly, I have made a decent living as an alternative physician. I have achieved either fame or notoriety, depending upon whom you choose to ask. If you choose to ask the physicians around the country who share my belief system, I am a 'very special person.'" He smiled.

"One of the reasons that I am *not* in bankruptcy is that I have had financial support from around the country *for standing up to Victor Herbert*. Nobody else has been willing to do that, because Victor Herbert, as reported in *Science Magazine*, is ruthless! He uses his legal degree like a saber and wields it mercilessly."

My God, Harris thought. *People thought Hamlet's soliloquy was so great. Shakespeare had nothing on Warren Levin!*

"That is exactly what it says about Dr. Herbert in *Science Magazine*, one of the most prestigious magazines in this country," Levin continued, elaborating on his former statement for emphasis. "Yet I elected to *subject* myself to the testimony that he gave and you listened to for *seven days*...because I knew the depth of that man's arrogance and ignorance."

At this point in the monologue, Sheehan stepped in. "Dr. Levin, I would object, as this is *beyond* the scope of the question."

No kidding, Harris thought. *If he wasn't* my *witness, I'd have stopped him after the first ten words.*

Sheehan rephrased his objection, telling Levin, "This is *not* responsive to my question. We are back on Victor Herbert."

Earlier in Levin's testimony, references to Herbert had either been made by Harris, Sheehan, or Levin himself; and the doctor had used *every one* of those opportunities to elaborate on something concerning his opponent.

They looked over at the judge, who was actually laughing. "I must say, Mr. Sheehan, you *did* ask the witness to answer the question any way he wanted."

"I said to answer the *question*, not to give me another…"

"My comment is that this has gone beyond the scope of the question. However, I have to caution both of you: Counsel for both sides are asking such open-ended and broad-based questions that it *invites* the type of testimony that we are getting."

Okay, Harris thought, *cut it off, judge. It hardly matters now. Warren was finally able to get the second part of his story out to all of them, on the record. We can both make our questions more specific. And, Mr. Sheehan, I really have to thank you for that one, for the opportunity you afforded my client.*

As usual, Harris and Levin took lunch down the block after copying Sheehan's last court transcript in the administration office. They were both pleased with how testimony had gone this morning. Harris would be continuing his direct examination once they went back in. He informed Levin of the direction his questions would take once they began the afternoon session. Since a lot of Herbert's testimony had focused on Levin's practice as a money-grubbing operation, doing useless tests in order to inflate income, he needed to let the panel hear otherwise. Levin agreed.

Back in position once again, Harris stood near Levin's witness chair as he asked him, "Did you derive any pecuniary profit from ordering *that* test," referring to a procedure discussed earlier, "or receiving the results thereof?"

"No," Levin responded.

"Please go on."

Levin turned to look at his lawyer. "To this day, I do *not* do the *routine* laboratory testing in my office. There are many, many physicians who have brought the machinery into their offices, making them profit centers; but I have held out all of these years. I believe that it is almost *impossible* to have good quality control for automated testing in a private physician's office." Levin knew he had to take the topic of money a bit further. "The question of what one does in order to make enough profit to survive in today's medical economic atmosphere is a problem that I submit besets every single physician. I know that self-referral for testing in one's own office is *always* a conflict of interest, and every physician has to deal with it with his own integrity. Yes, I do certain tests in my office when I believe that I will get the same or better results, and it's more convenient for the patient. However, I do not, in any way, perceive earning a profit on such testing as being inappropriate, immoral, unethical, incompetent, negligent, fraudulent, or any of the other 'lovely' words that have been used."

Harris wanted to follow up on the "self-referral" issue. "What is it that protects your patients from being exploited when you 'self-refer' them for tests or procedures which are done in your office and which will produce a profit for you?"

Levin sat up straight in his chair. He was not an imposing man, but he had an authoritative air about him. He dressed well and conservatively, favored bow-ties, and his thick, wavy, graying hair, beyond his receding hairline lent him a professorial appearance. He appeared credible, which Harris saw as an advantage.

"There are two things, Mr. Harris," the doctor responded. "Number one, I have to live with myself and my integrity. That is a *huge* concern for me. For over twenty years, my unwillingness to be 'one of the boys' and do what everybody else does has resulted in social ostracism, an incredible hassle in my life, deprivation of income, and obscene levels of personal vendettas and vindictiveness aimed against me. It has affected my family life, as has this process. I am here fighting because my *integrity* has brought me here. And it is my integrity that *insists* that I have a right, as a practitioner, to do that which I believe is helpful to my patients."

He sighed. "The second factor is that if a single test exists that would enable me to determine *which* patients I *can* help and which I am *unable* to help, I would *personally* shoulder the expense of that test, because I would then have one-hundred percent effective results. That would also bring me world-wide fame and proportionate income. In the meantime, I get my referrals *not* from establishment doctors but from *patients* who weren't helped by other doctors. Therefore, it is incumbent upon me to give service, get good results, and do it in a way that my patients are happy with. It just doesn't make sense for me to profiteer."

Harris wanted to focus on a specific test. "Prior to my last question, you were talking about having sent out samples for stool analysis."

"Yes, the last part of the stool analysis is what we call a qualitative microscopic examination, and that report is here. The reason why I stopped using that particular lab, though, was that I got the *same* report from them over and over. It didn't make sense."

Once Harris completed the segment of recross-examination, the judge turned the witness over to the panel members for questioning. Their initial queries were centered on Harris's last topic, the laboratory tests.

"When you do the glucose tolerance test in your office, Dr. Levin, how do you do it?" Dr. McAloon asked.

"We use a finger stick with a meter. It is extremely important, Dr. McAloon, because we have the option then of getting specimens in between times, so that we can get closer to finding the patients in their extremes," he responded, referring to blood glucose highs and lows.

The woman nodded. "In terms of hair analysis, my understanding of your testimony was that you've often gotten a falsely high result for a particular element because of external contamination, and that elevated levels in many situations do not reflect the true body state, whereas low levels are much more accurate. "

"For the specific minerals that I consider important: calcium, magnesium, copper, zinc, chromium, and probably manganese, and selenium," he responded, "but not for sodium, potassium, phosphorus, iron, and nickel."

"All right," McAloon said. "When I questioned you after the last patient, we were talking about chelation and, again, we were discussing trace elements; and you said, at that time, that the purpose of the Chelation therapy was to *remove* certain trace elements that had accumulated in toxic levels in the body. You specifically mentioned lead, aluminum, cadmium, and this morning you threw in mercury."

"Not mercury for EDTA. In vitro, it is easy to get precise binding constants that tell us the intensity with which a specific mineral is held in this sticky solution, and mercury is a very powerful binder in this complex. But that was twenty years ago. So from that *earlier* work we felt that we were able to use it for mercury detoxification for patients. It took some time for us to realize that the measurements didn't reflect it," he admitted, honestly, "and the explanation at the present time is that the intracellular binding is primarily organic with methyl mercury, and for some reason it isn't accessible to the EDTA once it *is* there. However, my belief is that when used simultaneously with exposure, so the mercury is still in the bloodstream, the EDTA would pick it up."

"I see," said McAloon. "So lead, aluminum, and cadmium are the three main elements you are attempting to remove with the chelation?"

"Yes."

"In Patient C," McAloon continued, "if you look at her hair analysis, her levels of both lead and cadmium were clearly below normal, even accepting that there is a range. She was way down."

Levin nodded. "In the toxic levels, what we have is acceptably questionable and toxic, but it isn't normal." Sensing McAloon's reluctance to accept what he had said, Levin decided to elaborate. "In other words, it is not a bell-shaped curve, but rather a question of a *cumulative* amount which at some point crosses a threshold and becomes toxic. The toxic threshold varies for different people and, generally speaking, when you are low, you are really low. Well, I went into that at some length before," he told her, reluctant to repeat his earlier, extensive testimony on the subject.

McAloon was not to be put off. "Her cadmium, for example, was less than 0.1, and the normal range is .1 to 1.8. So clearly an analysis of her *cadmium* level is lower than this lab's lowest range of normal. If I am interpreting what you are saying correctly, and you are saying that the hair reflects the total body, then her total body load of cadmium is very low."

Levin heard the doctor out and, once again, began to explain. "The low range is a function of the points at which the instrument begins to create static and is meaningless," he stated. "The optimum level of lead, cadmium, and aluminum at present, in my opinion, is zero. Again, if this patient had been a smoker for fifteen years, we know that smokers inhale significant amounts of cadmium on a regular basis, and that cadmium is absorbed through the alveolar membrane, then gets into the blood and is deposited into the body."

McAloon sighed in frustration. "I guess my question is this: If the tests that you order to access the body's stores of a given metal show levels as low as can be measured, yet you offer chelation to remove *toxic* levels of these chemicals, you have proven with the tests you chose that the condition you are treating *doesn't really exist.*"

Levin now appeared frustrated. "Dr. McAloon, I am unhappy that I *still* haven't been able to clarify this. I really tried. I'd like to think I'm articulate enough to do so, and I know that you are paying attention, so I apologize for not making it clear." Levin extracted information from a research article that had been entered into evidence explaining how mercury in fillings done in the teeth of live sheep had migrated into the animals' kidneys, pituitary and thyroid glands, gonads, and bone.

McAloon's frustration still showed. "I think that wasn't quite the thrust of my questioning," she replied, following his narrative. "One of the charges against you is inappropriate ordering of tests for patients. So, for this particular patient, I am focusing on the hair analysis test, which really didn't reflect anything significant, yet led you to propose chelation for the patient."

She was missing the point, Levin decided. "Hair analysis, besides testing for heavy metal toxicity, also looks for toxic minerals and essential minerals. It can point to a specific deficiency in zinc, copper, chromium, magnesium, for example, which I have no other way of demonstrating. If I find an elevated lead level, I can justify to the insurance company looking over my shoulder the process of proceeding with EDTA. Let's not forget that New York State has changed the ranges for various serum test levels. So you can have *significant* levels showing up in the hair without *ever* crossing the threshold in the blood. Frankly, hair analysis was *clearly* the best test we had back in 1976 for intracellular minerals. And, while it's still useful today, I supplement it with other tests."

Apparently satisfied, McAloon progressed to the stool samples that Levin would send to a laboratory in North Carolina. The discussion again involved a request for further elaboration on the significance of that and numerous other tests until the panel's medical professor was sure she understood the purpose of the tests in treatment of the specified patients. Following that, the prosecutor questioned Levin on how he made treatment decisions in his medical practice. "Healing," Levin responded, "means you have to stop doing the things that are *interfering*, and you must begin doing whatever is *healthful*. 'This is your life,' I tell a patient, 'and I can't tell you that you must stop smoking, and you must stop drinking. I can only tell you that it appears to me that those things are interfering with what you think you came here for—which is to get better.' So, in that sense, the patient has the final say in whether they elect to have Chelation therapy or not, as well." He looked at Sheehan, "I think that so long as we live in a society, Mr. Sheehan, where a woman can go into a cosmetic surgeon's office and say, 'I want to have my breasts enlarged, and I'm willing to subject myself to general anesthesia and all of its possible side effects plus the complications of silicone,' and that is perfectly okay, because the patient chose to do it. Then, for the life of me, I don't understand why that same patient can't come into my office and say, 'I've lived in New York City for so long that my insides are polluted, so I'd like to have Chelation therapy to rid my body of all of those toxins,' but New York State says, 'That's not okay.'" He looked at Sheehan and then shook his head in wonderment. "I see the analogy very clearly, Mr. Sheehan, and I'm sorry that you don't. If the patient wants a treatment, that individual is entitled to get it from someone who knows what he is doing and will do it properly."

Sheehan picked up one of the patient's charts and removed the intake questionnaire. "Dr. Levin, you have said that the protocols of your organization required a complete medical history, correct?"

"Yes."

"So," he read, "you're saying that a thorough, head-to-toe, hands-on, physical examination should be performed and recorded; relevant past medical records, including written reports of arteriograms, should be requested; if available, a complete list of current medications, including names, strengths, and frequency should be made; special note of allergies should be indicated; quality of arterial pulses should be recorded; presence and quality of arterial bruits; skin temperature of the extremities; hair loss of the extremities; mental status; and your form goes on and on to list what should be performed and recorded in the patient's chart—your own exhibit, which was admitted into evidence. Isn't it true Doctor, that your chart for this patient does *not* contain a record of all of that information? Isn't it true?" Sheehan repeated.

"Mr. Sheehan," Levin began, in a reasonable tone of voice, "that..."

Sheehan broke in. "Could you answer that 'yes' or 'no,' Doctor, without a six-hour answer?"

"I would say that the only thing missing are the *negative findings* on physical examination," Levin responded. "I have already testified to the fact that my current practice differs from what I did in 1976, fourteen years ago. I am proud to say that, except for that singular defect, I don't know many other doctors whose charts are as complete, thorough, and adequate as mine. I am proud of my medical care and of the charts that I maintain."

"Did you do a Doppler systolic recording?"

"No, because at the time that option wasn't available to me."

"Did you do all the blood tests listed on this document?"

Levin was losing patience. "Look, you are criticizing me for doing *too many tests*. Now, you want to be sure I did *everything* that piece of paper says."

"These are the protocols that you..."

"Mr. Sheehan, give me a break. This was published in 1989, last year, and you're looking at the chart of a patient I saw in 1976!"

"What protocols were you referring to when you previously ..."

"There was *no* protocol then, sir. It was one of the things I later helped to create!"

"Dr. Levin, on direct examination, did you not state that you did a hair analysis because the *protocol for chelation* says you are supposed to have the mineral status of the patient? If there were no protocols, what were you referring to?"

"What I referred to, Mr. Sheehan, were the things we discussed at our association meetings as to what constituted good practice. In 1976, we were attempting to *create* a protocol. Therefore, I was, at that time, adhering to a *non-existent protocol*."

From there, Sheehan decided to move back to the differences from laboratory to laboratory in parameters and results for hair analysis tests. Levin responded that he only trusted results from certain labs for that very reason, and he also explained that results were often given in different units of measurement, which seemed to mollify the prosecutor.

"Sometimes," Levin said, "the method of preparation varied from lab to lab. Some years back, a group of laboratories got together and formed a hair analysis standardization board *specifically* for the purpose of addressing these kinds of discrepancies. Before that, some labs used Atomic Spectrophotometry and ICAT, which is Inductively Coupled Argon Torches; so the results would differ from one laboratory to another due to the different methodology. So when you look at the results from early tests, you have to apply the standard deviation curves that the labs developed as they accumulated information."

Still focused on one particular patient, Sheehan smirked as though he were about to score a win. "You said that you did *not* base the chelation on the hair analysis test, in this case, but on the fact that the patient had compromised peripheral circulation, correct?"

"Yes."

"You also had the theory that the circulation problem was possibly caused by 'the works being gummed up' by these various minerals and things, correct?"

"Yes."

He moved in for the kill. "Isn't it true, then, Doctor, that if the circulation was compromised by an overabundance of these horrible minerals, you would expect the hair analysis or the urine test for minerals to *show* these elevated minerals that you are trying to get rid of? Correct? I mean isn't that just logical, Doctor?"

Levin gave a small laugh, as he looked at the prosecutor. "I appreciate your attempt at 'logic,'" he said, with a slight touch of sarcasm evident on the word, "logic," "but the answer is no."

"No other questions."

The committee chairperson then spoke, referring Levin to "a collection of letters" and asking what that exhibit represented. Levin couldn't have been happier with that reference.

"That collection of letters," he began, "is intended to represent my contention that the Office of Professional Medical Conduct brought me up on charges with the intention of taking away my medical license based on insurance company records, and that I didn't even have the opportunity, for the most part, to defend myself. I think that it's a terrible affront and a terrible intrusion." With the attention of everyone in the room fixed on him, Levin then stated, "It is also to document what I think is a basic part of these hearings and what we have been discussing for the last few days, which is what constitutes 'authority' and what constitutes 'standards.' Even if I were to temporarily assume the best possible motives on the part of the Peer Review Committee, their failure to be *consistent* is indicative of the serious problems that are represented in my particular case and what, in my estimation, makes this whole process an abomination."

The chairperson asked, "Do you feel that this is the genesis of these charges against you?"

"Objection!" Harris was on his feet in an instant. "That calls for absolute speculation and nothing more, since the state's witness refused to answer whether he pressed charges. Do you want Dr. Levin to guess?"

"I am simply asking for his opinion."

The judge asked the prosecutor if he wanted to contribute to the conversation.

Sheehan adopted a reasonable tone. "The witness, Dr. Levin, has pretty much said that these proceedings were the outgrowth of the insurance company problems with him," Sheehan said. "Now the question was directly posed, and Mr. Harris *objects* to it. This is unbelievable!"

It had been another endless day for the doctor-lawyer team. So they waited for the following morning before attempting to make a brief analysis of the proceedings, since most of the testimony was fresh in their minds. There were questions that allowed for broad-spectrum answers, they concluded, and Levin often responded in a circuitous manner, finding a route that allowed him to bring the committee along on a journey through the ten-year OPMC odyssey that had become a regular part of his life. Those opportunities gratified the doctor, since he hadn't been allowed to speak a word on his own behalf for so long. Sometimes, they both acknowledged, the committee members seemed to be working overtime, in step with the prosecutor, to find fault in medical practices the doctor may have subscribed to initially, when no better methods were available.

As always, the defense team concluded that the score was still even. For the moment.

CHAPTER 24

Levin succeeded in getting Abram Hoffer to agree to testify on his behalf, and he contacted Bob Harris to let the lawyer know about it.

"So, who is this guy, Hoffer?" Harris asked. "Tell me something about him."

Levin waved off his secretary, who was signaling another phone call from the doorway of his office. "His credentials are superb, and he's on my side."

"Great. That's a start. But you still haven't told me who he is."

Levin laughed. "The facts and only the facts. Now, you're starting to sound like the prosecution," he joked.

"Yeah, I know. But I also know, and so do you, that those are the guys whose job it is to tear our witnesses apart."

"True. Anyway, Abe Hoffer is a researcher with an M.D. and a Ph.D., a very smart guy," Levin added. "He is a pioneer in Orthomolecular Psychiatry and Medicine. He's Canadian, first of all, and he started out in agriculture and biochemistry, which led him to get a master's in agricultural chemistry. Once he had his Ph.D., that's when he became interested in human nutrition, so he became an M.D. and qualified in the area of psychiatry. He accepted a professorship and started to do research. When he and his co-workers discovered that megadoses of Vitamin B-3 were therapeutic for schizophrenia and also lowered cholesterol levels, this initiated the new paradigm in nutritional medicine, so vitamins were now being used for treatment, not just to prevent deficiency diseases. Anyway, he opened his own practice over twenty years ago and helped mental patients recover their lives without being doped up by tranquilizers all the time. He has written and published extensively, and he's a great guy. Besides having a good sense of humor, he tells people he has 'the hide of a politician,' saying that it's what sustains him, since he's constantly in conflict with the medical establishment. You know," he added, "kind of like me."

"Okay," Harris said. "The witness shall come forth!"

"I'll make the arrangements," Levin said.

The Administrative Officer called the meeting to order. "On the record," he began. "Mr. Harris, are there any preliminary matters?

"No, sir." Harris noted that the setup in the room was basically the same as it had been at the Eighth Avenue address. However, this Penn Plaza location worked better when visitors or witnesses, coming in on behalf of his client, were traveling from distant places and coming into Manhattan's Pennsylvania Station by railroad.

"Will you identify your visitors who are here today, Friday, May 17, 1991, and introduce them to myself and Mr. Sheehan for the record?"

"To my left is Dr. Abram Hoffer. To my right is Dr. Levin, the Respondent." Harris than introduced two recent law school graduates and a physician, who had come to observe the proceedings.

Robert Briber, chairman of the Hearing Committee, waited for Hoffer, the witness, to be sworn in and seated in the witness chair. Briber requested that Hoffer give his name and address to the court reporter. Harris approached the witness to begin his direct examination.

"Doctor, will you please state your educational background and your *curriculum vitae*?"

Hoffer was in his early seventies, slightly chunky, with coarse facial features and very little hair. From the committee's vantage point, he appeared bald.

"I received my Ph.D. from the University of Minnesota in 1944 in agricultural biochemistry," he told them. "I got my medical degree from the University of Toronto in 1959. I interned for one year at the City Hospital at Saskatoon in 1950, and then I joined the Department of Public Health for the province of Saskatchewan, located in Regina, in 1954. I received my qualifications as a psychiatrist, and seven years after that I became a Fellow at the Royal College of Physicians and Surgeons of Canada, my specialty being psychiatry."

Harris nodded his approval. "Did you have occasion to do any research in the course of your career?"

"Yes, I had done some basic research during my Ph.D. in the field of cereal chemistry. The problem, at that time, was that the American government insisted that flour be enriched for the diet of their troops overseas, but this was difficult to do because there were no standard ways of providing measured levels of vitamins in flour. One of my problems was to develop techniques for measuring one vitamin in particular, called Thiamin B-1. I did my dissertation on what happens to a wheat kernel as it matures, with the vitamins translocating from the leaves to the wheat kernel itself. Then, when I joined the Department of Health, as Director of Psychiatric Research for the province of Saskatchewan, it was my job to inaugurate a large-scale study of the problems of schizophrenia, which was one of our major issues at that time."

"What was your connection with the Rockefeller Foundation?"

"We had applied for a research grant in 1954 and were examined by the medical director of the foundation. On the basis of his on-site visit to our mental hospital, they agreed to give us a very substantial grant, with which we could enlarge our research program. The basic condition was that I would become a Rockefeller Foundation Travel Fellow, which was not very difficult to comply with," he said, smiling at the recollection. "I went off to Europe with my wife for three months, where we visited psychiatric research centers. The Rockefeller Foundation then provided support for our research for six years. We had about thirty scientists, a very good-sized research group."

Harris then reviewed Hoffer's stellar academic career, which lasted until the psychiatrist opened a private practice in 1967. At the lawyer's prompting, he discussed his publications, which consisted of more than four-hundred papers and contributions to seven books, the most recent being a textbook for physicians entitled, *Orthomolecular Medicine for Physicians*. Following this information, Harris probed into Hoffer's research with niacin and cholesterol levels, and Hoffer detailed a double-blind, prospective control experiment. Hoffer said he had been surprised to see such amazing results in rabbits with high cholesterol levels. The cholesterol readings had dropped appreciably with niacin, leading to its use with human subjects who, with two to three grams a day of niacin, had a *significantly* lower cholesterol level within forty-eight hours. He told the group that while his work was received with skepticism, after presenting his information at the Mayo

Research Foundation in Rochester Minnesota, where he was a Visiting Fellow for two weeks in 1956, the Mayo Clinic published their first paper on the topic, and interest grew in the use of niacin.

"Over the next thirty years," Hoffer said, "about three or four thousand papers were published. Finally, a seven-year, coronary heart study by the American government, involving fifty hospitals and about forty-five million dollars, showed increased longevity by two years in a population of men with a history of one coronary and who were between forty and sixty years old in the niacin group. They were testing about five drugs in a double-blind study," he added, "and after that niacin became, and still is, one of the major compounds for lowering cholesterol levels."

Having more than established the credibility of the witness for the committee and the prosecution, Harris decided it was time to get to the point. When Hoffer agreed to testify, Harris's staff had made copies of any testimony given by Victor Herbert and sent it to Hoffer to read. Harris now had a credible individual in the witness chair who would be helpful in discrediting Victor Herbert, and he was determined to take advantage of the situation.

"Dr. Hoffer, would you please tell us whether or not you believe that the state's witness's testimony is consistent with the work of a *legitimate* research scientist?"

Hoffer did not hesitate for a moment. "I would say that it is *not* consistent."

"Sir, the state's witness presented himself as an *expert* on various biochemical tests, and one of the tests that he indicated as *worthless* was a test called the 'mauve factor.' Are you familiar with that test?"

"Yes, I am," Hoffer responded, "and the reason is that *we* discovered it! If I might go back a bit: In 1960, while we were investigating the biochemical basis of schizophrenia, we discovered in the urine of the majority of schizophrenics a mauve staining spot. Let me explain," he said. "We didn't have a quantitative acid. We used a paper clotogram and then developed it—this is a technique for separating some of the chemical constituents of urine," he told them, looking at everyone to assess if they were following his explanation. "At eighty percent of the paper, we found a mauve staining spot, and it was consistently present in the majority of the schizophrenics but hardly ever present in the normal population. We called it the 'mauve spot,' because we hadn't yet identified it." Hoffer then elaborated on how the "mauve spot" came to be known as the "mauve factor"—a valid test for cholesterol.

"Did you have a chance to examine the chart of Patient C?" Harris asked next.

"Yes. I went over the entire chart but didn't study it in great detail last evening."

"Fine," Harris told him. "One of the charges against Dr. Levin is he used the mauve factor test with that patient, correct?"

"Yes."

"Would you comment on the appropriateness of using that particular test for that specific patient?"

Hoffer grinned. "Since I have been using this test myself for the past thirty years, I consider it *highly* appropriate. You see, people who have secreted large quantities of this compound have a double deficiency of zinc and pyridoxine, which is Vitamin B-6."

Harris then said, "The state's witness concluded from an examination of the chart, never having spoken to the patient, that the woman was *schizophrenic*; and it was professional misconduct on Dr. Levin's part, because he failed to treat her for schizophrenia. Do you agree with the state's witness's testimony in that regard?"

Hoffer paused a moment. "From what I read in the chart, it did not conform to my definition of schizophrenia."

"What is the definition of schizophrenia that you use?"

"The definition that I, and most psychiatrists, use is that schizophrenia is a syndrome with *two* main sets of symptoms: there are *perceptual* changes, called illusions or hallucinations; and there is a *thought disorder* that causes inappropriate behavior."

Harris asked a follow-up question. "Did you find any evidence of that syndrome in Patient C?"

"No, I did not."

"Are you aware that Patient C, who is still alive by the way, was caring for her two elderly parents, bringing them back and forth to medical offices, and arranging their diets?"

"Yes, I was aware of that."

"Is that kind of behavior *consistent* with somebody who needs treatment for schizophrenia?" Hoffer shook his head no. "Generally not," he answered, realizing the court reporter required a verbal response.

Harris proceeded to belabor the point a bit more, asking Hoffer whether the patient required the drugs Victor Herbert stated she should have been given for her non-existent schizophrenia. Sheehan objected to the question, claiming Harris had misconstrued the comment made by Herbert, as he had not read it directly from the record.

"Just *what* is it that I am misconstruing?" he asked the prosecutor indignantly. Then, almost as an afterthought, he added, "I think it is, perhaps, schizophrenia of the *state's witness* which is causing some of the problem in presenting appropriate counter-testimony!"

Sheehan sprang to his feet. "Okay," he said, sternly, "I *have* to respond to that!"

"No you don't," Harris countered.

"No, I *have* to!" Sheehan insisted. He turned to the judge, fury in his voice. "You can't let him castigate the state's witness in this totally improper, nasty, hostile, and slanderous way, and say…"

"Mr. Harris, be *quiet*!" the judge ordered, as he saw Harris open his mouth to interrupt.

Sheehan wasn't through yet. "First of all, instead of *apologizing* for lying about this question, he compounds the error by calling the testimony *irrational*, and he calls the witness *schizophrenic*! Who is going to put up with this stuff? Mr. Harris was told in the past that he is *not* to engage in this type of character assassination. He does it again…deliberately! I ask him *not* to do this type of activity. I don't call his client idiotic and childish, and I don't think he should call people or *anyone* names of that nature. It is illegal and improper and…impure!" Sheehan said loudly, after struggling to find another appropriate adjective.

The judge sighed deeply, once again. "All right, Mr. Harris. I am going to admonish you to leave the characterizations *outside* the hearing room." He turned to the Hearing Committee. "I am going to remind the Hearing Committee that Mr. Harris's statements are argumentative, they are *not* evidence, and they are *not* elements that can be used in the sustaining or the dismissing or the finding, one way or the other, of the charges." Storch turned back to the defense lawyer again. "And in the future, Mr. Harris, if you wish to ask this witness, or *any* other witness, to comment on the testimony of the Department's witness, you will read from the transcript citation *verbatim*."

Without further hesitation, Harris continued the direct examination of his witness, belaboring the issue of schizophrenia within the parameters of the judge's admonishment. When asked by Sheehan to establish a basis for a question to Hoffer, Harris offered to begin reading hundreds of pages of Victor Herbert's testimony back into the record to establish appropriate grounds for the question, since that was the way the prosecution wanted to play it.

Sheehan was still on his feet. "I will *object* to his doing that!"

Harris turned to Storch. His look was deadly. "I don't want to try my case this way," he declared emphatically." He jabbed his finger toward Sheehan. "*He* chose Victor Herbert. *He* brought him in!"

Storch wanted to keep things from escalating as they had so many times in the past. "Yes," he said, "and I have *sustained* the objection."

"Give me the record!" Harris demanded.

"I object to Mr. Harris being given *anything*."

"No, Mr. Sheehan," the judge stated, reasonably, "that is a public record. If he wishes to see a copy of the public record, the transcript, I am *not* going to deny him."

Mollified, Harris said, "Thank you, sir."

"Dr. Hoffer, are you familiar with the studies done by the state's witness in self-deprivation of folates?" Harris asked.

"I have some familiarity with it, yes."

"Can you tell us what familiarity you do have?"

Hoffer nodded. "I understand that Victor Herbert had placed himself on a diet that was totally deficient in folic acid or folates. I don't know how long he remained on that diet."

"Is it your opinion that medium- and long-term deprivation of folic acid in human beings provides any physical results?"

"Yes, it is my opinion that it *does* have physical results."

"Will you tell us, please, what results you believe that such deprivation causes?

"Well, it generally causes organic brain changes. I am talking about psychiatric changes. It tends to produce an organic brain change, a lot of depression and other changes in the psychological state."

"Have you, at my request, searched the peer-reviewed literature on this subject?"

"Yes," Hoffer responded.

"Is it your opinion that there is any likelihood that Dr. Victor Herbert is suffering from the *effects* of folate deficiency?"

Hoffer regarded Harris thoughtfully before answering. "I have never met Dr. Herbert," he responded, speaking slowly and carefully, "but I think any person, if they were to deprive themselves long enough of folic acid, is surely looking at that kind of change."

"You have never met Dr. Herbert," Harris began, "but have you had any scholarly exchanges with him?"

"Yes."

"Would you please tell the panel about those exchanges?"

His gaze switched to the panel's table. "Well, Dr. Victor Herbert has been known to have some very 'pronounced' views about the usefulness of using vitamins in larger than the RDA recommended dosages, and with this, he and I have been in strong disagreement. On many occasions, he has made statements in the medical literature which I couldn't agree with, and which were not substantiated by the data. I would then take advantage of this opportunity to write a letter to the editor, criticizing the statements made by Dr. Herbert and referring to the literature to bolster my position."

Harris smiled broadly. "And have you had those letters published?"

"Yes," Hoffer replied, "in every case."

"Can you comment on the topics of those disagreements?"

Hoffer rubbed his chin, thinking. "Well, let me give you an example. He made the statement that, based upon his own research, if you took Vitamin C, you destroyed the Vitamin B-12 in your stomach. It was shown over the next two or three years that this was *totally* false. A lot more sophisticated tests were done by competent scientists," Hoffer elaborated, putting strong emphasis on "competent" to Harris's glee, "who proved that Vitamin C had *no* effect whatsoever on the Vitamin B-12 levels. When his original view was put into the literature, readers didn't realize that subsequent studies showed that his work was not valid. My impression is Dr. Herbert must be a very unusual person, because he tended to reply with great anger and determination—something I had not seen with any of my other scientific colleagues. And then he would madly attack what I had said and would even indicate that there must be something wrong with *me* in order for me to have made any statements opposing *his* views."

As far as Harris and Levin were concerned, this testimony proved to be the highlight of the morning. They were both delighted that the committee was being treated to large doses of doubt regarding Victor Herbert and his credibility, courtesy of Levin's defense witnesses.

"Doctor, have you received any honors or awards or academic chairs for the work you have done?"

"Yes," Hoffer responded. "About three years ago, at the Ben Gurion University in Israel, a Chair was created called the Hoffer Chair of Orthomolecular Psychiatry."

Harris smiled at the witness. "Do you consider yourself an Orthomolecular Psychiatrist?"

"Yes."

"Would you tell the panel, please, what is the difference between 'psychiatrist' and 'orthomolecular psychiatrist'?"

Hoffer interlocked his fingers. "The orthomolecular psychiatrist uses *all* the treatments which are available to psychiatry in general, including the various elements of medication, psychotherapy, and counseling; but in addition to that, we pay *special* attention to the use of nutrition, special types of nutrition; we pay attention to the importance of allergies, reactions to different types of foods; and we pay special attention to the use of optimum doses of vitamins, those vitamins relevant for that particular case. And so I believe that our practice is broader than the practice of a psychiatrist who is not aware of the elements of orthomolecular psychiatry."

"Do you prescribe glucose tolerance tests for any of your patients?"

"Yes, I do."

"Now, the state's witness, talking about glucose tolerance testing, suggested that, if you do this test at all, a three-hour test would give you *all* the information you need. Can you comment on that?"

"The basic problem with a three-hour test is that you miss valuable data, since you have no evidence of what happens at the fourth or fifth hour, where you find your major decreases," Hoffer told him.

Harris proceeded to deftly engage the psychiatrist in a discussion of low blood sugar and psychiatric illness, and the doctor concluded saying that, "Low blood sugar is a very important factor in determining the operation of the brain."

"Doctor, as an orthomolecular psychiatrist, do you have occasion to treat yeast *candida*?"

"Yes."

"Will you tell us *why* a psychiatrist deals with yeast *candida*?"

Hoffer nodded his assent. "I think that is a good question," he said, explaining that an internist with whom he was friendly had shared some surprising results when treating this medical problem. "He told me that he had some schizophrenic patients with *candida.* To his amazement, as the infection cleared, so did their psychosis!" He shook his finger, reminding himself of something, and gave a case history of a depressed woman who failed to respond to treatment for two years. "So I began to look into the question of *candida.* Yes," he said, "that's actually how it started for me. She had discharge, changes in her mouth, sensitivity to sugar and yeast. So I put her on the Mycostatin program that we used at the time, very safe, a type of antibiotic. To my surprise, she came back a month later…normal! I kept her on the medication, and she was fine for two more months. I asked her to discontinue the Mycostatin, and within a month she had dropped into her previous depression. So, naturally, I put her back on the drug and had her remain on it for a year. So *candida* does play a *major* role in some patients who have psychiatric problems," he concluded.

Harris was delighted. "Dr. Hoffer," he asked, "is Mycostatin the same thing as Nystatin?" he asked, naming the drug that Levin used for the same medical condition.

The doctor nodded. "Yes, Nystatin is the trade name," he responded, "and Mycostatin is the generic term."

Harris moved in. "The state's witness testified that Nystatin is a *dangerous* drug. The words he used were '*very dangerous drug*.' Would you agree with that?"

"In my opinion, it is *not* dangerous. It is one of the more innocuous drugs."

Harris knew he could cover the remaining sticking points. "Doctor, you have done a lot of work with Vitamin C. Is that correct?"

"That's correct."

"And you have collaborated *extensively* with Dr. Linus Pauling?"

"Yes, I have."

"Can you tell the panel what 'metastatic oxalosis' is?"

"I don't know."

"Have you seen the term used *anywhere*?"

"I think I saw it in the transcripts."

"Other than the use of it by *Dr. Victor Herbert*, have you ever heard anybody else use the term?"

"No, I haven't."

"Is it your opinion that someone who gets megadoses of Vitamin C will develop increased deposits of oxalates?" Harris was referring to an abnormal condition characterized by the formation of calcium oxalate deposits in tissues throughout the body.

"To my knowledge, Vitamin C has *never* caused increased deposits of oxalates."

"So when Dr. Herbert said that taking large doses of Vitamin C will produce metastatic oxalosis, and therefore it is contraindicated, I assume that you disagree."

"I disagree."

Harris then took the doctor through a discussion of the use of vitamins, and Hoffer admitted using large doses himself at his present age of seventy-three. He also said that he prescribed them for his wife. Harris tried to explore the use of vitamin therapy in cancer treatment and was met by objections.

Harris geared himself up for a major speech, because he realized he had been afforded an ideal opportunity, courtesy of Sheehan's latest objection. "The basis of my latter questioning of this man about his non-conventional treatment of cancer patients has to do with the reaction of the peer-review establishment regarding people who achieve *fantastic* results outside of orthodox means. And it goes to the very heart of the case against Warren Levin, who is sitting here today." Out of the corner of his eye, Harris noticed Sheehan return to his seat.

"Dr. Warren Levin's defense all along has been: 'The reason I am here is because I am using tests and treatments that my conventional colleagues *don't* use, and they are angry about it, even though I am getting the good results that they were unable to get with the same patients.'"

He walked in front of the panel's table to continue. "Since you are asking me for *proof*, this man, Dr. Hoffer," he continued, pointing to the witness seated about fifteen feet behind him, "has achieved results in which he has extended the lives of people who had been written off with advanced cancer. Instead of being embraced by the entire orthodox medical establishment, they have *suppressed* him. This is the *same* phenomenon that causes the New York State Health Department to go after a guy like Warren Levin and bring him up on charges. Dr. Levin's crime is that he doesn't do what Victor Herbert, who believes he sets the standards of medical practice, *says* he should do."

He went to stand in front of the defense table, where his client was seated. "We don't have patients who are injured here. We don't have patients who are complaining. What this *really* is about is a doctor who *dared* to be different, who has treated patients who were *not* being successfully treated elsewhere."

He pointed to the panel members. "This panel has *dozens* of affidavits from people who went everywhere for years, who felt sick before, then came to Dr.

Levin...*and they don't feel sick now*!" Harris turned to face Hoffer. "Dr. Hoffer drew the conclusion that you can help people *without* killing them with the poisons used in cancer therapy. So the people who used to publish his original work...well, their phones suddenly got *disconnected*," he said dramatically, a look of disgust on his face.

"That same phenomenon is the reason that Warren Levin is here. I believe this panel, as well-meaning as they may be," he said to no one in particular, "is being asked to participate in a *political* trial. The very *least* you can do," he said, eyeing the panel members, "is hear one physician after another, who are not on trial or accused of wrongdoing, but who have experienced *exactly* the same thing that Warren Levin has."

He shook his head in exasperation. "Look at the lengths that the state has gone to in talking about Dr. Levin treating patients from the mid-seventies! Look at what is going on here." His voice dropped to a near whisper. "Think about this," he said. "At no time did they bring in a patient who claimed to be disgruntled, to say he didn't like Dr. Levin, who called Dr. Levin a dud."

"*Objection!* This is summation." Sheehan was shaking his head in disbelief for allowing it to go on for so long.

"Mr. Harris," the judge ruled, "you have *made* your point as far as the record is concerned. Let's go on."

"Thank you, Your Honor." *Thank you for giving me the opportunity to sneak in a bit of summation,* he was thinking.

"Dr. Hoffer, how long have you known Warren Levin?"

"I think around twelve to fifteen years."

"And in what connection do you know him, sir?"

"I first met him at various meetings we both attended, but my first really *clear* recollection was when I had invited him to speak at a meeting I was chairing. I recall the paper he presented. Since that time, we have had fairly frequent contact by letter and telephone."

Harris continued the questioning, establishing that Hoffer had testified twice before in similar cases. He also had the doctor make it clear to the panel that, in spite of his busy schedule, he had flown in from Canada especially for this hearing and that only his out-of-pocket expenses were being covered by Levin. He was not being paid to testify.

Hoffer told the committee that, "I was prepared to come to help a colleague who is practicing in a way which I consider part of the 'new medicine.'"

At this point, Briber, the committee chairperson, asked, "Mr. Harris, as a question of procedure, are you about done with the witness?"

Harris smiled benevolently. "I am sliding into home plate. I am very close."

Briber nodded and said, "We will take an hour for lunch, so we can be back here about 12:45."

Harris, Levin, and Hoffer went to lunch with the attorney's newly minted lawyer friends and enjoyed a lively discussion. So far today, the defense was leading the prosecution in points earned, as far as the group was concerned. Who knew how the score might change in the afternoon?

Cross-examination of the witness by Terence Sheehan commenced promptly at 12:45 that afternoon. He quizzed Hoffer about his academic appointments and about where he had hospital admitting privileges. Then he moved into the orthomolecular area.

"You would agree that you regard yourself as a proponent of orthomolecular psychiatry as it is commonly known, correct?" Sheehan asked.

"That is correct."

"And would you agree that, in general, the psychiatric establishment in the United States has *renounced* the efficacy of orthomolecular psychiatry?"

"That's correct."

When Sheehan picked up a book, read a quote about orthomolecular therapy and asked Hoffer to comment, Harris *strenuously* objected, since Sheehan refused to identify the book. An argument between the attorneys ensued, causing Storch to exert his authority.

"Please, gentlemen, keep it civil," he told them sternly. "Mr. Sheehan, identify the title, the author, the year of publication."

Sheehan regarded the judge sullenly. "I object to the procedure. I don't have to," he said, petulantly, "but I am willing. The book is *Mount Sinai School of Medicine, Complete Book of Nutrition*, Edited by Victor Herbert, M.D. Year of publication, 1990, I believe." Sheehan then turned back to the witness. "Dr. Hoffer, would you like me to read the sentence again?"

"Would you mind reading it in two parts?" Hoffer asked the prosecutor.

"Okay, Doctor. 'In fact, the *highly profitable* enterprise called orthomolecular therapy has grown up around the use of high dosages of vitamins to treat behavior disorders.' Do you agree?"

"No, I don't."

"The second statement: 'It has been found *without efficacy* by a task force report of the American Psychiatric Association.' Do you agree with that statement?"

"That is right. That was their conclusion."

Sheehan wanted more. "With respect to the first statement that you disagree with, why do you disagree with that? Is it just the author," he asked, referring to Victor Herbert.

"I disagree with the *financial* implications that this is a rip-off."

"And who do you think makes that allegation?"

"I don't know."

"Do you assume that it is Dr. Victor Herbert?"

"I am not going to assume."

"Well, it is *edited* by Dr. Herbert."

"That doesn't mean that he *made* the statement. He probably agrees with it, but I am not going to assume who made it."

Sheehan didn't stop there. "My question is, if *another* academic at Mt. Sinai was the one who made that statement and *not* Dr. Herbert, would you, under the circumstances, find any *additional* reason, perhaps, to determine that the statement is *partially* true?"

"No," Hoffer replied.

Levin, watching his colleague and friend testify on his behalf, imagined the degree of Sheehan's frustration at this point. The whole issue of alternative medicine was stuck in the state's throat, it seemed, an unpalatable type of practice they were desperate to discredit. And Sheehan actually had the gall to assume he would use other complementary practitioners to do his dirty work. *Sorry, Mr. Sheehan, you're really fishing for trout in a puddle.*

After several more forays and a re-visit to the area of schizophrenia and medication, Sheehan asked his final question in cross-examination.

"Doctor, what are your out-of-pocket expenses that Dr. Levin is required to pay...approximately?"

"Well, it will be my airfare and the stay at the hotel here in the city."

"Okay, thank you very much, Dr. Hoffer."

The panel took over, continuing the questioning and focusing on Hoffer's area of expertise: treating schizophrenic patients. The discussion centered on identification, treatment, remission, and relapse. The mauve factor test came up once again, with Hoffer admitting that no double-blind, controlled studies had been done with this test. With Dr. McAloon asking most of the questions, she progressed to the use of vitamins and minerals in therapeutic use. Hair analysis was then covered, prior to McAloon taking yet another turn and moving into the area of *candida* infections. Hoffer, as a psychiatrist, did not physically examine *candida* patients, he told her; he read the reports the patients brought from their family doctors and discussed the symptoms with the patients themselves.

McAloon was followed by Briber, the chemist, who quizzed Hoffer on the niacin and the earlier testimony regarding its use in coronary disease. While Hoffer didn't possess Pauling's penchant for wit and good humor, he nevertheless was similarly knowledgeable and unflappable and answered all questions thoroughly, backing his answers with examples of studies and published research.

As Harris watched the brusque chemist question Hoffer, he saw a sly look enter the committee chairman's eyes. Harris didn't have to wait long to hear what the committee chair was thinking. "Dr. Hoffer, one of the words bandied about in this hearing is the one word, 'quack.' Without bothering to try to define it, how do you *deal* with quackery in that context?"

Hoffer was too clever to fall for Briber's ploy. "I would like to define…I don't know the *legal* definition of 'quack.' I do know the *Oxford Dictionary* definition and the classical definition of a 'quack,' which is a person who *claims* to have an M.D. degree and doesn't. It is a person who *professes* to be a physician without having an M.D degree. Therefore, if this is correct, you can *never* label an M.D. a 'quack.'"

Briber changed tactics. "There are a number of elements in these charges being brought against Dr. Levin that we *haven't* discussed. You indicated that you were here because you wanted to support, I think your words were, 'new age physicians.' Would you define a 'new age physician' for me?"

"Yes," Hoffer said.

But Briber did not ask for the definition. Instead, he brought Levin's name into the mix. "Can you tell me in what respects *Dr. Levin* is a 'new age physician'?"

Hoffer looked at Briber, as though to deduce what the man hoped to gain from the answer he would give him. "I don't think it *is* a new age," he began, "as much as it is a new *type* of physician. It's a physician practicing orthomolecular therapy. In my textbook, *Orthomolecular Therapy for Physicians*, it's a physician who uses *everything* known to help his patients get well."

Following that, Briber used the tactics of a prosecuting attorney, asking a question in first one area, then in another completely different area, a small question, a major inquiry, moving at a dizzying pace, in a seeming attempt to throw the witness off track and into an admission that would damn the Respondent in the process. Hoffer was too clever. The tactic failed miserably.

Harris began his redirect examination, and after several forays was cautioned by Storch to confine his inquiries to questions asked by Sheehan in cross-examination or questions asked by the panel after that. Since megadoses of vitamins had come up so frequently in the hearings and had been added, almost as an afterthought, to Levin's charges by the state, Harris focused his attention there.

"Dr. Hoffer," he said, "let's talk about the segment of the population that does *not*, in your opinion, qualify for the dosages inherent in the RDA, the *Recommended Dietary Allowances.* What dosages of vitamins should they get and why?"

"Ideally," Hoffer began, "they should all get the optimum dose, but the question is: What is an optimum dose for each vitamin or for each condition? I should add that at a meeting sponsored by the National Cancer Institute in Washington last fall, the scientist who summed up the meeting claimed that we now needed RDA's for individual diseases, not just an RDA for health. For example, I think it's pretty clear that if you have chronic arthritis, you might need more vitamins than if you don't have arthritis. Schizophrenics might have their own needs, and alcoholics might have theirs. I can only go by the way I practice. I will assess a patient. If the person is under a large degree of stress, I will emphasize a large amount of Vitamin C, and those ranges will go anywhere from three to forty grams a day. With thiamin for alcoholics, I go from one-hundred to five-hundred grams, sometimes by injection, most of the time by mouth. In niacin for schizophrenics, the dose usually ranges between three and six grams, which are the median, but occasionally I will go as high as thirty grams. Other doctors have gone as high as sixty grams a day, which is an enormous dose of these vitamins. So each vitamin has its own required, optimal range. That is why I can't answer that question in a very simple manner."

Following Sheehan's recross-examination, Harris asked one of his special, broad-based, open-ended questions:

"Dr. Hoffer, can you predict what medical practice will be like in the year 2000?"

"I would think by the year 2000, there will be a major expansion of orthomolecular medicine into the whole field of medicine. You can see that now, in the medical journals on vitamins, where Vitamin E has been accepted as a respected, anti-oxidant and is now being used in megadoses, 800 units, for the treatment of tardive dyskinesia, where it has been shown that it can be effective." Hoffer was talking about a common side effect of certain psychotropic medications used for individuals with psychotic symptoms and causing involuntary, repetitive movements, especially of the lower face. "I am very optimistic that my colleagues in the field of medicine will adopt the use of nutrients in very large quantities. Yet I know that there is great fear from colleagues that they will be harassed and victimized if they start using this treatment approach."

As Harris was about to say something, Hoffer put his hand up to stop him.

"I would like to see what has happened in the state of Alaska happen all across the United States," Hoffer said, smiling broadly and looking at everyone in the room, one by one. "In Alaska, they have passed a bill which makes it impossible for their licensing board to go after a physician for the use of any alternative treatment, unless the board can prove that what that doctor did was harmful to the patient!"

"Thank you, Dr. Hoffer!" Harris said, and he really meant it.

The witness was excused. Judge Storch turned to Harris and inquired about the pile of copied documents that had greeted him in the morning.

Harris shrugged. "They are additions to the increasing exhibit of patient affidavits in support of Dr. Levin's 'candidacy for licensure,'" he stated matter-of-factly.

"No objection," said Sheehan.

Storch pursed his lips. "I am going to incorporate them into Respondent's exhibit. However, I am going to preclude you from putting any more in. I counted them up this afternoon. I came up with approximately fifty-five affidavits already in that exhibit. I think that is sufficient to make your point. Any additional ones will just be cumulative."

Harris didn't like what he was hearing. "We are seeking a few from medical professionals, and I think they really ought to be added."

"I object!" Sheehan said. "It is becoming a filibuster, and I think that an inch of these things is enough!"

"I don't know whether an inch or ten inches is enough! This was a concession, a result of my request to have patients testify," Harris said.

Storch said, "I have the authority to limit cumulative testimony."

"This is in place of cumulative testimony," Harris countered.

"I will allow you up to six more for your professionals…if you find them."

"Fine," Harris agreed.

Five additional hearing dates were agreed upon, taking them to the end of July. At that point, more than two years would have passed since the Levins had met with Bob Harris in the lawyer's office on the Fourth of July. More than two years, with countless hearings, testimony of over forty-three-hundred pages at the end of today's proceedings, witnesses, direct examinations, cross-examinations, redirect, recross, lost income for Levin, lost hours with Susan and Erika, endless expenses and legal bills, and still no indication of how it would all end.

Levin took a series of quiet, deep breaths before he rose from the defense table to leave the hearing room. It was the middle of May 1991, and he was endlessly being forced to focus on whatever he may have said or done fifteen years earlier. He wondered how well Sheehan, Storch, any of the committee members, or the Commissioner of Health himself would do if they were asked to attend sessions such as these and provide experts to justify their long-past actions.

CHAPTER 25

Susan walked into the kitchen. She put on coffee and glanced at the calendar on the wall. The last day of Passover was twenty days ago, April sixth. For the very first time, Erika was able to actively participate in the holiday. Susan's parents had come up from Florida to visit and share the holiday. As they had done at Chanukah, the Levins once again kept the celebration small. They infused the meaning of Passover into the rituals, attempting to be as observant as possible, so that Erika would begin to understand her rich, religious and cultural heritage.

The little girl had studied her grandfather and father as they put on their yarmulkes. Her grandmother had covered her head with a scarf as she recited a quick *barucha* over the Sabbath candles, since the evening of the first Seder, ushering in Passover, fell on a Friday night. Erika was given small tasks to assist, as Matzo ball soup was prepared in the kitchen. The table was laid with the divided Passover plates, and the grandparents reveled in explaining these meaningful parts of the ritual to their adored granddaughter, much as they had taught her mother decades earlier. The adults all read from the Levins' beautiful, personalized *Haggadah*. Erika asked the four questions, with a bit of assistance from her parents, and her parents and grandparents beamed proudly as each took a turn answering one of the questions. The little girl squealed with delight when she discovered the *afikomen*, the hidden matzo. The adults managed to put aside their worldly concerns as they drank wine and considered the deep purpose of the holiday, which resulted in the Jews' eventual flight out of Egypt and slavery.

Susan recalled the moment when she picked up an egg-sized bundle of bitter herbs and dipped it into the *charoset*—the pasty concoction of apples, pears, nuts, and wine—trying desperately to keep focused on the ancient ritual and not draw parallels with the bitterness that the never-ending process of disciplinary hearings had brought into their lives, overshadowing so many aspects of routine, family existence. She said a silent prayer, beseeching the Lord to grant them the freedom that had become elusive for so long. She yearned to return to the carefree lifestyle she once knew, but was aware that she would settle for a life that had fewer worries than her present existence. She prayed that the endless inquisitions and black clouds would disappear from their reality once and for all.

She suddenly became aware of the forgotten coffee pot in her hand, remembering that she had come into the kitchen to prepare breakfast. As she lifted her head, the calendar appeared once again in her line of sight, and she sighed deeply to break the spell she had briefly fallen under as she reminisced. She had written all of the remaining hearing dates on the kitchen calendar, including the agenda. Today, April 26, Dr. Herman Richard Casdorph would be testifying in support of Warren. She hurried to fill the pot. She wanted to be sure that her husband was fortified enough to sustain himself through whatever unguided missiles flew his way today. He had gotten home late last night. He would have slept at the office, except that he insisted upon sleeping in his own bed the night before a hearing. She hoped that Bob's presentation of today's expert witness would shore up Warren's wall of defense.

She put two slices of whole wheat bread into the toaster. Casdorph had flown in from California yesterday and had met with Warren and Bob for an extended period of time in preparation for today's hearing. Susan hadn't been awake when he slipped into bed last night, so she never heard any details about the meeting. He'd just have enough time for a hurried breakfast this morning before he had to get to the train station, so she'd have to wait patiently for him to return this evening to learn how things went.

Casdorph was a bright guy, Susan recalled Warren telling her when he first contacted the physician to testify on his behalf. He had both an M.D. degree and a Ph.D., an enviable combination attesting to great scholarship and competitive ability. He did his residency in internal medicine and cardiovascular disease at the Mayo Clinic in Rochester, Minnesota. While he was there, he conducted a research project which led to his Ph.D. through the University of Minnesota in medicine and physiology. Interestingly, the Mayo Clinic requested that he remain an additional year as a staff member in the cardiovascular section. He then sought licensure as a physician and opened a private practice in Long Beach, California.

Casdorph held certification by both the American Board of Internal Medicine and the American Board of Chelation therapy. Susan hoped that his credentials would favorably impress the Hearing Committee.

Levin listened to his lawyer establish Casdorph's reputation as a physician published in peer-reviewed journals and didn't miss Bob's smirk as he observed the members of the hearing committee as they took in the details.

"In addition to the journal articles you referred to," said Casdorph, addressing Harris, "I have also edited a medical textbook on the subject of lipid metabolism." The doctor offered the title and the publisher of the book.

Harris paused for a moment before asking his next question. "Did there come a time when you undertook Chelation therapy as a treatment modality?" he asked.

"Yes. About eleven years ago, I chose to evaluate Chelation therapy and subsequently offered it as an option for my patients." Casdorph answered in a matter-of-fact tone of voice. He was a tall man, trim, in his early sixties, and had a soft Southern accent from his boyhood in West Virginia. From the age of twelve, Casdorph knew he wanted to become a physician, and he had told Harris and Levin in their meeting the previous evening that he had found his year of internship at Indiana University Medical Center in Indianapolis to be both a fun experience and an exhausting one. He told them interesting stories about things that had happened during his rotation through numerous medical specialties, peppered with the real-life excitement of riding through questionable neighborhoods in an ambulance with lights flashing madly and sirens blaring. That got Harris started on his own experiences as an ambulance driver for Morrisania Hospital in the Bronx, which preceded his first real career as a social studies teacher—a short-lived period with unforgettable students, fabulous stories, and low pay—prior to his entry into law school.

Harris asked Casdorph if he had written any articles about his work with Chelation therapy. Levin noticed that the committee members exchanged glances at this point. He wondered what they were thinking.

"I had done some preliminary studies which I believed were significant," he responded, "since they illustrated the efficacy of EDTA Chelation therapy, but when I attempted to get these published in the usual medical journals and in letter form, they were all rejected."

"And why was that?"

"I didn't realize it at the time, but over the past decade I've come to understand that this therapeutic procedure has become a political issue in which organized medicine, for whatever reason, has decided to oppose Chelation therapy or any positive discussion of the subject. Hence, no publications, no papers."

Harris nodded. He certainly understood this pattern; he had heard it often enough from numerous physicians with stellar credentials. "Do you have hospital privileges?"

"Yes, I do."

"Do you generally have patients in the hospital throughout the year?"

"Just about all the time."

At this point, Harris engaged in a line of questioning that demonstrated to the onlookers the fact that here was a physician who used a procedure that his client used—and was being prosecuted for using, who had hospital privileges, yet had *never* been sued, nor had his license been threatened by the authorities, nor were his privileges ever revoked. Casdorph also explained that he had appeared in court on only one previous occasion in defense of another physician whose license was being threatened.

Harris wanted the committee to understand that while Victor Herbert, the state's witness, seemed to always be available to a disciplinary body determined to strip a physician of his license, Levin's witnesses *rarely* appeared on behalf of a defendant. "Dr. Casdorph, just *why* are you here?" Harris asked.

Casdorph stared straight ahead at the committee members as he responded. He wanted to be sure he had their full attention. "I hold Dr. Levin in high esteem because of his activities in the field of preventive medicine over the last decade," he said, his admiration for Levin quite obvious. "It is my opinion that Chelation therapy has merit, so whenever it comes under scrutiny, I feel that I should give my testimony."

His tone was mild and not challenging, Levin noted, yet his pedigree was impressive enough to add weight to his words. Levin breathed a deep sigh of satisfaction, realizing that there had been far too few of these moments over the years of hearings. Obviously, most of them occurred during the testimony of the witnesses appearing on *his* behalf.

After establishing the point that Casdorph had been asked to testify in Indiana several years earlier when the issue of the validity of Chelation therapy was raised, Harris asked, "Doctor, to the best of your knowledge, is the use of Chelation therapy considered professional misconduct in the state of Indiana?"

"It is *not* misconduct, no."

"Is it illegal in Indiana?"

"It is *not* illegal."

"What made you begin to investigate the use of Chelation therapy for your patients eleven years ago?"

"My whole interest has been in vascular disease," Casdorph told Harris, "and for that reason I did my Ph.D. work in cholesterol metabolism and established my office adjacent to Long Beach Community Hospital twenty-five years ago. Mine is a typical hospital-oriented practice in internal medicine and cardiology. When I began to hear repeated reports of the apparent benefit of EDTA infusions in patients with vascular disease, I decided that my research background put me in a good position to evaluate the efficacy of EDTA therapy, so I began to do studies for that purpose."

"Would you tell us about those studies?"

"I would be happy to do that, and I would like to have the opportunity to show slides that will graphically illustrate the studies."

Harris requested a slide projector, which was then brought to the hearing room. When he asked Casdorph to identify the presentation for the record, Sheehan jumped in.

"Is there a *question* pending of this doctor, or is he just here to give a slide show?" There was more than a little sarcasm in the question, Levin noted, and he observed the prosecutor slyly eyeing the panel, as though to forewarn them that they needed to heed his objection.

To his credit, Casdorph was not put off by Sheehan's knife thrust and simply began explaining his work as though the lawyer had not spoken. "Before I even conducted the studies," he began, I gave EDTA Chelation therapy in the hospital to patients with a variety of disorders—primarily heart disease, stroke, and Alzheimer's disease—and the initial results seemed very positive. As a matter of fact, they were *so* positive," he continued, smiling as he recalled the circumstances, "that it was *too good*! I thought there might have been a placebo effect, so I set up a study in twenty patients. Each patient would serve as his or her own control in order to have some *objective* measure that the patient had actually *improved*."

Casdorph continued smoothly, explaining the qualifications of the physicians conducting the studies. He then presented and explained all of the technical details involved.

At that point, Sheehan voiced an objection, requesting a scientific paper to corroborate the results of the studies. "The doctor *must* have written a paper to summarize his findings and methodology in this case," Sheehan interjected, "and if he did, why doesn't Mr. Harris just introduce *that*? Rather than just looking at *random slides* that could be from *anywhere*—and we don't know *whose* they are or who *took* them—could we determine whether or not there *was* a paper published?" Levin was disgusted by the smug look on the prosecutor's face.

The judge asked Harris to respond. "Judge, we really don't have a medical issue here. We have a *political* issue. No political journal would take the doctor's write-ups nor would the various peer review journals." Harris was deliberately averting the issue.

"*This body* will take the article right *now*," Sheehan said to Harris, calling the defense attorney's bluff.

Harris's jaw tightened with anger, and he addressed the judge, not Sheehan. "May I request that counsel talk to the *judge* and *not* to me? I don't wish to have a chat with him about this," he said, motioning toward Sheehan with his head.

Briber decided to intervene. "You are *both* instructed to do that," he told both attorneys.

"That is a *fine* idea," Storch echoed.

Levin was watching Harris very carefully. He realized that his attorney *needed* to bluff his way out of this unfortunately reasonable request for published results. Harris did this type of thing well, Levin knew.

Harris strutted around, fixing the panel, Sheehan, and finally, the judge, with a malevolent stare. "I don't believe that there is *any* requirement that we produce *anything* that counsel dreams up *sua sponte*," he began. "The doctor is here!" He pointed at Casdorph dramatically. "If there are questions as to time, date, efficacy, he is here to be asked about them. There is *nothing* in the law of evidence which is superior to live testimony by the actor involved in the discussion at hand."

Levin groaned inwardly. Harris had completed his statement with both arms outstretched, like an Olympic gymnast after a difficult routine, then slowly pivoted, an expression of innocence plastered onto his face, as though to doubt his confident presentation would be ridiculous and questionable.

As he had many times before, Storch sighed deeply and briefly closed his eyes. "Mr. Harris, why don't you lay some foundational testimony about the slides so we can get over this?" he said in a weary voice.

"Thank you, Judge." Harris struggled to keep from laughing aloud. "*Who* took the slides that you wish to show, Doctor?"

"The slides were prepared by a professional photographer in Long Beach. In the case of the brain flow studies, we took the computer printout form the hospital and had slides made."

"Were all of these made under *your* direction and guidance?"

"Yes, they were."

"Do you agree that they *accurately* reflect what you had them created to show?"

"Yes."

"The study which you spoke about as being represented on some of these slides, did you have occasion to write it up?"

"Yes, I did."

"Did you submit it to peer review journals?"

"Yes."

"Did you submit to the *same* peer review journals that published your papers on hyperlipidemia and lipid metabolism over a period of fifteen or more years?"

"Yes. I also attempted to present this at the national medical meetings whose organizations I belonged to, but it was not even accepted for *verbal* presentation. For example, I am a fellow of the American College of Physicians, and they would not even allow me to *talk* about the subject, so the studies were subsequently published in the *Journal of Holistic Medicine*."

"Do you believe that these slides fairly and accurately reflect the protocol and results of your study?"

"Yes they do."

Harris smiled. "I offer the slides," he said, simply.

Sheehan was not about to let this happen without a fight. He requested a brief *voir dire*, so he could question the witness. He proceeded to ask a series of questions which Casdorph answered unflinchingly.

Sheehan then seemed to borrow a technique or two from Harris. He paused for a moment, looked everyone over, then turned back to the physician. "Do you *have* the study with you?"

Casdorph looked him in the eye. "No."

The prosecutor spun on his heel to face Storch. "I object!" he shouted. "This is absolutely unbelievable! The man is here as a *scientist* having performed a study which he claims establishes the efficacy of a treatment modality which is at issue in this hearing. Does he bring the study? No! Why not? I object to another word out of this witness's mouth about this study. The *least* he can do, if he is going to testify about a study before a group of experts," he said, gesturing to the members of the panel, "is to let the experts *see* the study."

Levin wished he could just disappear at this point...and take Casdorph along with him. This was humiliating, and Levin was sorry he had subjected the man to a tongue lashing that had apparently just begun. Sheehan's face was bright red with indignation, and Levin was certain that escalation would be the next phase. Hopefully Bob, king of the spontaneous and outrageous rejoinders, would come to the doctor's rescue.

"There could be glaring, obvious *defects* in the methodology," Sheehan declared. "Who knows *who* selected these patients, *how* they were selected? Who knows what kind of *control* was given to these patients? Who knows if the proper *measurement* techniques were done? This would all be reflected in the *study*, and this witness *deliberately* did not bring the study, but he brought *little pieces* of the study: namely, some *slides* which he *claims* mean something!"

Harris took a leisurely stroll up to the side of the prosecutor. He looked at the aggravated man for a moment, while exuding a calm and confident manner.

Levin was holding his breath.

"I believe the study is in the book that is *already* in evidence," Harris told the judge, his voice little more than a whisper. As he swiveled his head to look back at Sheehan, Harris's eyebrows were raised, as though in total surprise at the angry, flustered appearance of the prosecutor.

Levin quickly extracted his handkerchief from his pocket and pretended to wipe his mouth. He pressed hard. He was afraid he'd burst out laughing.

"Why didn't you *tell* us that?" Sheehan demanded. He appeared on the verge of apoplexy.

Harris snorted. "I wanted counsel to finish his *insults*. If he had done his *homework*, he wouldn't have *insulted* this witness in the way that he did."

"I *heard* your response to Mr. Sheehan," Storch said tiredly, looking to end the latest piece of courtroom drama rapidly. The judge reviewed the exhibits and checked with the witness, to be sure he was looking at the proper articles. "Would it help out in your testimony to have the articles in front of you for your review?" he asked politely.

Casdorph shook his head. "I don't *need* them in front of me, since I wrote them."

Storch overruled Sheehan's objection and directed Harris to continue with the testimony. Harris turned to Casdorph with a flourish, and the doctor began to explain each of his slides in great detail, as they were projected in the room. Harris could see that the physician was hugely enjoying the process, and he believed a part of the pleasure was a result of Sheehan's annoyance with allowing the "slide show" to begin with.

Casdorph gave the gender and age of the patient represented on each slide, the condition being treated with chelation, and the results of the therapy as portrayed on follow-up slides. The age range of patients was considerable. "This elderly gentleman, ninety-two years of age, had cerebral atrophy by brain flow," he explained, "an extremely abnormal situation. After six IV's, *just six IV's*," he repeated, "we see that the brain flow pattern is starting to normalize." He was referring to the blood flow to the brain.

Casdorph also showed a severely infected foot in a diabetic patient and the healing that was prompted by the Chelation therapy administered. The medical people on the panel understood the implications in this case: had this foot not healed well, it would have led to amputation, as was the case with numerous diabetic patients with ulcerated toes, feet, and legs.

His study was broad-based and included not only blood flow to the brain and lower extremities but also to the heart. He presented a patient whose chest pain led to a discovery of occluded coronary arteries requiring coronary artery bypass surgery. However, the patient elected to begin chelation treatment prior to undergoing the operation. The chest pain disappeared after several sessions, and the totally occluded right coronary artery had opened *completely* after only five months of treatment.

"In the patients with heart disease," Casdorph told them, "we use the heart wall motion study, which gives us an objective measure of the ejection fraction. As you can see, after twenty infusions, the ejection fractions all go up; they are clinically improved. These data were analyzed by a statistician at the University of California in Long Beach and found to be statistically significant. That means that the improvement in the ejection fraction of the heart could *not* have occurred by chance alone."

Casdorph had the attention of everyone in the room, and he pressed that advantage. He spoke of the work of Daniel Steinberg, M.D., Ph.D., a prominent lipid researcher published in the *New England Journal of Medicine*, who was being considered for a Nobel Prize. He quoted from the research, citing treatment strategies that were also used by the respondent in the hearing room, Warren Levin. Casdorph left nothing to chance and was very clear when he drew the parallel to Levin's work.

"So, in summary," Casdorph concluded, "we all know that arteriosclerosis may involve various aspects of the arterial tree. Obviously, if it involves the leg arteries, we will have peripheral vascular disease. If it involves the heart, we will have coronary artery disease. If it involves the brain arteries, we will have manifestation of cerebrovascular disease." He looked at the judge, the prosecutor, and each of the panel members. "When EDTA is given," he stated with the utmost confidence, "it is ninety-five percent excreted through the kidneys, and we *always* urge proper monitoring of the renal function for this reason. The fatty portion of the plaque and the diffused ionic calcium are both picked up in the infused EDTA. We realize that the effect of picking up other trace minerals, such as iron and copper in the tissue, may have the effect of inhibiting arteriosclerosis where it really begins." He ended by spacing his words very carefully for maximal impact. "And this, of course, is published in one of the *leading* medical journals of the world."

The lights in the room were turned back on. During the entire period of Casdorph's testimony thus far, more and more individuals, supporters of Levin, had entered the hearing room. Finally, Storch refused to let others join the seated group, agreeing to leave the door open, since there was no confidential testimony being given, and promising to secure a larger room for the next session.

Harris, believing that Casdorph had done an excellent job thus far of proving the worth of his client's treatments and validating the procedures with scientific proof of his own and of other researchers with unimpeachable credentials and published results in prestigious journals, resumed his stance near the witness. The lawyer elicited from Casdorph an admission that the doctor had received over one-hundred chelation treatments himself and had administered the therapy to *thousands* of patients over the past eleven years. In fact, Casdorph had treated both of his parents, now in their eighties, with chelation.

"Dr. Casdorph, are you a fellow of the American College of the Advancement of Medicine, ACAM?" Harris asked.

"Yes, I am."

"When you administer Chelation therapy, is there a protocol to which you adhere?

"Yes. ACAM has a protocol which has been approved and which the members do follow. It is a rigorous protocol."

"Doctor, I would like to read you from the testimony of the state's witness and ask you to comment on it. The state's witness has said that it would *not* necessarily require a peer-reviewed, double-blind study to support a form of treatment. He suggested an alternate method when he said, 'You simply do an arteriogram and show the narrow coronary arteries by arteriogram and then administer your proposed therapy: chelation or whatever it is, and then show by a *subsequent* arteriogram that narrow coronary arteries have been widened. That is not a double blind study, but it demonstrates efficacy.' Doctor Casdorph, could you comment upon that testimony of the state's witness?"

"Well, I agree that a double-blind study is *not* always necessary for a treatment modality to be administered. It just so happens that a double-blind study evaluating Chelation therapy has been performed and published in a peer-reviewed article: namely, the *Journal of the National Medical Association*, Volume 82, No. 3, page 173, entitled 'Pilot Double-Blind Study of Sodium-magnesium EDTA and Peripheral Vascular Disease.' The senior author of that was James P. Carter, who is on the full-time faculty of Tulane University," said Casdorph, invoking the name of one of Levin's future witnesses. "In addition to this small study that is finished and published, there is a large, double-blind study in progress in the United States at this time at two army hospitals."

Harris was satisfied that he had proved his point, using his witness's expertise. Now, it was time to further build on that platform. "Doctor, doing an arteriogram involves risk, does it not?"

"It does."

"Is it fair to say that the risk is increased in patients whose vascularity is compromised?

"It is, yes."

"Are there non-invasive techniques which can give you objective indications of the circulation in the body?"

"Yes, that is the reason we use the radio-isotope studies, which are non-invasive, yet give us useful information."

"You are familiar with a plethysmograph?"

"Yes, I own a plethysmograph machine, which gives an accurate indication of peripheral vascularity in the extremities. I believe it is accepted by vascular specialists across the country."

Harris smiled. "Was it accepted as such in 1975?" he asked.

Casdorph thought for a moment. "It was *accepted*, but not used as widely then as it is now."

"Would you say that Dr. Levin's use of it in 1975 illustrated a man a little *ahead* of his time?"

It was Casdorph's turn to smile. He looked directly at Levin as he spoke. "Yes, I think that is one thing that is noteworthy about Dr. Levin. He has attempted to be on the forefront of preventive medicine as long as I have known him, which has been eight or ten years."

Levin smiled back at him. He believed that Casdorph's testimony was on target and illustrated essential points that the committee needed to hear from someone other than himself.

"Did you have a chance to visit his office yesterday?" Harris asked.

"Yes, I did visit his office."

"Can you tell the panel what observations you made regarding Dr. Levin's office, with regard to its efficacy, modernity, and its position on the cutting edge of medicine?"

"I object to that question on the grounds of relevance!" Sheehan said. "The respondent is *not* charged with being architecturally and aesthetically improper. He is charged with actions related to specific *patients* and *treatments*."

"I will sustain the objection," said Storch. "Let's move on."

"Doctor Casdorph," said Harris, clearly miffed at not being allowed to pursue his line of questioning, "did you *see* any evidence of fraudulent misconduct or grossly negligent practices when visiting Dr. Levin's office?" Harris knew that the question was a real stretch and would draw an objection, but he asked it anyway, figuring he might be able to slip in a less objectionable query, by contrast, down the line. In fact, he planned to play this out as long as he could.

"Objection! The witness was there *yesterday*. The fraud did *not* occur yesterday. Therefore, he would have *no* relevant information regarding those charges!"

Harris was not to be deterred. He turned to Sheehan, the fury apparent on his face, taking this drama as far as it would carry him. "That brings up a little problem," he said through clenched teeth. "The medical license that is in jeopardy is the license that he has *today*! Since the state waited first from 1975 and then *after* the Court of Appeals spoke in 1986 to do *anything* about this, the reality is if he *stopped* doing whatever the state found objectionable in 1975, there would nonetheless be the issue of his *continued* practice in 1991. So, his *present practice*, and the extent to which it speaks of appropriateness or inappropriateness, *also* seems to be an issue to me."

"I disagree!" Sheehan said, and Harris couldn't blame him.

"Objection sustained."

"Let's take a brief break," said Briber, in an effort to allow the antagonism to leak from the room during a recess in proceedings.

Several people in the crowded hearing room sighed, Levin among them. *It came across like a group sigh*, he thought.

When they reconvened, Harris took Casdorph through a collection of quotes by the state's witness, Victor Herbert. The testimony by Herbert was centered on the treatment specifics of several of Levin's patients, whose charts had been requisitioned by the state. Casdorph had reviewed the records last night in the presence of both Levin and Harris, who had elicited feedback from the man on some of the sticking points in the state's case. So, the dialogue moved smoothly back and forth in the hearing room today. The lull was broken when Harris read a passage from one of his *own* arguments.

Sheehan was on his feet in an instant. "I object!" he shouted. "Mr. Harris is reading his *own* colloquy. It is *improper*! That isn't testimony. It is not part of the record. It is just statements by counsel and not part of the evidence. And I object to him reading his own previous statements in the record. I mean, he is *not* one of the witnesses in this hearing."

"I am going to sustain the objection. If you have testimony that is sworn and on the record that you wish your witness to comment upon, we will hear it, but you are *not* to merely read your own statements!" Storch declared, emphatically.

Harris was not letting go of this one. "Before you rule," he responded mildly, "could you hear my argument on an issue?"

A big sigh. "Mr. Harris, I am *not* going to allow you to read your own statements into the record!"

Harris tried to paste a reasonable expression onto his face. "I am not suggesting that you don't have a *right* to make any decision you want…which may or may not be a correct judgment," he added, only half-jokingly. "What I am asking is this: If you are going to listen to counsel's objection, maybe just for the appearance of *propriety*, could you permit me to make *my* point on the record, so if by chance you make the *wrong* decision, some judge above you will be able to know what you did and what I said and, therefore, correct it?"

Sheehan shook his head in disbelief as he addressed the judge. "I object to Mr. Harris's deliberate, sarcastic remark that you should listen to him for the 'appearance of propriety,' as if you are not upholding the standard of propriety. I submit that is an improper remark to make in a quasi-judicial proceeding."

"I would like to make a comment," Harris said, paying no attention to Sheehan's speech.

Another deep sigh. "Go ahead, Mr. Harris…briefly," the judge added.

"You ruled that Dr. Victor Herbert, who has *never* offered patients Chelation therapy, was *qualified* to testify for several hundred pages about what he *didn't* know. So I need to ask my current witness to comment on the state's assertion that 'Chelation therapy and anyone who is an expert in it are all fraudulent.'"

The judge held the sides of his head and offered up yet another sigh. "Ask him the question, Mr. Harris, and *don't* re-read your own non-sworn statement into the record." He sounded resigned.

"Thank you, Your Honor. Dr. Casdorph," Harris began, turning to face his witness once again, "is it your point of view that Chelation therapy is a *fraudulent* therapy, and any expert on this form of treatment who might come in to testify would, therefore, be a *fraud*?"

Casdorph pulled his lips into a tight line and shook his head. "That is *not* my opinion, Mr. Harris. I *disagree* with that statement."

Having won that victory, Harris continued to probe further into Herbert's testimony, checking out various statements with Casdorph, who did not agree with *any* one of those assertions. Once he had discredited enough of Herbert's testimony on the issue of Chelation therapy, he then turned to the topic of hair analysis.

"Doctor, in your practice of medicine, do you utilize the technique known as hair analysis?"

"Yes, I do."

"For what purpose do you use that technique?" Harris probed.

"I feel that it is an important modality in evaluating the trace minerals of the body."

"Did you have occasion to review some of the laboratory results on Dr. Levin's patients yesterday evening?"

"Yes, I did. As I recall, the patient was a stained glass worker and had a history of occupational lead exposure."

Harris assumed an innocent expression as he asked, "Did you find anything *unusual* in those results?" he asked, drawing out the word, "unusual."

"Objection!"

Harris wasn't surprised that Sheehan voiced an objection to that very open question.

Sheehan continued, "Unless we are talking about something *in evidence* that the witness reviewed, I object. If it is something that is *not* in evidence, and the witness reviewed it, it is *incompetent evidence* and *not* part of this hearing. I don't remember a stained glass worker as being included in *any* of the charges."

"Are you referring to documents which are in evidence?" asked the judge.

"I am *not* referring to documents in evidence," Harris responded, preparing to lecture the hearing room on points of law. "Before documents *get* into evidence, they are *not* in evidence. *Then* you lay a foundation for them, and then they *become* evidence. I am attempting now to lay a foundation for the admission of these."

Once again, Sheehan wasn't going to let Harris slide by and was annoyed enough to address the other lawyer directly. "You're 'attempting to lay a foundation,'" he parroted, "except that you asked him what he found when he reviewed them. That is *improper*. The documents are *not* in evidence."

"That is not a foundational question," Storch stated.

Harris smirked. "I agree."

Now it was Briber's turn to get annoyed, and Levin was gratified to see the annoyance directed against the prosecuting attorney. "Please, Mr. Sheehan," said the chairperson of the committee, "address your comments to the Administrative Officer, and not to Mr. Harris."

Sheehan glared at Briber. Levin enjoyed the moment. He saw that Harris was about to continue.

The defense attorney pursued his attempt to have the witness demonstrate that hair analysis was a more reliable way to detect lead deposits years after exposure, more accurate than blood tests, and his questions led up to Casdorph's summary.

Casdorph cleared his throat preliminarily. "In the case of the lead exposure that you referred to, the blood levels will *only* be elevated *immediately* after exposure. But for *years* in the future, the deposits of lead will be *in the body*, *in the brain*, and will be *detectable with hair analysis*, which indicates what is found in the *tissues* of the body. I might add that this individual received Chelation therapy, which mobilized lead *from* the tissues, and serial determination of urine lead excretion did indicate a *marked* mobilization of lead *after* the therapy. That's the second way that you can document lead in the tissues *a long time after* the initial exposure."

Levin watched as the interplay of lawyer and witness continued and was satisfied that, not only had Harris elicited solid probative information regarding the useful nature of hair analysis in detecting lead levels, but he succeeded in moving Casdorph to a place where he was able to elaborate on the *value* of hair analysis and the use of Chelation therapy to solve the problem of harmful lead in the tissues of the human body.

Having overcome the opposition and achieved his purpose of laying the foundation for his evidence, Harris said, "For the limited purpose of demonstrating this phenomenon in a vivid way, I offer these lab results in evidence." Harris was pleased with himself.

Sheehan looked to wipe the smirk off his opponent's face and objected to the introduction of the documents unless they were first certified, which Harris said would be done. The objection was sustained until Harris could present them to the court as certified. So Harris had won a point, then temporarily lost that point, but would win it back again shortly.

Since Levin was not being charged with malpractice or with causing harm or death to a patient, Harris wished to simply explore the process of Chelation therapy, which was pronounced as both harmful and dangerous by Victor Herbert. Levin was pleased to hear Casdorph emphatically state that he knew of no deaths from the treatment and, considering the thousands of patients he had chelated and the patients who had received the same treatment from his colleagues, he knew of only two cases of temporary kidney failure from which the two patients recovered and survived.

As Harris proceeded with his questions, Sheehan voiced an objection to the style employed. The prosecutor was growing impatient with Harris's technique of reading the questions asked and the answers given by Victor Herbert over a one-thousand-page span in the record.

Harris had his answer ready. "We have a four-thousand page record so far," he responded. "Because of the enormity of the record and the complexity of the task, we have done hundreds of hours of work in order to relate for the panel what our experts believe are inaccuracies, untruths, or misstatements by the state's witness."

"I will overrule the objection," was Storch's response. "But I am going to ask you, Mr. Harris to operate in the most expeditious way. Just do it in the form of a summary question." Harris proceeded with his direct examination until the lunch recess, jumping back into the role immediately following the break.

"Dr. Casdorph, is it fair to say that you are clearly in favor of the use of chelation in applications which are *not* generally accepted by what are described as your 'orthodox colleagues'?"

"Yes, I think so."

"Do you have any explanation for *why* the vast majority of physicians who you describe as well-meaning individuals would *refuse* to utilize a modality which clearly seems to you valuable in the treatment of some of their patients?"

Levin leaned forward. He didn't want to miss a word of Casdorph's response.

"Well, I think there are a couple of reasons," the doctor began. "One is it is not generally accepted by the majority of physicians and is not taught in medical school. However, there is a subset of physicians who find it fascinating and would like to chelate, but they are threatened by hearings such as this. They see what is happening to physicians who did chelate or who do hair analysis, and I think there are a significant number of doctors who find it more comfortable *not* to get involved in controversial areas."

"Like hair analysis?"

"Yes."

"Have other physicians reluctantly confided to you their desire to use Chelation therapy?"

"Yes."

"Could you tell us about some of those instances?"

Sheehan rose. "I object! It is really egregious hearsay."

"I will sustain the objection. It is really going down the road, Mr. Harris."

Harris raised his eyebrows questioningly. "The egregious hearsay objection?"

"No, the collateral issues," said the judge.

Harris nodded. "If it *is* true that your well-meaning colleagues *don't* do it because it is not generally accepted," he said to Casdorph, "that still leaves the question of why what *you* consider to be a therapy valuable enough to administer to thousands of patients is *not* generally accepted by your colleagues."

"As I stated earlier," Casdorph began, "I believe in the past decade it has been made a political issue and ceased to be a scientific issue. There is so much pressure from organized medicine and the various societies to *suppress* Chelation therapy in this country, that it is more comfortable for most physicians *not* to get involved. No one really knows why organized medicine set out to suppress Chelation therapy, because we *do* know that in the first decade of its use, there were many positive articles written about it by well-known researchers published in peer-reviewed journals, so the *real* answer is not available. My hunch is that the chelation process was abused by physicians who did not do it properly, found that it could be a money-making device, started running patients through without appropriate evaluation, and organized medicine felt that this was risky, and that they had to control it, even if it meant suppressing it entirely."

Levin nodded with satisfaction. He couldn't have said it better himself.

"So instead of controlling the abuse, they attempted to *eliminate* the use as well as the abuse?"

"Yes, I believe so."

"I have no further questions," said Harris, lowering himself into the chair next to his client.

Storch looked toward the prosecutor. "Mr. Sheehan, cross-examination?"

Sheehan stood and requested one of the exhibits admitted by the defense. He immediately focused his questions on the study underlying the slides that Casdorph displayed and explained earlier in the day.

"Looking at this article," said Sheehan, "wouldn't you agree that *anyone* reading it would assume that the study you *claim* to have done in that article was done in the year 1988?"

Harris jumped up. "Objection!"

"Mr. Harris?"

"He is asking for this witness's opinion as to how some *imaginary third party* would draw a conclusion from a set of facts. Dr. Casdorph is *not* an expert on magic!" Harris stated emphatically.

"I sustain the objection." Storch then suggested to Sheehan that he rephrase the question, which the prosecutor proceeded to do.

"Objection! It is *exactly* the same question. He hasn't even changed the words!"

Now it was Sheehan's turn to sigh. "Withdrawn."

Sheehan took an extra moment and seemed to be studying the floor. When he lifted his head, his eyes were narrowed. He began to pursue the doctor with a vengeance, Levin noted, wishing he could pound the table in front of him and yell his objections. The prosecutor was stuck on the article representing the study illustrated by the slides. The article itself was contained in a textbook that had already been introduced into evidence. However, Casdorph explained that he had not read the book itself nor had anything to do with its publication. The book contained a compilation of articles, Casdorph said.

Sheehan moved toward Casdorph. "Up until this moment, neither I nor the panel, I'm sure, knew that this book was a compilation of articles...that could be ten, twenty, thirty, or even forty years old!" he said, dramatically. "If you look at this book, there is no way to tell. I am pointing out to you that this is one of the hallmarks of the *sloppiness* and *lack of rigor* that characterizes the so-called 'alternative' type of medicine, *especially* as it relates to chelation." He turned to the panel and promised, "I will show *other* deficiencies that are apparent in this book through this witness." There was a nasty edge to his tone. "I think it is *all* relevant on the issue of whether or not there is any science to support the use of chelation."

Levin closed his eyes. They were really taking it on the chin. Not only that, but he always felt absolutely awful when his expert witnesses were flayed by the prosecution. These were intelligent, scholarly men, and they were made to feel...

Storch signaled for attention. "All right," he said. "Whether or not there is a statement in the book that identifies whether or not this book is a compilation of articles, or whatever, can be determined by the committee. They all have copies of the book. I don't think it is particularly relevant to explore that line of questioning through this witness."

Levin said a silent prayer of thanks. There was a semblance of fairness in the room. He watched as Sheehan tried to trap Casdorph to no avail regarding a teaching position he had formerly held at a medical school, prior to switching to the issue of his hospital privileges at two facilities in Long Beach. Casdorph admitted that, outside of the chelation treatments he administered at a hospital while he was doing his study, neither of the two hospitals currently offered chelation treatment; Casdorph administered that therapy only at his private office.

After belaboring the details of the study Casdorph had done, he switched gears very suddenly, asking for Casdorph's opinion regarding the efficacy of Levin's treatment of patients with diagnoses of mental illness.

"This is *not* an area of my expertise," Casdorph told the prosecutor once, and then again, when the question was repeated. Harris joined in, saying the question was asked and answered twice.

Sheehan then decided to ask questions about the other cases in which Casdorph had been called to testify. Since the doctor had not discussed the subject matter with Harris the previous day and believed it did not relate to the current testimony, he engaged in a brief exchange with the judge over the issue, and no significant information emerged. So Sheehan returned to the topic of Chelation therapy.

"Would you agree that one of the reasons why you did *not* charge Dr. Levin a fee for testifying here today is because this issue is of direct influence on *your* practice, *your* income, *your* reputation, vis-à-vis chelation? Correct?"

"Objection!"

"The basis, Mr. Harris?"

"The state of California does not consider Chelation therapy to be unprofessional conduct. The state of New York…"

Sheehan moved in. "I object to Mr. Harris testifying! This is a serious matter. He is *influencing* the board now on a legal issue which he claims is a fact. He is *not* entitled to make these verbal statements to the panel. It is improper!"

"Withdrawn," said Harris, smoothly. "The state of New York has *no* jurisdiction over Dr. Casdorph. He is *not* a practitioner here, nor does he hold a license here. To assert that his testimony will somehow assist or hurt his practice in California is just to make a good guy into a bad guy. That's all."

Sheehan addressed Harris directly. "I am allowed to challenge the witness's interest, his bias," Sheehan said, tightly.

Harris had adopted the angelic little boy look again. "Withdrawn." Levin couldn't help chuckling.

"Wise choice, Mr. Harris," said Storch. "Please answer the question, Doctor."

Levin and Harris, sitting next to each other, watched Sheehan actually strut back to the witness's chair. He seemed very pleased with himself.

"Doctor," he began, repeating and rephrasing his prior question, "isn't it true that you didn't charge a fee for being here and gave up two days of your practice because it is in *your* personal interest that the disciplinary bodies of a significant state, such as New York, do not make rulings that criticize or outlaw or denigrate Chelation therapy in general? Isn't it true?"

Casdorph looked the attorney directly in the eye, a serious expression on his face. "No, sir, I really wouldn't agree with that statement. I think it is most *unfortunate* that this action has been filed against Dr. Levin in the past and is pending against him for the past two years. I have known him for a number of years. I gave my reasons in *earlier* testimony for coming to testify." Casdorph wasn't about to allow the attorney to intimidate him.

Sheehan leaned his face close to Casdorph's. "One of those reasons is *not* your own self-interest...in your opinion?" he badgered.

"It is *not* my self-interest. As a matter of fact, I stated that I prefer to *avoid* this type of activity. I am involved *only* to the extent that I am in favor of *good medicine* anyplace in the country. Dr. Levin, whom I have known for eight or ten years, called and asked me if I would come and testify, so my acceptance to do so *hardly* constitutes selfish behavior."

So Sheehan went around the same circle again, working overtime in an attempt to discredit Casdorph's study, which he had already attacked repeatedly. He decided to characterize the physician's research as an "experimental study" rather than a "research study." Hearing the doctor's responses, which were both appropriate and convincing in their combined opinion—which they scribbled on notepads on their table—the defense duo shared a satisfied wink.

Then a minor glitch occurred. Somehow Sheehan had discovered that Levin was paying Casdorph five-thousand dollars in expenses to cover office operations and provide medical coverage for his practice during the two days of work Casdorph would miss. For some reason, Sheehan found the fact fascinating and explored every word of that agreement repeatedly, in detail. The defense lawyer and his client were puzzled by this unseemly interest.

Coming full circle yet again, Sheehan returned to the subject of Chelation therapy. "The long-term effects of EDTA are not really known in the scientific literature, are they?"

"I know of no studies on the long-term effects. But the nice thing about EDTA is that we have thirty years of experience with it now, and secondly, it is very rapidly eliminated from the body. In a patient with normal kidney function, the biologic half time is one hour." The doctor eyed the prosecutor meaningfully. " I would think if there were any long-term effects, they would have shown up after thirty years of use." Casdorph couldn't help but smile after stating this.

Bravo! thought Levin.

Sheehan recovered quickly. "Doctor Casdorph, would you agree that the state should *prevent* physicians from prescribing therapies that are *not* effective?"

Casdorph looked at the prosecutor and sighed. "Counselor, I don't mean to be difficult, but you *are* getting into an area that is *very* difficult to answer. I am concerned about the state coming down on selected individuals when..." He broke off and started anew. "I serve on the medical mortality review board of my hospital, and I see cancer patients who are literally *killed* by conventional drugs, like chemotherapy. That's why it's so difficult to answer your question." He looked at Sheehan, then said, "I *know* what you want me to say, but..."

Sheehan shook his head in exasperation. "Could I ask the Judge, *again*, to request that the witness *not* try to psychoanalyze me, but to answer the questions? He was asked questions related to this on direct examination, about the patient's freedom to choose. He was wonderful! Now, I am asking him a *specific* question to see how far he is willing to go on a specific issue, and the witness, for some reason, is sliding around like an eel! He is a smart man. He understands the question. He just won't answer it!"

Levin marveled at how petulant Sheehan sounded. He wondered if the man would get down on the floor and start throwing a tantrum.

Storch turned his attention to the witness. His gaze was stern. "Dr. Casdorph, you are under oath. You are *required* to answer the questions that are put to you, not to analyze, not to tell counselor where you think his question is going. Counsel is *allowed* to lead on cross-examination."

Casdorph nodded, and then he attempted to explain himself. "My introductory remarks are just to indicate my resonance about this area regarding what the state has a right to do. If you want a yes or no answer: If a drug is proved to be *totally ineffective*, yes, I think that the state has a right to inform the public."

"That *wasn't* the question," Sheehan complained. "The question was, does the state have the right to *prohibit* a physician from giving the drug or modality to a patient *even if* the patient asks for it?"

"Yes, probably so, if they apply the same philosophy to *all* physicians and *all* drugs."

The prosecuting attorney and the doctor continued their dance for awhile longer. Casdorph retained his cool, as the prior defense witnesses had done;

Sheehan often showed his frustration. The prosecutor labored mightily to discredit Casdorph's publications, questioned the use of angiograms to test the efficacy of Chelation therapy, and jabbed whenever he thought he had found an opening.

Finally, "No other questions, Dr. Casdorph. Thank you." The prosecutor took his seat.

Briber said to the witness, "Doctor, the way that we proceed now is that the panel may have questions to ask you."

Dr. McAloon wondered aloud why organized medicine and the editors of peer-review journals reject articles on Chelation therapy.

So do I, Dr. McAloon, so do I, thought Levin. *And so does every other alternative medical practitioner in the country. Thank you for asking!*

McAloon then asked the witness a series of questions about his study. The questions were reasonable, Levin thought, and the witness's answers were forthcoming and thorough. She then tried to clear up her own confusion about chelation chemicals, attempting to understand the difference between magnesium disodium EDTA and calcium disodium EDTA.

By the nodding of his head, it appeared that Casdorph interpreted the question as reasonable in nature. "Calcium EDTA was the *original* chelator used for treatment of lead poisoning," he told her. "Now, when you want to take calcium *out* of the body, you *don't* use the calcium salt, you use the *sodium* salt. That was the original work that was done in the 1950's. And subsequent to this, in the interest of intracellular magnesium, it was found if you *add* magnesium sulfate to the solution, it goes in as *magnesium sodium EDTA*, so that the magnesium is *released* to enter the cell, and they appear to have a beneficial effect over using just sodium EDTA alone."

McAloon pursued the idea of chelation a bit further before she was completely satisfied. Casdorph referred to one of his slides in responding that "the purpose of Chelation therapy is not to take calcium out of the *body* but out of the *abnormal deposits*, out of the arterial walls." McAloon followed this discussion with questions about hair analysis, once again pursuing the matter until she was satisfied that she had enough information to evaluate the process in deliberations.

Dr. O'Connor followed with two quick questions, and Casdorph's response involved two quick answers. Briber focused on Chelation therapy, wondering why the California hospitals where Casdorph had privileges did *not* allow the treatment to be given to patients on premises. Casdorph's answer was predictable: the fear of a malpractice suit.

On redirect examination, Harris decided to elaborate on *why* Casdorph was unable to chelate patients in the hospital setting. Referring to the other case in which Casdorph had testified, Harris asked: "Dr. Casdorph, after you testified in the state of Washington, what *consequences* did you experience as a result of that testimony."

Casdorph clearly did not expect that question and shifted uncomfortably in his seat. "Well," he responded, "this subject hasn't come up before, but as a result of prior testimony in the state of Washington, it came out in the hearing that I was *giving* Chelation therapy in a hospital, in a municipal hospital. The opposing attorney, after the hearing, took it upon himself to *write* to Medicare of Los Angeles and tell them that he felt I was doing something that was *inappropriate*, and they in turn contacted my hospital, which caused a series of hearings and committees to be set up. At first, they decided in my favor, and later they decided that I should *not* be allowed to do chelation in the hospital. So, it *did* result in sort of an embarrassing situation for me as a result of my testimony."

Harris nodded. "And a deprivation of chelation to your hospitalized patients from that point on?"

"Yes, it limited their right to receive it. The sickest patients were due to receive chelation while they were in the hospital."

"How many years had you been administering Chelation therapy in the hospital?"

"A couple of years."

"During that period of time, had there been *any* episode in which a patient had an adverse reaction or adverse consequences?"

"No, there were no problems at all."

"Had there been any instances were a patient *improved* as a result of the therapy?"

"Yes."

Harris rubbed his hands together. "So, as a result of that prosecutor's zeal and vindictiveness," Harris stated, glancing quickly at Sheehan, "your hospitalized patients, the ones who needed it the most, no longer could get it until they got well enough to be *out* of the hospital?"

"Correct."

"Doctor, are you a proponent of *preventive* medicine, *including* Chelation therapy?"

"Yes, as *part* of a practice."

"Would you describe how Chelation therapy can be *used* for prevention?"

"Well, for example, patients with vascular disease, stroke, can have Chelation therapy to *reverse* the deposits that are there and *prevent* further difficulty down the line."

"Do you believe that somebody who *doesn't* have a stroke or a problem would *benefit* from taking chelation as a preventive?"

"Yes," Casdorph answered. "As I said earlier, the time may well come in which this is *incorporated* into mainstream medicine."

"I object!" cried Sheehan. "It is *not* responsive to the question! The question is, does he believe in *doing* it? It doesn't ask him to *hypothesize* some great future."

When Harris attempted to learn whether Casdorph would be willing to chelate an *asymptomatic* patient requesting the treatment, Sheehan objected to the phrasing.

"This is cross-examination to get the witness to change his answer!"

Harris looked at Sheehan. "I just want the *truth*."

"No, you want your *answer*, but you have to take it as it comes."

"Objection sustained."

"I'm finished," said Harris, walking away from the witness.

CHAPTER 26

Briber opened the meeting. "It is May 24, 1991, and we will resume the hearing in the matter of Warren M. Levin, M.D. Mr. Harris, you have another witness?"

"Yes, sir, I am calling James Carter."

"Just a moment," interjected Sheehan. "Can we go off the record for a moment?"

Given permission to do so, Sheehan walked Harris off into a corner of the room. "James Carter?" the defense attorney inquired. "You said you'd be calling Chaim Schwartz, and I was just about to ask for his c.v. Who *is* this James Carter?"

"We'll be giving you his c.v.!" Harris said, barely able to contain what would surely amount to explosive laughter.

"What are talking about?"

Harris was enjoying himself hugely. "Come on, Terry," he said to his opponent. "Don't you get it?"

"Get what?" Sheehan responded, uncomfortable at his disadvantage. "You told me last week that you were bringing in this Dr. Chaim Schwartz. I wasn't able to find anything out about him, either, so I was about..."

"Schwartz!" Harris looked at Sheehan and realized that the prosecutor wasn't "getting" anything, so he finally took pity on him. "Good Lord, Terry, don't you know *any* Yiddish at all? 'Schwartz' means 'black.' Dr. Carter here," he said pointing toward the center of the room where the witness was waiting to be sworn in, "is black. Even *you* can see that!" Harris laughed.

Sheehan backed away from Harris, no trace of amusement on his face. He was shaking his head in disbelief, his mouth open, as he walked back to where the others were and asked that they go back on the record. Harris just looked at Levin and winked, and Levin realized that his lawyer was reveling in the fact that he had thrown the state's prosecutor off stride at the start of the morning's session.

The witness was sworn in, his C.V. submitted to the court, and his educational accomplishments detailed for the record. After medical school, Dr. Carter had done residencies in pediatrics, a two-year stint in the U.S. Navy, followed by additional education at Columbia University's School of Public Health and Administrative Medicine, with a year in residence as a graduate student, and a summer studying nutrition as part of his fellowship in tropical medicine. He earned a master's degree in parasitology at Columbia, after which he was awarded a doctorate in Public Health, also from Columbia. Board-certified in pediatrics, Carter now worked at Tulane University's School of Public Health and Tropical Medicine, heading the nutrition division and teaching public health students, as well as medical students.

"I deal with nutrition as it interfaces with the practice of medicine," Carter said.

Harris then asked the doctor's destination at the end of the day. "I am going to the Sudan as a consultant to the World Health Organization," Carter stated, matter-of-factly, having done similar work for the State Department in the past.

The defense attorney moved smoothly into the area of chelation, which was of particular interest to Carter, who proceeded to relate a story about a practicing family physician he encountered in 1983 whose cholesterol reading was nearly 900, over 700 points above the acceptable level for cardiac safety.

Prompted to elaborate, Carter said, "He was seriously ill with coronary artery disease and had experienced multiple heart attacks. He had unstable angina," referring to chest pain that came and went periodically, "and in those days, the surgeons were not doing triple and quadruple bypasses. In any event, due to the extensive blockage in all of his coronary arteries, they refused to operate on him."

"What happened then?" Harris asked.

"The doctor went off to a clinic in Alabama where he received Chelation therapy. He returned to Louisiana free of chest pain, reopened his office, and began offering Chelation therapy as a part of his medical practice."

"What did *you* do then?"

"I made contact with some of the doctors who were doing chelation. I approached it like I would any other problem open to analysis and the use of scientific methods to establish its efficacy. Then I wrote a proposal to conduct a retrospective study of the effectiveness of Chelation therapy in the treatment of coronary artery disease," Carter explained.

Harris asked him what the study showed, and Carter laughed softly.

"I could not get funding for the study," the doctor stated, shaking his head at his own foolishness for trying. "But eventually *another* doctor, who was facing coronary artery bypass surgery, had Chelation therapy, and got a good response, so *he* approached a foundation in which he was influential. Money was made available and matched by the doctors who made up the American Academy of Medical Preventics. *That* study is now in progress at three army hospitals," Carter said.

At Harris's request, the doctor spoke of another collaboration that followed and a published paper that resulted, reviewing 2,800 cases of patients treated with EDTA Chelation therapy. He described the parameters of the work and the double-blind, crossover study that was constructed immediately afterwards. The administration protocol was designed by the organization he had previously referred to, which by that time had changed its name to its present form, ACAM, the American College for Advancement in Medicine. The chelation protocol that Carter referred to was the one that Warren Levin had testified earlier to helping create. Carter explained that ten sodium magnesium EDTA chelation treatments were given to half the patients, and when the code was broken, those were the patients whose conditions had *improved*. In the "crossover" piece, the control group—which had originally received only vitamins and minerals or additives before—had chelation *added* to their protocol and also showed improvement.

Carter then explained a puzzling fact. "We submitted an article for publication to the *Lancet*," he said, citing one of the world's leading general medical journals, with specialty journals in oncology, neurology and infectious diseases. "I got a very interesting letter back from them, which stated, in effect, that 'We are not going to publish this, but we want you to understand that there is nothing *wrong* with this study. We just think that you do not have a large enough number of cases for us to go out on a limb and counteract the prevailing opinions with regard to the use of Chelation therapy.'" Carter shrugged his shoulders. "We thought it was interesting. We kind of lost...but we won, at the same time."

"I *object* to quoting from a document unless Mr. Harris intends to offer it," Sheehan said. "I submit that the document does *not* say what this witness just said! He is quoting from a document that *none* of us have seen."

Bob Harris took advantage of the prosecutor's wording. "Counsel just stated, 'I contend that the document does *not* say what the witness *claims* it says.' I would like to know the basis for that contention." Levin watched his attorney gather steam. "Since an officer of the court has an obligation to act in good faith, and since I know that the letter has never been *seen* by counsel, I think it is fair to ask the basis of that contention." Harris still wasn't through. "He is calling this witness a *liar*!"

Sheehan came back at him immediately. "What is the basis for *your* stating that I never *saw* the letter, Mr. Harris?"

"Tell me I'm wrong!" Harris challenged.

Sheehan's jaw came forward. "*You* can say things, but *I* can't?"

The judge could sense it coming...again. "Mr. Sheehan, please, let's not," he pleaded.

Harris responded instead. "I think this is a *very* significant issue."

Storch was not to be put off. "Mr. Sheehan, Mr. Harris, I am speaking. Do *not* interrupt. I don't want this to degenerate into personal attacks. Hearsay evidence is *admissible* in these types of proceedings. It will be given the weight that the committee believes it is due."

"My objection is to not having the document for the *panel's* review."

"If you are making a request for production, leave out all of the emotional language."

"That is what I am asking," Sheehan said, annoyed at being chastised when he felt that the opposing attorney had provoked him.

Carter agreed to make the letter available when he returned from his trip to the Sudan. Harris then requested details on two other studies involving chelation.

The doctor told him, "The pilot, double-blind study was eventually published in April 1990 in the *Journal of the National Medical Association*."

Harris put out the bait. "Is that a *throwaway* journal, a throwaway *rag*?" he asked, with the hint of a smile.

Carter sniffed, disdainfully. "I *read* that comment from Victor Herbert in the transcript. The *Journal of the National Medical Association* is a publication that was established by the *black* physicians in this country, and I think it *very* disparaging for him to comment about it as though it were a throw-away journal," Carter said, referring to Victor Herbert.

Like most lawyers, Harris was schooled not to ask his witnesses questions unless he knew the answers in advance. He looked at the doctor in the witness chair with approval. Nearing sixty years of age, Carter was a tall, good-looking, black man, who was well-spoken and intellectually curious. Living in the South, he was known as Jimmy by those close to him. He took endless ribbing when his "namesake," Jimmy Carter, was elected president. He was comfortable in his own skin, but had been annoyed by Victor Herbert's comment calling the medical journal a "throwaway" publication.

Sheehan was on his feet in an instant. "I *object* to the question and move to *strike* the question *and* the answer!" He looked at the members of the panel and said, in defense of the state's witness, "Victor Herbert *never* said it was 'a throwaway rag' to my recollection, just that it is *not* the equivalent of peer-reviewed journals."

Harris cut off the judge, who had begun to respond. "I will *quote* from the testimony of Dr. Herbert," he declared.

Storch paid no attention to the interruption, addressing the prosecutor instead. "Mr. Sheehan, you *know* I don't have the power to strike testimony."

Sheehan *should* know that, Harris thought. It had come up numerous times already, and Storch always made the same comment.

Sheehan took a different tack. "The *second* part of my request is to direct the panel to *ignore* the question and the answer. That is what Hearing Officers *routinely* do," he said, petulantly.

Storch took a conservative approach. "Based on the next question, I will decide whether to instruct them."

"Fine," Sheehan said, his tone making it clear that it was *not* fine, at all.

The judge allowed Harris to read Victor Herbert's pertinent comments from the transcript. Setting the stage, Harris began by asking Dr. Carter if the *Journal of the National Medical Association* was peer-reviewed and listed in the *Indicus Medicus* of the United States, referring to the massive source of medical reference works and journals, including those involving forensic medicine. Carter replied affirmatively. Harris stated the transcript page number and line, and then began to read.

> **Harris:** "Dr. Herbert, *what* journal was this article published in?"
>
> **Herbert:** "In a journal that has *trouble* getting articles and will take *anything*."
>
> **Hearing Officer**: "Just answer the question."
>
> **Herbert:** "The *Journal of the National Medical Association*."
>
> **Harris:** "Is that a journal of the American Medical Association?"
>
> **Herbert:** "No, it is a journal of the National Medical Association, a *much* smaller group."
>
> **Harris:** "Could you tell us whether that journal is *respected* in your field as a *reputable* journal?"
>
> **Herbert:** "No, it is *not*. It is basically a very *poor* journal, almost '*a throwaway*,' and it is a journal whose members *can't* get something published in a good journal. So they submit stuff to it, because they'll take *anything*, since they don't get much. And Carter *has* to be a member of the National Medical Association."
>
> **Harris:** "Did you find the article itself *persuasive* in any way with respect to the advisability of performing chelation on patients?"
>
> **Herbert:** "The article is *worthless*.'"

Harris read a few more lines from the transcript and then stood looking at Storch, waiting for a ruling on admissibility. Sheehan renewed his objection, claiming that Victor Herbert hadn't *exactly* said what Harris had *originally* claimed. The judge proceeded to overrule the objection.

A self-satisfied smile on his face, Harris practically glided back over to the witness chair. For his own part, Levin couldn't entirely suppress the positive feeling that the whole interaction had evoked.

"Doctor," Harris asked his witness, "did you have a chance to read Dr. Herbert's testimony *prior* to coming here today?"

"Yes, I did," Carter responded, a slight look of annoyance crossing his features.

"Would you care to comment on it?" Harris asked, innocently.

"Dr. Herbert uses this word 'fraud' very, very loosely," he told Harris, relating several international studies with statistically significant results that were dismissed by Herbert. He followed that with case histories of people too sick to continue working, whose lives were dramatically altered for the better following chelation treatments. Carter then admitted to having the procedure himself as a preventive measure, due to a strong family history of diabetes.

"I have had at least fifty bottles," Carter said, referring to the intravenous solution, "if not more. The initial series, in other words, followed by boosters." Carter then spoke about a study he had conducted, polling the members of the American College for Advancement in Medicine, ACAM, and learning that at least one-quarter of the member physicians had become interested in chelation due to their own illnesses, such as angina, heart attacks, and coronary artery disease.

"We also found," Carter elaborated, "that ninety-six percent of the members not only *gave* chelation to their patients, but they *took it* themselves. And that, to me, is unheard of!" he declared.

Having had breakfast with Carter that morning, where he observed the doctor downing countless vitamins and other pills, Harris had posed the question in the courtroom, in an effort to illustrate that proponents of alternative therapies practice what they preach. When Sheehan's objection to the question was overruled, Carter listed the numerous antioxidants he regularly ingested, followed by a scholarly presentation of their role in attacking free radicals, which damaged cell membranes. He ended by stating that "taking antioxidants is the wave of the future with regard to what you, as an individual, can do to help retard the aging process."

Harris nodded when Carter ended his explanation of the value of dietary supplements, then he asked another question involving Victor Herbert. "Are you familiar with Dr. Herbert's lawsuit against the National Academy of Science?"

"I am not too familiar with it. I did hear that he was suing the organization, but Herbert has a reputation for suing *everybody*."

Levin was surprised that Sheehan didn't object to the statement and ask the judge to have the panel not consider it. He speculated that Sheehan had finally learned that whatever the panel members heard, they heard, and he had to hope that they judged things the same way *he* did.

For his part, Harris had decided to continue the job of taking apart Victor Herbert's testimony, sentence by sentence, with the intention of rendering it as worthless as he judged the man himself to be. "Dr. Carter, on page 959 of the testimony, Victor Herbert says, 'I want to make a broad charge that *all* vitamins were not indicated. I don't care whether they are injected, oral, or applied to the skin. I submit it is *irrelevant*.' Have you had a chance to read the patient's chart in this case?"

"Yes," the doctor replied.

When Harris asked whether the vitamins were justified, Carter proceeded with an explanation that earned an objection from Sheehan, saying that the doctor had presented a "scientific thesis," not a responsive answer. Harris's next question applied to *any* of the patients' subpoenaed charts, wherever Levin had used vitamin and mineral supplements, inquiring whether those actions constituted professional misconduct.

"The answer is no," Carter stated. He continued by elaborating on his prior scientific explanation in response to Harris's follow-up question, which had laid appropriate groundwork.

"Doctor," Harris asked next, "one of the treatment suggestions Dr. Levin made, as part of a clinical ecological approach, was the dust-proofing of a room. On page 695 of the record, Dr. Herbert calls that a 'fad.' Do you agree with that?"

"No, not at all. I think that any allergist will stress the importance of controlling dust in the environment. The comment is just so far out, it doesn't even merit an answer," he concluded, his opinion of Victor Herbert clear. "Those of us in public health are concerned with disease in the family and in the community—the environment, which constitutes clinical ecology."

"On page 675, Dr. Herbert says, 'I am the *world authority* on Vitamin B-15.' Do you agree with his self-evaluation?"

Carter laughed at the statement, shaking his head from side to side in amazement. "I think Dr. Herbert is usually *wrong*, not by reason of what he says, but by reason of what he *excludes*." He thought a moment, then added, "I don't consider him a world authority on *anything*...except Victor Herbert!" he said, looking at the people in the room.

"Dr. Herbert has been referred to as 'a legend in his own mind.' Can you comment on that?"

"I object to that statement," Sheehan said, forcefully, "since *no* witness in this hearing said that *except* Mr. Harris, *repeatedly*, as part of his character assassination!"

"Sustained."

At this point, Harris decided to enter the arena of patient choice, something that had come up frequently during the trial. He hoped that Carter's answer would be thorough and not interrupted by objections. Groundwork, once again, needed to be laid.

"Dr. Carter, if I am a forty-five-year-old male living in New York City and feel *fantastic* and have no symptoms of illness but decide, for *prophylactic* reasons, that I wanted to have Chelation therapy; if you were my doctor, would you give it to me?"

The doctor considered Harris for a moment—a middle-aged attorney fighting to save the licenses of embattled physicians, a stressful job, obviously overweight, an ideal candidate for a heart attack—and began his response. The committee members, Harris noted, since he had them in his peripheral vision as he queried the doctor, had leaned forward in their seats, something he noted that they tended to do when a question captured their interest.

"I think the answer to that is *yes*, Mr. Harris, but I would like to clarify it. When chelation was introduced into New Zealand, it happened to be in the right place at the right time, although it was introduced by the *wrong* people. It was introduced by non-physician practitioners. But the New Zealand government was looking at more costly ways of treating patients with arteriosclerosis. After media and press coverage showing that patients were getting *better* after chelation, the government invited Dr. Ralph Lev, a cardiovascular surgeon from New Jersey—one of the few who uses Chelation therapy—to come over as a consultant. After that visit, they decided to give chelation to the *sickest* patients, and I shared my original proposal with them for a retrospective study, using several criteria. I suggested that they take the design we had written and do a prospective study, offering *both* groups conventional treatment and adding the chelation to *one* group only."

Carter said that New Zealand was still looking at the design of the study. "In the final analysis, it is the *cost*, the dollars spent versus the outcome, that is going to determine the survival of chelation," he speculated.

"In your work with the World Health Organization and with other international groups, have you learned of the use of Chelation therapy in countries *other* than the United States?"

"Yes. There have been two official governmental commissions on alternative medicine: one in Sweden and one in the Netherlands, and there is also a non-governmental commission on complementary medicine in the United Kingdom. Prince Charles, who is the titular head of the British Medical Association, has made repeated appeals for the incorporation of alternative therapies into the National Health Service."

Carter shrugged his shoulders. "We don't even *have* a commission, because we have, in its place, a network of councils on *health fraud*," he said, "where alternative therapies are *discouraged* and prevented from ever coming into the marketplace." Since no one objected, Carter decided to continue. "You will see large sums of money coming from the National Pharmaceutical Council and other sources. It is *my* opinion that Victor Herbert plays a *major* role in the operation of that network. We filed a petition with the FTC, the Federal Trade Commission, on March thirty-first accusing certain organizations of *restricting* free trade by not informing people that there is an *alternative* to coronary artery bypass surgery and other types of vascular bypasses. We are asking the FTC to conduct an investigation. I think Dr. Herbert plays a *key* role in this network, as I stated before."

Harris then asked, "Do you believe that a cardiac surgeon has an obligation *prior* to operating on a patient to inform him that there is an *alternative* therapy which has a significantly lower mortality risk than the proposed surgery?"

"*Objection!* This is *beyond* the scope of this witness's competence. He is board-certified in *pediatrics*. I don't believe that extends to making professional judgments about *cardiac surgeons* and the propriety of their treatment of various conditions."

"Do you wish to respond, Mr. Harris?" asked the judge.

"Dr. Herbert is board-certified in *internal medicine*," Harris began. "He testified on *everything* from potato soup to arteriosclerotic heart disease, to EKG's in which electricity comes *through* the machine, to Chelation therapy, although he has *never* used chelation in the treatment of these conditions in his life. To suggest, after presenting Victor Herbert as their *primary* and *only* scientific witness—if you want to call him that," he added, derisively, "that Dr. Carter should be constrained... I don't have anything else to say!" Harris glared at the judge, waiting for his response.

"I am going to *overrule* the objection. You can answer the question."

Carter told them he believed that one day cardiac surgeons were going to be *required* to inform patients about less-invasive options of treatment. Harris was thrilled.

"Dr. Carter, some of the patients who are the subject of the charges in this hearing was patients that Dr. Levin treated in the mid-1970's. On page 1077 of the record, Dr. Herbert testified that 'The standard cry of the *quack* is that he is a scientist ahead of his time.' Do you believe that Warren Levin has been *ahead of his time* in terms of the medicine that he has been practicing?"

"Yes," Carter stated, without hesitation.

"Do you believe that he is, by inference—based upon the 'Victor Herbert standard'—a *quack*?"

"No, I don't, but I am not sure of the *definition* of a 'quack,'" Carter said, honestly.

Harris moved closer to him, a smile playing at the corners of his mouth. "Let me make it easier for you," he told the doctor. "I'll ask if you think Dr. Levin is described by any of the common synonyms for 'quack.' *Charlatan?*"

"No."

"Fraud?"

"No."

"Bum?"

"No."

"How long have you known Warren Levin?"

"Since 1983 or 1984," he responded.

"Have you had occasion to talk to Dr. Levin about aspects of his practice, to have substantial discussions?"

"Yes, at meetings, and from reading his charts I found him to be a lot more thorough than I had been able to perceive from our discussions. He is *very* thorough.

When Harris began to quiz Dr. Carter on treatment for *candida* in women, the doctor alluded to what had recently become known as the "*Candida* Yeast Syndrome." "One of the suspected etiologies of this syndrome is the fact that the *candida* organism secretes a toxin which is immunosuppressive; it alters the function in the balance between the immune cells, the helper cells, and the suppressor cells. It is this *toxin* that the person is reacting to. So that person is not only sensitive to the presence of *yeast* in the vagina or yeast in the intestinal tract, but they are also reacting to yeast in *foods* in their diet. There are *lots* of foods and nutritional supplements that contain yeast, so attention would have to be paid to diet," said Carter, echoing statements that Levin himself had made in defending his treatment of *candida* patients. Carter also upheld the use of Nystatin in treating the condition.

With that out of the way, and another point scored for the defense, in Harris's opinion, he returned to an earlier strategy. "I would like to continue reading from the record," he said, "page 2159, during Dr. Herbert's direct examination by the prosecutor. In speaking about Dr. Carter here," he said, motioning toward Carter with the page from the transcript, "Mr. Sheehan asked Victor Herbert, 'Could you tell us what your *opinion* is regarding his abilities as a reputable researcher?' Herbert responds, 'He is *incapable* of telling fact from fiction, as I pointed out in a review of an article that he published in the journal, *Food Technology*.'" Harris looked at the committee members to ascertain whether the full effect of Herbert's slanderous remark about his current witness had reached them. He was pleased to see a few sets of eyes drop, in what he hoped was embarrassment.

"Let me skip down," Harris then said. "Mr. Sheehan asked, 'First of all, what did the article by Dr. Carter concern?' Herbert says, 'It promoted Evening Primrose Oil as a remedy for various human ailments. He based it on studies carried out by a promoter of the Evening Primrose *fraud* who was under fire by the Federal Government.' Then Herbert adds," Harris said, a smug smile on his face, "'and I was a *witness* for the Federal Government in the case.' So the prosecutor followed with, 'What was the *result* of that litigation?' Herbert said, 'We took Carter apart.' Then, 'Was the promoter allowed to *sell* that remedy?' 'No, no,' Herbert responded, 'it was enjoined from sale.'"

Harris stood quietly for a beat. "At that point, I shouted, *'Objection! Objection!'*" he related, looking down at the page, obviously anxious to read further. "So, of course, our judge here," motioning to Storch, "asked, 'What is your objection?'" Since Dr. Carter had not been present during the many days of Victor Herbert's testimony, Harris turned toward Carter to make sure the doctor didn't miss a nuance of his objection argument. "I said, 'In the testimony just given, we heard a *scientist* testify in a courtroom for reasons which may or may not be related to his testimony. The second part of my objection is that the witness began to quote himself! He sits here and says, '*I* wrote an article that said such and such.' It is as if he is quoting an authoritative source. *We are hearing the same person testify twice!*" Harris read the words with the same amount of indignation in his voice as he had used when he made the original argument, hoping for maximal impact in the moment.

Storch shook his head. "Mr. Harris," he sighed, "why don't you focus on the testimony? We don't need to hear the objection."

Harris responded with light humor in his voice. "But the objection was so *brilliant*, I wanted to read it!" A few titters in the courtroom.

Harris put a serious look back on his face. "Anyway," he continued, "Mr. Storch then told us to 'move on,' so…"

"He is going to say it *again*, I think!" Sheehan interrupted.

Harris looked up over his glasses at Sheehan, eyebrows raised, then continued. "So, when I cross-examined Dr. Herbert," he began, putting the first page he had read face down on the defense table and selecting the next one in the pile, "I asked, 'Doctor, the substance that Dr. Carter supported was called *what*?' 'Evening Primrose Oil,' he answered. 'What is that?' I asked. 'Gamma-linoleic acid,' he responded. So I followed with, 'He supported this as useful in what connection?' So Herbert starts talking again. 'He put his name on an article as an author of an article which was *obviously* authored by the *promoter*, because it had appeared under the promoter's name *alone* previously, without Carter's name listed as a co-author. The article was published in the *Journal of Food Technology*, making various allegations of fact with respect to treatment of human disease. I wrote a letter to the editor, which they published, in which I dissected the article and pointed out that *none* of the conclusions of facts stated in that article were supported by any evidence, and *that* is why my letter to the editor was published in that journal. And I also corresponded with Carter, who is a very nice guy, and I see him when I go down there.' Then Herbert says," Harris pointed out, making sure he had everyone's attention, "'I teach nutrition at *his* medical school where he is a professor, and they sort of keep him out of the way because he is...he really can't tell fact from fiction. He is a very nice guy, a very pleasant guy. He doesn't know his rear end from second base scientifically.'"

Although everyone present in the hearing room at the moment, with the exception of James Carter, had been in attendance when Victor Herbert had originally uttered those words, the sharp intakes of breath informed Harris that the statements made by the state's witness were having a *greater* impact the second time around, with the object of Herbert's invective, Dr. James Carter, sitting in their midst.

Sheehan broke the silence. "*I object to this reading!* Mr. Harris can ask Dr. Carter questions like, 'Did you *publish* such an article?' without reading this. It is *unnecessary* for us to listen for a second time...as *great* as it is, to Dr. Herbert's testimony," he sniffed.

The judge agreed with Sheehan. "I think, at this point, Mr. Harris, you have probably gone pretty far enough. Why don't you ask the witness some questions? Why don't we get some testimony out of the witness?"

It was Harris's turn to sniff. "His objection was one paragraph from home plate, anyway." Turning to his witness, Harris asked, "Dr. Carter, first of all, does Victor Herbert *teach* in your medical school?"

"No, he does not."

"You are there twelve years. Has he *ever* lectured at your medical school in twelve years?"

"I think he gave a talk on health fraud at the Veterans Hospital, which is part of the overall medical complex at Tulane. But he does *not* teach nutrition at our medical school."

Harris saw an opening to slip in something extra. "In the last twelve years, Doctor, when Victor Herbert came to teach in your medical school—*that he doesn't teach at*," he added emphatically, "did he come to see you?"

"No."

"I object to that question and move to strike!" Sheehan shouted, his patience wearing thin. "The witness indicated that he is *not* in the medical school but in the School of Public Health. This is an inaccuracy!"

"The objection is overruled. I *don't* have the power to strike," Storch responded, matter-of-factly, repeating himself yet another time. Storch then added, "The witness's responsibilities also include teaching nutrition to the medical students."

"Teaching nutrition to the medical students, but he is *not* on the faculty of the School of Medicine!" Sheehan wasn't giving up.

Carter spoke up. "Correction," he said softly. When Storch asked for the correction, Carter told him that he *was*, indeed, on the faculty of the medical school.

Harris resumed. "Has Victor Herbert *visited* you in New Orleans in the last twelve years?"

"No."

"Have you seen him *anywhere on earth* in the last twelve years?"

"No, and we have *not* corresponded. Had he written to me to find out *what* we were doing in the way of research with gamma-linoleic acid, which is found not only in Evening Primrose Oil but in other sources, he would not have made those statements in honesty."

Harris nodded. "Doctor," he said, then, "Herbert talks about the Evening Primrose Oil fraud. Gamma-linoleic acid is found in *other* substances as well, isn't it?"

"Human breast milk, Borage Oil, and Black Currant Oil are all sources," Carter responded.

"So, Doctor, are you *still* doing work in this area?"

"Yes. Our last publication, which is in press with a journal entitled *Women's Health*, is called 'The Effects of the Combination of Gamma-Linoleic Acid in

Evening Primrose Oil and Fish Oil vs. Magnesium and Placebo in Preventing Preeclampsia in Pregnancy.' The fatty acids prevent a clinical condition which is characterized by high blood pressure, edema, and protein in the urine, most often during the first pregnancy," he explained for the sake of the non-medical listeners.

Harris then directed Carter to remove the newspaper under a pile of papers near the witness chair. "That is the *New York Times* of May 24, 1991, correct?"

"Yes, this morning's paper," Carter responded.

"Would you read the name of the article we noted this morning, please?"

Carter read: "'Why Drugs Cost More in the U.S.'"

"Can you tell me *why* you took special note of that article this morning?"

"Out of my experience with chelation, I am writing a book that deals with racketeering in medicine and some of the underlying reasons for the escalating costs of health care. One reason concerns the ability to *control* what gets into the marketplace, like in the case of Evening Primrose Oil or Chelation therapy. Those controlling techniques probably fall under the RICO statutes: Racketeering Influenced Corrupt Organizations," he explained. "That was the reason we filed the petition, listing those organizations, with the Federal Trade Commission for them to investigate."

Carter seemed to hesitate when asked to name names, so the judge instructed him accordingly. "The National Council on Health Fraud," Carter blurted out.

Harris was waiting for this. "You wouldn't happen to mean the *same* council that *Victor Herbert* heads or is a 'prime player' in would you?"

"He *is* a principal player," Carter admitted.

When Harris segued into an issue concerning treating patients with arthritis, and Sheehan objected, since there was no mention of that condition in the patient charts subpoenaed from Levin, Harris sought to find relevance. "This is a *political* case!" he stated, in a strong voice. The reason why the Commissioner of Health chose to bring this case against Warren Levin is *not* because Warren Levin was giving chelation and there was anything wrong with chelation!" he declared. "It is because he was giving chelation, and there are *billion-dollar interests* in this country who *don't* want chelation given. And, all along, we have seen that the various things Dr. Levin is doing have *economic roots* in the opposition to them," Harris added, tangentially.

"I object!" Sheehan appropriately declared. "This has *nothing* to do with my prior objection! This is an overall *summation* that he has given *many* times. That is why this hearing is taking *forever*, because Mr. Harris is expanding this into a global conspiracy between Dr. Herbert, the AMA, and various other people who are also guilty of racketeering." Sheehan was really gathering steam now. "It is not legal and proper. We have charges. The evidence has to *relate* to those charges. If we are examining a whole other issue, this case is totally open-ended, and it will *never* end."

Sheehan was right, and the panel members were nodding in agreement, as was the judge. Levin cringed. His lawyer was often outrageous, he acknowledged, but he *did* trust him. He had done a fine job getting the defense witnesses to repudiate Victor Herbert's baseless allegations. He wondered if the defense would lose ground if Bob Harris's antics continued.

"All right, enough!" said the Administrative Officer. "Two points: As a strict technical matter, this case was *not* brought by the Commissioner of Health. It was brought by the State Board for Professional Medical Conduct. Second, whether or not there are political implications to this case, I am not prepared to say. It is not my role to say."

Storch looked at the prosecutor for an answer to his next question. "There are no charges about Evening Primrose Oil that I am aware of, are there?"

"Excuse me, Judge!" Harris interrupted. "Not only are there charges that he used it, because he *did* prescribe it to one patient, but this man," he indicated Carter, "with double doctorates was *character-assassinated* in this room. My job is to present Dr. Carter to the panel as what he is: a credible, reliable, decent researcher and physician!" Harris was indignant.

The judge attempted to call a lunch break, asking that he be shown the charges relating to the primrose oil during that recess. He made a point of refusing to entertain the notion of "global conspiracy," however, unless Harris could relate it *directly* to the charges brought against Levin.

"You don't think this is *related* to the charges?" Harris asked, incredulously.

"Don't argue with me, Mr. Harris."

"I am *not* arguing with you, Judge," Harris argued. Then he added, "Don't point your finger at me! It is not appropriate behavior for a judge." Harris *was* arguing with the judge; it was apparent to everyone.

Levin groaned inwardly. He was glad it was time for a lunch break.

When the afternoon proceedings began, the primrose oil issue and the conspiracy theory were back on the floor, resulting in a volley of comments between Storch and Harris. Levin watched, his head following each speaker.

Sheehan walked to his seat, saying, "I will *withdraw* the objection, because the argument is getting much longer than the objection would have achieved."

Harris smiled. "Just to make you *comfortable*," he said, "there is an allegation in the Amended Charges which says that Dr. Levin is guilty of 'prescribing the following treatments which were not medically indicated.'" Harris threw his hands up in the air, the pages he held fluttering noisily. "They list just about *everything* you will find at a *health food store*, and one of the things in the list is *Evening Primrose Oil*. I just wanted to increase your comfort level," he said to the judge and Sheehan, in a mocking tone.

Storch sighed with resignation. "My comfort level is extremely high, Mr. Harris. Mr. Sheehan has withdrawn his objection. You can proceed."

When Harris had exhausted the topic, he then had the doctor speak about the patient whom Victor Herbert had labeled "schizophrenic," and Carter stated that he saw *no* evidence of a mental health diagnosis in that patient's chart. Harris then smoothly moved the doctor into a discussion of the six-hour glucose tolerance test and the diagnosis of hypoglycemia, both proclaimed *worthless* by Victor Herbert; they were upheld as valid by James Carter, the witness. The defense attorney also verified that, like Dr. Hoffer, a prior witness, Carter was *not* being paid to testify; only his out-of-pocket expenses for airfare and hotel were covered.

Carter was given the opportunity, through one of Harris's special, open-ended questions to speak at length. He used that chance well. "I have a lot of respect for Dr. Levin as an individual," he said, "for what he's trying to do, how he treats his patients. I happen to believe that it is better to *prevent* a disease than it is to wait until it occurs and is full-blown. I also believe that it makes more sense to spend three-thousand dollars for a series of intravenous chelation treatments, which—as near as I can tell—work a hell of a lot better than a coronary artery bypass, which costs on the average about $35,000."

Harris appreciated the testimonial. "You spent several hours last night reviewing Dr. Levin's charts and court transcripts with him. Did you find any omissions or commissions rising to the level of *fraud* or *professional misconduct*?

"No. None, whatsoever." His response was firm.

Sheehan commenced his cross-examination of the witness. He established that Carter had a dual appointment at Tulane: Clinical Professor of Pediatrics in the School of Medicine and professor and head of the Nutrition Section at the School of Public Health, which was his primary appointment. Sheehan then moved to the topic of Carter receiving his degrees from Columbia University, questioning which division of the school had actually awarded the credentials. The prosecutor determined that Carter had never been in private practice and then asked whether he had been in a practice partnership.

"Right now," the doctor answered, "I am an employee of several physicians, and I provide nutrition consultation. I also look after patients with alcohol and drug addition."

"You have never given chelation to a private patient who came to you with a medical problem for which you thought chelation was indicated. Is that correct?"

"That is correct."

Changing gears abruptly, the prosecutor attempted to explore the issue of racketeering in medicine. Harris objected, asking the judge to inform the witness that he did *not* have to answer the questions.

Storch looked at Harris. "*No*, I will *not* make that statement," Storch said, wondering where Harris was going with this. "He *must* answer all questions that are put to him, as is the case with *all* other witnesses."

Storch's internal question was answered by Harris's reply. "That *wasn't* the case with Victor Herbert," Harris said, staring into Storch's eyes.

A brief debate followed, and Storch directed Carter to answer. Sheehan seemed surprised when the doctor labeled the National Council on Health Fraud as the AMA's "surrogate," intimating, but not directly stating, that one of its targets was alternative medicine.

The doctor exhaled loudly. "The AMA is the second most powerful lobby in this country," he said, without hesitation, "second only to the National Rifle Association. It is one of the largest contributors to political action committees. I think they have been very effective in using the political process in an open way and also in a covert way to control the medical marketplace. Period!"

Sheehan took an interesting direction. "Doctor, would you agree that you do not particularly like Dr. Herbert as an individual?"

The surprise was plain on Carter's face. "No, not at all. That is not true."

"Then you like the guy, right?"

"I haven't seen him for over twelve years," Carter said, reasonably.

Sheehan worked at trying to get him to admit that Victor Herbert's critiques of Carter's articles, via letters to the editors of two journals had, in some way, influenced Carter's view of Herbert. Sheehan then moved to admit Herbert's two letters into evidence, one addressed to the editor of *Food Technology* and the other to the editor of the *Journal of the American Dietetic Association*.

This time it was Harris's turn to wonder where Sheehan was going with *his* line of questioning. Nevertheless, he believed he had a valid reason to object to the letters' submission.

"These letters have been faxed from the Bronx VA! Your *independent, neutral witness*," Harris spat, referring to Victor Herbert, "faxed this stuff to the prosecution for the state! You are letting things in on ego," he accused the judge, "and not on examination."

The argument failed. The letters were admitted into evidence anyway.

"Do you agree," Sheehan asked Carter, "that this hearing and its charges were brought in *good faith* against a physician who certain officials believe is not practicing properly?"

"I don't believe the charges were brought in good faith," Carter smoothly responded, "but I think the members of the panel are *acting* in good faith."

"The charges were brought in *bad* faith, then?"

"I believe so."

"To achieve what overall gain," Sheehan wondered.

Carter didn't hesitate. "The charges were brought to make an example of a physician practicing a particular style of medicine." Given permission to elaborate, Carter said, "There is a tendency on the part of various organizations to use the legal system to resolve questions in science and as a means of sanctioning the physicians whose practices may be different from what is usual and customary—even though that practice may be doing a great deal of good, may be focusing on health promotion and prevention, which in the long run will be the only way that we will be able to curtail and bring down the spiraling—ever-spiraling, health care costs. I am saying there is *collusion*—using the legal system for this purpose: to eliminate, to almost seek out, search, and destroy!" He was clearly annoyed by what he believed was going on.

"Fine," Sheehan said. "One question, Doctor: If academic medicine and the medical establishment and everybody else in power are so opposed to keeping down these various alternate therapies, such as chelation and the other things you espoused, how is it that *you* managed to still have a high-level job, apparently in a medical school? Isn't that kind of inconsistent with your overall argument of a mean conspiracy against knowledge in this regard?"

"Not at all," replied Carter. "I am in a school of public health, concerned about preventive medicine, about illness and pathology in the community, about access to health care. I am concerned about the application of knowledge and technology in medicine for the benefit of the prevention and treatment of disease in the population."

"The question was, Doctor: How come you *still* have a job if the whole world is against *people like you*?"

"I never said that. *You* are saying that," Carter told him, eyeing him severely.

When the topic turned to Chelation therapy once again, and Carter was asked about an American study of the procedure with a large number of subjects, Sheehan appeared shocked to discover that the results were published in December 1956, in the *American Journal of Medical Science*. "How about offering something, Doctor, that is not in ancient history?" he asked.

"I object!" Harris stated. "As long as the study was done *prior* to the time that Dr. Levin treated these patients, it is relevant. The notion that a scientific study, that

is efficacious when done, loses its efficacy over time, simply through the passage of time, is *ludicrous*," he stated, eloquently.

Sheehan turned to the subject of an upcoming cost-benefit analysis study that would be spearheaded by a postdoctoral student at Tulane during the coming summer. The proposal would require approval and funding from the Office of Health Policy, a government entity created in December of 1990, Carter told him. Sheehan pressed for more information.

Carter nodded. "We are designing a study to look at the cost of Chelation therapy versus the cost of bypass surgery in relation to the achieved outcomes and the quality of life: a study that would be done simultaneously in this country, in New Zealand, and in the United Kingdom."

When Sheehan had completed his cross-examination, the session was turned over to the committee members. Dr. McAloon verbally ran an entire list of tests past the witness, questioning whether they were appropriate tests to routinely perform on a patient coming into a private physician's office. With the exception of Darkfield Microscopy, Carter's responses were either "appropriate," "take it or leave it," or "appropriate for a patient living in New York City." Dr. O'Connor, the retired gynecologist, focused several questions on Carter's use of the term "*Candida* Syndrome," requesting elaboration. Carter was specific about the protocol to follow in diagnosing and treating the syndrome and responded to O'Connor's point that "males are subject to *candidiasis* just as much as females, but perhaps not as frequently."

Briber then weighed in, asking about the effectiveness of Chelation therapy for rheumatoid arthritis. "Are there any contraindications for Chelation therapy?" Briber asked.

Carter nodded. "Patients who have compromised renal function, and patients who have congestive heart failure," he responded. Then he added, with a smile, "Most of the contraindications are in the *protocol*."

"How would you feel if chelation was offered *without* cost to the entire population over age forty-five?" Briber asked.

"I think it is an academic argument," Carter told the chemist, shrugging his shoulders. "I don't think it is going to happen."

"I have no further questions. We will meet again on June fourth. Please be prepared to talk about the conduct of this investigation afterwards. Dr. Carter, thank you very much. Good luck on your trip to the Sudan."

The meeting ended at 3:20 p.m. When Carter walked out of the hearing room with Levin and Harris, he asked the defense lawyer a question.

"Bob," he said, a look of puzzlement on his face, "what were you and prosecutor talking about during that huddle you had in the corner of the room before we began this morning?"

Harris looked at the tall, distinguished physician as they shook hands prior to parting. Levin sucked in his breath noisily, since Harris had explained the little joke he had played on Sheehan regarding "Chaim Schwartz," and he was worried about how Harris might respond to Carter.

"To tell you the truth, Jimmy," he said, a touch of mirth in his voice, "it just concerned a little bit of 'black humor.'"

CHAPTER 27

"Good morning," Storch said. "Before we proceed with the testimony, Mr. Harris, you have some preliminary matters?"

As the morning began with the typical opening procedures, Warren Levin occupied his usual seat, firmly ensconced at the defense table, eyeing the notes he had made during the past two hearings. He looked over what he had written during Hoffer's and Carter's testimonies on his behalf. His *modus operandi* was rigorous. He would take copious notes for himself during the sessions, jotting his impressions, as well as noting information to prompt his attorney during the proceeding itself. He would carefully review the notes afterwards, either on the train home or while commuting back into the city the following morning, scribbling reminders in the margins, underlining significant sections, or marking areas with asterisks. He was then able to call Harris's attention to specific passages, which the attorney would then locate within his own copy of the actual transcript, unless Levin had already cross-referenced the portion for discussion. That attention to detail is what made the defense team of Harris and Levin so effective in the strategic planning department, he thought. It also kept the significant happenings of the day fresh enough in his mind to discuss with Susan, who invariably waited up with dinner, anxious for an accounting of the most recent hearing room dramas, hoping to hear more positives than negatives. Considering that Levin generally went from his lawyer's side directly to his medical office to see a backlogged schedule of patients, he often got home very late. He knew better than to eat dinner and sleep on a full stomach, so the discussions with Susan served a triple purpose: he kept her current on the progress of his fight, emptied his mind of the day's events so they wouldn't keep him awake at night, and allowed his body's digestive system sufficient time to function. They agreed that both Hoffer's and Carter's testimonies were helpful to his cause, and they were also gratified that visitors from various alternative medicine associations occasionally attended a session to show support. He told Susan he believed that the past two sessions had advanced his defense admirably—if for no other reason than fattening the record with "testimony disguised as objections," which was how Sheehan frequently referred to Bob's courtroom style.

Bringing his attention back to the proceedings, Levin heard his attorney respond to the judge in the affirmative.

"Yes, Judge, I do have some preliminary matters. First of all, Dr. McAloon had asked for any articles we had on how food allergy causes hypoglycemia. I offer this photocopy of an article in a book called *Brain Allergies*, put out by Keats publishing, which deals specifically with that subject."

That excerpt, plus a copy of Victor Herbert's speech to the insurance company directors, were two items Harris handed to Storch, who moved to mark and admit them into evidence—until Sheehan voiced his objections. The prosecutor, annoyed because "as usual" he was being shown new material "a second after it's offered," noted the missing copyright page of the book chapter and the fact that Victor Herbert had not been at the hearings for months, yet a speech he had given was being offered as evidence. Sheehan also complained that no witness had authenticated the book first, which was the acceptable procedure to follow, and the age of the book was in question due to the missing copyright page. Harris argued that the book made reference to material published as late as 1986, therefore it was a current edition; and he submitted that the speech was listed on Dr. Herbert's c.v. and was critical in this case for its effect on health insurance companies and their reluctance to reimburse for Levin's procedures, leading to the completion of the "circle theory" that resulted in the prosecution of Levin.

The next order of business involved the introduction of two of Levin's patients and one of the doctor's employees, all prepared to testify in the hearing, who introduced themselves—as per Storch's instructions—only by their initials. During an immediate break for a brief executive session, Harris successfully admitted Victor Herbert's speech into evidence, a satisfying move for the defense.

Now, Harris's upcoming task concerned a creative scheme he was planning to initiate as a defense tactic. Sheehan, knowing a few of the particulars, spoke out to halt the upcoming drama before it could gather momentum.

"I think Mr. Harris already has some kind of medical events taking place outside," he began. "Before he decided to subject these people to *whatever* type of invasive situations that are going on out there," he said, pointing to the exit door of the hearing room, "he should have gotten approval from the panel as to whether or not he can introduce that evidence. I have very *strenuous* objections to this entire scenario that Mr. Harris thinks he is going to play out *without* objections!" Sheehan, who normally held himself in a dignified manner, even while engaging in verbal battles with the defense, seemed agitated, Harris was pleased to observe. "It is *improper* to bring in human subjects and subject them to anything for purposes of this hearing. These people are *not* part of the hearing or patients in the case." He looked at the members of the panel, fire in his eyes. "I have *never* had a hearing where we have subjected outside parties to any type of medical procedure in order to prove a point!" Harris noted the nervous looks that the panelists were giving one another, and he felt *doubly* pleased, if for no other reason than he believed that Sheehan's "performance" was an ideal "opening act" for the "drama" he hoped would unfold.

Sheehan went on to elaborate about "fancy squiggles" on a slide, patients with slides of few or many "squiggles," all in an attempt to prove that Darkfield Microscopy was not an effective test for identification of *candida* infections. "In addition, we have to take it on *faith* whether one patient has the condition and another doesn't. What do we do?" he asked, his voice rising, "A complete physical examination to *see* if they have the condition or not?" He calmed himself a bit, and then continued. "This is a lot of bells and whistles with all kinds of fancy microscopes and fancy monitors here and wires and lights that really add up to *zero* from the point of view of the probative value. And," he continued, slyly, "it is a little scary if something goes wrong with the drawing of blood, leading to some kind of infection. Is the state implicated here?" Sheehan eyed Storch, waiting for a response.

Harris had watched the panelists' faces during the prosecutor's speech. These people were *more* than a little curious, he noted, and Sheehan's warm-up act only got them more interested...until he squished their hope with the threat of legal liability. *Damn him!*

"Mr. Harris?" asked Storch.

"Does that require a response?" Harris asked, disdainfully.

"Yes, it does. Mr. Sheehan has objected to your proposed line of testimony and demonstration."

Harris was fired up. "As far as patients providing finger stick samples outside of this room, that is *not* the panel's business," he began. "One of the charges against Dr. Levin is that he did a *worthless* test: Darkfield Microscopy. Dr. Levin is here, and his technician—who has been performing this test for six years—is here, and both are available to testify about the patients' histories and provide blood samples." He walked to the panel table, his tone moving into the reasonable range. "What are we supposed to do?" he asked the group. "We have an accusation that this is a worthless test…because *Victor Herbert* says it is worthless. I thought that Dr. Levin's idea of bringing this in was very creative. He has had patients who had been to *ten* other doctors before finally being diagnosed with *candida* by Dr. Levin…because of the efficacy of *this* test." He threw his hands up in surrender. "If you don't want us to do it, fine. We'll pack it up and go home!" he said, walking away from them.

Storch admitted that the demonstration would be interesting to watch. He then made a point of saying that the Hearing Committee would not be making the *final* determination in the case.

Storch said, "The record will have to be preserved and reviewed by the Commissioner or designee and the Board of Regents, and I am worried about the reproducibility of this demonstration."

Harris had thought of that in advance. "That's why I brought a camera," he told the judge, a huge smile lighting up his face at the thought that he'd be allowed to proceed, "to take photographs of that screen." He pointed to the setup on one of the tables in the room.

Nevertheless, Storch ruled against him. "I am going to preclude you from presenting the demonstration," he said.

Harris knew he was beaten, but planned to salvage what he could from the situation. "I would like to have noted for the *record* that we have present here today two people with *known* high counts of *candida albicans* in their serum, along with their medical charts, which they *volunteered* to make available to the panel. And we have a technician who, several moments ago, did a finger stick on each of them, in order to make slides, since fifteen to twenty minutes must elapse before a slide is usable. Those patients are volunteers who are *willing* to be questioned, under oath, about *anything* the panel wants to ask them. We have present in this courtroom a Nikon Opti-Shot, Darkfield Microscopy unit, together with a video attachment and thirteen-inch monitor so that, had your ruling permitted," he eyed Storch, balefully, "the panel would have been in a position to *see* on the monitor what was on the slides; and I would have been able to photograph the screen for evidentiary value with the camera I brought." He pointed again to the table, making certain that all attention was drawn to the complex and expensive items that would be pressed into service if the experiment was allowed to proceed as planned.

Levin had listened carefully to what his attorney had been saying and believed Harris had done his best to get as many details as possible into the record, since the demonstration would probably be barred from taking place. He didn't think that Storch would reconsider and relent. On the other hand, Levin noticed that Harris was still not through.

"So *that* is what we would have done had you permitted it, Your Honor." He shifted his glance from Storch to the committee. "The Health Department *waited* from 1975 until 1989 to lay charges against Dr. Levin. Many of the people who were either his patients or his technicians are either long gone or dead!" he dramatically stated. "The idea that we should somehow bring in the *original* patients and perform the demonstration on them, *assuming that their status had remained the same for fourteen or more years*—even if they were alive and available—is so ludicrous that it is not worthy of further discussion. *That's it!*" he ended, with emphasis. His comments related to Sheehan's objection that the patients who had come in to be part of today's demonstration were *not* the ones whose charts had been subpoenaed.

The judge, moved by Harris's appeal, relented slightly and said that he was willing to allow the lab technician to re-enter the room and be sworn in to testify about the particular test in question. Harris felt that the testimony would be useless to his defense of Levin without the planned experiment that would have clarified the issue for the panel and made it all come alive right in the hearing room. He refused to agree with Storch's compromise.

Sheehan stepped forward. "Mr. Harris chose to not only sweep the table clear of the *fancy* electrical equipment, but he also chose to sweep the table clear of an apparently, possibly relevant, *witness*. That was *his* decision." Sheehan lifted his chin and pointed it toward his legal opponent. "I want the record perfectly clear on that."

"I move for a mistrial!" Harris demanded. "When *you* make a speculation about what a Respondent is *not* bringing in, you create a *negative inference* out of an offer that has *never* been made. This is fatal flaw in this hearing, an absolutely

fatal flaw. That is prosecutorial misconduct of the worst kind, and he knows it," Harris told Storch. "It puts Dr. Levin in an *impossible* situation."

Levin wasn't sure he agreed with the implications of the argument, but he was amused by how much mileage his attorney was able to squeeze out of every presumed affront. He also understood the reasoning behind Harris's moves: others would be reading these transcripts. If the committee's recommendations were not favorable, there would be plenty of information in the record to assist the Respondent at the next two levels of review.

"I will overrule the motion for a mistrial, and that is *all* I am going to say about that," Storch decided, after hearing the attorneys bat the subject about for another fifteen minutes.

Harris smoothly segued into another topic of interest to the defense: Victor Herbert's statement that a laboratory in Chicago had been enjoined from performing cytotoxic testing and hair analysis on specimens of patients from New York, since those tests were allegedly *illegal* in New York State. "I *demand* to know the name of that laboratory in Chicago and the reference showing that these tests are *illegal* in New York. It is *not* a crime, and there is *nothing* that I can find in any statute which says you may not do this!"

Sheehan cleared his throat. "With respect to its legality, there is no specific regulation that says that," Sheehan admitted, adding something about it being a lab policy, and saying that he was willing to call in an individual from the state lab—familiar with the antecedents of the policy in other states—on rebuttal.

Upon hearing that Sheehan would also provide the name of the Chicago lab to him, Harris conceded that the prosecutor could bring in *any* witness he so desired. Harris then asked to have four videotapes admitted into evidence, claiming they were informative tapes given to patients who had certain types of treatments done in Levin's office, saying each tape was under an hour's viewing time. When the Hearing Officer agreed to accept copies of the tapes as soon as Harris had them made, he also asked for the titles to be recorded and marked for admission.

Sheehan picked up one of the tapes and read the title. "This one reads, 'Herbert's Hobby,' he told Storch, in amazement. "What exactly could *that* be? What that has to do with giving patients medical information is beyond me." He glanced at Harris. "I am sure it is not too complimentary to my witness," he tentatively ventured. Coming to some sort of silent conclusion, he then said, "I don't think these tapes are all that relevant to the charges. If they are full of misinformation or accurate information, they don't change one iota the nature of the treatment contained in the charts in evidence. I'm also sure that these tapes were *not* seen by the patients in question, unless Dr. Levin keeps the *same old tapes* around for five, ten, fifteen years. Besides, I don't recall those patients talking about *seeing* tapes during the time they received chelation."

Harris stared wordlessly at Sheehan, as the prosecutor continued to think aloud.

His mind made up, Sheehan then said, "If they are going to be introduced into evidence, here is another problem. The Commissioner or his designee and the Regents *all* have to sit down before a VCR for a *minimum* of four hours to look at this stuff. Reviewing charts is different. To review a tape, you have to sit there like a dummy and go through totally irrelevant parts and wait for something you think may be relevant. I submit, it puts a *burden* not only on the panel but on future reviewers to have to sit through this."

Harris responded. "Dr. Levin has been accused of *misinforming* his patients and *defrauding* them, of doing tests they *don't* know about or understand and wouldn't agree to if they did. They're charging him with *professional misconduct* for recommending that one patient, in view of her condition, have her mercury amalgam fillings removed." Harris began to enumerate the videocassette tapes. "One of these tapes is from '60 Minutes,' which did a piece on the controversy surrounding mercury amalgam fillings, so patients can evaluate the issue for themselves. There is a tape here called 'The Sugar Film, which addresses the state's accusation that Dr. Levin *wrongfully* does glucose tolerance tests and diagnoses hypoglycemia, which they've called a 'silly diagnosis.' These films are playing all the time in his office," Harris told them.

Suddenly, with renewed fury, Harris said, "I don't give a *damn* if the Regents have to spend four hours on these tapes. You are talking about deliberating in a month or two the issue of *stopping this guy from treating patients!* Maybe these films will educate the Regents, since I certainly have found them educational." Harris knew they were waiting to hear something about the Victor Herbert tape, so he took a deep breath in preparation. "There is also a *short clip* from the show '20/20,' part of a composite film Dr. Levin made, showing one of the things Dr. Herbert said here in testimony being refuted."

Following the descriptions of the tapes' contents, "The Sugar Film," "Our Drinking Water"—both produced and sold to physicians and others;

"The Composite Tape"—which had the Victor Herbert clip, and "Exploding Nutritional Myths" were given admission designations. Harris was pleased... but only for the moment.

Sheehan stepped forth with something completely unexpected. "If you *look* at the charges," he said, intimating that Harris hadn't really "looked" closely at the charges that were hanging over his client's head for over a decade, "we *never* alleged that Dr. Levin did not seek informed consent from any of the patients before he subjected them to whatever tests or anything that he did. Informed consent is *not* in the charges. In fact, it is apparent that a lot of these patients were totally *willing* participants in these types of—in the state's view—," he amended, "improper, fraudulent practices. A lot of these patients *asked* to be misled, they *begged* for it. Dr. Levin told us that those are the type of people he *wants*, who *believe* in this stuff." Sheehan's tone of voice came across as extremely mocking at this point. "So, really, these tapes are essentially *irrelevant*. These are classic 'hearsay,' produced by a third party. Dr. Levin is *not* on these tapes." He snorted. "If this is offered as expert testimony, it can't be done, because I can't cross-examine them...unless you want to get the person who appeared on '60 Minutes' in here, like you did with the other experts." He brought his face close to Harris's, knowing he was right. "You *can't* throw in these taped statements and expect me to sit here like a dummy and not be able to cross-examine," he concluded, emphatically.

Harris was quick to respond. "I am not offering these as expert testimony or anything," he countered. "They are merely offered because they are shown to patients, and the panel said they wanted to *see* what patients in Dr. Levin's office actually look at. Virtually *every* patient at some time during the course of treatment in that office sees these tapes and is offered audio tapes to take home."

Storch called an executive session with the members of the committee, so the meeting momentarily went off the record. Once back on, Storch announced the result of the private conference, which was *not* to accept the videotapes into evidence after all. On the other hand, Storch publicly informed Harris—for the sake of the court reporter—a set of audiotapes submitted earlier, featuring Levin as the speaker, gave the committee members the information they were seeking.

"However," the judge continued, "there *is* an excerpt from *one* videotape which Mr. Harris wishes the committee to see, and Mr. Sheehan concurs. It is from a program called, 'Inside Edition.' It involves an interview with Dr. Victor Herbert and includes some statements Dr. Herbert made which are going to become part of the record. Mr. Sheehan has set the tape to the section of the program containing those relevant statements, and we are going to play that segment for the Hearing Committee. The reporter," he instructed, looking at the court reporter, "will *transcribe* the statements made on the tape, so that the record is preserved."

Briber asked for the broadcast date, and Harris estimated it was after the hearings began, possibly in June or September of 1989. "It refers to a physician who is in active practice," he added.

All eyes went to the television monitor in the hearing room. The interviewer is heard asking Victor Herbert, "Doctor, what is your mission in medicine?" Herbert says, "Well, medicine is my *business*, and fighting *quackery* is my hobby." The voice in the background says, "Dr. Victor Herbert of the Department of Veterans Affairs Hospital in the Bronx, New York, is a renowned biochemist and nutritional scientist. He has written many articles and won awards like this one from the Federal Food and Drug Administration for exposing fraudulent medical practices." The award is shown to the viewing audience in a close-up shot, after which Sheehan stops the tape.

Levin was delighted that the segment had been viewed by the prosecutor, Hearing Officer, and members of the Hearing Panel. He was also gratified that the words spoken by Herbert on network television were officially written into the notes being compiled in his endless hearing and attempted prosecution by the state of New York.

Prior to the close of the session, the chairperson of the Hearing Committee, Robert Briber, made a request: "I would like to talk briefly about our course from here on out," he said.

So would I! Levin thought.

So would I! Harris thought.

CHAPTER 28

Levin rolled over gently and snapped on his bedside lamp. Seconds later, Susan did likewise. The LED reading on the clock atop the bureau directly across from their bed read three twenty-five. Moonlight peered through the partially opened slats on the stylish, fabric-faced vertical blinds.

"Well," she said, speaking softly, "since neither one of us is sleeping, should we talk for awhile?"

"I guess so," he responded, rubbing his eyes and reaching for his glasses.

They propped up their pillows and scooted toward the head of the bed into a semi-reclining position.

"How do you think it's going?" she asked.

He had no doubt what Susan was referring to. The hearings occupied a portion of every day's conversation for the past eleven years, sometimes taking a second or two and other times going on for hours, often broken into bite-sized segments, depending on their respective schedules. "It's hard to say," he admitted. "There are times that Bob and I walk out of that place smiling, other times barely able to contain our laughter, and oftentimes upset or infuriated. It's become the 'room of mixed emotions.' I usually go in hopeful, just because that's who I am. I never know what shape I'll be in when I come out."

She thought about what he was saying. "I don't know how you do it, Warren." She smoothed her long, straight hair back from her forehead and gathered it into her left fist before allowing it to fall behind her ears and onto the pillow.

"What is it that I'm doing?" he asked.

"You know. Going to work every day, seeing patients, paying attention to what's going on with them, talking to their family members, dealing with the staff. *Focusing*, I mean. Focusing on your work, on *medicine*, while all of this other garbage is going on…is *constantly* in the background." Sometimes his strength baffled her. Although she wasn't directly involved in the battle, the indirect role she played was enough to keep her feeling raw and vulnerable. Some days, she felt she couldn't take any more of the tension and presence of the omnipresent black cloud over their heads.

"I'll tell you something, part of what keeps me going." He covered her hand with his own. "*Your* support, Susan, is critical to my survival in this fight," he said, giving her hand a squeeze, "and my strong belief that I was *specifically* 'chosen' by New York State to fight the good fight for my brand of medicine. I love what I do and know that I'm practicing a type of healing that makes the kind of difference I, as a doctor, *want* to make in people's lives." He sighed deeply. "It's unfortunate that it's taking so many years to get through this battle, since all I'm *really* doing is fighting for the right to keep working at my job."

She nodded in understanding. "How much longer will it continue? Do you have any idea?"

He laughed. "You know, at the end of every session in the hearing room, Briber always says something about, 'We'll have to figure out where this is all going,' or 'I would like to talk briefly about our course from here on out,' or something to that effect. Sheehan complains every so often that things are dragging on; he usually blames Bob. For me, this continuing saga means preparing Bob for each upcoming session, and digging up research and articles, writing letters, calling people, trying to raise funds—all in addition to keeping the practice viable. As for our family life, I think it's the thing that's taken the greatest hit, what's gotten gypped the most. I get home so darn late, I don't see Erika a whole lot, and you and I have so little time together that isn't focused on something related to the hearings. I don't know what to say anymore. I really don't."

Susan was silent, listening, thinking. Finally, she said to him, "Erika starts kindergarten in the fall. I can try to come into the office more, take some of the pressure off you there."

"You're already handling the business end of things."

"To tell you the truth, Warren, I've been a little worried about things from that perspective. Sometimes I wonder how we're going to keep up with everything financially." She kept her voice neutral and her comments general. Her concerns were valid, but he had enough to worry about without knowing all of the harsh details of what she was increasingly realizing. She needed to make payments of sixty-five hundred dollars a month toward the twelve-year loan they had taken of $850,000 dollars to design and construct the office. The rent on Park Avenue was astronomical. Staff salaries and benefits ate a huge chunk of income. Then there were the mortgage payments on their home, travel and accommodation expenses for conferences, malpractice insurance, other insurances, food, clothing, child-rearing expenses, utilities, taxes, and the day-to-day costs of living. Entertainment and vacations had become distant memories. Then there were eleven years of legal bills, which continued to mount. Where was the money supposed to come from? The Legal Offense Fund had been helpful in staving off bankruptcy so far. How much longer would they survive and keep the business viable? True, it was a medical office, but it was *still* a business, so both profit and loss had to be carefully calculated.

"Somehow, we'll manage," he responded, ever the optimist.

Susan decided to let that topic drop but not the issue of her increased presence in his office. Seeing one another more frequently throughout the day might be therapeutic for them both, she thought. "So, like I said before, maybe I'll just try to come in a bit more often...to stay more on top of things," she added, "and not even wait until the fall. After all, Bob still doesn't want me at the hearings; he thinks I'll be a distraction to you. Maybe he's right," she ventured.

At the mention of the hearings, something was triggered for Levin. "I've often thought about doctors who get sued for malpractice, whose actions have caused a death or disfigurement or some sort of permanent damage to a patient. Those trials, that have huge monetary settlements attached, probably go a lot quicker; they're probably over in weeks." His voice was pensive. "Here I am, not charged with malpractice but with something that the Board of Regents of the state of New York loosely calls 'professional misconduct,' and it's an ongoing saga of so many years." He sounded puzzled.

Susan asked him what the state considered *professional misconduct*; since she had long ago lost sight of the precise reason *why* New York State inserted itself into their lives like a knife with a serrated blade that was so entrenched it was nearly impossible to remove.

"Good question," he responded, with a chuckle. "The way I understand it, and I'm really not sure I even understand anymore, they believe I've ordered excessive tests or done excessive treatments on patients and have used diagnostic or therapeutic methods that deviate from 'accepted and scientific standards of medical practice.' So for routine lab tests, an insurance company pays *other* doctors but not *me*, since if *I've* ordered such a test, it couldn't *possibly* be necessary. The way I envision it," he told her, "is that PROFESSIONAL MISCONDUCT is printed on a huge, monstrous umbrella in big letters, and underneath that umbrella are standing a collection of alternative, holistic, complementary, orthomolecular, or eclectic medicine physicians, all of us under suspicion by the state and its henchmen and executioners. Guess who's holding the umbrella," he asked, with a laugh.

"How about that guy who practices *nutritional preventive medicine* in New York City; the guy I'm sitting in bed next to?" she answered. They sighed jointly. "So, do you think I'd be a distraction to you if I started attending the hearings?"

"You'd probably be fine when my expert witnesses are testifying under direct examination," he said, thinking about it. "They have great credentials, they agree with my diagnoses, they agree with the tests I've ordered, and they believe my treatments were correct. When Sheehan starts cross-examining them, quoting some of the nasty stuff Victor Herbert has said about me, about my practice, tests, diagnoses, patient care, and on and on, I think …"

"It would be too much for me to hear, to stand for," she finished. "Bob's probably right. I know we've discussed this before. I just wondered if maybe. . ."

"Mmmm," he murmured, noncommittally. "You know, the initial week of testimony, those horrific one-thousand pages from Victor Herbert, is what Sheehan uses for fuel *every day*. He continues to dig through the guy's words in an effort to hang me and discredit my witnesses, who are amazing individuals, well-qualified, well-respected professionals. For example, Herbert says that I treat 'nonexistent diseases' with 'worthless therapies' that are lucrative for my practice but can be 'harmful' for patients. Then Sheehan will cross-examine people like Linus Pauling or Abe Hoffer to learn whether my diagnoses even exist, are valid, and if I treated the patients adequately. Victor Herbert looked at my charts and diagnosed my patients without examining these people, and he gave them mental illnesses they don't have. Sheehan tries to entrap my witnesses using Herbert's old testimony. It's crazy, Susan."

"Do you think Bob is doing a good job defending you?"

"He really works at it; that much I can tell you. He sounds like he knows what he's talking about as far as the medical terminology goes. In fact, he's become very comfortable with the whole philosophy and the junction at which conventional and alternative medicine interact. Sheehan's not half as good." Levin started to laugh.

"What?"

"Bob's pretty outrageous sometimes, I gotta tell you. I'm thinking of one example, but I'm sure I can dig up about another dozen without trying."

Susan was in the mood for a laugh. "Tell me," she prompted.

"One of the visitors in the courtroom had a name similar to Sheehan's. I'm not sure what it was, but when Briber or Storch asked the guy to state his name for the record, the guy told them his name and spelled it. So Sheehan says, 'Rehan, like Sheehan, right?' since the names rhymed. Bob says under his breath: 'Like Sheehan, only better!'"

"Oh, my God," she said, laughing.

"That's not the best part. What happened is that the court reporter *wrote Bob's comment into the transcript*, and Bob and I were reading it later when we were reviewing the testimony. We cracked up!"

They laughed together.

"You know how we've been claiming collusion in this trial?" Levin asked.

"Uh-huh," she said, turning over on her side to face him. "What happened there?"

"Victor Herbert's been out of the picture forever, but Bob thinks, and so do I," he added, "that Sheehan's probably still talking to him. We're sure the state has him on tap. We found out that Herbert already collected $100 an hour for reviewing my charts, another $100 an hour for having come in to testify, then an additional $250 a day plus expenses to be available on the days the hearings are conducted."

"You're joking, right?"

"Not at all. And on the days of the hearings, they pay his expenses, whatever that's supposed to mean, when he's on call from eight in the morning until four in the afternoon, and they give him an hour off for lunch."

Susan shook her head. "Unbelievable."

"So, do you remember the day we had Jimmy Carter come in to testify for me?"

"Sure."

"Okay, Jim is black, and the German or Yiddish word for black is 'schwartz,' as you know. Bob tells Sheehan that the witness we're calling in that day is 'Chaim Schwartz.' So Sheehan must have contacted Victor Herbert, who had *no idea whatsoever* who this Schwartz guy was. Bob calls Jim to the stand, and Sheehan says, 'I thought your next witness was named *Schwartz*.' Bob goes over and whispers to him, 'He is 'schwartz,' Mr. Sheehan; even you can see he's black!'"

"I love it!"

They laughed together, their mood lighter.

"You know, it's funny," he told her, "that some of things I've been saying and doing are becoming more and more acceptable. For example, studies are now being done with chelation and atherosclerosis, for one thing. And one other thing is even *more* significant. You know how I've counseled my patients and their families not to simply accept that one of them has Alzheimer's disease just because they've received that diagnosis from another practitioner?" he asked. "I always suggest intensive nutritional therapy, especially Vitamin B-12 shots, and I like them to start immediately."

"You've said that even if the person *doesn't* have pernicious anemia, which would immediately suggest a B-12 deficiency, that some symptoms pointing to Alzheimer's *resolve* with these shots, proving it *wasn't* Alzheimer's to begin with. Did I get it right?"

He chuckled. "You've heard me tell these stories so much all these years that you are remembering *exactly* right. Some people start having problems with physical coordination, a bit of dementia or symptoms of other unexplained neuropsychiatric disorders. Countless times, I've had patients respond to the vitamins, and the patients and their families are in tears, they're so happy. They came to my office hoping to hear something *different*, have something *good* happen."

"That's probably what you find so exciting about your work."

"That's a big part of it, Susan. Anyway, I have an article from the *New England Journal of Medicine* that came out three years ago, where nine researchers within *mainstream* medicine are advising doctors to consider the Vitamin B-12 therapy for cases such as these. Nevertheless, you've got someone like Victor Herbert stepping up and calling anything out of the ordinary 'fraud' or 'quackery.' It really gets discouraging sometimes. I think back sometimes to how I even had the nerve to open my practice right in the heart of the city and then put my advertising dollars into one-minute spots on a classical radio station, for goodness' sake. Yet word got around and people came, and I've made a good living. But now ..."

"Now, Warren, you're literally engaged in the fight of your life. But, like Bob told you many times, you're not alone. You've got me, and you've got Bob. You've also got so many alternative practitioners, groups, and journal editors on your side, willing to testify for you, support you with calls and letters, and contribute to your Legal Offense Fund. Even your patients have come through with written testimonials and a willingness to testify. They've given you money out of their pockets, for goodness' sake, even though many of them privately pay your rates due to lack of insurance coverage for your tests and therapies. Well," she considered, "you were brave enough to go public with this and, as hard as it's been on all of us, I'm sure it will be worth it...once it's over."

He took his glasses off and carefully placed them on the nightstand. He rubbed his eyes and pressed the switch on his bedside lamp. Susan closed her light, too. They slid into comfortable sleeping positions. Maybe her ears were playing tricks on her, but before she drifted off to sleep, she thought she heard her husband mutter softly under his breath, "*If* it's ever over."

CHAPTER 29

Due to the busy weekday schedules of the committee members, the prosecutor, and the judge, Levin was on his way to the hearing room on a Saturday morning. He hadn't had a chance to read the *New York Times* since Wednesday's trip into the city. It had been more important for him to prepare for the meetings he and his attorney had scheduled with Dr. Robert Atkins after hours on Thursday and yesterday. So he packed three days worth of newspapers into his briefcase and had the luxury of spreading everything out on the adjoining seat in the nearly empty train this morning.

Levin prided himself on being well-informed and staying current with significant world events. He sighed with pleasure as he started reading an article carrying the dateline: Moscow, July 10. "With a fanfare of trumpets, a patriarchal blessing and a dollop of politics, Boris N. Yeltsin was inaugurated today as the first freely elected President of the vast Russian federated republic. 'Great Russia is rising from its knees,' Mr. Yeltsin said after taking the oath of office before a Kremlin assembly in the cavernous Palace of Congresses that included President Mikhail S. Gorbachev, leaders of his Government and the Russian Orthodox patriarch. 'We shall surely transform it into a prosperous, law-based, democratic, peaceful and sovereign state.'"

Levin sniffed and shook his head in disbelief as he read, thinking, *I* live *in a "prosperous, law-based, democratic, peaceful and sovereign state," but where has it gotten me? It's as though* my *particular "state," New York, doesn't want me to be "prosperous." In fact, it doesn't even want me to be able to earn a living. As far as it being "law-based," it seems like the "laws" are "based" on the wishes of mainstream medicine, and the rest of us be damned. "Peaceful?" My life hasn't been truly "peaceful" for all the years I've been battling the state to retain my medical license.*

His mood had turned sour while reading the initial article, he realized. *Damn New York State, the Department of Health, the Commissioner, and the Office of Professional Medical Conduct. You've managed to ruin my commute and the pleasure of reading the papers...just like that!* He took several deep, calming breaths and studied his reflection in the window of the train. *Buck up, man! You look haunted...hunted...whatever. That's not the way you should look when you walk into that room this morning. Calm yourself. Let peace show through. Yes. Better. Much better. He smiled self-consciously at his reflection, which he now thought portrayed the image he needed to accompany him into the hearing room.*

Reading through the newspapers rapidly, he scanned the headlines and absorbed as much information as was possible during such a short trip. Walking from the train to the hearing room at Penn Plaza, he thought about his meetings with Bob Atkins. The tall, trim, affable physician referred to himself as a "nutritionist." Yet he had done residencies in internal medicine and cardiology, then he went on to specialize in both cardiology and complementary medicine, opening an office on the Upper East Side in Manhattan in 1959, which later became The Atkins Center for Complementary Medicine. He had done quite a bit of research on ketosis and had developed the "Atkins Nutritional Approach" or simply, the "Atkins Diet," into which countless Americans hooked themselves, as they counted carbohydrates and enjoyed the pleasures of heavy protein and fat intakes, including saturated fats, with the addition of leafy vegetables and dietary supplements.

Levin thought of how relentlessly Atkins had pursued his career, writing numerous books and gaining extensive popularity. In fact, Levin had to laugh when he recalled Atkins telling him that he didn't get around to marrying until four years ago, at age 56! Atkins had told him and Bob Harris his personal story, declaring that life had really begun for him in a meaningful way back in 1963. "You know, guys," he said, laughing as he spoke, "I was up to 224 pounds because all I was existing on was junk food, the junkier the better: cookies, cake, muffins, candy, ice-cream, pretzels, kind of like teenagers often do. Then one day I read about a low-starch diet in the *Journal of the American Medical Association.* I tried the diet for myself, had no problem losing weight, then I thought I'd give it a shot with my patients. When sixty-five of my overweight patients dropped a ton of weight, well not quite a ton, but you know what I mean," he chuckled, "I ended up on the *Tonight* Show. That was in 1965. And it got me a *lot* of publicity. Then, when I wrote an article about my results for *Vogue* magazine in 1970, everybody started to call it the 'Vogue Diet,' until I published *Dr. Atkins' Diet Revolution* in 1972."

Levin remembered his lawyer asking, "Didn't that book go on to become a best-seller?" "Believe it or not," Atkins had told him, "it sold *millions* of copies. I really don't think I expected anything like that to happen." He laughed again. "But I can't say that I wasn't happy about it. Me and my bank account."

His philosophy of weight control was simple: carbs were bad, making the body overproduce insulin and making people feel hungry. His initial book enjoyed such immense popularity for so long that he had followed up with *Dr. Atkins' Diet Cookbook* in 1974, *Dr. Atkins' SuperEnergy Diet* in 1978, *Dr. Atkins' SuperEnergy Diet Cookbook*, also in 1978, *Dr. Atkins' Nutrition Breakthrough* in 1981, and *Dr. Atkins' Health Revolution* in 1988.

He's a pretty impressive guy, Levin thought, and *a known quantity. I'm sure he'll resonate with the panel. They'll all know* who *he is, since he's a real public figure. I hope that works to my advantage.*

The session opened with Harris submitting a number of articles and other documents into evidence. There was no objection.

"Mr. Harris, could you give us an idea of what you expect today?" Briber asked.

"Yes, I can. I expect to offer the testimony of Dr. Robert Atkins."

"How long would you expect that to take?"

"All day," Harris responded, his look challenging Briber.

Suddenly, Sheehan piped up with something Harris had not anticipated, something which threatened to dilute the power of the presentation of Robert Atkins, something insignificant and not relevant to the proceedings of the day. Sheehan complained that a letter from a medical journal, addressed to Dr. Carter, a former witness, did not *say* what Sheehan had been led to believe it would say. "It says that 'your paper did not seem quite strong enough to defeat the opposition.' That's what it says!" Sheehan announced.

Harris was really annoyed at this diversion tactic and decided to make short work of it. He swiveled to face the judge. "Number one: that *sure* is a stony remark after something 'inappropriate' has been admitted. Number two: if that is *testimony* from the prosecutor, I *object* to it. The letter says whatever it says. And number three: Mr. Sheehan's 'subtlety' should be one of the 'arts' taught to professors in their initial training. In any event, the panel can make its *own* evaluation." He turned a quarter turn to look toward the committee members. Levin watched, studying Harris's grim profile as his attorney slowly turned his head, staring down each panel member in turn, as though challenging them to draw a conclusion other than what he expected of them.

Levin made sure his mouth didn't drop open nor did he allow himself to inappropriately laugh aloud as he watched Harris say his piece and work a practiced, intimidating look to his advantage in a truly arrogant performance. Levin shifted slightly to look past his attorney and at the judge. Storch's mouth twisted in various directions, maybe to stifle a laugh, maybe not.

"We will take the remarks from both of you under advisement," the judge muttered, his hand partially covering his mouth.

Levin watched as the room filled to capacity with spectators and supporters. The judge had ruled that once all chairs were occupied, the doors to the hearing room would be closed. When the visitors were identified by initials for the record, many of them stated that they were complementary physicians, chiropractors, respiratory therapists, or neutropathic physicians. Atkins' wife was also present.

Under direct examination, Atkins stated that his practice of medicine, which had begun as internal medicine with an emphasis on cardiology, was the same today as it had been in the beginning, "except that more of the subdivisions of internal medicine became of interest to me."

"What subdivisions were those?" Harris asked him.

"Well, it started off with an interest in nutritional medicine, and then, gradually, over the years, evolved into medicine based on a *different* medical model than that on which I had been trained. I then realized that what I was practicing was something which, in Europe, had been given the name, 'complementary medicine,' because that term really means 'using *all* of the healing arts,' including orthodox, allopathic medicine, and integrating them into a system where each and every healing art, if and when it is valid, would make a complementary contribution to patient management."

Under Harris's careful inquiry, Atkins spoke of his particular interest in metabolism and metabolic disorders, and the management of obesity and blood glucose disorders. The panel heard about Atkins' initial book, which sold ten million copies in various languages, and was pronounced "one of the best-selling books of all times."

After Sheehan made an objection to the introduction of the book into evidence, Harris, ever the dramatic player, said, "He is about to tell you," pointing to Atkins in the witness chair, "if you will *permit* him, what organized medicine *did* in response to the book that was outsold only by the Bible in this country!" He finished the phrase with his arms outstretched, as though he had just offered a rousing sermon to a voracious congregation.

Sheehan wasn't about to accept that sitting down. In carefully measured speech, he stated, "This is *not* a conspiracy trial in federal court, involving various defendants and plaintiffs, including Dr. Atkins. This is a *professional, disciplinary hearing* involving *one* physician, Dr. Levin, and particular patients and particular issues. If Dr. Atkins has nothing to say regarding issues relevant to *those* parameters, then he shouldn't be here as a witness. We cannot expand this into a Dr. Atkins case!" Levin absolutely hated it whenever Sheehan said something he believed was insulting or demeaning to one of his colleagues, who was kind enough to take the time to appear on his behalf. *Of course*, he thought, *Bob did make a mess of Victor Herbert…but that was different.*

"I will sustain the objection. Let's move on to the next question."

Darn it, Levin thought. *Come on, Bob, rephrase. Get an answer!*

Harris didn't let him down. "As a result of your book, Doctor, did any medical associations convene any conferences?"

"*Objection! Irrelevant.* He is asking the *same* question a different way!"

Storch sighed and nodded. "Sometimes asking a question in a different way makes it acceptable," he said. "The objection is overruled."

Way to go, Bob!

Atkins looked over at the committee members and spoke to them directly. "The American Medical Association formed an *ad hoc* committee to evaluate my book and to send out press releases."

"Did the *ad hoc* committee come to any conclusions?"

"*Objection! Irrelevant.* We are going into the *same* area. How certain doctors regarded Dr. Atkins' book is *not* an issue in this hearing. If it is, we will go through all of the other six or seven books and talk about the *same* irrelevant information for about two or three hours! I object to this lengthy, protracted hearing."

"Mr. Harris?"

Harris responded to the judge. "Judge, it may take days, but it *will* go in. There is *no* reason why this man who wrote the second best seller in this country, and was persecuted for it by his orthodox colleagues, can't discuss it. This is a precursor for showing that Dr. Atkins practices the *same* kind of medicine that Dr. Levin does… and you're looking to take Dr. Levin's license away! If *this* is not relevant to what is going on here, I must have been somewhere else for the last two years," he said, totally indignant.

Sheehan was at him again. "It isn't relevant. You can only do *one* case at a time."

"Dr. Atkins has one of the *largest* medical practices in the city of New York," Harris responded. "His medical practice is *very* similar to Dr. Levin's."

The judge told Harris, "Then, maybe we should be hearing about that."

"Fine," Harris said, still somewhat miffed. "Except that the issues all along in this case have been, 'Why does a physician who is classically trained wind up using alternative methods?' And, number two, 'If these alternative methods are so good, how come the bulk of physicians don't use them?'"

"That is *your* characterization of the issues," said Storch. "I dare say that Mr. Sheehan's characterization would be somewhat different." He quickly put his hand up to keep Harris from interrupting him. "Nevertheless, I am going to *sustain* the objection. Let's move on."

Harris turned to his witness. "Did there come a time when you began to practice a *different* approach to medicine than you had *prior* to writing your book?"

"Yes," the doctor answered.

"Why?"

"Because I learned, from the actions of the American Medical Association, that scientific accuracy was *not* a part of their game plan, at least as pertaining to my own research and my own work. They *misapplied* the scientific literature in order to show that my work was incorrect. I can only cite an example in order to make this hearing go as quickly as possible. My diet, that I had researched on ten-thousand patients with really successful results on the majority of them, was a ketogenic diet—meaning that it was *so* restricted in carbohydrates that the body releases free fatty acids and ketone body agents as an alternate fuel source. They said that it had been shown in the medical literature that the ketogenic diet produces weakness, faintness, and inability to conduct one's work."

Harris nodded to Atkins to encourage him to elaborate. "The study which *they* used involved bivouacking soldiers in the Arctic who were found eating nothing but pemmican. These were *slim* soldiers, who were engaging in heavy Arctic work, so they were *not* the obese, keto-resistant individuals for whom the book was intended. This sort of scientific inaccuracy led me to question the motivations of the American Medical Association in forming that *ad hoc* committee to send out press releases all over the country. And so, at that point, my attitude changed. I had practiced medicine so orthodox that my own first book had taken an adversarial position *against* people practicing alternative medicine. I even mentioned, 'Beware of doctors who use ACE, adrenocortical extract," which is probably the only statement in my book of twenty years ago that I no longer can stand behind. Every other statement has stood the test of time, and subsequent research has shown it to be scientifically accurate even though I only had certain preliminary articles to support the scientific basis of my book when I wrote it."

"So, as we established a few moments ago, after you wrote your book you began to practice medicine differently. Dr. Atkins, could you please elaborate on that a bit?"

"Yes, I became open to other healing arts. When people approached me with a nutritional alternative to the pharmaceutical approach, which I had been taught in my training, I looked at it with the willingness to try the nutritional therapies. The first lesson I learned was that nutritional medicine is consistent with the Hippocratic dictum, "First, do no harm." I felt comfortable that I was able to practice an effective form of medicine which provided patients relief from problems I had been previously unable to tackle using consensus medicine."

"Go on," Harris directed him.

"If a treatment carries no risk, I am open to securing as much information as I can about its use. With complementary medicine, the fact is that the patient is in the office *today*, seeking help *today*, for a problem which is *current*. And if there is no proven, effective therapy, it is unethical for me to send the patient away because I might have something to offer that hasn't yet been proven."

Harris established that Atkins' practice existed in two Manhattan locations, one being largely used for testing. Atkins favored glucose-tolerance tests of five or more hours, the listeners learned. The doctor also shared the fact that one-third of his patients experienced *candida* problems, for which dietary change was part of the treatment protocol, as well as Nystatin and Nizoral. He believed in doing swabs from the colon area and also live blood analysis to detect *candida*. His laboratory did cytotoxic testing, since Atkins required these results prior to doing nutritional counseling.

As Levin sat and listened to all of this testimony, he sincerely hoped its impact on the committee would be positive. As Harris was leading Atkins through the paces, the witness was describing tests and therapies he used on his patients which were *identical* to those used by Levin. Surely the panel could understand that, while the OPMC might come after a "little guy" like himself, who didn't have a best-selling book out nor radio programs like Atkins did, they would never chase after Bob Atkins' license with the same determination and zest. It would end up garnering them too much bad press. However, in their pea-brained minds, it was perfectly acceptable to wreak havoc with Warren Levin's practice, his life, his income, his peace of mind. Surely, someone on that committee had the good sense to draw the parallels and make it right. He hoped.

"Despite the fact that it is unpopular," said Atkins, referring to the cytotoxic test, "despite the fact that insurance carriers basically won't reimburse my patients for it, I believe it is a *good* investment on the patient's part because they have the greatest probability of getting better clinically when they abide by the restrictions suggested by the findings on the cytotoxic test."

"The state's witness, Dr. Victor Herbert, testified that cytotoxic tests cost the testing physician three or four dollars, that it is a test primarily done so that *fraudulent* physicians can make money from their patients." Harris had prepared Atkins for this question, so he wasn't hesitant to ask it. The observers in the courtroom had leaned in expectantly when Harris took one of his famous, dramatic pauses to its limit before finally blurting out, "Dr. Atkins, are you a *fraud*?" Levin was aware of the sharp intakes of breath from around the room but he, too, had expected the question so he wasn't startled by the collective reaction.

"I shouldn't answer that question, but I will!" Atkins responded, looking stern and severe, playing his role in the drama to the hilt. "I've met Dr. Herbert, and his statement is intellectually dishonest." *Nice phrasing,* thought Levin, *and, oh, so politically correct!* "The cost of the test is calculated in *technician* time, which is two hours of a high-level technician. My technicians are instructed to look at *each* slide for thirty seconds to one minute. The reagents cost sixty to one-hundred dollars for a series used for a *single patient.* The purpose of the test is to get meaningful clinical information to improve patient management and care. It enables the physician to pick out those foods from a patient's diet which are causing a reaction in the body. The bottom line is what happens to the patients when they go on the avoidance diet suggested by the cytotoxic test. It has been one of the *greatest* sources of increasing the patient responses since I started my practice of complementary medicine."

As Levin sat and listened, although he knew that Atkins' practice methods were similar to his own, he felt like cheering as he watched the impassive faces of the committee members and the prosecutor. *See,* he felt like standing up and telling them, *see? You* know *who this guy is, everybody does, and he's telling you that he depends on the* same *tests and treatments I do, and you want to take my license away for doing those things!*

Harris took Atkins through his use of the Doppler plethysmograph for peripheral vascular insufficiency, blocked arteries, and stenosis of arterial circulation, offering Chelation therapy as the most effective treatment. His office had been offering that therapy for the past eight years, and Atkins estimated that approximately one-thousand patients had received it, with no need to hospitalize a patient for an adverse reaction and no morbidity resulting from its administration. He said that anyone board-certified in Chelation therapy *knew* how to appropriately administer and monitor the infusions. Atkins said that he estimated, from speaking to colleagues who also offered the treatment, that *eighty percent* of patients with cardiovascular disease experienced either subjective or objective evidence of improvement.

"Those who are symptomatic with intermittent caudication or angina, which is chest pain, will report increased exercise tolerance, increased time to angina, increased time to having to stop walking due to the caudication," Atkins elaborated.

"You make extensive use of vitamin and mineral supplements in your practice, do you not?"

"Yes, I do."

"Is it fair to say that the overwhelming majority of physicians in this country ignore or largely ignore nutrition with regard to the treatment of most ailments?"

"That is true."

Why do you think that most of your colleagues *don't* utilize some of the things which you have clearly found to benefit large numbers of your patients?"

Atkins took a moment to reflect on the question. "I think there have been some efforts to *suppress* the communication of this sort of information. There are many published statements that are seemingly authoritative which say that vitamin therapy or nutrition therapy is a waste of time, something some people even call health fraud. I think doctors really tend to respond to that which they are taught and don't like to look into new projects in which they don't have the support of their medical colleagues. I think it has become political, that there are economic interests supporting the use of a pharmaceutical medicine. So a competing therapeutic which is non-pharmaceutical is not going to receive the financial support...and it does take financial backing to reach physicians. Physicians are reached mostly through medical journals which accept advertising mainly from pharmaceutical clients, and a position contrary to theirs is not likely to be accepted." He offered an example about a journal editor asking him to delete a phrase from an article he contributed for publication so as not to offend a pharmaceutical sponsor.

Harris decided to focus on Atkins' radio programs, a local one hour broadcast live at ten o'clock at night from New York City and a syndicated program that covered the Eastern seaboard, the West Coast and several places in between. Harris had already appeared a number of times on the local program, so he centered his questions on the other show.

"Dr. Atkins, would you tell us, please, what the subject matter of that show is?"

"It revolves around the fact that there are *two* kinds of medicine that a doctor can practice, and two kinds of *doctors* that a patient can choose...and that the patient should have the right and the freedom and the wherewithal to make *choices* as to how his or her own or the family's health matters are run."

"Doctor, *when* do you get into your office in the morning?"

"I see my first patient at 7:30 a.m."

"So why do you do a radio show from ten to eleven at night?"

"Because this point of view, freedom of choice in medical matters, is something about which I have passionate feelings. I believe the view must be disseminated, and I was given an opportunity to be one of the voices representing that viewpoint, and that is my interpretation of the meaning of my life and the reason for my existence. And I just wouldn't give it up!"

Levin was ecstatic when he heard Atkins express exactly what he himself felt and believed. He couldn't help himself. He began to applaud, loud and clear. The spectators in the packed hearing room craned their necks and twisted in their seats to see where the applause was coming from.

"Dr. Levin!" Storch said in a no-nonsense voice. "I am going to ask you to refrain from that sort of thing. This is *not* a show! This is a *hearing*. Applause is *not* appropriate."

Since Storch addressed him directly, Levin decided to milk the moment for its value. "I am sorry. What he described is *my* life also, and I appreciate Dr. Atkins expressing it so well."

Storch nodded but did not remove his stern gaze from Levin as he said, "Let's proceed."

"Doctor, in addition to your radio show, are you involved in any other activities intended to educate the public about complementary medicine? "Well, certainly, there are my lectures and my writings."

"Have you written any books related to complementary medicine and an explanation of the modalities that you use?"

"I have written one book which is about complementary medicine, and it is about the type of medical practice that Dr. Levin has and that I have."

Levin watched Harris, knowing what to expect at this point, and the lawyer didn't disappoint him. Harris did his little march, eyeing each panel member in turn, looking out at the assembled viewers in the room, before returning his gaze to Atkins. "Doctor," he began, "if I were standing on the moon looking down at your office and Warren Levin's office, excluding the architecture, is it fair to say that what goes on in your office is, for the most part, similar as what goes on in his medical office?"

Atkins nodded his assent, and said, "For the most part, it is similar."

"Let me ask you, what was the purpose of writing *Dr. Atkins' Health Revolution* a few years ago?"

Atkins broad smile seemed to light up the courtroom, Levin thought. "To let the world know that there are *two* kinds of medicine: there is *consensus medicine*, which I spent half my career practicing; and *complementary medicine*, which can get *better* results in terms of patient response. I wanted that point to reach the public, allowing them to compare them point by point, to decide which type of practitioner they wanted to entrust their health and the health of their families to."

When Harris attempted to admit the book into evidence and Storch refused, since the witness was available to testify, Levin knew there would be a spontaneous and outrageous strategy originating in his lawyer's mind. Once again, Harris didn't disappoint him.

"Doctor, since the judge has ruled that the book *cannot* come into evidence, and the basis of his ruling is that you are here to *testify*," Harris began, setting the scene for the drama to follow, "I am going to start with the table of contents, page one. As I give you the topic, I would like you to please give us your testimony on that subject."

Sure enough, Sheehan jumped up, his mouth tight, barely contained anger showing through his non-verbal movements. "*I object to that!* He is asking the witness to *read* the book since he can't get it into evidence legitimately! That is *totally* improper."

Harris assumed his innocent, "who me?" look, and in a soft, reasonable tone said, "I am not asking him to read anything. He doesn't even have to *open* the book. The basis of the Judge's ruling is that Dr. Atkins is here to summarize his writing. He is here to testify, and his live testimony is an appropriate substitute for admitting the book into evidence. I don't see the problem with that." He spun around rather gracefully to face the witness again. "Let's go!" he said, rubbing his hands together enthusiastically, accompanied by titters in the hearing room from the overflowing audience of visitors.

"I object! The witness is here to give *probative* testimony based on the issues in this case, not to summarize nor paraphrase one of his books for us. That is *not* the function of his presence here!"

Harris turned to the prosecution table once again. He smiled broadly. "Well," he drawled, "the *only* disagreement that Mr. Sheehan and I have concerns the issues in this case. While the state has framed them as a series of *charges*, my point of view and that of Dr. Levin is that the charges have very *little* to do with the case. The unstated agenda in this case all along has been this 'parallel universe' of medicine, as Mr. Sheehan derogatorily describes it, and Dr. Atkins is certainly one of the members of the 'parallel universe.' And I think that if we plan to ask Dr. Atkins' opinions about Dr. Levin's treatment of certain patients, then part of what we *need* to do is clearly and thoroughly define what that 'parallel universe' contains. I thought we could do it succinctly, so we brought along seven copies of this book for the panel to peruse at its leisure...and even perhaps learn something from," he added snidely. "But, absent that, we will just go through the book and..."

Sheehan was really angry now. "Mr. Harris has said that he is *not* here to discuss these charges. He wants to discuss this 'conspiracy theory.' If that is the case, I suggest that Mr. Harris draft his *own* charges, serve them on his client, accuse him of being a victim of the conspiracy, then he can hold his *own* hearing about the conspiracy aspects."

Levin shook his head as he listened. Sheehan was beginning to compete with Bob Harris for the "Most Outrageous Attorney Award." *What a show! And the judge doesn't want to allow applause?*

Sheehan wasn't finished. "He *has* to respond to the state's charges! If he is *not* going to do that, it is an admission by him that this evidence is not relevant," Sheehan said to Storch. "Therefore, you should *not* allow it!"

Harris was ready. "Dr. Atkins is here having read each and every page of each and every chart that was introduced into this hearing!" he declared.

"Good," Sheehan countered, "so let him talk about *that*!"

"He is here to comment on each and every one of the charges against Dr. Levin. Since that is the game we are playing, and I use the word 'game' advisedly, I think that *part* of that game is where the witness is entitled to describe his *own* background, his *own* practices, and the *basis* for his conclusions."

The Judge must have felt that he was being excluded from the game, Levin thought, since he finally weighed in. "First of all, no matter *how* you wish to characterize it, and I recognize you may be playing to an audience," he said, glaring at Harris, "but this is a hearing..."

Harris didn't let him finish. "This is *my* audience," he said, gesturing to the full hearing room and the exit doors, where many, many more spectators were standing, hoping for an opportunity to take a seat inside if someone had to leave early.

Storch looked as though he wanted to pound his fist through the table. "This is a *hearing*! It is *not* a game! We take this very seriously, as I know Dr. Levin does. I do *not* consider this to be a game or a matter of gamesmanship in any way, shape, or form!"

Harris shrugged. "Then you will agree with what I am doing."

Storch shook his head. "You will *not* have the witness read the book into the record. We will *not* spend the whole day discussing the book! If the witness is here, and you told us that he is prepared to discuss the charged patients, let's get on with *that*."

Harris must have realized that he couldn't pursue his plan any further, so he took Atkins through a philosophical discussion of medicine through the ages, beginning with Hippocrates. He spoke of empiricism being a results-oriented approach which, if successful, becomes acceptable medicine, whereas the rationalist approach requires an acceptable form of medicine to be explained.

"The empirical tradition in medicine is what's on trial here," Atkins explained, "because Dr. Levin practices it. I believe that the empiricists can get better results, as I did."

Harris nodded in agreement. "Dr. Atkins, you have described complementary medicine as the 'health revolution.' Why?"

Atkins laughed. "One *needs* a revolution if one has an idea whose time has come, and it exists in the context of an entrenched, powerful, dominant establishment. And the idea whose time has come is the idea that there are natural therapies and nutritional therapies which work, which have worked for centuries, and which are not getting publicized to the physician because of the economics of the pharmaceutical dominance of medicine. I estimate now that ninety-eight percent of the therapies that are administered to patients today are therapies with synthetic chemicals which were developed some time in the last seventeen years for the purpose of potent protection of pharmaceutical profits. And that whole double-blind control experiment really works against anyone who hasn't got the money to support a study, and in so doing works against *all* natural and nutritional forms of medical care which simply will not get the economic support to be studied."

After the introduction of a number of articles that Atkins used in his practice, along with his books and pamphlets, to educate his patients, the lunch recess was called. Harris, Atkins, and Levin went down for a quick lunch and a discussion of the afternoon's strategy.

Refreshed, Harris opened the afternoon session with the topic of Chelation therapy, and Atkins offered a brief history of its use for heavy metal toxicity and the accidental discovery that it was effective in cardiovascular disease.

"It's interesting," Atkins said, "that the treatment was withdrawn from use for cardiac patients because there was a relapse into the same state of cardiovascular disease that existed *before* once treatment was withdrawn." He chuckled and looked at the committee members, since there were two doctors on the panel. "This was another breach of scientific logic," he told them, "tantamount to saying that *insulin* is no good, because once you stop taking it, diabetes once again goes out of control!" His logic succeeded in raising several eyebrows.

Harris segued into the subpoenaed charts, which Atkins had had in his possession for four weeks and had read thoroughly.

"You have had a chance to review the charges against Dr. Levin by the state of New York. Can you comment on the charges in relation to those charts?"

"Yes. I would say, without exception, that each and every charge leveled against Dr. Levin is for engaging in a practice which is standard and appropriate operating procedure for a practitioner of the *other* kind of medicine, of complementary medicine. By the standards of complementary medicine, there is not a single example in all the charges and all the charts of Dr. Levin doing something which would be considered incorrect or inappropriate."

"Let's go to the standards of orthodox medicine," Harris said. "In the sense of the thoroughness of history, testing, diagnosis, treatment, prognosis, do you find any fault with Dr. Levin's work?"

"None at all. I find a pattern of thoroughness. I would imagine that anyone who has been at these hearings would have to agree that here is a doctor who practices by the rule of thoroughly investigating difficult patients."

"Is it fair to say, Dr. Atkins, that much of your patient load is *similar* in nature to much of Dr. Levin's patient load?"

"Absolutely true."

"Is it also fair, for the purposes of time, to say that a significant percentage of patients who come into your offices come *after* visiting many other practitioners numerous times?"

Atkins nodded enthusiastically, then shrugged. "Virtually *every* patient has gone through the mill with a series of visits to practitioners of consensus medicine and sought my help because they had *not* been getting relief of symptoms or turnaround of their illnesses with conventional medicine."

"Dr. Atkins, is it fair to say that you and Warren Levin are friendly competitors?"

"We *are* competitors," Atkins said. "A lot of times people that I think should have come to *me* go to *him*!" The courtroom broke out in spontaneous laughter. Atkins continued, "Throughout all of these charts, by the way, it looks like Dr. Levin *beat* me to my conclusions by having arrived at these conclusions *long before I did!"* The statement was made in pure admiration of the physician under fire by the state of New York and carried no guile.

From his seat, Levin smiled and nodded his appreciation to Atkins, who returned the courtesy. When Harris asked Atkins if he used ACE, adrenocortical extract, in his practice, nothing that it had been taken off the market for a number of years in the past, Atkins said, "Actually, when I wrote this book, that's about the time that I met Dr. Levin. I remember him telling me, 'I think you made *one* mistake in your book. You really should look into ACE.' And twenty years later, I agree with that evaluation. I began using it, and I found that it was an *excellent* support for patients who suffered a variety of stress reactions, including the stress of hypoglycemia."

Harris picked up some papers from the defense table. "Dr. Herbert described Dr. Levin's administration of ACE in five cc doses to one patient with a questionable psychiatric status to be 'professional misconduct.' He then blamed the death of Patient A on Dr. Levin's treatment, because Patient A died *six months after the last injection of ACE.* In Dr. Herbert's mind, the death and the termination of ACE treatments were somehow related."

Atkins shook his head in disgust. "The testimony given by Dr. Herbert is *preposterously* irresponsible! I think this is an example of a person who carries a pathologic prejudice against the sort of clinical nutrition that Dr. Levin and I practice. I really don't believe that the man could know *that little* about a subject in which he purports to be an *expert.* Therefore, I leave it up to the panel to make a judgment as to the integrity of the deponent. We complementary physicians believe that we should be treated as the *respected opposition* and not as people practicing quackery or health fraud."

Thank you, thank you, thank you! thought Levin, smiling broadly.

"Dr. Atkins, why are you here today?" Harris asked, bluntly.

"Because I see a potential miscarriage of justice in the very fact that a competent physician has to defend himself and go through the majority of his net worth just because he can't turn back and practice a kind of medicine which is not as effective as what he has learned through his personal experience. This, I think, is a *pivotal* case. If this miscarriage of justice were allowed to go on, I think it would be very destructive to progress in clinical medicine."

Harris smiled with satisfaction and turned to Sheehan. "Your witness," he said, returning to his seat next to Levin and exchanging a smile with his client.

"Thank you," Sheehan said, getting up and buttoning his jacket. "Doctor, one reason why you regard the case as 'pivotal' is because you feel that if Dr. Levin loses this case, someone like yourself may be next. Correct?"

"Yes."

"So your reason for being here is *not* totally lacking in self-interest, correct?"

"That is true."

Levin figured it must really have made Sheehan happy to get that positive answer, since he tried to establish a motive of self-interest in the actions of every one of the witnesses who appeared on behalf of the defense so far and would do so with those who would appear in upcoming weeks. *To what avail?* he wondered.

Sheehan took Atkins through his early training in medicine and cardiology, establishing that the doctor was board-eligible but had never taken the board certification exam in cardiology. He then had Atkins admit to taking the boards in internal medicine, passing the written but not the oral portion of the exam.

Levin's thoughts were the same as before. *So you tried to embarrass my witness. To what avail?*

"You never attempted to try to pass again, correct?"

"No, because I was in practice and no longer interested in either a job change or an academic career. In those days, board-eligible and board-certified were interchangeable," Atkins stated.

"How have you tried to help Dr. Levin in his predicament?"

"On my radio broadcast, I have made appeals to the public for money to help Dr. Levin with these incredible financial responsibilities that go with defending oneself. I have actually given him money out of my own pocket."

"Do you regard Dr. Herbert as an expert in nutrition?"

"I regard him as the complete *antithesis* of an expert in nutrition."

Harris wanted to clap and cheer at that statement and predicted that Levin also had the same impulse and was struggling to control it.

There was a near glitch in the proceedings when Sheehan asked Atkins if he considered himself an expert in nutrition, and the doctor said no, because he thought the title too arrogant. Sheehan asked that the witness's entire testimony be ignored by the panel, since Atkins was brought in as an expert witness and was not willing to be thought of as an expert. The onlookers gasped as a group, aghast at what they were hearing. Harris stated that *he* was declaring Atkins an expert. The audience laughed.

Storch simply said, "Dr. Atkins is a licensed physician, licensed to practice in this state. We will hear his testimony. The weight that it will be given will be something for the committee to decide in its deliberations in the case, but we *will* hear his testimony." That succeeded in ending the word-play between the lawyers.

In an effort to prove that Levin *routinely* ordered the same set of laboratory tests for every patient who came into his office, Sheehan—in spite of Harris's objections—began to list a number of tests for Atkins, who had already stated that it was standard practice in conventional and alternative medical offices to have a set of tests by which to thoroughly assess a patient, no matter what the complaint. Atkins also admitted to giving asymptomatic patients Chelation therapy for preventive reasons, if the patient requested it.

Harris stepped in. "There are *no* charges against Dr. Levin for treating asymptomatic patients, so *why* are we discussing Dr. Atkins' philosophy about whether or not Dr. Levin should have treated patients who he is *not* accused of having treated?" There were nodding heads and murmurs from the crowd.

Sheehan's rejoinder was swift. "This witness's *credibility* is at stake in this proceeding, and I am allowed to ask him questions." Once again, there was a collective intake of breath from the observers.

Sheehan spun around to glare at the group seated behind the prosecution and defense tables. "I object to the audience acting as a Greek chorus to everything I say concerning Dr. Atkins!" he stated, angrily. "That is *not* their function," he told the judge. "I would ask that they be directed to be quiet, or if they want to continue, I ask that they go *outside* with the doors closed!"

The judge looked at the visitors. "I will instruct the spectators present that your continued presence will be allowed so long as you maintain order. If you become disruptive, I will have the room cleared. Let's proceed."

Levin marveled at how Storch always seemed able to maintain his even demeanor. He might get frustrated, but he never erupted in long, angry tirades or spoke in a threatening manner. He simply stated the consequences if his instructions were not followed. Levin had to hand it to him. He wasn't so sure he could pull it off as well as Storch did.

Sheehan began a line of cross-examination based on one of Atkins' books, to which Harris strenuously objected, since the book had not been admitted into evidence. However, the judge ruled that a witness can be cross-examined on anything that he has written. When Sheehan began to introduce the topic of vitamins, Harris geared up for a major dramatic performance in front of a sold-out house, so much so that Levin, himself, was cringing inwardly once again.

"These products do not have FDA approval, do they, Doctor?" Sheehan asked.

"*Objection*!" Harris shouted, rising to his feet rapidly, nearly knocking his chair over in the process.

"Mr. Harris?" asked Storch.

"When did you stop beating your wife?" Harris said, directing his outlandish comment toward Sheehan. "Vitamins don't *need* FDA approval. That is a question designed to mislead the panel into thinking there is something *wrong* with Dr. Atkins. The vitamins don't have the approval of a Lubavitch rabbi. So what?"

Storch rubbed his palm over his face. Levin wasn't certain whether it was to keep from laughing or because he was tiring of the drama. "Do you wish to be heard, Mr. Sheehan?" he asked.

"I will ask another question," Sheehan responded, with a deep sigh.

He had opened up the topic of Atkins' sale of vitamins to his patients, some of whom lived out of state and ordered refills from him by mail. From there he moved to FAIM, Foundation for the Advancement of Innovative Medicine, an organization of seventeen-hundred people, which included fifty professionals. Atkins was president of this group, which had a licensed lobbyist in Albany, Monica Miller. Harris was annoyed at the direction Sheehan had taken.

"This whole line of questioning seeks to find wrongdoing and inappropriateness," Harris complained. "If he wants an acknowledgement that FAIM looks into things that affect beleaguered physicians like Dr. Levin, the answer is, *yes*, they do. Now, *what else* is there to talk about?"

"The objection has *nothing* to do with the question," Sheehan told the judge.

Briber, the chairperson, was visibly agitated. "The expense and the opportunity for us to hear this witness and to carry this case further is too important to get it caught up in that kind of Mickey Mouse," the chemist said. "Let's just stop that! We are dealing with an important issue, and we have important people in the room." He eyed the packed hearing room significantly. Calm and order were restored.

Sheehan proceeded to discuss FAIM, trying to elicit opinions from Atkins about handouts that were distributed at various meetings of the organization. Harris voiced lengthy and loud objections to the questions.

Sheehan held up one of the handouts. "I submit," he said, "that this is inflammatory and totally unprofessional. I think it should be seen by the panel to understand what type of documents and theories this *expert* witness—*in Mr. Harris's words*—agrees with.

"Judge, that is McCarthyism!" Harris shouted.

Sheehan looked at Harris. "Will you stop those terms?"

Harris shook his head. He began a mocking paraphrasing of what had just transpired, once again, playing to the audience, "his audience." "The witness said, 'I never saw it before. I am told it is handed out at a meeting of an organization I belong to where there are one-thousand or more people.' The state then says, 'Do you agree with any of it?' 'Yes, I agree with some of it,' Dr. Atkins responds. 'Now, I offer it in evidence, because it is a rag, it is a piece of garbage, and I want to show the panel what kind of garbage he agrees with.'"

Sheehan's face was red. *"That's right!"* he shouted.

"That *shouldn't* go in!" Harris countered.

"It won't," said Storch. "The objection is sustained."

"Just as Mr. Harris cross-examined Dr. Herbert on his involvement on the Council against Health Fraud, I should be allowed to cross-examine Dr. Atkins briefly on this same issue," Sheehan said to the judge, petulance once more in his voice. "I submit that you are *not* allowing me the same leeway up until now as Mr. Harris, in his conveniently protracted cross-examination of Dr. Herbert that he enjoyed…"

"I didn't enjoy it!"

"Leave your editorializing," said the judge.

Sheehan proceeded with an introduction of the FDA Act and tried to get answers to questions from Atkins. In an effort to protect his witness, Harris asked the judge to advise Atkins that he could choose not to answer, for fear of incrimination. When Atkins refused to answer the question, Sheehan suggested that the panel be told to disregard Atkins' testimony, as it could not be stricken from the record.

Harris stood. "The Civil Practice Law and Rules in the state of New York say that when a witness testifies in a civil proceeding and refuses to answer a question on the grounds of the Fifth Amendment, that the panel or the one who tries the facts may draw a negative inference with regard to that question and that lack of answer. Those are not grounds for striking testimony. The truth be known, Dr. Atkins doesn't *know* what the FDA Act specifies."

"Wrong!" Sheehan declared.

"As a matter of fact," Harris responded, "the state's witness, Victor Herbert, refused to answer a question, and the Health Commissioner reinstated the hearing!"

Storch said, "I am going to reserve my ruling on Mr. Sheehan's motion to have Dr. Atkins' testimony disregarded by the committee. I am requesting briefs on the subject from counsel for both sides."

Harris shook his head. "It is not going to be necessary, Judge," he told Storch. "I am going to ask Dr. Atkins if he knows the FDA law. I *know* he doesn't know it."

Sheehan pressed his lips together in frustration. "You are now leading the witness, Mr. Harris, asking him to change his testimony. He said he didn't want to answer the question. It is over. You can't get him to change his testimony."

Storch was not to be deterred. " I want briefs on the subject to be in my office in eleven days, by the close of business on July 24, 1991," he said. "If you have no further questions, Mr. Sheehan, we will take questions from the committee."

Dr. McAloon asked the witness to define a nutrient versus a pharmacological agent or drug. Atkins said that a drug becomes a "blocking agent, which basically is an enzymatic poison," whereas nutrients are either present in our normal diet or in supplements. He labeled them as "a blocking agent versus an enabling agent." McAloon then asked Atkins about protecting consumers from alternative medicine.

He looked at the amply endowed physician and said, "Some of the complementary physicians are not very good; some are excellent." He then looked over at Warren Levin. "It is ironic that the Defendant in this action today is one of the very, very good ones."

McAloon twisted her lips to the side skeptically. "Do you think the government should have a role in safeguarding the public or educating the consumer about some of these alternative therapies?"

Atkins snorted. "Unfortunately, the government has already taken sides and has appointed the academics to be their counselors. And, in appointing the academics, their history of action is to absolutely *not* include practitioners of the other persuasion. I still believe that alternative practitioners have a right to be heard by people who understand what they are doing. If *we* were on the board, and there were a bad apple among us, you can be sure that we would get his license revoked *quicker* than you would, because the one thing we don't want is somebody giving our movement a bad name!"

What a spectacular finish! Harris thought. *I couldn't have done better myself... and that's really saying something.*

O'Connor asked a brief question, following which Briber asked Atkins, "Doctor, how does the complementary medicine community discipline its members, or does it?"

Nice, thought Harris.

Atkins shrugged. "We don't have occasion or power to discipline our members. We are hoping for that power. We have absolutely no way of implementing the fact that there may be some practitioners who have shown questionable morality or ethics of whatever. Such physicians would have to be disciplined by the existing structure."

"Dr. Atkins, to practice complementary medicine, why did you say that the person first *had* to be a physician?" Briber asked.

Atkins smiled broadly and nodded enthusiastically. "That is a *wonderful* question," he said, "wonderful question! I think the discipline of medical training is absolutely mandatory. I have always said that to be a good complementary physician, first you must be a good physician. You have to understand the mechanisms of illness, the organ interrelationships, and the pharmaceuticals for which we hope we have an alternative. But to provide an alternative, you have to know how the alternative compares with the majority of the alternatives of pharmaceuticals or surgery."

"Have you used, or do you now use, a Heidelberg capsule for gastric analysis?" Briber asked.

"I have, and I do when I suspect that the dysfunction is one of hydrochloric acid secretion in the system. I have used it for the primary question, which is, 'Can it measure the Ph accurately in the stomach?' It does. We get this information with fewer traumas to the patient than the usual way of putting down a stomach tube and studying the gastric acid. This is very pleasant and easy to take and relatively inexpensive."

"Thank you," said Briber. "I have no further questions."

"Re-direct, Mr. Harris?" asked the judge.

"Dr. Atkins, your diet, which was the basis for your *Dr. Atkins' Diet Revolution* came from the medical literature, did it not?"

"As a matter of fact, it did."

"So that is the diet that the AMA convened an *ad hoc* committee about?"

"Yes."

Harris took a moment to look deeply into the eyes of everyone in the room, especially the members of the panel. He wanted it to sink in...deeply.

"Doctor, the vitamins and nutrients you sell under your name are not the only ones you sell from your office, are they?"

"No, and my patients also know that they can go to stores and buy my products or others' products."

Harris nodded. "If somebody comes into your office on a prescription drug, do you hesitate to continue to prescribe that medication?"

"Not at all. When they are on a prescription drug, and there is no appropriate reason for me to discontinue it, I will renew that prescription, especially when I don't feel confident that there is a nutritional alternative."

Harris then established that, although Atkins did not have hospital privileges, patients in his office who experienced acute episodes were transported to an emergency room within eleven minutes. "Not only that," Atkins stated, "but among my personal consultants are some of the finest hospital-based physicians in the city, and my relationship with these people is at the highest level. There is a great mutual respect. As a matter of fact, my greatest satisfaction comes from these interrelationships with people who are practicing orthodox medicine and our ability to create a really good teamwork situation."

"Thank you, Dr. Atkins, I have no further questions."

On re-cross examination, Sheehan once again began harping on one of the handouts given at a professional association meeting that Atkins had attended.

Harris got to his feet. "Is this question going to determine in any way Warren Levin's fate? Because, if not, I would like to go on to the next question in the hopes that it might be probative on the issue."

A big sigh from Storch. "Mr. Harris, save your editorializing for closing."

Sheehan had the floor again. "Dr. Atkins, is it your opinion that nutritional medicine can treat or cure cancer and multiple sclerosis?"

Atkins appeared thoughtful. "Well, treat, yes. I don't want to use the word 'cure,' but certainly treat effectively."

"No other questions."

Briber had a last question he wanted to sneak into the proceedings. "I am interested in the extent to which you devote resources to research, distinct from patient care."

"I can only answer your question by saying that the practice of complementary medicine is not very profitable, and my banks don't always loan me the money that I try to borrow from them to keep myself from going into Chapter 11, or whatever it's called. Complementary medicine is extremely time-consuming to the physician. I cannot, and this is what Dr. Levin taught me," he said, glancing over at Levin, "I cannot do a patient contact in less than thirty minutes, even with an old patient. There are too many things that have to be covered."

As the doctor spoke, Harris thought, *Okay, all of you, if you aren't physicians or alternative physicians, just think about the amount of time you get from a doctor during a patient visit: five minutes, ten, less? Think about it, guys and gals. Think about what traditional, establishment medicine is really offering you.*

Atkins was still speaking. "Meanwhile, the insurance carrier assumes a ten- or fifteen-minute patient contact, particularly Medicare, and it is impossible to show a profit practicing this kind of medicine, and yet we do it because of the satisfaction of seeing patients get better. So my answer to you is, I would very much like to conduct research, and I hope that one day I will have the funds to do it. I hope to create a foundation, and the profits, when they exist, from that foundation will be earmarked for doing research of the kind that you are talking about."

Briber nodded at the thoroughness of the answer. "I have no further questions, Dr. Atkins. Thank you very much."

As Harris, Levin, and Atkins exited the building, they walked toward the parking garage where Harris had parked in order for him to put the litigation bags stuffed with books and documents into his trunk. "What do you guys think?" Harris asked. "I'm sweating like a pig because it's so damn hot out here, but I feel like flying!"

"I think you did a great job today, Bob, the lawyer," Levin laughed, "and you were superb, Bob, the doctor," he said to Atkins.

"Why don't two Bobs and a Warren go have a bite together?" Harris asked. "It's all about nutrition, you know." The doctors laughed as they looked at the defense lawyer, the sweat pouring off his face after taking a few, short steps.

CHAPTER 30

The summer rolled by at a dazzling speed for Levin, the hearing of July 26 not particularly significant, as far as he was concerned. When he entered the hearing room on September 5, Susan was with him for the very first time. It promised to be an interesting day, since the state—which had earlier declared that *only* Victor Herbert could *possibly* testify as an expert—had suddenly invited in a *new* witness, Michael Victor Herman, M.D. Once again, there were an appreciable number of visitors in the courtroom, in addition to Warren Levin's spouse.

What's with these state witnesses all named Victor? thought Harris. He refrained from making the crack aloud.

Once the witness was sworn in, Harris made a request to the judge. "Your Honor, I would like to request that Dr. Herman's testimony be severely time-limited," he stated. "On page 203 of the record, counsel for the state indicated that *any* witness other than Dr. Victor Herbert would be 'purely ancillary and 'very minor in significance.' Then, on page 1088, he described any other testimony other than Dr. Herbert's as 'superfluous.' I take him at his word," he said, looking at the audience for effect, since none of the observers had been in the hearing room at the time those words had been uttered by Sheehan. "If this testimony is to be 'superfluous, ancillary, and minor,' then I would like it time-limited," he repeated, again for effect, this time looking toward the panel, to drive his point to home base, "so we are not listening to *superfluous, minor, ancillary* testimony all day."

Storch looked at the prosecutor. "Do you care to respond, Mr. Sheehan?"

"Merely to state that I agree that it is unnecessary to buttress Dr. Herbert's testimony in any way," Sheehan stated, so as not to embarrass himself regarding his position on Herbert's value. "However, since the *other* side presented an entire retinue of 'experts'—which I do not believe were experts, I just felt that it would be appropriate to spend an hour or so on the rebuttal case, presenting another *similar, stellar* expert to just underline what Dr. Herbert had to say."

"Very well, Mr. Sheehan," said Storch. "Mr. Harris, we will hear the witness, and it will take as long as it takes. I will just note in passing that while Mr. Sheehan may have made those statements on the record on pages 203 and 1088, we are up to page 5000 and thereabouts. There has been a *lot* of testimony in between, so there may be other areas to explore."

Sheehan stepped up to the witness. "Dr. Herman, could you tell us what specialty you have, if any?"

"My specialty is internal medicine and cardiology."

"Where did you go to medical school, and when did you graduate, please?"

"At the Peter Bent Brigham Hospital in Boston, Massachusetts. I had a residency in internal medicine and a two-year fellowship in cardiovascular disease at the same hospital. Then I served two years in the United States Navy as a physician in San Diego, California. I subsequently returned to Brigham Hospital, which is affiliated with Harvard Medical School, and was a staff cardiologist there from 1968 through 1974."

"What did you do in 1975?" Sheehan asked him.

"I left Boston in 1974 and came to Mount Sinai in New York City, where I became Chief of Cardiology and Professor of Medicine. I was there until 1980," Herman said, "when I became Chief of Cardiology and Professor of Medicine at New York Medical College in the Westchester County Medical Center, which is my present position."

"Could you tell the panel whether or not you have published at all during the course of your career?"

"Yes, I have published around one-hundred and fifty full-length articles on various aspects of cardiovascular disease, research studies in cardio-vascular disease."

"Have you had a private practice?"

Herman nodded. "I have a small private practice in cardiology."

When Sheehan introduced the topic of Chelation therapy, Harris asked to conduct a *voir dire* of the witness, regarding his knowledge of the treatment. The line of questioning rapidly shifted to a discussion of arteriosclerosis, due to Harris's challenge.

Herman took a deep breath. "Arteriosclerosis is a pathologic disease process that involves the arteries in the body and develops due to certain risk factors such as family history, hypercholesterolemia, hypertension, cigarette smoking, and genetic factors which damage the arterial wall. This initial damage causes a process of blood clotting, platelet aggregation—cellular in growth—and lipid deposits. Plaque is then formed, first microscopic, which builds up over the years on the arterial wall. This arteriosclerotic plaque disrupts blood flow and can cause occlusion and blockage of various arteries throughout the body, resulting in problems in the organ served by those arteries."

Sheehan looked at his notes. "Could you tell the panel what treatment modalities have been employed over the last twenty years or so in treating this condition?"

"It depends on what organ you are speaking of. Take the heart, for instance. First, the risk factors that cause the problem have to be controlled: stop smoking; and get hypertension, hyperlipidemia, hypercholesterolemia, and all of the associated lipid problems under control. That is the primary therapy. The secondary therapy deals with how that process assists blood flow and affects the various organs that are involved. It we are speaking of the heart, it is heart attack, damage to the heart muscle. Direct approaches include bypass surgery, angioplasty, arterectomy, and balloon angioplasty—a whole gamut of approaches."

Sheehan closed in on his target. "During the course of your professional career, Doctor, have you become aware of a modality known as Chelation therapy?"

"Yes, I have."

"Could you tell us whether there are one or more specific conditions for which that modality is an approved and recognized treatment?"

"Objection!"

"Basis, Mr. Harris?"

"What is the basis of Dr. Herman's knowledge?" he countered, his mouth tight and his left eyebrow raised above his eyeglasses.

"Objection overruled. You can explore that in cross-examination, I am sure, Mr. Harris."

When Herman asked for the question to be restated by the prosecutor, Sheehan amended it to include a broader area. "Could you tell us whether there is any type of heavy metal condition or any other condition that warrants treatment with Chelation therapy, in your professional opinion?"

"There are several conditions, and these involve, as you have mentioned, heavy metals, such as lead poisoning; such as high levels of calcium in the bloodstream, hypercalcemia, where Chelation therapy is indicated for the removal of that particular condition."

"How long has chelation been recognized as a treatment for these types of conditions?"

"At least twenty years."

"In your professional opinion, during the last twenty years, has chelation been recognized in the medical community as a treatment for arteriosclerosis?"

"No, it hasn't been recognized as a treatment," the doctor admitted.

Sheehan grinned. "Aside from what the medical community thinks about it, in *your* professional opinion, do you believe that chelation is a valid, effective treatment for arteriosclerosis?"

Herman shook his head. "No, I don't believe it is."

Sheehan picked up three patient charts and showed them to Herman. "Are those the names of the three patients whose charts you reviewed at my request?" he asked.

"Yes, sir," the doctor answered.

Sheehan selected one of the charts. "Could you tell us *what* precisely this patient was being treated for? In other words, what was the treatment plan for this patient?"

"I really couldn't determine that," the doctor said, shaking his head.

"In any event, you were able to determine that chelation treatments were rendered to this patient, correct?"

"That is correct."

"Let's assume that the treatment was given for arteriosclerosis. Based on your review of the chart, was that medically indicated?" Sheehan asked.

"No, because I don't feel that is an accepted therapy for arteriosclerosis or arteriosclerotic heart disease."

Sheehan proceeded to show the remaining two charts to Herman, asking the same type of questions and getting the same answers as he did for the first chart. The prosecutor got Herman to endorse the view that the charts were not maintained in the way that a licensed, medical professional *should* compile patient charts: the diagnosis was not clear nor the treatment plan. The doctor found no reason to give chelation treatments to any of the three patients who, incidentally, belonged to the same family.

Interestingly, Sheehan asked a hypothetical question that Harris would have enjoyed posing. The prosecutor wondered whether Chelation therapy, if shown to be effective for arteriosclerosis in a study by a respected researcher and published in a medical journal, would be a treatment that Herman would use in his own practice.

Without hesitation, Herman said, "If this was scientifically proved by reputable studies appropriately, I would use it, most certainly. Proven efficacious, proven safe and effective, absolutely, I would use it. But I have found no such evidence."

"Doctor, would you and other cardiologists that you know ever place your own self-interest over that of your patient's by deliberately suppressing a treatment modality which you *know* to be a cure?"

"I would hope not!" Herman said, seeming surprised by the directness of the question. "If something is effective and it is new, I would use it. My gracious, that is what we are here for. We are here to *treat* patients and take care of them."

"Doctor, the claim also has been made during the course of the hearing that everyone who lives in a big city over, say, the age of fifty would benefit by having Chelation therapy rendered to them. Would you agree with such an opinion?"

"No, I don't think there is a *shred* of scientific evidence to support such a claim," Herbert told Sheehan.

"Do you know of Victor Herbert?" Sheehan then asked.

"I know of him," Herman responded.

"How do you know of Dr. Herbert, please?"

"Dr. Herbert and I were both on the faculty of Mount Sinai when I was at Mount Sinai in the 1970's," he responded.

"Have you spoken to Dr. Herbert in any way about the Dr. Warren Levin case?"

"I have not spoken to him since the 1970's, actually," Herman said, thoughtful.

Sheehan smiled a tight little smile. "Could you tell us what your opinion is of Victor Herbert as a scientist and physician?"

"Why, he is a…"

"*Objection!* He says, 'I haven't seen him since the 1970's.' He doesn't even say he knows what he *looks* like. Now, he is going to give an *opinion* about what a *genius* he is!"

"Overruled."

Herman blinked rapidly several times, collecting his thoughts. "I feel he has made excellent scientific contributions. He is recognized as a leading physician and expert in his field."

Sheehan nodded with satisfaction. "Doctor, who requested that you review records for this agency on this case?"

Herman appeared puzzled. "You did," he said, hesitantly.

"Aside from your contact with me, have you had contact with any *other* individual concerning this particular case?"

"No one."

"Thank you very much, Doctor," said Sheehan, returning to his seat. "I have no other questions."

Harris hefted himself up, prepared to begin cross-examination. Levin surprised himself by hoping that Susan would get to witness some of the courtroom theatrics that the defense attorney had employed over the past two years of the hearing and which lost some of their excitement in the telling.

Harris walked over to Herman. “Doctor,” he boomed, formally introducing himself, “I am Robert Harris. I am Dr. Levin’s attorney. How did it come that you are here today?”

“I received a phone call from Mr. Sheehan asking me to join him,” Herman responded.

“Have you ever testified for the state before?”

“Not for this department,” he said.

“Did you ask Mr. Sheehan this question: ‘There are thousands of cardiologists in New York. How come you are calling me?’”

Levin knew Harris’s pattern. The lawyer was just warming up. Susan was going to see some fireworks, he was willing to bet.

“No,” the doctor responded.

Harris moved his face closer to the witness’s, and with an incredulous expression, repeated, “You didn’t ask him?”

“No.”

“Did you ask him, ‘Where did you get my name from?’”

“No.”

Harris stretched his mouth, looked out at the audience to be sure he had everyone’s attention. “The state doesn’t pay you very well, someone with all of your degrees and accolades. No big deal, money-wise, right?”

“That is right.”

“So why did you come?”

“Because I am a teacher and researcher. I am interested in things like this, and I believe in the good practice of medicine for those reasons.”

“Did you give Mr. Sheehan a *curriculum vitae*?”

“I believe I did,” Herman replied, shifting uncomfortably in his seat.

Harris raised his long arm and pointed to the ceiling imperiously. "I call for the production of it!" he declared.

Sheehan murmured, "I would have introduced it, but I couldn't find it today. I think the doctor's secretary may have sent me one a long time ago. Since I couldn't find it this morning, I just relied on the witness's verbal description."

Harris snorted at Sheehan before returning to the witness. "Was the subject of Chelation therapy as a treatment for various arteriosclerotic diseases ever discussed in your training?"

Herman shook his head. "Not in medical school."

"Did you ever *see* chelation used on a patient during the four years that you were in medical school?"

"Not for arteriosclerosis."

"In medical school and at Peter Bent Brigham did you ever *talk* to anybody who had used Chelation therapy for arteriosclerotic problems?

"No, I didn't."

"After Brigham Hospital you went to Mount Sinai?"

"Yes."

"Is it fair to say that Chelation therapy is *not* a treatment of choice for dealing with arteriosclerotic problems?"

"That is correct."

"At Mount Sinai or afterwards, where you are now Chief of Cardiology and Professor at Westchester County, did you ever talk to *anybody* who had used Chelation therapy to treat arteriosclerotic heart disease?"

"I never have."

"You said that you wrote about one-hundred and fifty articles. I ran a Medline search and came up with one-hundred and twenty-one. Would you accept that as fair?"

"That is fine."

"Out of these titles, is Victor Herbert an attributed author on any of them?"

"No, sir."

"Is there a reason that you were on the same faculty with him for years and never once chose to do any research with him worthy of writing up?"

"It is a very large faculty. He was at one institution, I was at another. That is probably why we would have never met for research."

"You were talking before about the National Institutes of Health, and *all* the people there and how they are anxious to improve the *world* by doing studies and finding out the truth, right?"

"That is correct."

"Would you feel that I was way off base if I called the NIH a *political cesspool* in terms of the way a potential test or experiment has to go through land mines to get funded?"

"We would have to debate this," Herman responded. "I understand what you are getting at. It is difficult to get things through, to get them reviewed."

Harris then postulated for Herman the following: a group of morbidly obese men over age sixty enter Westchester County Medical Center with hypertension. Then, suddenly, the condition disappears. The *only* difference is that those individuals are now chewing sugar free bubble gum.

"Would you think," continued Harris, "that recommending sugar free bubble gum to morbidly obese people would require double-blind, randomized, controlled studies in order to suggest that it might have some efficacy?"

"I think it would. I would require that," said Herman.

"I object to the hypothetical as being *totally inapplicable* to this proceeding. It has no meaning whatsoever," the prosecutor insisted. "It reduces the entire intellectual discussion of the issues to a cartoon!" Sheehan was getting wound up again. "Talking about bubble gum and five-hundred pound people just doesn't compute. It is an invalid, meaningless, dumb hypothetical. If Mr. Harris wants to talk about chelation and the anecdotal reports and ask the doctor questions whether they satisfy his scientific requirements, I have no objection. But bubble gum? This is ridiculous and absurd!"

Interestingly, Storch overruled the objection, and Harris delightedly proceeded with his bubble gum analogy, asking whether Herman would add bubble gum to the regimen of patients who fit the previous parameters. Levin turned briefly to wink at Susan.

Herman shrugged. "If the bubble gum is clearly shown to be benign, I might, after a lot of trials."

Harris belabored the point of the 'trials' the doctor was insisting on. Then he abruptly dropped the topic.

"Dr. Herman, by the way, in your one-hundred and twenty-one articles, how many times does the expression 'Chelation therapy' appear?" Harris eyed the committee as he asked the question.

Herman glanced at the floor for a moment, seeming to study the attorney's shoes. "Probably never," he muttered.

Harris then held up a handful of the doctor's published articles and began to quiz the witness on points made in article after article. Sheehan voiced objections regularly and was often overruled.

Sheehan stood up. "This cross-examination is not cross-examination," he stated. "We are bogged down in meaningless scientific detail which has *nothing* to do with this case at all!"

"Mr. Harris?" asked Storch.

"I have nothing to say. I will go by your ruling."

"I am going to allow the question."

Harris rephrased, Herman answered, and this pattern continued for a protracted amount of time. When Harris summarized the results from the slides shown by Dr. Richard Casdorph and asked for an opinion from Herman on the effectiveness of chelation, the doctor was reluctant to stamp the process with approval.

"Dr. Herman," said Harris, "Is it fair to say that the consensus indication for doing bypass surgery is either high-grade stenosis of the left main artery or three-vessel disease?"

This question led to a period of inquiry and response to clarify several points. Then Harris pointed out another article where bypass surgery resulted in one-hundred percent brain damage for the patient. Harris looked pensive. "I am puzzled," he told Herman. "This man didn't have high-grade stenosis of the left main artery or three-vessel disease of the kind that would normally cause one to have an operation, did he?"

"No, but he had a very positive stress test at a low work load, which has a very bad prognosis. I think that would *certainly* be an indication for surgery."

Harris established that the small private practice that the doctor maintained was a hospital-based practice. "How do you know what doctors do in their private office if you have never had a private office in your life?" Harris asked him, shaking his head in utter disbelief.

"Every day, I deal with doctors in private practice. I talk to them and visit them."

Harris was beginning his warm-up, Levin noted. "Do you go to visit them and say, 'Listen, let me take a look at your charts and see if they are up to snuff?'"

"No, I don't." Herman was beginning to look perturbed.

Harris made the point that medical charts in a hospital setting have multiple entries made by numerous individuals who have contact with the patient, unlike the charts in the office of a private physician. Herman had his own philosophy.

"I think there are certain *criteria* for charts whether you are in a private practice, institutional practice, or whatever," Herman said. "You have to have some format for keeping records so that, on review, it is apparent what you were doing. There are certain basic guidelines that one needs to follow, wherever you are."

Harris walked Herman through the essentials of a medical chart: a history, presenting symptoms, treatment plan, tests ordered, and test results. Then Harris asked, "Is the problem with Dr. Levin's charts that they are sloppy?"

Herman shook his head no. "I really can't find, on reading them, what the main problems of that patient were and what the treatment plan and its rationale were. I do not find that."

Harris confirmed with Herman that there was a regular chart review process in an institutional setting that dictated a specific format for medical charts. The thoroughness of the chart became critical if a patient in a hospital died.

"Are any of those needs requirements of a private practitioner?" Harris asked.

"I think the private practitioner's chart should meet the same standards, because he is responsible for the care of his patients. I must say, in the future, I think we are going to come to that."

Harris looked at the doctor questioningly. "In the future? But this is a *1976 chart*, which *is* the future from, say, 1921." Harris decided to postulate once again. "I would like to make you the Health Commissioner for a moment. Can I do that?"

"You can."

Harris asked a question which he believed was key to the hearing and made sure, as he frequently did throughout the proceedings, to pin each member of the committee with a significant look. "Would you take a physician's medical license away from him because you believed his patient charts were sloppy?"

"I object as irrelevant!" shouted Sheehan, who was forewarned by Harris's gaze at the committee.

"It is hypothetical, and I am entitled to ask it!" Harris retorted.

"It has to have some *relation* to the case and some *probative value*," Sheehan lectured him. "What this witness would do if he was Commissioner has *nothing* to do with this case. He is here to give his expert opinion on the adequacy or inadequacy of the treatment rendered to particular patients and his knowledge about certain modalities that were discussed during this hearing. His philosophical approach to disciplining doctors is absolutely uninteresting to the panel and to the Commissioner of Health, who has to review this panel and to Regents who have to review it. Ultimately, I object to the question as being *preposterous*!"

Levin always enjoyed watching Sheehan get hot under the collar. While Sheehan didn't indulge in broad gestures and dramatic stances, he did increase the volume of his delivery, as well as its pace. Being fair-skinned, he tended to get red-faced, as well, making him look more like a blushing schoolboy than a prosecuting attorney. His arguments were generally standard, though, and never as creative as Bob's. On the other hand, when Sheehan made a good point, it usually spurred Bob on to even greater heights: sometimes they caused Levin to cringe and other times to smile. The audiences generally enjoyed the theatrics…sometimes too much.

This time, Storch's sigh was directed at Sheehan. "I wish you hadn't used the word 'preposterous,'" he said, rather weakly.

Sheehan continued to face Harris. "Why don't you call him 'King,' and ask about people who commit subway crimes?"

"Relax," Storch told the prosecutor. "Whether or not this physician is of the opinion that one level of discipline or another should be rendered is not relevant. It is up to the committee in its deliberations to decide what penalty, if any, should be imposed if any charges are sustained."

If Harris's strategy was simply to get Sheehan all riled up or for the committee to hear that—if no other charges could be indelibly pinned on Levin—perhaps the Commissioner would pull Levin's license for sloppy charts, then perhaps the defense lawyer's objective was accomplished. Harris simply said, "Withdrawn," which was met with the simultaneous exhalation of breath from a number of the spectators, who then shifted in their seats as evidenced by the creaks and groans of the wooden chairs.

Harris then moved the discussion to the angiogram, used to diagnose cardiac conditions, to see if disease is present and how severe the situation might be. In an angiogram, a thin tube called a catheter is inserted into the femoral artery or vein in the groin and threaded through the vessel until it reaches the targeted area. An iodine dye is injected into the vessel to provide contrast for x-ray films, taken by a tiny camera, of the blood flow in that artery or vein.

"So the angiogram, which you say has some morbidity and mortality consequences, is really done to provide a road map for a surgeon, correct?" Harris asked.

"That's one reason," responded Herman. "But sometimes the diagnosis isn't that apparent, so it is often used for diagnostic purposes. For example, if someone's occupation was such that it was important to know if there was underlying disease, and by all the other modes of testing you didn't have an answer, then an angiogram would be done."

"Could you give me an example?"

"Airline pilot."

"So, as the head of a service, you need to have the patient's informed consent. Do you go to the airline pilot and say, 'We can't be one-hundred percent sure that you don't have blocked coronary arteries, so we are going to risk killing you to find that out'?" Harris waited, his eyebrows raised high.

"No."

"I object," Sheehan said, calmly, this time around. "Whether or not certain accepted modalities have a risk factor has *no* relevance to the issue in this hearing which is, namely, whether a specific modality which may have no risk value has an efficacy. That is what this case is about."

So that's what the case is about in the eyes of the state, thought Levin, his wife, and his lawyer, simultaneously. *Nice of them to finally let us know that all of those pages of charges and nonsense all boil down to this one sentence. You could have said that a lot sooner, guys.*

Sheehan was still voicing the remainder of his objection. "The fact that other methods of diagnosing or treating conditions have a mortality factor or a risk factor is not relevant unless we are dealing with chelation, which we say has *no* proven efficacy, so we cannot compare risk factors. We are discussing whether a modality has *any* scientific merit. This is what the discussion *should* be about, not this totally tangential, irrelevant discussion of medical ethics and philosophy of treatment."

Sheehan's actually got a point, thought Levin, begrudgingly.

"I agree with Mr. Sheehan. I will sustain the objection."

Calling for a lunch break, Storch requested a brief meeting with both attorneys. When the hearing reconvened, Storch told the committee something very interesting.

"The Department has *withdrawn* three charges having to do with alleged failure to maintain records which accurately reflect the evaluation and treatment of Patients A, B, and C, since the regulation came out in 1981 and was *not* in effect during the time treatment was rendered," Storch said.

Levin and Susan looked at each other. Harris had refrained from sharing this news over lunch. However, their relief was cut short.

"That isn't a complete description of our discussion at all," Sheehan said. "The Regents, in the past, and the courts, in the past, have allowed charges such as that one—even in the absence of a specific regulation dealing with medical records on the grounds that they violated the generally accepted standards of medical practice. There are court cases in the Education Law that have upheld that interpretation, and *that's* the interpretation we relied on.

"However, this is a case that will go to the Regents, who in recent times have taken a *contrary* position: namely, that they will *not* allow use of generally accepted standards of medical practice in the absence of a specific regulation in effect at the *time* of the alleged conduct. So, knowing of the Regents' attitude toward those types of interpretations, the state agreed, once the Hearing Officer raised the issue, to *withdraw* those three charges on the assumption that the Regents would follow their current thinking and not call them in," Sheehan said.

Boy, what a tight-ass, thought Levin. *Couldn't he have simply let me enjoy the gift guilt-free? No, he had to cover his own ass, just in case the Regents* doesn't *do what it's been doing and decides to stick it to me on the charts, as well.*

Sheehan had muddied the judge's pronouncement so badly that Storch needed to clarify. "The bottom line, Mr. Sheehan: *You* have asked to delete those charges from the allegations. Is that correct?"

"That's the bottom line," Sheehan responded.

Harris wasn't going to let this pass so easily. "The problem with 'the bottom line,'" Harris said, "is the clear implication that 'Dr. Levin is guilty, but since there is some technical nonsense, we're not going to charge him with it.' That's not appropriate for a prosecutor to do! It prejudices the panel. The state brings charges that are not going to be sustained, they agree to withdraw the charges, but instead of simply withdrawing them, Mr. Sheehan goes through a tautological argument which is intended to tell the panel, 'This guy is as dirty as mud, but we just can't hold him on that one.'"

Briber, as panel chairperson, responded. "Mr. Harris, the panel is *not* prejudiced."

Harris looked each panel member over for a moment, then said, "You *look* prejudiced to me!" The audience appreciated the comment.

A deep sigh from Storch. "Mr. Harris, the committee is now aware that these charges have been withdrawn. There have been no findings on the charges."

Harris shrugged. "I think my point has been made," he said. He turned back to the witness to continue cross-examination, still wondering why the state selected this particular witness.

"So you *didn't* ask *where* he got your name and just said, 'Of course. It will be my privilege to serve.' Right?"

"I think I said, 'I would like to see what the issue is, and then I will let you know.'"

"What did he tell you the issue was?" Harris asked, referring to Sheehan.

"I think it is as he has been questioning me today: the issue was the inappropriate use of Chelation therapy."

Harris nodded. "You came here today to testify about Chelation therapy and Dr. Levin's use of it, right?"

"Yes."

Harris smiled at the witness. "You're a bright guy," he said. "You know what this hearing is about, right? It is challenging a physician's right to practice medicine in the state of New York. Did you *read* anything about Chelation therapy?"

"Objection!" Sheehan was on his feet. *"When?"* he asked. "In response to my call or *ever*?"

Harris nodded at the prosecutor and turned back to the witness. "Since the time that you agreed to testify about Chelation therapy until now, one o'clock in the afternoon on the fifth of September. Did you *read* anything about Chelation therapy?"

"Yes," said Herman, in a small voice.

"*What* did you read?" Harris asked him.

"I read a variety of documents that I have saved over the years."

"Can you tell me *what* they were?"

"First of all, I read the package insert from the EDTA itself to refresh my mind about the substance. I read a couple of articles, one by Alfred Sofer that dealt with the issue of chelation. I reviewed a position paper that I had from the New York State Medical Society on Chelation therapy. I think that is about it."

Harris had perfected the incredulous look, and he applied it to his face rapidly. "You have a computerized Medline search engine in your institution, don't you?"

"Yes."

"You have an extensive medical library in your center, don't you?"

"Yes."

"Did you *run* a Medline search for chelation within the universe of arteriosclerosis or cardiovascular disease?"

"No, I didn't."

"When you talked to Mr. Sheehan about this, did you *inquire* as to whether or not there had been defense witnesses who spoke *in favor* of chelation?"

"I don't believe I did."

"Were you *told* that Patient C is still alive, her phone number is available, and you could speak to *her* about her treatment?"

"I wasn't told that."

"The fact that the *package insert* on EDTA doesn't mention using Chelation therapy for arteriosclerotic anomalies doesn't *stop* a licensed physician from using it for that purpose, correct?"

"That is correct."

"Doctor, I would like to ask you a hypothetical question. You have the opportunity to present speakers at Grand Rounds. So I come to you and say, 'Doctor, the issue of Chelation therapy is really becoming topical, and I would like to give a talk in your hospital on Grand Rounds, so that your residents and attending physicians will be familiar with the subject. I have *never, ever spoken* to anyone who has used Chelation therapy for *any* aspect of heart or vascular disease. I have *never* dealt with a patient who has been *treated* with this therapy. I have *not* searched the peer-reviewed literature. But I have read the *package insert*, an *article*, and a *position paper*. I really don't know a *damn thing* about the subject. Would you *permit* me to address your physicians on Grand Rounds?"

"We probably *wouldn't* invite you," Herman simply said.

Harris got in the doctor's face. *"What the hell are you doing here?"* he shouted.

"I object to this line of questioning!" Sheehan said, in a loud voice.

Harris smiled and stepped away from Herman. "Withdrawn."

"Is it fair, Doctor, to say that *you* don't know a damn thing about Chelation therapy?" Harris began again.

Herman's jaw muscle jumped. "I know *a lot* about it!"

"You know *a lot* about what you *think* you know about it!"

"Objection! Argumentative."

"Sustained."

Harris softened his tone. "*Tell* me what you know about it," he challenged.

"*Objection!* Improper question. Ask a *specific* question."

"Tell me, Dr. Herman, what is the *theoretical basis* for the physiological process of EDTA?" Harris asked, drawing on his tutelage from Levin.

Sheehan intervened. "In treating *what*? In *doing* what? Lead poisoning?"

Harris was ready for that. "Improper question," he told Sheehan. "*You* don't understand the subject matter any better than your witness does!"

Dr. Herman was instructed to answer the question. "I *will* answer that. It chelates bivalent and trivalent ions. Thereby, as it is excreted from the body, removes those ions."

Harris then took the doctor through a number of ions to establish what category each fell into. Then he started making comparisons.

"How is the action of a calcium channel blocker distinguishable from sodium dicalcium EDTA?"

The doctor launched into an explanation and concluded it by saying, "You don't *remove* calcium with a calcium channel blocker. You alter the way it enters and exits cells. You are literally typing up calcium in the bloodstream wherever the

EDTA can meet up and take that ion and remove it from the bloodstream itself. But I don't know that you are doing anything for those plaques. I seriously doubt, from the knowledge that I have, that you are doing anything, but I don't know."

Harris took a moment to look around the hearing room, pacing as he did so, and began to recount certain facts. "You *don't* know," he repeated. "You *didn't* search the literature, you don't know *anybody* who uses it, and you don't know anyone who has *had* the treatment. Please," he said, dramatically, holding his hands out, palms up, "*please* tell the panel *what* your expertise is that makes *your* opinion worth listening to in a...license...revocation...hearing," Harris asked Herman, spacing out the final three, and most significant, words in his question, for maximal effect.

The witness was definitely annoyed by the attorney's gratuitous plea. "My expertise is that I have been practicing cardiology in an academic center for over twenty years, treating patients, doing research, looking for new therapies, interested in any good therapy that would come along. Based on *my* review, *my* experience watching it for over *twenty years*, I don't feel that Chelation therapy really offers *anything* to the patients, based on the current knowledge that we have."

Suddenly, from the defense table, Levin pounded his fist. *"He didn't even look!"* he shouted.

Harris swiveled around to face his client, concerned that Levin would upset the legal process Harris was currently engaged in, one that was aimed at discrediting Michael Victor Herman, M.D. as an expert witness. "I want you to go outside," Harris said to Levin, in a no-nonsense tone.

"You *bet* I am going outside!" Levin responded, immediately getting up and leaving the room.

Susan wanted to go out with her husband and comfort him. He rarely allowed his irritation to show, and she could totally understand his public display at this particular moment. However, she chose to stay, so that she could see how the attorney she had selected to save her spouse's license would handle the situation.

"I *share* his sentiments," Harris announced, "but *not* his behavior." He turned back to the witness. "You say your evaluation is based on your 'experience.' *But you don't have any experience.*"

"I object!"

Harris rapidly swiveled toward the Hearing Officer, but his finger was pointed straight at Sheehan. "*He* put this man on the stand! I spent all morning listening to this *nonsense*. He has *no* idea what he is talking about. This is a *disgrace*!" He turned, so that the pointing finger was now aimed at Herman. "I will bet you," he began, looking at the spectators, "that he is one of the nicest, classic cardiologists in Westchester. *But he doesn't know a damn thing about this subject!*" The finger moved toward Sheehan again. "And *he* has the temerity to present him!" The finger was aimed at Herman. "He comes in here to talk about something he has never seen, used, researched, or looked up, and says, 'Hey, I have a big professorial title in something that has *nothing* to do with this. If it was good, I would use it, but it is *no* good, so I don't deal with it.' It is an *insult* for him to be here. It is an insult to *me*, because I have better things to do than to listen to somebody who has such a formidable background spending the last four hours saying, 'I don't know what the hell I am talking about. I don't want to go through all of these articles and pages to convince the…"

"Mr. Harris is out of order!" Sheehan shouted, playing the role of judge, not prosecutor.

Harris, completely fired up, totally ignored him and continued to play to his spellbound audience. Susan Levin was getting to see what her husband had promised: an Academy Award-winning performance. In fact, Levin had quietly re-entered the courtroom, attracted by all of the shouting he heard within, and resumed his seat at the defense table.

"To come here to a license revocation hearing to testify against a guy on a subject that he has *no* experience with…"

Briber slammed his palm on the table in front of him. "That is *enough*, Mr. Harris!"

At this point, Storch intervened, his voice calm, in contrast to those of the preceding speakers. "The question was repetitive," he stated, as though Harris had merely asked a question, not uttered a series of scathing remarks. "Ask a different question, if you have one." Then, to make sure he wouldn't be seen as a judge who couldn't control the proceedings, he added, "Save your tantrums for another time."

"I apologize." This was from Levin.

"I don't!" from Harris.

Storch ignored both of them and repeated, "If you have another question, ask it."

"I have *many* more questions. If I have to demonstrate this man's *ineptitude*..."

"I object to *testimony* by Mr. Harris!" said Sheehan.

Storch took off his glasses and rubbed his eyes, tiredly. "Ask another question *without* any further editorializing on your part," he directed Harris.

Harris took several deep breaths to center and calm himself, a technique he picked up from Warren Levin. Then he began to ask the doctor questions, culled from Herman's own published articles. This led to objections citing relevance, however the judge directed the witness to answer the questions time after time. When Harris's line of inquiry shifted to other areas of the chart that the witness had not testified to in direct examination, the prosecutor's objection was upheld. Harris then attempted to read portions of Victor Herbert's testimony and elicit feedback from the witness, which infuriated Sheehan, who voiced vehement objections and supported them with generous backing.

Harris then turned back to the issue of Patient A. "You read this chart over and saw a diagnosis of, among other things, hypoglycemia. Did you notice that?"

"Yes."

"Do you recognize hypoglycemia as a *legitimate* diagnosis in view of appropriate findings?"

"Yes, he seemed to have a low blood sugar terminally in his prolonged glucose tolerance test. That fulfills the diagnostic criteria."

"Were you given copies of the hospital charts relevant to this man's admissions *after* he saw Dr. Levin?"

"I don't believe so."

Harris whirled around and faced Storch. "I move that Dr. Herman's testimony be stricken! He has *not* testified based upon the complete chart of these individuals. How can *any* conclusion be..."

Sheehan cut him off. "Dr. Levin didn't treat those individuals in the *hospital*. What it shows in the hospital record does *not* bear upon what he *should* have done when he saw these patients. Whether or not this witness received any hospital charts is still a question," he finished, weakly.

"If you want to assert that you sent them to him, I am willing to accept your word. Then I will be glad to stop talking. If you did, *say so*."

Sheehan blew a noisy breath. "I *didn't* send him hospital records. You objected to some, but other hospital charts were sent from that hospital in New Jersey, although I did not discuss those charts with the doctor."

"Let me withdraw my motion. I don't want to push that issue."

"Good idea, Mr. Harris," the judge murmured.

Harris faced Herman again. "If you found out that this patient wound up in the emergency room comatose, obtunded, and that they put fifty-percent glucose and water into him, and he sat up and whistled 'Dixie' would that increase your certainty as to whether or not this man was hypoglycemic?"

"I think that would be a pretty firm way of establishing that diagnosis," Herman answered.

This brought a smile from Harris, who was ready to insert another reference to Victor Herbert into his next question. "If I were to tell you that *Victor Herbert* testified that the man *didn't* have a problem with hypoglycemia, and that hypoglycemia was basically a *nonsense* diagnosis, would you disagree with him?"

"*Objection!* Did he have a problem with hypoglycemia at the time he went into the hospital or at the time that Dr. Levin treated him?"

"Both!" Harris stated.

"Go ahead, Doctor," said Storch.

"Based on the information that you gave me, I would say it sounds like hypoglycemia," Herman responded.

"I have no further questions of this man," Harris said. He strode confidently over to Levin at the defense table and resumed his seat.

Dr. McAloon addressed the witness. "You stated if a scientifically valid study on Chelation therapy was submitted to one of the peer-reviewed journals, you believe that it would be published?"

"Absolutely."

"You don't feel there is a subtle discrimination that perhaps goes on when unconventional subjects or studies are written about and submitted for publication?"

"I don't think so. In fact, I think the journals would welcome this. They would *like* to settle this issue. As part of the editorial board of *Circulation* and the *American Journal of Cardiology, I* would like to see it settled, positively or negatively," he told McAloon.

Briber was next. "You are concerned about the controversy that surrounds Chelation therapy?"

"Yes."

"What is the harm in the use of Chelation therapy?"

"I view it this way," said Herman. "It is totally unproven that it has any benefit right now. The harm or any side effects are from the EDTA itself. Also, it is the false hopes that this can raise. Besides, when it is used, other forms of therapy are disregarded, so you may not use the established, proper therapies because of this. These are my concerns."

Harris had a few more questions to ask on re-cross examination. "Doctor, *what* are the side effects of Chelation therapy?"

"Side effects?" repeated Herman. "Well, first of all, in that it chelates the ions we have discussed already. It can cover levels of calcium; so hypoglycemia, not directly but indirectly through the kidneys can cause potassium loss; tie up magnesium, which is an important element. So, from an electrolyte standpoint, those things can happen. You can have nephrotoxicity, hepatotoxicity. We talked about myocardial depression: You raised that issue. With someone with heart disease, chelation can depress the myocardium, decrease contractility. And there are simple things, like nausea and vomiting."

"Do you know what percentage of patients receiving Chelation therapy protocols have *experienced* any of the side effects which you just said could occur?"

"I don't know that, because I don't think that data is collected or available."

Harris smirked. "How would *you* know if it is collected or available if you didn't even look up what has *already* been written on it?"

"Mr. Harris!"

"Withdrawn."

Harris leaned in toward the witness again, his eyes narrowed. "I wonder *how* you've been able to continue to sit here for this last hour , as an 'expert' without walking out to save your self-esteem. I wonder how you have been able to *testify* as to what *could* happen, when the fact of the matter is that you don't have the slightest idea of *what* happens. You don't know if chelation has been used in fifty cases or millions of cases. You don't know what the peer-reviewed literature has said about it. You don't know what the tests have said about it. You don't know what the non-peer-reviewed articles have said about it. How do you have the *gall* to sit there and say, 'Listen to me!' and 'Based on what *I* am saying, consider allowing Dr. Levin to retain his license to practice medicine'!"

"I object to these personal attacks that are disguised as questions!" Sheehan said.

Harris shook his head in disgust. "I have no more questions."

Storch looked at Sheehan. "If you have nothing further, Mr. Sheehan?"

"Nothing."

"Thank you very much for your participation," said Briber, politely, to Herman. "You are excused."

When the hearing room was cleared, Storch spoke to the two attorneys and the three committee members. He reminded them that, during Dr. Atkins' appearance as a witness for the defense, Sheehan asked that the entire testimony be stricken due to a refusal by Atkins to answer a question.

"Mr. Sheehan requested the opportunity to brief the issue, which I granted," said Storch. "I subsequently received a brief from Mr. Sheehan. Mr. Harris placed his argument on the record at the time of the motion and decided *not* to submit any additional documentation. I have reviewed Mr. Sheehan's brief. It is now *my* decision that Dr. Atkins' testimony should *not* be stricken." Storch reiterated that he didn't have the authority to strike testimony anyway, he could only have directed the committee to disregard it. "But disregarding the entire testimony of the doctor is not appropriate under the circumstances, and the motion is denied. That is all I have to say on that matter."

As they stepped outside into the mid-afternoon heat of early September, they all looked spent: Harris, Levin, and Susan. Somehow, they didn't even feel like discussing anything that had happened during the day. They each wanted to do a bit of soul-searching to try to figure out where everything stood in this increasingly confusing and endless process.

CHAPTER 31

Storch opened the proceedings. "All right, why don't you bring in the witness, Mr. Sheehan."

"Would you please give your name and address to the court reporter," said Briber.

"Robert Rej. I am Director of Clinical Chemistry for the Wadsworth Center of Laboratories and Research, New York State Department of Health, Albany, New York."

"What are your responsibilities?" asked Sheehan.

"We are responsible for carrying out clinical laboratory tests in the area of clinical chemistry, endocrinology, enzymology, toxicology, therapeutic substance monitoring, blood gases, and related areas specific to a clinical laboratory. We organize and administer the Proficiency Testing Program that is part of the Lab Licensure Program, sponsored by the Wadsworth Center. The Proficiency Testing Program ensures that all laboratories within or outside of New York State which accept specimens from New York residents are issued a permit by the Department of Health, so we can assess the quality of those laboratories. By sending clinical specimens to these laboratories, we are able to judge and monitor their performance, so we can recommend whether or not the Clinical Laboratory Evaluation Unit should even issue a permit to conduct clinical laboratory measurements in those areas."

"You have published a number of scientific articles?"

"Yes, approximately seventy-five full papers, either in peer-reviewed journals or book chapters and over one-hundred abstracts, letters, reviews, and similar other papers. Most of them are in my c.v.," Rej said. Rej was in his mid-forties and had a studious face topped with a shock of dark hair that spilled over his forehead on the right side, and he wore super-sized spectacles. He had earned his Ph.D. in Biochemistry from the Albany Medical College in 1976.

"Doctor, are you familiar with the subject of hair analysis for medical purposes?" Sheehan asked.

"Yes, I am."

"Could you tell us whether, at any time during your involvement with the State Department of Health, any investigation or study was undertaken regarding hair analysis?"

"Yes, several times over the mid- and late 1980's. The Department received an application for a permit from at least one laboratory that requested a permit to do multi-element hair analysis to assess nutritional status."

Sheehan nodded. "In order to perform such testing, was a license or permit required to be issued by your office?"

"Yes, a permit is required of all laboratories in New York State or those out of state which are doing business with New York State physicians and residents," Rej replied.

"If the Department reached a conclusion about whether or not multi-element hair analysis should be licensed by the state, could you tell us about it?"

"It did reach a conclusion, and I was involved in that process. Multi-element hair analysis is, at very best, a research technique. Many of the elements which were purported to be measured by these laboratories had no clinical utility."

Sheehan looked at Rej for a moment. "Therefore, *was* a permit issued with respect to this application for hair analysis?"

"No, it was not."

"Could you tell us whether a permit allowing multi-element hair analysis for nutritional status evaluation has *ever* been issued by the New York State Department of Health?"

Rej shook his head negatively. "Not to my knowledge."

"Will the New York State Department of Health, if it knows about it, *issue* a permit allowing any laboratory in the state of New York to perform multi element hair analysis for nutritional evaluation?"

"No, we would not."

"Doctor, prior to our coming to the hearing today, did I send you certain excerpts, single pages here and there, from various medical charts that are in evidence in this hearing?"

"Yes, you did."

"If a lab *outside* of New York State conducts such tests and solicits samples from New York physicians, does the Department of Health have a *policy* regarding such a practice?" Sheehan asked.

"Yes," Rej said, "and I believe there were some legal cases to support that. Such laboratories *must* seek and obtain a permit similar to laboratories that are physically located in New York State."

"Even if the laboratory is *outside* the state?" Sheehan asked, to drive his point home.

"That is correct," Rej responded.

Following an objection from Harris, Sheehan addressed the Hearing Officer. "At one of our last sessions, Mr. Harris *demanded* of me that I back up my claim made many months ago that there have been cases where we have *stopped* laboratories from performing either hair analysis or cytotoxic screening on New York State residents even though the lab was out of state. He said," Sheehan continued, pointing to Harris, "*Name one case!*' I said, 'I don't know the case, but I will get it for you,'...and now I *will* get it for you."

Harris countered, "The claim was made that a laboratory out of state had been *stopped* from doing cytotoxic testing and hair analysis, and if the laboratory that is being discussed in *this* case was stopped from doing those two things, then I don't have an objection." Harris looked toward the judge. "But I know that it's *not* the case, because I checked it more thoroughly than *he* has." Harris jerked his thumb in Sheehan's direction.

Sheehan backpedaled, after shuffling through several pages and cross-checking his evidence, and claimed that he had proof that of one particular lab that had been stopped from doing cytoxic testing and another that was prevented from doing hair analysis. Harris was ready with a clever retort.

"What has happened in the past," he said with a laugh, "is that we have a claim of a one-hundred-and-ten-story building, and then we are offered two fifty-five story buildings." He illustrated the height differences with his hands to show what he considered to be a major difference that the prosecutor just wasn't getting. "So I don't think it is appropriate for the state to make a representation of something and then come back …" Harris broke off for a moment. Then, "It is reminiscent of Dr. Herbert with his '*thousands* of articles that include something,' and it turns out that it's only *one single article*…and *Herbert* was the one who wrote it! Same thing."

"Your objection is overruled."

Harris just shook his head in disbelief at the judge's willingness to allow Sheehan's witness to present unrelated facts and then compound the error by overruling the defense's objection. *Conspiracy,* he thought. *Warren is right. This whole thing just smacks of conspiracy.*

Sheehan began by questioning Rej about clinical chemistry, chemical analysis, the principals underlying various medical tests, investigative standards, and evaluation of scientific claims to establish the man's expertise in response to an objection by Harris that a platform was not appropriately laid for inquiry.

"When you were requested to investigate the question of multi-element hair analysis, were you able to apply those principles of scientific study?" Sheehan finally asked.

"Yes, I did."

Sheehan then requested that Rej summarize the testing process for multi-element hair analysis. Rej explained that he had undertaken a thorough review of the literature, and learned that the majority of the studies did not support the clinical utility of the test. "The primary concern was of contamination, since hair is a dead tissue and there is no active metabolism, unlike with blood, live tissue, or urine. So the ability of hair to asses a current condition is limited. Most of the utility of such data tends to be for epidemiological studies with residents who live near an ore-refining plant, so there will be elevated levels of some metals in the hair in that population compared to a control population living far from such manufacturing facilities. I stress the *multi-element* hair analysis because some elements, like zinc, can be measured on an individual basis and the preparation technique differs."

"Were you able to find a scientific validity to the claims made by the proponents of hair analysis in relation to a person's nutritional status?"

"No, we couldn't." Rej referred to another lab that did the test but had not applied for a permit. He said that when reference values were compared, using plasma emission spectroscopy for measuring the elements in the hair, the results produced were vastly different from lab to lab.

"Getting back to a question I asked you earlier regarding excerpted pages from medical charts that I sent you…"

Harris immediately objected, saying that a witness should not be asked to testify without having seen the *entire* record, which was a ruling made against the defense earlier.

Sheehan nevertheless continued. "I think it is still relevant that a laboratory which a physician used was unlicensed to perform the requested service. And the test was found by the Department of Health to be totally valueless in the way it was done. Just as *you*," he pointed toward Harris, "have introduced today articles published in 1991, allegedly in support of what Dr. Levin did in 1970 and 1975."

Storch said, "It is already in. The committee will have to make a determination as to whether or not a decision that was rendered in 1986 is relevant to the patient care rendered in 1976. We are attacking the test your client ordered as medically valueless."

We are attacking the test your client ordered as medically valueless. Levin would have loved to jump up at the moment and ask, "*We?* Who are *we*?" *You're the judge, no matter who is paying your salary. Are you forgetting that when you say 'we'? Well, at least the 'attacking' part of your sentence is accurate.*

The attorneys continued to debate the entire situation, as the lab in question was told by New York State to *stop* performing the tests and was fined twenty-thousand dollars, as well. However, no litigation resulted, as Sheehan pointed out. Harris's rejoinder was that the lab's "capitulation" to the state may only have indicated that the lab didn't have the state's infinite resources to fight the charges.

"That doesn't mean that hair analysis is good or bad," Harris said. "Just because the lab agreed to stop doing the procedure means *nothing*: maybe it wasn't profitable. We haven't determined a *thing* about hair analysis."

"I agree," Sheehan responded, "but it is introduced to support my contention that *you* disputed. It is *illegal* in New York State."

Harris was quick to parry. "It doesn't *say* it is illegal."

"We stopped them from doing it," Sheehan argued.

There's the "we" again, Levin thought. *The whole bunch of you, tied together, one following the other so you don't stray from the path of conspiracy. What a bunch of winners!*

"They *agreed* to stop!"

Sheehan looked at his opponent in frustration. "Be *quiet* for one second," he ordered. "When I said, on cross-examination of your witness that these tests were illegal, you said, 'Sez who? *No one* says that.' You disputed when I said we even went after labs *out of state*. You said, 'It isn't true!' This case is to show, number one, that it is the *policy* of New York State that hair analysis is *not* legal for labs to do; and number two, and it is the policy to even go after *out-of-state labs* which do the test on New York State residents' specimens. So this is all to substantiate the claim I made."

When Sheehan started to question Rej on the licensing of labs to conduct cytotoxic tests, Harris objected, since Levin did that particular test in his office and did not require a license from the Department of Health to do so. When Storch allowed certain items to be admitted into evidence, following the lawyers' discussion, Sheehan asked the question he had been attempting to ask prior to the objections and delay.

"Dr. Rej, does the New York State Department of Health have a *position* regarding whether or not cytotoxic testing is a *valid* test to be performed by any laboratory in New York State or any laboratory out of state on New York State residents' specimens?"

"Yes, the Department *has* such a policy. It is that this is *not* a valid clinical laboratory test."

"Thank you. That is the end of the testimony."

"All right, Mr. Harris," said the judge.

Harris had been reading over the documents that Sheehan had just proposed submitting into evidence. One of those papers had Levin's name in the letterhead as a member of the advisory group to a laboratory in Florida.

Harris stood in front of Storch, the letterhead in his hands. "Judge, I cannot figure out *what* the relevance of these papers is to this case. Yes, Dr. Levin's name is here as a member of the lab's advisory group. This is correspondence between the lab and New York State. What does that prove?"

Storch motioned to Sheehan. "Mr. Sheehan, I would like to hear your response."

Sheehan launched into a protracted explanation of how the documentation supported the testimony just given by Rej regarding lab licensing issues and legality of the performance of certain tests as pertaining to New York State residents. Then he went a bit further.

"It turns out," Sheehan told the judge, "that the Respondent is listed on the very letterhead of a laboratory whose *specialty* is this cytotoxic testing. I don't know *what* Dr. Levin's connection is: member, advisor, owner, but his name is on *every* piece of communication that goes out of that lab. That very lab had been *denied* a permit to do the very test the Respondent was in here saying is a 'terrific, wonderful test, and I don't know any reason why I shouldn't be allowed to do it, and I don't know that the Department of Health *says* I can't do it' is why this document is relevant to the case. It is relevant on the issue of credibility. It is relevant on the issue of this witness's direct testimony about this test. And it is relevant to rebut Mr. Harris's contention that there is *no set policy*. So on all three grounds, it is relevant information."

Storch studied the documents a moment more, then spoke to Sheehan. "Unless you can demonstrate some ownership interest on Dr. Levin's part, some reason that he would have knowledge of the specific application that you seem to be referring to, I am not inclined to allow the letter in."

"I can't," Sheehan admitted, "and the witness's direct testimony is sufficient on the issue." The prosecutor turned toward Rej. "Thank you," he said to the witness. Walking back to his seat, he said to the panel, "I have no other questions of Dr. Rej."

Harris was anxious to begin his cross-examination. He quickly established that Rej had worked for the same laboratory ever since receiving his Ph.D., and verified that the lab director had no patient contact at all.

"Dr. Rej, have *you* ever *done* hair analysis on a person?"

"I have not."

"Have you ever *seen* hair analysis done? In other words, watching a sample taken from a patient and put through the necessary procedures to yield results?"

"I have seen the results from various hair analyses, but I have not seen every bit of the process from collecting and washing the sample and the process of analysis."

Harris questioned Rej about testing a hair sample for lead, which could have been picked up through an external environmental situation and not be indicative of lead in the body's tissues. The topic of zinc in the hair was also discussed, since shampoo could leave a residue of zinc.

"Environmental contamination is well-known and a significant source of error," Rej said.

Harris countered by saying that environmental contamination might lead to a higher reading than normal, but if the analysis showed a low level of zinc, it could have diagnostic value for a patient. This was followed by Harris's presentation of an article regarding a study on hair analysis that started a lengthy give-and-take between Harris and Rej but yielded nothing of value for either side.

Finally, Harris got to the point. "What I *am* trying to ask you, Doctor, is this: You came in here to testify, I presume, as an *expert* in hair analysis, correct?"

"No, that was never raised."

"Are you prepared to say that you do *not* have expertise in hair analysis?" Harris asked, his famous incredulous look in place.

"I would say that I am an expert in the field of clinical chemistry, the measurement of elements in a variety of biological fluids or tissues. Because of the quantitative and clinical difficulties in using hair as a specimen, it is simply an unreliable specimen; and the body of literature just does not exist for performing these tests or interpreting them in any meaningful way."

Harris then established that the forty-four-year-old witness had gotten his Ph.D. in 1976 and had not had *any* educational training in hair analysis. "Dr. Rej, isn't it true that you don't know any more about hair analysis today than you did in 1976? So you got your degree and read articles of work done by others, and then you came here to testify as an 'expert' on something that you don't know a darn thing about. Is that a fair thing to say?"

The man shook his head. "No, I would say if there was significant scientific evidence to demonstrate that hair analysis was clinically useful, then it would certainly be an area that I would pursue. All of the papers we have seen are very typical of the one you submitted into evidence." Rej had determined that the paper Harris had asked him to read showed a poorly controlled, poorly defined study with no clinical relevance

Harris picked up a pile of documents from the defense table. "I have copies here of *every* paper you have ever written," the lawyer said, waving the thick set of papers near the scientist's face. "Would you please take these and show me *where* the words 'hair analysis' are found…unless you know in advance that the expression doesn't exist anywhere in your articles." Harris glared at the witness challengingly.

"I would say that is fair to say," Rej admitted, in a small voice.

"So you've gone through a working lifetime banging out these papers, never *once* working on a patient, and after writing *all* these peer-reviewed articles, you haven't felt that the subject of hair analysis is either important enough or that you have enough expertise in the area to write *one word* about it. Is that correct?"

"Again, I haven't seen anything in the literature that would convince me it would be worthwhile pursuing," Rej replied, his voice calm, his non-verbal language anxious.

"I want to turn your attention for just a moment to cytotoxic testing. Have you ever *done* cytotoxic testing?"

"No, I have not.'

"Have you ever *seen* it done?"

"No, I have not."

In a mocking tone, Harris began a familiar litany. "So, Doctor, your expertise, once again, is…"

Rej didn't allow the lawyer to complete his sentence. "The reason for my coming here was only to testify about what the Department's opinion was. I did not actively participate in those decisions. I am only aware of it in my role as Director of Clinical Chemistry and my interaction with the unit that issues permits to laboratories."

"Doctor, does your office regulate what tests a physician can do in his office?"

"It does not." Harris stood near the man for an extra moment, just looking at him and saying nothing. It seemed to have the desired effect, however, because Levin noticed the man shifting in his seat, licking his lips, blinking hard, averting his eyes from Harris, and increasing his non-verbal indications of anxiety by the second. Levin noticed a twitch at the corner of Harris's mouth before he stepped away and looked through Rej's published articles once again.

Ceremoniously extracting one of the scientist's articles from the pile, Harris began to quiz him about vitamins, which produced an objection from Sheehan as being beyond the scope of the witness's direct examination, a viewpoint upheld by the judge. However, Harris wasn't about to lose an opportunity to get his thoughts on the topic into the record.

His strong voice reverberated in the hearing room. "The state's first and seminal witness testified, among other things, that functional vitamin tests were *valueless* and were done solely for the purpose of making money for the doctor doing them. Part of the charges against Dr. Levin is that he did functional vitamin testing. Now, here is an obviously *brilliant* man of science. He has written *all* of these papers," he continued, his fist filled with the impressive collection, "and *one* of those papers talks about functional vitamin testing and how it is done, what its value is, and all of that stuff. So the inconsistency between the 'brilliance' of the first witness and brilliance of the second witness occurred to me," he stated, semi-sarcastically, "and I thought it should be pointed out to the panel. I want to make the panel aware that *this* witness has written extensively on this very important subject, which the *previous* state's witness says is baloney!" Harris was referring to Victor Herbert, not Michael Victor Herman.

Sheehan stood up. "The witness said he never used the term 'functional vitamin tests.'"

"We are talking about the *concept*, not the term," Harris countered.

Storch was signaling for their attention. "Mr. Harris, I am sorry, but you are out of line," he admonished. "The objection is sustained. There was nothing in this man's direct testimony today that had *anything* to do with this subject. He is presented as a rebuttal witness on a limited area regarding your direct case. You are opening this up into an entirely different area in which he did *not* testify on direct examination, and I am *not* going to allow it." Storch stopped speaking and thought for a moment. "If you wish to call him as your *own* witness, I don't know what Mr. Sheehan's response would be, but as the Department's witness, he is here to testify on a limited area, and this is way beyond the scope of this morning's testimony."

Harris laughed, knowing he had made the point he set out to score. "Let's stop," he said.

He turned back to Rej. "Thank you, Dr. Rej," he said, still smiling, "this is a *brilliant* article. It should go into the Hall of Fame."

"Hall of Fame," Sheehan repeated, disdainfully.

Briber, chairperson of the committee, asked the witness a question about single-element hair analysis, which Harris found interesting. Rej responded, explaining the usefulness and appropriate circumstances for such a test. The discussion was soon over.

The judge asked Sheehan if his rebuttal case was concluded, and the prosecutor answered in the affirmative. As Sheehan walked the witness out, Harris took a moment to offer a collection of articles into evidence. Sheehan returned and Storch asked whether either attorney had any more witnesses to call, and when both said that they did not, he suggested a lunch break, after which closing arguments would be presented.

Over lunch, Harris and Levin agreed that Rej had done nothing to advance the state's case. In fact, his presence had been practically useless. Harris was delighted that his ploy had worked to get the committee to hear that Rej had written on a topic dear to Levin's heart: functional vitamin tests. Therefore, doctor and lawyer were pleased that the state's third witness turned out to be more useful to the *defense* than to the prosecution. They looked at their watches and hurried back to the hearing room.

CHAPTER 32

Majid Ali walked into the hearing room with an air of relaxed self-confidence. He was probably in his 50s, a Pakistan native, a very handsome man with a comfortable, self-assured presence.

Dr. Ali had become a surgeon in Pakistan. He later moved to the United States where he became a citizen and also a pathologist. For most of the last two decades he had been the Chairman of pathology in a hospital in New Jersey and had held an adjunct professorship in pathology at the Columbia University College of physicians and surgeons.

He had achieved five patents and had a few more pending; had written nearly a score of books—some for physicians and some for non-physicians. He was the credited author of approximately 65 peer-reviewed journal articles and the number of articles which were not peer-reviewed.

He and Warren had come to know one another in both a social and professional context over many years prior to the hearing.

When one thinks of physicians one thinks of pathologists as the straightest kind of people imaginable. Their work involves surgery on bodies and assessing cells in petri dishes and through a microscope. Important work indeed but avant-garde not at all.

There was another side to Majid Ali. He had a private practice and in New Jersey which he maintained after his hours in the hospital and on some weekends. From listening to his description of his practice he apparently had some very sick folks as patients. It would not at all stray from the truth to describe him in his private practice as an alternative or complementary or integrative physician.

He testified that he was board certified in anatomic pathology; a diplomat of the American Board of clinical pathology and a fellow of the Royal College of surgeons in England.

His substantive testimony began with the fact that he was not being paid to be there. Rather, he came to shed what light he could on the matters at hand

Dr. Ali talked at great length about chelation therapy and his belief that it was a valid modality for treating patients. After he discussed the subject he was asked by Sheehan whether or not he believed that chelation therapy should be used on patients who show evidence of arteriosclerotic heart disease. He said that he did and that he has concluded that it has a great deal of value in treating such patients. Sheehan then asked him whether he treated patients for arteriosclerotic problems in his practice in New Jersey. Ali's face dropped and with a great deal of pathos he said that he did not because the New Jersey Board prohibited it. He said that he sent those patients to doctors in New York. He then aired a moment of his opinion that that situation was, from a scientific standpoint, absurd.

Dr. Ali then testified at length regarding his belief that in many ways the bowel was the most important functional part of the body. He quoted Dr. Burkitt who said that the social choice was to have large hospitals and small stools or large stools and small hospitals. He discussed his ideas about the fact that every living thing contains aging oxidant molecules which signal the organism that it is time to die. He hypothesized that without these everything would live forever and we would soon be overrun. He then discussed his ideas of how we can attenuate some of the effects of these molecules when it comes to human beings.

Ali commented on the charts that live in was being prosecuted over. He said that he found no departure from good medical practice in any of them. He also remarked that many of them were very difficult cases and that in his opinion Levin was doing everything that anyone could do to help them.

The subject then turned to the use of a dark field microscope to diagnose Candida. Ali said that he used a dark field microscope in his laboratory and had looked for Candida many times in the dark field. He would see something which he could not prove was Candida but when the patients were treated he would look again and whatever it was that he was looking at was gone. He concluded that what he saw was Candida since the patients involved were all suffering from.

Although the state of New York had brought in a so-called scientist who with regard to cytotoxic testing which Levin regularly used that it was an invalid process, Ali testified that while he did not use cytotoxic testing as such, he had obtained the patent on a process to improve the classic cytotoxic test.

Ali said that he used intravenous therapy containing a number of substances among which are magnesium, molybdenum, vitamin B12 and vitamin C. He stressed that he was not treating for deficiencies but using large doses of these and other vitamins for treatment purposes.

Harris asked Ali what he thought of a state's witness statement that a patient reporting that he was feeling better should be ignored because some of his test results did not show significant improvement. Ali responded that the notion of ignoring a patient's report was utterly absurd and that the physician has an absolute duty to listen to his patient.

Ali was asked whether he favored a cytotoxic allergy test as opposed to an ELIZA allergy test. He responded that he has no criticism of using cytotoxic testing but since he invented the ELIZA test he was partial to it!

Harris had been on his good behavior all day. Dr. Ali was not a confrontational guy and it was absolutely clear that he was unwilling to exaggerate or lie for anybody.

Toward the end of the hearing Harris asked Dr. Ali, in essence, since Levin is accused of pretty much doing everything wrong that a doctor can do wrong in the practice of medicine, the state asserts that his license should be taken from him in order to protect the public. Did he think that the public needed to be protected from Warren Levin?

His response was succinct and to the point. "No, I don't think Dr. Levin is the type of physician that anybody needs to be protected from."

The hearing was concluded and Harris walked over to Dr. Majid Ali and summarized his testimony simply," Doctor, it has been an honor to know you!

CHAPTER 33

Briber opened the afternoon session. "We will proceed now with summations of arguments. You have no further evidence to admit, Mr. Harris?"

"No, sir."

"Mr. Sheehan, do you have any further evidence to admit?"

"No."

"All right, Mr. Harris."

Harris decided to remain seated, next to his client, during the summation portion of the hearing. He had timed his presentation and knew that it would take him a full hour. He suspected that Sheehan's would be briefer, since the prosecutor had suggested that summations be done prior to breaking for lunch.

Harris assumed a soft, collegial tone. He was certain that a number of his ploys had irritated panel members from time to time, so he wanted to present a friendlier side of himself at this point, for the benefit of his client.

"It is a little more than three years since we first met, and because of that fact, I think one or two personal comments are in order. I do believe that there is probably a lot better way to adjudicate the behavior of physicians, but right now and during these last three years, *this* has been the way. I think that the willingness of this panel to endure all of these sessions for, in essence, no pay, is a superlative exhibit of public-mindedness.

"I firmly believe that some of the quiet civic participation that occurs, which people aren't even aware of is what somehow enables society to function at all. And I, as a representative of Dr. Levin, thank you for being as diligent as you have been with your questions, note taking, and patience with all of the 'enthusiasms' that tend to take place in a hearing."

Levin was seated to the right of his attorney and was able to comfortably observe the Hearing Officer and prosecutor across from him and the panel to his left. They all seemed relaxed, but that was often the case after lunch. He wondered if O'Connor would fall asleep, as he had done in the past.

"I have appeared before a lot of Hearing Officers and judges in nineteen years of practice. Judge," he said, looking at Larry Storch, who was seated directly across from him. "You have somehow managed to be level-headed and a gentleman through three years of difficult deliberations, and I can simply say to you, while I haven't agreed with every one of your rulings, they have always been made after consideration by a true gentleman, so the term—Your Honor—fits you very well." Storch nodded his thanks.

"Mr. Sheehan," he said, shifting his gaze to the right, "all I can say is that this would have been an impossibility to endure if I didn't have a competent adversary, which you certainly have been." Sheehan inclined his head in acknowledgement.

"The German philosopher, Schopenhauer, said that 'All truth passes through three stages: First it is ridiculed; second, it is violently opposed; third, it is accepted as being self-evident.' On page seventy-one of the record, in colloquy, Mr. Sheehan indicated that Victor Herbert was an 'expert in quackery' and was aware of the work of Dr. Levin and, therefore, would be able to adequately testify."

Harris swiveled his gaze to include the members of the panel, as well as the prosecution table. "From the very beginning, when I first met you, I stated that this was a trial about being 'different.' It was a trial of medical politics and economics, and it was a trial of a group of people who have the temerity to challenge and try to expand what physicians are doing for their patients in this chaotic world." He opened his palms and shrugged. "Several thousand pages of testimony later, I believe that the evidence has shown that I was *correct* in that observation.

"Thomas Edison once said, 'The doctor of the future will give *no* medicine but will interest his patient in the care of the human frame, in diet, and in the cause and prevention of disease.' Edison died in 1931, but those words were echoed almost verbatim by Linus Pauling who came in here and who basically said, 'I am here for the same reason. I think Warren Levin represents the kind of doctor that I *hope* future physicians will be like.'"

Harris paused a moment in thought. "I would like to give some attention to the topic of the state's witnesses right now and comment on each."

Oh, oh, thought Levin, *here we go!*

"It probably would have been a lot easier to conduct this hearing if the 'brilliant mind' of Victor Herbert was not also a *mad mind.* That's the impression he left on me: a brilliant but mad individual. I think we are all the losers because the madness overshadows the brilliance. I think it is fair to say that if you take the sum total of two-thousand pages of Dr. Herbert's testimony, you cannot really rely upon it to make a decision in this case. While it is true that Dr. Herbert knows a great deal about many things, he is unwilling, and probably psychologically *incapable*, of relating to what it is that he does *not* know. Brilliance has been defined as 'knowing what it is that you *don't* know.' Using that definition, Victor Herbert possesses *no brilliance at all.* In fact, time after time, he was willing to exaggerate, overemphasize, or distort his testimony outright because of an unwillingness to say something that this panel could have easily accepted. I just don't know."

His eyes swept over the panel members. "I think, probably, that a clearer example of the fight that Warren Levin and people like him have been engaged in for all these years is a fight which was adequately described this morning by Dr. Rej as 'a circular reasoning.'"

He now moved onto the state's next witness, turning him into an ally for his *own* client in the process. "I think that Michael Herman was probably the *best* witness for Warren Levin that has appeared in this room in three years. I saw him as a bright and well-educated man who wants to do the very best that he is humanly capable of doing for his patients. He's a good investigator who has written many papers, and with all of the layman's knowledge that I have acquired about medicine, I couldn't understand the titles of more than half of them, so I have to assume they are complex. Dr. Herman basically told this panel, 'I don't know what I don't know, and I am willing to stake my reputation on it.' His basic reasoning was simple: 'I don't use Chelation therapy and none of my friends do, so therefore the treatment is no good. As the chief of the department, if I don't use it, no one in the department will do so either, which is additional proof that it isn't any good, because we use whatever is good for our patients."

He nodded his head slightly, seeming regretful. "While I condemn the ignorance that is inherent in that line of thinking, I don't condemn the man. I think that it is that very approach to medicine in the 1980's and 1990's that *allowed* this schism to develop between doctors who are practicing what is called 'conventional' medicine and those who are practicing 'alternative' or 'complementary' medicine.

"Actually, I define medicine as 'an attempt by decent and educated physicians to keep their patients healthy and to help those patients get well when they are sick.' With that definition in mind, what Warren Levin is doing in his practice *shouldn't* be the subject of charges before the Health Department!" Harris's tone of voice had taken on an extra layer of seriousness. "Many of the things which he was *condemned* for since the time that the issues were raised have *now* become standard practice—and others should be included in what is considered 'standard' for physicians. I call to mind the amusing and idiosyncratic former patient of Dr. Levin who had never had the surgery his cardiologist recommended because of the chelation treatments he had at Dr. Levin's office. Remember how he lifted his shirt up and displayed his torso in the hearing room, saying, 'Look! I don't have any scars. I had chelation and *never* had the operation they wanted me to have, and I am just fine ten years later!' When I called him, he could not figure out *why* the state had found it necessary to intercede on his behalf when he was so *happy* with the outcome of his visits to Dr. Levin's office!" He looked at each of them in turn as he made the following statement: "I am *still* trying to figure out how decent physicians could send somebody for coronary bypass surgery without *first* trying Chelation therapy!"

Levin was pleased to see the thoughtful looks on the listeners' faces. He knew they probably didn't agree, but at least Bob had given them something to think about...again.

"You know, even if you *don't* believe it's effective, with no risk factor, the only thing chelation can do is fail to solve the problem. But if the treatment is successful, maybe it will save the lives of the people who will never get off the operating table due to mortality risks. And, yet, Warren Levin has been defending himself for an awful three years against the charge that he tells people to try Chelation therapy *before* undergoing bypass surgery."

He let that idea percolate for a moment before beginning his next topic. "The *only* testimony attacking cytoxic testing that we've heard in three years came from Victor Herbert...a person who doesn't *do* and hasn't *done* cytotoxic testing! You know," he said in a chatty tone, "Hippocrates wrote about delayed reactions and allergies to food, and in his writings we actually find evidence of what is today called an 'elimination diet.' Those strategies are being used today. But allergists and immunologists are unwilling to give up the patch testing and the desensitization shots for economic reasons. The traditional form of desensitization often does more *harm* than good and produces asthma in a lot of patients. Yet one of the major charges against Dr. Levin concerns the different cytotoxic tests that he conducted.

"Dr. Rej came in here. I think, in a certain way, he is like Dr. Herman, except I am not convinced that he has the knowledge or the ability that Dr. Herman does. I don't think he knows very much about hair analysis at all, and I definitely think he knows *nothing* about cytotoxic testing. In fact," he said, a sincerely puzzled look on his face, "I can't really figure out *why* he was here today—except that the state of New York relies upon what are supposed to be 'learned opinions.'

"Hair analysis can be valuable, but the state—instead of insisting on standardization and issuing guidelines so that the technology be used in a limited and appropriate way—decided to can it completely! It isn't a panacea, but it is a cheap, non-invasive test which may indicate significant low levels of calcium or zinc, magnesium, selenium, and potassium—all of which can indicate serious consequences, or even death, for a patient."

Harris nodded to the panel, wanting to be sure they comprehended the seriousness of not using such a valuable test. "Now, we all heard Victor Herbert talk about chronic fatigue syndrome, calling it *psychological*, saying it was a diagnosis made by quacks. *I suffered from it*," he shared with them, "but I *didn't* have a psychological problem." His glare was designed to ensure that no one doubted his latter declaration. "Here we are, in 1991, understanding the relationship of red blood cell magnesium and chronic fatigue syndrome. It tells us that what Warren Levin was doing about this condition *fifteen years earlier* is *now* being documented as real and scientifically valid!"

He snapped his fingers, as though a thought had just occurred to him. "If you look at what was scientifically valid in the past, much of it is no longer valid. In fact, I wonder if either of the physicians on this panel *ever* sent a patient with ulcers to have his stomach frozen. That was appropriate treatment, based on valid knowledge, some fifteen years ago. The only problem was: *it didn't work*, and it caused more trouble for the patients. In the 1940's and 1950's, if a child had a sore throat several times within a short period of time, the tonsils and adenoids would be removed. Now, in 1991, we know that it was *completely wrong* to do so. Another example: When x-rays were first invented and Roentgen did his studies, people stood up while the x-ray was taken. When those pictures were compared to ones of the patient lying down, it was determined that the organs *dropped* when you stood up. So in the 1800's, good, decent, surgeons, who wanted to do the best for their patients, did hundreds of thousands of surgeries to *elevate* the organs in the body cavity. By today's standards, they'd be called 'quacks,' but they weren't quacks then. They were acting upon the best truth and knowledge that was available to them at that time."

Harris was really on a roll. "Do you remember reading that, at the turn of the century, the treatment for poliomyelitis in children was to put them into a body cast as soon as the acute phase was over? The muscles would atrophy. Sister Elizabeth Kenny from Australia, in response to a virulent outbreak of polio in 1904, worked to rehabilitate the ones who did not have bulbar polio, by putting them on crutches. She also used massage, passive resistance, and warm water in the other three phases of her four-phase treatment. Those in body casts ended up in wheelchairs the rest of their lives and *never* walked again. Yet she was booed out of a meeting of the Royal Society of Physicians, where she went to give a presentation! President Franklin Roosevelt, when he came down with polio, had Sister Kenny brought to Warm Springs. He was soon able to walk with crutches. Within one year, it was considered *professional misconduct* to put a body cast on a child!" He scanned their faces. "*That's* medical progress."

It was time to speak directly about his client for awhile. "When Warren Levin looks out at the world and sees a *better* way to treat patients who have gone to numerous physicians and not been cured, he will use nutritional investigatory techniques because he recognizes that there are relationships in the body that are *not* susceptible to healing by administrations of prescription medications. He realizes that *environmental influences* play a role in illness, that diet and exercise, self-image and psychological factors *all* influence people. So he deals with them at that level."

He picked up a medical chart. "The state subpoenaed charts from people they decided to 'protect,'" he said, a touch of amusement in his voice. "The first two patients no longer required protection. They were dead," he added. "Then Victor Herbert made his most vitriolic comment in two-thousand pages of testimony when he accused Dr. Levin of *causing* the death of one of them through a rebound effect from a withdrawal of adrenocortical steroids...*six months after the last administration of ACE was given!*" Harris couldn't resist adding an editorial comment. "It didn't make sense. It wasn't science. It was just that the diseased and distorted mind of the man thought he could have Dr. Levin's license taken away if he convinced the committee that the doctor *murdered* a patient. It was a rotten thing to do...particularly since Dr. Herbert didn't even know the *difference* between ACE and cortisone."

He picked up another chart. "The next patient had brought herself and both of her parents to Dr. Levin. Her parents are dead, and this woman has had *years* to reflect on her own treatments at his office. She wrote two letters *praising* Dr. Levin's work. Since Dr. Levin publicized his situation so widely, *hundreds* of patients came forward to speak on his behalf, and we submitted as many affidavits as we were *allowed* to offer. Sure, one angry ex-patient did come in and complain about his digestive problems, saying they were not resolved...because he didn't follow Dr. Levin's recommendations—that is until he went to another doctor, who recommended *the same thing*!"

Harris spoke about Herbert's assertion that it was "illegal" to use EDTA chelation for arteriosclerosis. Yet the FDA itself put *no limitations* on the manner in which a physician used approved drugs. The article that Harris quoted had come out in 1982.

"Dr. Levin has given Chelation therapy to *thousands* of patients who feel better because of it. I don't think that there is anything else required of a physician than using something he believes will be helpful to a patient, then continuing to use it when it *does* prove helpful. Dr. Levin has been doing alternative therapy since 1974, and there have been no complaints to this department by anyone claiming to have been harmed.

"Victor Herbert says that people don't require vitamins if they eat an adequate diet. But he's suing the FDA because that's what he does if he doesn't agree with you...or he testifies against you. The other day I read in the *Medical Tribune* that elderly people need *more* Vitamin B-6 than the RDA suggests. *Warren Levin said that in 1974*, before there was a *Medical Tribune.* We brought in Linus Pauling, who certainly believes that Orthomolecular Medicine is the direction of the future. He says that when physicians are focused on *wellness* instead of illness, that we will, for the first time, have a fighting chance at providing medicine at an economically achievable level in this country."

Harris spread out his palms and shrugged, holding the shrug for an extra second. "Okay, you can't blame physicians for their points of view. They are taught in medical school that they are going to *cure* illness, when in fact they help God to cure, if anything. So *preventing illness* may be their biggest calling. Yet that is the area in which they are most lax. If they spent as much time as doctors like Levin do on preventing illness, we might have a better situation in this country."

He fixed Sheehan with a pitying look. "On page 959, Mr. Sheehan says, 'I want to make a broad charge that *all* vitamins were not indicated. I don't care whether it is injected, oral, or applied to the skin. I submit it is irrelevant.' I don't think Mr. Sheehan was given a great case here. I don't envy the job he was asked to do by the state of New York. But I think that the remark, which is reflective of the advice given to him by the state's 'expert,' shows what a demented and ignorant view the state has on this entire subject area. The fact of the matter is that when you look at medical journals these days, you'll see that numerous articles discuss treating cancers with nutritional approaches that five short years ago were thought of as complete quackery."

Harris sighed. "Majid Ali and Abram Hoffer weren't willing to lie for Dr. Levin. They answered truthfully. Reasonable physicians can agree or disagree on approaches to disease, but if a physician acts in good faith with a rational belief in what he is doing and causes no harm to the patients over a long period of time, there is *no* reason for the Health Department to be involved."

Harris launched into a review of Levin's successful protocol for *candida* next. Following that he attacked Victor Herbert's credibility vis-à-vis that doctor's claims of board certification in nutrition, then segued to Herbert's claims as the author of countless articles and the investigator of numerous trials, plus his hospital position, attendance at conferences, and his constant presence in the courtroom, while testifying against someone or launching a lawsuit.

"I don't know what is true or false about Victor Herbert and neither do you," he told the panel. "I don't envy your job. I think that the public is entitled to be protected from quacks. I think that even this cumbersome system has as its root the goal of weeding out those who would harm their patients or who would unduly capitalize on their medical license and take advantage of patients. I will tell you, though, that in defending physicians and dentists and other health professionals for a working lifetime, I have *never* met anyone, anywhere who gives informed consent to patients to the extent that Warren Levin does. I do not know of a physician's office where you are handed your chart at every visit and given copies of all your lab results. I do not know of a physician's office where, when you are sitting for chelation, you are given a whole array of educational tapes, some of which I found very interesting and informative. I do not know of a doctor who tape records his consultation with you, so you can take it home in case you forget something, so you have a ready reference. I do not know of anybody who hands out the amount of literature that Warren Levin does.

"When Dr. Carter examined the charts, he felt that Dr. Levin's patients were getting what they required. I don't think Dr. Carter was lying. Dr. Casdorph, the witness who came from California with all the slides, did some of the seminal work on Chelation therapy. I don't think *he* was lying. Robert Atkins, who has written one of the world's best-selling books, comes in and says, 'Listen, whatever Warren Levin does, I do in my office, but *he does it better* in a lot of instances.' But the state won't go after Atkins, with the power of the airwaves at his disposal through his radio show. You pick on Warren Levin because he was one of the founders of this approach to the treatment of human beings. If you can break *him* down and take away his license, then you can beat up *all the rest* of the people who are making progress in the treatment of health and disease." Harris's pace had quickened. "The witnesses who came in for Dr. Levin weren't paid, except for their expenses. The state's witnesses were *all* paid: Dr. Herbert, Dr. Herman, Dr. Rej."

Harris shook his head in amazement. "Semmelweis died a pauper in Bedlam for the crime of telling people to wash their hands in between examining women. Surgeons who were routinely subjected to the screams and cries of their patients fought the use of nitrous oxide, the first anesthetic; it took a year to overcome their resistance."

He looked at his client, who was seated quietly next to him. "I think Dr. Levin is going to be vindicated no matter *what* this panel does. I think it would be preferable to have that happen during his *lifetime* rather than posthumously." He looked at the panel. "You *cannot* find against Warren Levin. You *cannot* find against truth. It would be *tragic* for this panel of bright, wonderful people to add its endorsements to the perverse teachings of the establishment that tries to get patients into operating room, to force prescription drugs where vitamins will do the job."

Harris took off his glasses and rubbed his eyes before putting them back on. "There has *got* to be a better way. *This* way is *not* the way to determine the validity of Warren Levin's therapies. *Nobody* has been willing to come in here and say, 'I was hurt by Warren Levin.' He has seen *thousands* of patients in thirty-five years. *Nobody* was willing to come in here and say, 'I was defrauded by Warren Levin.' I think beating up on Levin has been a state sport for a long time. I think there is a tremendous amount of resentment because Levin went and stood up for his constitutional rights all the way to the Court of Appeals…twice."

Now Harris's look was a pleading one. "I believe that you folks have an opportunity," he said. "I believe that by exonerating Warren Levin on each and every count on each and every charge brought against him, that there is message to the New York State Health Department that says: 'Being different *isn't* being dishonest or fraudulent.'"

He smiled at everyone in the room. "Thank you for everything that you folks have contributed to this. I…am…finished." He sighed deeply and took off his glasses.

"Thank you, Mr. Harris," Briber said. "I would urge you to consider submitting some of this in writing. Your reference to specific quotations and citations to those will be helpful for the panel."

The floor was turned over to Sheehan. "I also would like to thank everyone. Maybe I'm a masochist," the prosecutor said, "but I seem to have found the hearing *enjoyable* for some reason. I thought it was an interesting case. Mr. Harris drove me crazy…but he was a lot of fun to work with," he said with a nod to his opponent.

"With respect to the *charges* in this case," he began, launching directly into attack mode with no need for a warm-up, "I submit that they represent the most *insidious* type of professional misconduct. I believe the record is clear that Dr. Levin is a very smart person and doctor, so we are not saying that he doesn't have the ability or knowledge to practice properly *if he wanted to*, not at all. He is *so* smart that he *knows* what he is doing, and he is *deliberately* doing it! What we are alleging is that there was a deliberate pattern of practicing fraudulently in this case, in addition to gross negligence, which I submit is irrefutable. Even Dr. Levin's own experts said, 'Doctors don't normally do this, it is not accepted, it is not in the peer-reviewed literature, it is not orthodox medicine. But it is good medicine because I and some other people say so.'

"What we are saying in this case is that Dr. Levin knew that what he was doing was *not* within the standards of practice, was *not* proven, was *not* part of accepted medicine, was *not* legitimate medicine, but because he could made a good buck at it, and he had a lot of people who wanted it, who were true believers in this type of stuff, he got into this kind of medicine and stayed in it. I submit that this kind of *deliberate, knowing, intentional* misconduct on a long-term basis constitutes the *worst* type of professional misconduct.

"I submit that Dr. Levin's practices and those of the doctors he calls to defend him are engaged in an attack on the very *concept* of scientific truth. They have determined that in order to insulate their lucrative practices from any type of scientific scrutiny, they have to *destroy* the very hallmark of medicine and science: the scientific method. I submit that these doctors in alternative medicine or, as I would characterize it, *fraudulent medicine*, are involved in an active strategy to *destroy* the public's faith in the scientific method and to destroy medicine's and science's ability to rely on the scientific method to create standards to discipline doctors who don't adhere to those standards. They set up these parallel medical specialty boards and journals, which are *absolute shams*.

"This politicizing of the issue has been unfair, cheap, fraud, meretricious. I submit it is a symptom of the alternative doctor's knowledge that what they are doing is inherently *wrong* and *unsubstantiated*, but it is a sign of their desperation to maintain these lucrative, easy practices. Legitimate medicine means tons of hard work. He got into alternative medicine with less competition: he told us there was hardly anyone doing that in New York City. So he got into this field as a way to make money, knowing that this type of medicine was *not* legitimate. However, he knew that there was a ready clientele, anxious and eager to seek out any physician who follows this type of alternative medicine. Therefore, he got on the bandwagon.

"The patients who came into his office hardly *ever* saw Dr. Levin. They saw people who gave them test after test, day after day, then during the two-hundred and fifty dollar interview for an hour or more, it was an august moment, because *Dr. Levin* came in and went over all the tests and recommended additional ones. You can run a facility like that just like a factory. That's why Dr. Levin is so strong about attempting to protect this practice. He is an *excellent* salesman.

"Another strategy they used to destroy the scientific method was to assassinate the character of those good physicians who had the guts to stand up and point out the logical deficiencies and the inherent disbelief of alternate medicine's precepts. You saw Dr. Herbert come in here and criticize alternate medicine and Dr. Levin's practices, and he was subjected to the most scorched-earth cross-examination that has *ever* been allowed in an OPMC hearing! His character was *assassinated* before he even got on the stand, and it *continued* to be assassinated even after he left. Why? Because the doctors who follow this lucrative type of fraudulent practice are *so* anxious to maintain their stranglehold on these patients, these deluded patients, that they will go to *any* lengths to destroy and intimidate *anyone* in establishment medicine who has the guts to stand up and say, 'Listen, this stuff doesn't wash scientifically.'

"We are not a bunch of simple-minded jurors who don't know anything about medicine and can be misled by any expert. Here, the panels are composed of experts themselves, so luckily we don't have that problem. I submit that you *have* to find Dr. Levin guilty of negligence and gross negligence. The issue of fraud is separate. It requires knowledge on the part of the doctor that he is deceiving people, or he is following deceptive practices, or the treatments he recommends and engages in are not valid, truthful, legitimate modalities. Dr. Levin *knew* that his practices were a lot of bull. He *knew* there was no scientific theory to support all of this nutritional type of practice. He *knew* there was no reason to subject all of these patients to these batteries of tests. And I submit that it was done *deliberately*—to make money, *not* to help the patients. One last example of the way they are attempting to foist this totally bogus philosophy on the public and on science is when they attempted to get Section 230 of the Public Health Law amended so that panels such as yours would have to include a member practicing alternative medicine! It is the most brazen attempt to *destroy* physician discipline that one can imagine. It is the *worst* type of professional misconduct that we have here. This panel should strongly reject it.

"I submit that Dr. Levin's license to practice medicine *should be revoked*. But, more importantly, I submit that the panel should issue a determination fining Dr. Levin ten-thousand dollars, which is the absolute maximum, *per specification sustained*. Because this is not, as I said before, simple negligence or incompetence or failure to know exactly what is expected of one, or being unable to do it. *This is financial crime*. It is a *deliberate* crime, and money is at the root of it, so a fine is appropriate in this circumstance. Thank you very much."

The room was silent when Sheehan finished. The sheer malevolence of his closing argument seemed to have shut down everything and everyone for the moment. Briber broke the spell. "We will take these matters under advisement," he said, somberly. "You will hear from us in due course."

Harris and Levin were absolutely stunned. They had not expected such a vitriolic presentation from the previously mild-mannered prosecutor, who was always proper in his technique. It was with numb fingers that they gathered their materials and left the hearing room.

"We're screwed, Warren," Bob told his client once they reached the sidewalk.

"Don't I know it," Levin agreed, his head down against the wind gusts. "All this for nothing. For absolutely nothing."

CHAPTER 34

As he walked out of the florist's shop, Levin was thinking back on the past few months. He carefully placed the healthy rubber plant on the floor of the back seat of his car. Levin had already spent the whole summer with his mind split in multiple directions: his family, his practice and, of course, wondering where things stood with the Hearing Committee. Following the April hearing, there was the one session in July, then the recess until early September. It was as though the hearings were designed to hit every season of every year, a "gift" from the state designed as a seasonal spoiler. They had scheduled the state's last joke of a witness for yesterday morning, and Sheehan had actually wanted to move *right* into deliberations without the fortification of a lunch break. Sure, Sheehan had his summation prepared for a one-punch delivery: GUILTY as charged, so let's mash Levin right into the ground. Fortunately, Bob, who knew he needed a huge chunk of time to wrap up his defense, didn't allow it to happen. *Not that it mattered one iota,* he thought.

All summer long, he had forced himself to concentrate on whatever the task at hand happened to be. If it was a weekend and he was at the playground with Erika, he did his best to stay in the moment and enjoy the four-year-old's gleeful shrieks as she slipped out of the mouth of the tubular slide into his waiting arms. As he pushed her on the kiddie swing, he directed her gaze to a flock of birds or a passing airplane. He listened to her laughter and thought of his role as a father… and, inevitably, as a provider. That's when he had to *stop* thinking. Unfortunately—his mind would inform him at those unwelcome moments—his continuing role as a provider was currently in the hands of two doctors and a chemist: three "stellar" representatives from the state's disciplinary board.

When he and Susan went out for an evening, to the home of friends, to a charity event, to temple, or to a play or concert, he reminded himself to concentrate on how pretty Susan was, how much he loved her shiny hair, her sparkling personality, how important she was to him, how proud he was to be seen with his young, vivacious wife. He was determined not to shortchange her by undermining their moments together with any of his foreboding thoughts.

As upbeat as he tried to be, he didn't want the loss of the case against him to come as a total shock to her, so he had made a conscious decision to try to prepare her. He brought the plant into the house and set it near the French doors in their sunny family room, which faced the rear of the house. Susan was out, bringing Erika to a friend's for a sleepover. She would like the plant, he knew. That's why he had bought it. He would show it to her when she got home. *Put a smile on her face before we get into the car.* There were few distractions when they were on the road, so the car was generally an ideal venue for the types of discussions they needed to have relevant to the proceedings. He went to get dressed, so he'd be ready to leave when Susan got back.

"What do you mean, 'It doesn't look good'?" Susan asked, her brow creased with anxiety. She turned toward the driver's side to look at him.

"Just that, dear, nothing more, nothing less. It doesn't look good. Both Bob and I felt the same way when we walked out of the hearing room after summations yesterday. You'll see what I mean," he had told her.

"*When* will I see what you mean? *How* will I see what you mean?" Each question was asked at a greater volume level. "When you lose your license? When the practice goes down the tubes? Is that when I'll *see* what you mean, Warren?" She was breathing rapidly, and tears had already come to her eyes.

They were driving into Manhattan. For a change, he had taken Saturday off. He had immediately decided to do that once he was informed of the final scheduled hearing. It was pretty chilly today, even for late October, so he flicked on the heater. He had bought theater tickets for *Phantom of the Opera* at the Majestic Theater in advance, wanting something to look forward to the day after the hearings ended with the attorneys' summations, and they were booked at a hotel in the Theater District.

"No, Susan, that's *not* what I mean." He struggled to keep his voice calm. He was teetering at the edge, as well, but knew he had to be the one to keep things on an even keel. She just allowed her anxiety to show. As long as it didn't spill over, it was probably a healthier way of dealing with things, he realized. "The prosecutor asked the court reporter to have the transcripts expedited. I'll stop in to pick up a copy on Monday," he told her. "Then you can draw your own conclusions."

"What *conclusions* am I supposed to draw from the transcript, Warren?" She twisted to her left as much as her shoulder harness allowed in order to read him better as he drove, his eyes fixed on the road ahead. "*What* can I figure out from reading a couple of hundred pages more of that stuff that you can't tell me *right now*?"

He held the wheel with his left hand and reached for her hand. "Susan," he said, his hand providing warmth and, he hoped, comfort, "I simply can't remember everything that was said yesterday. There was a lot. Bob was great. He was respectful and flattering to the committee."

She laughed, thinking of Bob. "Probably for the first time in years," she joked.

"Well…" he trailed off, chuckling. "Probably. Then he did his best to review the testimony of the state's witnesses, working hard to continue discrediting Herbert, as usual. The thing is, Herbert was really the *only* witness for the state, in Bob's eyes, since that was how he was originally portrayed. Interestingly, Bob saw Herman more as a witness for *me* than for the prosecution. And even that guy who came in at the end, the lab director for the state, was probably more helpful to us than to them…that is, if he was helpful to anyone. Frankly, I just saw him as utterly tangential. In fact, he was brought in simply because Bob had challenged Sheehan on a point earlier on, and Sheehan just wanted to do the 'pissing contest' thing with Bob. You know, 'Well, you said "*prove it*," so I'm proving it' type of thing. At least that's how Bob saw it."

"Really?" She was puzzled.

"Yeah, that's just how it all seemed to him. Anyway, he then pleaded my case, asking them to find in my favor. You know, the usual stuff a lawyer would say at the end of a trial. They may call it a 'hearing,' but it's still a *trial* for all intents and purposes," he added.

"Hmmm," she acknowledged. "How about Sheehan's summation?"

Levin tried to change the subject at that point, first to interject a funny story that happened with Erika, then to ask a question about their daughter's pre-school class night. *Boy, what a wimp you are, Warren,* he chided himself. *Weren't you thinking, just a short while ago, about how great it is to be able to discuss difficult topics in the car? So why are you avoiding things?* Susan listened to the story, answered his question, and then asked her own. "Warren, *why* are you avoiding my question?" She watched his eyebrows rise in surprise.

"Your *question*? Did I miss something?" he asked innocently.

"War-ren." Her voice carried a tone of warning.

He sighed deeply, not wanting to spoil their evening out. "Sheehan's summation. Okay, it was shorter than Bob's," he answered noncommittally, knowing full well that she wasn't asking about its length.

She played along for the moment. "How much shorter?"

"It was one-third the length."

"One third? How long did Bob speak, for goodness' sake?"

He laughed, twisting his neck to the right to glance at her. "How about one full hour!"

"You've got to be kidding!" That really surprised her. "I mean, this wasn't a murder trial with a jury of twelve of your peers and a judge on a high bench with robes and a gavel in a richly paneled hall of justice or anything."

"No," he said, drawing out the syllable a bit. "It was a plain old room with a few tables and lots of chairs, an Administrative Law Judge in a suit and tie, and a small area between tables that Bob would have filled up had he paced around or marched around," he said, recalling one of several rooms initially on Eighth Avenue and later at Penn Plaza that he had spent countless hours in over the past three years. "Bob actually stayed seated. And I'm glad he did. It just made things seem less adversarial…for the moment. It gave me a chance to look across at Sheehan and Storch and also to my left to see the panel members."

"Okay."

"But don't say it wasn't a murder trial," he told his wife. "The whole thing is 'attempted murder,' as far as I'm concerned." He glanced her way again briefly. "The state of New York is making a very valiant effort to *murder* my career."

Susan nodded somberly. However, she was still not ready to let go of her initial inquiry.

"So?" she asked.

"So?" Levin responded.

"Warren, come on!"

"Okay, okay," he said. "You'll read it all in the transcript, but I'll give you the bottom line."

"Which is?" she prompted.

"Which is that Sheehan made a mess out of me."

She could hear the abject dejection in his voice, something she rarely heard, even with all of the relentless attacks he had experienced inside and outside of the hearing room over the years, even with the inquiries from the local medical society, the badgering and requests from the insurance companies, even when their prized controller had hidden unpaid bills for their insurance coverage in the ceiling tiles of Warren's medical office, or when some chiropractor out west tried to extort them. This time, he sounded deflated. If not for her own anxiety and need to know more, to know it *all*, she would have let the topic drop…at least for the evening. But not now. She *needed* to hear it all.

"What did he say?" Her voice was so small, it was barely audible over the road noise. Had he been able to look into her eyes, he would have seen the fear, the panic, the unshed tears threatening to spill down her cheeks and stain her pink silk blouse. Had he been in a position to listen to her heartbeat with a stethoscope, he would have been alarmed. Had he observed the sudden pallor of her skin, which actually showed through her artfully applied makeup, he might have pulled over onto the side of the road and simply held her. But he didn't do any of those things. He was watching a scene engraved into his internal memory but staring diligently at the highway in front.

"Sheehan quoted some article from *Forbes* magazine that gave an excerpt of a forthcoming book. He mentioned the *Frye* rule, whatever that is, and used it to tell the committee to reject what he called the 'anecdotal' and 'unscientific evidence' that he said my witnesses presented. He said I was guilty of the *worst* type of professional misconduct. That I *deliberately* practiced fraudulently, was *grossly* negligent, that I *consciously* did all of this *only* because it was profitable. He called our journals and medical specialty boards 'parallel universes' and 'absolute shams.' That we were 'politicizing' everything and crying 'conspiracy' because of our 'desperation' to hold onto our 'lucrative, easy practices.'"

"*Lucrative? Easy?* What is he, crazy?" Susan was incensed. "Let him come into your office and follow you around for a week, or even for a *day*. He'll see how hard you work, all of the things you do!" Her panic was rapidly being replaced by cold, hard anger. *Maybe that's better*, Levin thought. *Her fear and pain are too much for me to bear.*

"Yeah, well, that's what he said." Now Levin was feeling the burn of anger. "You'll *love* this one," he told Susan. "Sheehan said, and I quote, 'Legitimate medicine means *tons* of hard work, so *he* got into alternative medicine.' What a load of crap! He said I run my office 'like a factory,' and to add insult to injury called me an 'excellent salesman.' Anyway, enough of Sheehan's garbage. You ready for the bottom line yet?" he asked.

"May as well. I've heard every other line so far."

"He wants them to charge me with negligence and gross negligence and save the issue of fraud as a special category, because I *knew* that my practices 'were a lot of bull,'" Levin told her.

"He said that? 'A lot of bull'?"

"He said *exactly* that." He cleared his throat and asked again. "So…the bottom line now?"

"The bottom line," she agreed.

"Revoke my license to practice medicine and fine me ten-thousand dollars

per specification sustained." He said it in a resigned, totally emotionless voice.

"Revoke your license? Ten-thousand dollars per item they find you 'guilty' of? They've *got* to be kidding." She was absolutely horrified. "Can they *do* that?"

"Apparently they can, or Sheehan wouldn't have asked for it."

"Oh, my God!" Susan exclaimed, hiding her face in her hands. "Oh, my God!"

They sat quietly in the moving car for a minute, thinking, absorbing, grieving, clearing their minds, doing it all at the same time then in cycles. Finally, Susan broke the silence. "Warren, I think we have to consider filing for bankruptcy. It's the last thing I wanted to talk about tonight, the one time you took a Saturday off in…I don't know, in *forever*. The one time we decided to stay in the city for the night. But maybe that's what we need to talk about, since we have some time to ourselves."

"Bankruptcy." It wasn't a question, it wasn't an answer, it was just a statement. He repeated it. "Bankruptcy." He took a long, deep, noisy breath. "That's a word I've used loosely, thinking that our Legal Offense Fund and all of the generous contributions from colleagues and, embarrassingly enough, patients would keep us solvent. Bankruptcy. Oh, God, this is awful. Too awful to even consider."

She was the calm one now, the voice of reason. "*I'm* the one who did the taxes with the accountant back in March and April, the corporate and the personal taxes. It didn't look too good then, Warren. I didn't want to worry you unnecessarily. I thought that maybe things would go better."

He wasn't really listening. He was thinking. Then he began to think aloud. "You know something, Susan, we still don't know *how* this thing is going to go. All right, it was awful to sit there and hear all of those things said aloud, all at once, by a prosecutor who should have been somewhat swayed by the evidence we presented, by the impressive retinue of witnesses who came to my aid, by the patient testimonials, by the fact that I've never harmed a living soul and have helped so many over more than thirty years in the field of medicine. I really don't understand why Sheehan wasn't influenced by everything he heard on my behalf for so long. His presentation was *poisonous* in nature. I never really hated the guy in all of this time. Okay, he's just doing his job, I thought to myself, time and again. And he's really not a bad sort of guy. Bob would joke around with him before we got started or when we had a recess or whatever. Bob would refer to him as Terence Cardinal Sheehan and the guy would give a short laugh and blush a bit. I didn't think he would *viciously* attack me the way he did in summation… and add a recommendation for *additional* financial penalties to his directive to pull my license. I mean, what for? You want me out of the business. That's obvious. I don't understand it…yet I *do* understand it. The Commissioner, your boss, has charged you, Mr. Sheehan, with helping him do the job of blowing alternative medicine off the planet, or at least out of the state of New York. So if you make an example of this guy, Levin, maybe some of his 'admirers' or 'worshippers' or however his colleagues think of themselves, will 'do the right thing' and return to orthodox medicine, to the established ways, where they'll medicate, operate, and radiate. They'll pay no attention to whatever their patients put into their bodies, they'll decide not to do the non-invasive tests that will yield the richest results and information and simply stick with the painful old ways. Then, if the patient dies, it's okay, because the insurance companies will be happy and not complain, the pharmaceutical companies will continue to fill their coffers, and all the doctors will be doing things in the old-fashioned tried and true ways. No innovative techniques. No new cures. No great results. No more getting to the root of a problem. They'll just palliate the symptoms, as usual. They'll call it 'treatment.' And if anyone who has heard of alternative medical techniques and practitioners wants to find a physician of that type to treat them, they will have to check the laws of other states to see *what* is allowed *where*. Or, worse yet, they'll simply go to a *real* 'quack,' someone who *doesn't* have a medical education at all but is willing to chop up ants and roaches to make a 'healing powder' or something like that."

They had arrived at the parking garage, with Levin so focused on his monologue that he was surprised when the valet tapped on his door, which was still locked. He held up his hand to put the guy off for the moment and turned to Susan.

"I'm sorry, sweetheart," he told her. "I guess I just went off on a tangent. I know you're probably right. I suppose we do need to talk to our lawyer about bankruptcy." She nodded. "But not tonight, okay? Let me take you 'out on the town' for a change. Let's have some fun. God knows, it's been a long time since we've done something like this. You can call and make an appointment on Monday once I see if I can get home early one day next week. Are you all right with that?" She nodded again.

"Warren, I just want to ask you one more question," she said, eyeing the impatient valet, who was looking at the cars lining up behind theirs.

"Sure."

"What did Bob say?" she whispered.

He took a very deep breath before he quoted his defense attorney's comment upon leaving the hearing room yesterday. "'Warren, you're screwed.'"

Warren, you're screwed, she thought. *We're all screwed. You. Me. Erika. Your medical practice. Screwed by the state.*

CHAPTER 35

Thanks to the generosity of friends, colleagues, and patients, Levin kept *somewhat* current with his financial responsibilities to his attorney. Besides the money he still owed to Harris, Levin realized that, more importantly, he owed him a real debt of gratitude, something he tried to acknowledge to his stalwart defender on a regular basis. No matter how it all turned out, Levin knew that he had the right man in his corner. What had begun as a routine medical defense case for the lawyer had ended up as a mission that took endless hours, thus reducing his hourly fees to pennies on the dollar. Fortunately, Harris was the managing partner of his firm, so he usually didn't have to justify his business decisions. Otherwise, Levin knew he would have already been in bankruptcy proceedings.

Susan meticulously recorded any contributions to the Legal Offense Fund and carefully documented where each dollar went. They hadn't been as lucky with their personal and business expenses, however, and things were getting really tight. The discussion they had in October regarding their dire financial straits had resulted in a consultation with their bankruptcy attorney. For Levin, the thought of ever having to give up his Park Avenue office, his dream, was too much to bear. *I was in hock for almost one-million dollars in 1982, two years after investing all that I owned and could borrow in my version of Camelot—the first holistic center in Manhattan. By 1986, I grossed just under two-million dollars with a staff of thirty-five in this sixty-five-hundred square foot facility on Park Avenue and Thirtieth Street. I already had another medical doctor working with me, as well as nutritionists, physician's assistants, exercise therapists, and numerous many others. For many years, I helped my competitors get started in one way or another. Once the OPMC brought me up on charges, however, I've been unable to attract any other practitioners to share my space and my reputation—which had previously allowed me to enjoy significant passive income. New York State has already spent more than a million bucks in their unyielding efforts to take my license away. And here I am, going broke, risking everything, and for what? Just to keep on fighting New York State as the "chosen one," the representative of alternative medicine, for the privilege of retaining the medical license that I earned and have honorably used to assist the sick for over thirty years, and may go bankrupt to preserve.*

As he rode the railroad into the city, Levin looked out at the passing view. It was December. Snow looked so pure and white when it first settled, darkening unattractively as it was scraped from the roads and was piled alongside the passing train. *Why do positive things turn negative?* he wondered, unable to keep his mind from focusing on his own precarious situation, where his license was constantly suspended above his head just out of reach. He decided that his commuting time would be better spent with some guided imagery, a pleasant scene, to relax his mind and center his psyche before he got to the office, the office that he might eventually be forced to vacate. He closed his eyes.

As he walked from the station to his building, he barely noticed the dirty piles of snow that had gotten him thinking bleak thoughts in the train. He was focused, instead, on the day ahead. He breathed deeply, the cold air refreshing and cleansing. He shut out the noise of the Manhattan traffic circulating around him and simply enjoyed the wide expanse of Park Avenue as he maintained a brisk stride. It was as though his surgery had never occurred, he thought. His recovery had been uncomplicated, and his tests showed no recurrence of the cancer that frightened him and Susan into thinking that he'd never wake up from the operating table or that he'd be facing life as half the man he had been. He nodded to himself: There was no minimizing the effects of clean living, megadoses of vitamins, mineral supplements, and chelation therapy…no matter what those assholes at the OPMC and their hired guns tried to say. *Hey, keep your mind out of the gutter,* he thought. *That's exactly where those folks are trying to put you: out on the street, into the gutter. Just make sure you don't do the job for them.*

He knew that the committee members were engaged in deliberations during these very days and wondered when they would finally issue their decision. Meanwhile, it was business as usual at the office. The one difference was that he no longer had to arrange his schedule around hearing dates, or work around Bob's schedule for essential planning meetings, where they studied the transcripts for clues on further medical instruction for Bob or strategy thrusts. Ever since he walked out of the hearing room for the last time six weeks ago, he tried to keep from revisiting the scene in flashbacks, but often his efforts met with little success. So, in his mind, he imagined Bob employing an alternate technique at a specific point or responding to Storch or Sheehan somewhat differently or bringing up something new and even more shocking when cross-examining one of the state's witnesses. He imagined his own witnesses, who had all done a splendid job, had super credentials, and were unflappable under the state's farce of a cross-examination shining even *more* brightly, blinding the committee with their brilliance and being ultra-convincing in their testimony in support of Levin and his medical practices. Whenever he got into one of these moods, it drained the energy out of him and left him spent. At this point, he had the transcripts in his possession, but they didn't give any hint of people's facial expressions or their reactions to something that was said. Frankly, he had paid such close attention to the words being spoken in the hearing room that he sometimes forgot to glance around and check how a phrase or expression was being perceived or received.

Chanukah had come early this year, December 2, and once again he and Susan hadn't felt up to entertaining and kept their celebration small and intimate. Erika told the Chanukah story to them once again, and this time she knew far more facts. They had both marveled at how mature she sounded. She continued to be a mild-mannered child with a rather grown-up way about her, since there were no other children in the house. Susan tried to arrange play dates every so often and had become friendly with some of the other mothers whose children were in Erika's kindergarten class. Most of those women didn't work outside of the home, however, and Susan often went to Warren's office to oversee the clerical staff and manage the finances. She also assisted with the quarterly newsletter that Warren distributed and brought some of the work home when necessary. Whereas the other women dropped their children off, ran to the gym, went out for coffee, took a short shopping trip, met for lunch, Susan really couldn't relate to that carefree lifestyle. Her concerns were serious. She hoped that they would remain solvent enough to keep the practice going, considering the monthly payments on the construction loan and salaries and benefits for the staff.

The bankruptcy attorney, Marcus Rabinowitz, had advised them to continue making the mortgage payments on their home, since taxes and homeowner's insurance were also included in their monthly payments. It was a struggle, but they managed to follow his advice. So, for Susan, mixing with the wealthy residents of their community was more a stressor than a pleasure. A few of the other mothers of children in Erika's class were married to doctors, as well, but she was quite certain that their spouses weren't engaged in the fight of their lives, as Warren currently was. Nevertheless, she did arrange play dates for Erika occasionally, and since the children were doing more than just parallel play at this point in their development, the routine changed from last year, and the moms would drop their little ones off at their young friends' houses and not be obligated to stay and chat with the parent. Susan was glad of the new rules; they suited her purpose far better.

They had a few people over for New Year's Eve, something to break the monotony. Susan had thrown herself into the planning, glad to get her mind off her problems. They took a week off later in January and went to Florida. Last year's trip was restful but necessary, due to Warren's surgery. This year, they both needed recovery time from the heavy burdens they were forced to carry continuously. They took Erika with them.

And so the months passed, with no word from the Hearing Committee, no decision, no hint of what was to come. Spring came and went, and Erika turned six. The school year started, and suddenly, Erika was no longer a little girl: She was in first grade and riding the yellow school bus. Susan had insisted on driving her back and forth to kindergarten last year or having her housekeeper assist with the transportation, but it was time to let go a bit. Erika's excitement made it all worth it, as the bus stopped right at the base of their driveway and the motherly driver welcomed the little girl for her first ride of the year several weeks ago.

There was a chill in the air as Susan walked Erika down the driveway this morning. They were both wearing warm sweaters. Susan's was a thick, cable-knit that her mother had made for her when she started college, so she often wore it for sentimental reasons—especially since that was the first and last time her mother had ever picked up a pair of knitting needles. Erika's was a multi-colored pastel that Susan had crocheted for her only child, after buying herself a large crochet needle and an instruction book that took her from the initial creation of a crocheted chain to the completion of a sweater for a small child. While she never made another item and couldn't even recall where the leftover yarns and needle were, she had carefully packed this sweater into a gift box with a cloud of tissue and saved it for just this occasion. Erika was thrilled by the gift this morning, still too young to understand that her mom's handiwork might not be the latest fashion on the first grade runway.

Susan waved at Erika as the bus left and pulled her sweater tighter. It was the first day of fall, September 22, and it was much chillier than she liked. *I hope this doesn't signal a heavy winter,* she thought, heading for her car. She promised Warren she'd spend the next few days at the office.

Susan walked in and greeted the receptionist, who handed her a bundle of mail. "He's in one of the examining rooms with a new patient," the woman told her, in response to Susan's silent question. Susan walked into Warren's office and piled the mail on the table, separating bills from checks, throwing the junk in the waste basket, and placing the contributions into a separate receptacle for logging.

Over lunch, they talked. After reviewing the basic necessities of office operations during the next three months, the phase-out period, they briefly discussed their finances. Things were tighter than ever. The worry they hid from the rest of the world was plainly etched on both of their faces. The question that arose every day for the past nine months was once again uttered, something they seemed to take turns doing. "Nothing from the committee yet?" "No." "Deliberations were completed over nine months ago." "Yeah, I know." The only thing that changed in this litany was the number of months, which were growing like Jack's beanstalk. Bob had no idea why the decision was taking so long. "No news is good news," is the only comfort he could offer, but the Levins already knew that their attorney held little hope of a comforting verdict in the case. They finished the lunch that Susan had brought for both of them and turned to their afternoon responsibilities.

Wednesday, Thursday, and Friday were days that they spent in a similar fashion. There was only one significant difference. The envelope arrived in the mail on Friday. The envelope from the Office of Professional Medical Discipline.

Levin had no patients scheduled for Friday afternoon. Susan brought the envelope into his office at lunch time. Just seeing it had been enough to cause her to lose her appetite. He looked up as she walked into his office and immediately saw the large manila envelope in her hands. That and the expression on her face were enough for him. He hastily packed up the lunch he was laying out for both of them and shoved it into his small refrigerator.

He stepped out of the office for a moment and told the receptionist he was not to be disturbed under any circumstances. He locked the door when he walked back in. Susan was at the table with the envelope. She had put every other piece of mail elsewhere.

He moved his chair next to hers and slit the envelope open with a letter opener. The document was thick, over one-hundred-and-twenty-five pages. Susan put her hand up and flipped to the last page to check the date. September 22, 1992, she read. The very day I gave Erika her new sweater. The first day of fall. Three days ago, the committee members completed this project that had taken them nine whole months, the entire gestation period of a human infant. The question was, what did they produce in those nine months? A masterwork? A prize-winning publication? An exoneration? Or a death sentence for her husband? She looked at the hand holding the pages up: it shook involuntarily. She could feel her heart racing, as her chest rose and fell rapidly. Her eyes were half-closed from the pressure of the anxiety she was experiencing.

Levin put his hand over hers. "Susan," he said, gently. It wasn't a question. It was a statement. He just wanted her to know that she wasn't facing the contents of the envelope alone; neither of them was. She looked at him, her eyes full. He took her hands from the document and moved his chair even closer. He reached out to her, and she leaned into him. They needed the closeness and warmth of each other. They remained motionless for several minutes.

"Okay," he said, finally. "Let's do it. Just promise me one thing. No matter what's in this document, it won't destroy us. If they take everything else away, and they may do that. Promise that they won't take us away from each other."

Tears streaming down her face, she simply nodded, wordlessly.

Levin placed the document, in its spiral binding, on the table between them. They read silently, and Susan turned the pages when he nodded. Every so often, one or the other of them commented on something written on a page or read a passage aloud. The whole thing began with a long list called, "Summary of Proceedings," which started with the June 20, 1989 Notice of Hearing and Statement of Charges, and continued through the final hearing of October 25, 1991 and listed all of the players who had participated in the two-and-a-half-year drama. In the "Statement of Case" area, it read: "The Department has charged Respondent with practicing the profession of medicine fraudulently, with gross negligence, and with negligence on more than one occasion, failure to comply with a subpoena, moral unfitness, failure to maintain accurate records, and failure to provide a copy of a patient's medical record upon receipt of a written request from the patient. It mentioned that Victor Herbert did not have to answer as to whether he had made the complaint about Levin. It summarized that over five-thousand pages of testimony were elicited and several hundred exhibits were introduced. The committee even wrote about Sheehan's introduction of the *Forbes* article that cited the *Frye* rule regarding the scientific method to reject the anecdotal and unscientific evidence offered by Levin and his witnesses.

As they read, they both grimaced when it was stated that the committee recognized Victor Herbert as an expert in the fields of nutrition and vitamin therapy. They laughed when they saw that Herbert's testimony about certain aspects of Levin's practice was found to be "biased and inflammatory," even quoting where Herbert said, "I therefore believed him [Dr. Levin] to be a liar and still so believe..." and "Medicine is my business and fighting quackery is my hobby."

Reading on, they saw that Majid Ali, M.D. was found to be "credible," whereas Robert Atkins, M.D. was "not accepted as an expert witness," and James P. Carter, M.D. "did not convince the Committee of the soundness of his scientific judgment." They ran through Levin's other witnesses, and it hurt him to see that Linus Pauling's testimony as a scientist "was not germane to the issues in the case."

Susan looked at Levin when she read that, "Warren Levin, M.D.'s testimony, like Dr. Herbert's was biased and inflammatory. His testimony about his management of his patients was colored by his elaborate system of self-justification." He shrugged in response. They read further, and Levin snorted at their comment concerning all of the fine, educational material that he offered his patients. "A careful review of his patient education material indicates that the material, in the committee's judgment, is a biased, one-sided presentation of his practices, not the balanced presentation of information that can elicit true informed consent." Levin smiled when he read that, "Respondent has many satisfied patients." They noted that the exhibits tendered "contain lengthy and sincere testimonials from over fifty patients and shows the extent and depth of their support for Dr. Levin."

Levin had told the committee, when they were questioning him about his reluctance to place a diagnosis in the patient's chart that, "It is my belief that there is no acute or chronic illness that can't be benefitted if there is a way of improving the nutritional status of the patient." He had told them that writing a diagnosis often caused a problem with the patient's job, since the health insurance was provided through the workplace, so he only did so if the insurance company insisted on it and the patient agreed. The committee didn't forget to include all of that in their report.

Susan read, "As part of his evaluation of his patients, Respondent obtains a very detailed nutritional history, utilizing a 1200-item, computer-analyzed questionnaire. The Committee finds this emphasis on good nutrition commendable." She looked at him. "Well," she said, "it seems as though they think you did a few things right." He nodded in response.

The report then focused on Levin's dietary treatment of four conditions: hypoglycemia, *candidiasis*, nutritional deficiencies, and food allergy/addictions. They questioned the existence of the conditions and considered his treatment of them as inappropriate medical practice. They attacked his use of Chelation therapy and Cytotoxic Testing.

Finally, they got to a section entitled, "Conclusions of Law." Here, Levin decided to read aloud.

"The following conclusions were made pursuant to the findings of fact listed above. All conclusions resulted from a unanimous vote of the Hearing Committee unless noted otherwise." He swallowed noisily. He quickly read over the "Factual Allegations," noting which they had decided to sustain. Then he moved to the "Specification of Charges" section, seeing which of those were upheld, noting that the allegations in parentheses were meant to support the specification it followed. There was even a brief, very brief, section listing charges that were *not* sustained. *Big deal,* he thought.

They found his four patient witnesses credible "to the limits of their recollection of events." He went through every painful detail, took a deep breath, and then read: "Recommendations. The Hearing Committee, pursuant to its Findings of Fact and Conclusions of Law herein, unanimously recommends that Respondent's license to practice medicine in the State of New York be ***revoked***." Levin fought hard to keep his voice working evenly. "This recommendation was reached after due consideration of the full spectrum of available penalties, including suspension, probation, censure and reprimand, *or* the imposition of civil penalties of up to $10,000 *per* violation. As noted above, the Hearing Committee concluded that the deficiencies in the medical care rendered by Respondent demonstrated gross negligence, negligence on more than one occasion, fraud and moral unfitness to engage in the practice of medicine. Any individual who receives a license to practice medicine is placed into a position of public trust. Respondent used his position of trust for his own gain, to the detriment of his patients' welfare. His conduct constituted a serious breach of the public trust. No mitigating evidence was offered by Respondent. The Hearing Committee unanimously concluded that a penalty less than revocation would *not* be appropriate. It is unlikely, if not impossible, that Respondent could be rehabilitated, given a period of suspension with retraining. His repeated, willful and cynical behavior demonstrated that such re-education would not be successful."

They sat there at the table, as the hours passed, as the darkness of the September night set in, as the staff and patients left the office, as the sounds on the street outside quieted down. They sat there and sat there. Numb. Breathless. Spent.

CHAPTER 36

Susan hung up the phone and sat down to think. She had been crying a lot, sleeping poorly, and felt at her wits' end ever since they had received the decision of the Hearing Committee. They wanted to revoke his license. They wanted to fine him, too. They wanted to destroy her husband.

She had just spoken to her good friend, Jill, a psychologist who lived in Arizona now but still communicated with some of her New York colleagues. Susan had pleaded with Jill to ask around on her behalf to try to find a therapist, someone she could talk to about the anxiety and distress she was experiencing, especially since she had nearly passed out in temple last week. She had experienced the first panic attack of her life and thought she was having a heart attack. "Warren," she had whispered, her eyes wide with fear, "we've got to leave…right…now! Please!" He had taken one look at her and had ushered her out of the crowded row in record time. She stood outside the entrance doubled over and gasping huge quantities of air. "Susan, what is it? What's *wrong*?" he had asked repeatedly. She had been unable to respond. "Home," she gasped. "Take me home." He laid her on the couch and went to get his stethoscope. She hadn't wanted to go to the emergency room, and he had honored her request to go straight home. He suspected that she was having a panic attack. He was right. "Susan, you need help," he had told her. "I know; I know," she had responded.

Well, now she had an appointment in one hour with a psychologist whom Jill told her had come highly recommended. He was great with anxiety disorders. He was smart, insightful, and calm. Best of all, he was in Connecticut, close to home. She didn't know what to wear to her first appointment. She didn't want to seem like a basket case. She wanted to look put-together and stylish. She settled on a light blue silk blouse, a silk scarf and dark blue slacks with a sharp crease. She completed the outfit with a pair of navy pumps and checked the results in the mirror. She brushed her hair until it was gleaming, grabbed her jacket and keys and set off.

She sat out in the parking lot of the professional building. She didn't want to appear any more anxious than she already was. Going into the waiting room twenty minutes early would be a big mistake. But what if he had paperwork for her to do first? What if she was supposed to get to the first appointment early? What if…? She was giving herself an extra dose of agita for nothing. She waited five minutes then entered the building. The sign on his suite read "Michael T. Rothman, Ph.D., Psychologist." Below that was another sign: "Waiting Room. Please Come In." She opened the door slowly. The office was on the lower level of an old brick building, and the waiting room was paneled in dark brown faux-wood. There was a wall with a deep shelf built in and recessed lighting from below. There were two ceramic statues in both corners of that shelf: a Greek Evzone and a Greek Amalia. She looked closer and realized that these ceramics once housed the potent Greek anisette drink, ouzo. For some reason, that made her laugh softly. It seemed like the psychologist must have a sense of humor.

There were a few pieces of interesting art on the walls, she noticed. Then she saw a manila envelope on one of the chairs that lined three walls of the waiting room to the right. There was a Post-It note on the envelope: "Susan, please fill this out before we meet."

She sat down, glad she had come in fifteen minutes before her appointment. There was a white noise machine in one of the corners outside of the door that said, "Office. Private." Yet another door said, "Restroom Inside." She sat down and rapidly filled out the forms. She was glad that Dr. Rothman didn't have the 1200-question forms that Warren had in his medical office. She rushed to the restroom and returned seconds before the therapist opened the door to his private office.

After her session, on the ride home, she decided that she really liked the gentle, young psychologist who listened patiently as she spoke, whose quiet manner calmed her racing heart and wordlessly encouraged her to slow her rapid speech. It felt good to unload the burden of her dark thoughts and fears, to tell it all to someone who wasn't living the nightmare with her, as Warren was. She had made another appointment to see him in three days. Just the thought of the upcoming session was a calming influence.

At the same time, Levin was talking to his defense lawyer on the phone. "Warren, we have the right to submit something called a 'Proposed Decision,'" Harris told him, explaining that it would be a document that expressed exactly what *Levin* would have liked the Hearing Committee to say, rather than the scathing and horrific document they had sent him. "I know the case as well as I know my own life history," Harris told him, "so I'll put something together over the next day or two and fax you a copy. We'll have to send one out to Storch and one to Sheehan. That's the way this works."

"Do it," Levin told him.

Harris sat at the large table in the conference room. He had one of the law associates join him. Over five-thousand pages, fifty-one hundred and eighty-eight pages to be exact, of testimony littered the entire expanse of the table, separate hearings bound by plastic spirals. Harris began writing. He used a legal pad and wrote in longhand. He had never learned to type and knew it would slow him down to use a computer as he hunted the keyboard frantically for each letter of every word. As he completed a page, he'd number it and toss it to the other lawyer, whose job it was to search through the sections and locate the page number of each citation Harris had marked with an asterisk. He had used a red pen to place a hint of the date or the name of the witness who was being examined to make the search easier. After a few hours, the document was complete, the proper pages cited, and it would soon be put into the secretary's hands for immediate typing.

Harris called Sandi into his office so that they could review Harris's version of how the decision should have been written together. The face sheet read, "Proposed Findings of Fact and Conclusions," submitted by Respondent Warren M. Levin, M.D. It had the targeted agency's name at the top: State of New York, Department of Health, State Board For Professional Medical Conduct. In the lower right-hand corner, it read, "Robert H. Harris, Esq.," with the firm's name, address, and telephone number below.

Harris began by stating, "Respondent was licensed by the State of New York on June 30, 1959 to practice medicine and surgery. Said license has never been suspended or revoked and remains in force to this day. In the initial Statement of Charges, Respondent is accused of dozens of very serious breaches of legal, moral, and ethical rules, purportedly arising from his treatment of several patients during the years 1976 to 1988. No patient treatment issues in this group occurred after 1983." He proceeded to say that, "In his opening statement, Respondent's counsel asserted bad faith prosecution (pp. 25-30) including the fact that several charges were brought based only on insurance company records (pp. 22-23) resulting in State's witnesses not knowing what some of the items in the charges were (p. 272). Although the State contended that the standard breached by Respondent was merely 'minimally acceptable standard' (pp. 12-13), Respondent indicated that in fact *no* standard had been set forth by the prosecution (p. 2864ff)."

Harris made a point of saying that in Levin's thirty years of practice, the state was only able to make a charge of "withholding" a chart from a patient when, in fact, the chart had been lost. Such an issue would ordinarily *never* have come to the attention of the OPMC which, in Levin's case, held the charge up for examination with great enthusiasm. Harris made certain to insert Sheehan's "parallel universe" term into his document, since the prosecutor constantly wanted to illustrate the gigantic schism that he believed existed between conventional and alternative medicine, although practitioners of both were held to the same standards and had earned Doctor of Medicine degrees.

When Harris brought Victor Herbert's name into the arena, "the soul of the state's case," he refused to let a single misstep of Herbert's escape as he recalled each of the doctor's "gems" on paper. In writing his own "decision," Harris said, "Based on the foregoing, the panel finds the testimony of Dr. Victor Herbert uncertain, confusing and prejudiced and that it is therefore excluded from our deliberations."

Then he continued, citing Dr. Herman. "We likewise choose to ignore the testimony of Dr. Michael Victor Herman because of his total lack of familiarity with the subject matter he was attempting to testify about," and followed that statement with multiple citations. In his document, Harris also dismissed Dr. Robert Rej summarily, as his testimony was "unrelated to this proceeding." He also illustrated why the testimony of the patients called in by the state had absolutely no validity.

"We, the panel, conclude that the Health Department has failed by any reasonable evidentiary standard to prove any element of the various charges brought against the Respondent," wrote Harris. "We, the panel, disagree with the prosecution's conclusion concerning Respondent's experts. We found each of them to be credible, knowledgeable in their fields, having a point of view but willing to be challenged, and behaving consistently with the concept set forth by Francis Bacon, 'Truth is the daughter of time—not of authority.'"

Harris acknowledged that certain points *could* be considered "matters of honest scientific debate, not misconduct." He honestly believed that his client was a physician who was truly prescient regarding many of his medical strategies. "He was clearly ahead of his time in terms of evaluating for triglycerides, high density lipoprotein, and in recommending ideal levels of cholesterol rather than averages for over a decade before the National Heart, Lung and Blood Institute arrived at the same conclusion." He further discussed Levin's use of vitamins, minerals, and Vitamin E, and explained how his understanding of the role of free radicals twenty years prior to its becoming public knowledge had benefitted Levin's patients. Harris didn't forget to relay the important fact that many of Levin's formerly "questionable" procedures had become *standard practice* over the years as the hearings continued. He also explained how the testimony of the defense witnesses upheld Levin's medical practices, which were also supported by one-hundred and thirty-six exhibits and fifty affidavits from patients "applauding his treatment methods."

Harris ended his twelve-page document with the following sentence: "It is the recommendation of the Hearing Panel to the Commissioner of Health that all charges against Respondent be dismissed."

Harris and Sandi finished reading the prepared document, discussed the changes that each saw as necessary, tweaked the language a bit for smoother flow, and gave a marked-up copy back to the secretary with instructions to make the corrections and send out the three copies, saving another three for their files.

"Sandi, let me tell you a little story," Harris said, chuckling. "I wasn't about to write this in that document, but reviewing the salient points in the case brought something funny to mind. It's about Michael Victor Herman."

Sandi held a finger up, indicating that she'd be back in a minute, which she was, a cup of coffee in her hand. "I'm listening," she told the firm's managing partner, knowing that his story would be interesting but not brief.

He proceeded to relate a "gem," as he referred to it, from the half-day of testimony given by Herman, an incident he treasured. At one point, Harris had taken Herman through each significant career decision the doctor had made, from medical school through residency and from position to position until he attained his current status, asking at each juncture: "So, Dr. Herman, did you *study*, *give*, *see* someone receive, or *talk* to anyone who administered Chelation therapy?" Of course, Herman had answered, "No" for each portion of his professional life, as

Harris knew he would, while under oath. Finally, when Harris got into Herman's face and shouted, *"So what the hell are you doing here today, testifying against one of your colleagues in a hearing to revoke his medical license? You know* nothing *about Chelation therapy, and that's one of the things the state is harping on. Just what the hell are you doing here today?"* The committee members, in unison, had uttered, "Mr. Harris, Mr. Harris, please!" which failed to have an effect on Harris, who kept his angry face directly within Herman's line of sight. Finally, *"I don't have to take this anymore!"* Herman retorted, leaving the witness chair and grabbing his coat. This time, the committee's chorus was, "Dr. Herman, Dr. Herman, please!" It was only Storch's even demeanor and conciliatory words that had brought the physician back into the chair he had summarily vacated.

Harris picked up the phone. "Warren, I just want to let you know that your copy of the Proposed Decision will be arriving in a few days. Sheehan's and Storch's are going out this afternoon, as well." Harris left the office. He had dinner plans.

Susan looked at her watch. It was time for her second appointment with Dr. Rothman. She had just finished reading over the document Bob had prepared on Warren's behalf and it made her feel a little better. *That's the way the committee* should *have written the decision in the first place,* she thought, as she backed the car down the driveway.

Susan was smiling as she left Dr. Rothman's office. She wasn't quite sure if it was her own idea or if he had suggested it, but she knew where she would concentrate her "energy," which was the psychologist's expression for her runaway anxiety. A meeting of ACAM, the American College for Advancement in Medicine, was coming up soon. She couldn't *wait* to get home and contact the program director. She wanted to stand in front of all of those wonderful supporters, many of them her husband's colleagues and friends, and thank them for all of their help and assistance. Susan dashed into the house, made her phone call, and then rushed into her office to start typing.

She continued to see Dr. Rothman twice a week for several more weeks and even delivered her little speech in front of him for practice. When he told her to cut back to weekly sessions, she was pleased that he had acknowledged that she had gotten herself under tighter control.

She stood in front of her closet. She wanted to pick just the right outfit to appear in at the podium of the ACAM meeting. She had a chocolate brown suit she had selected from Barney's in New York. It fit her to perfection. She pinned back her long, shiny hair and eyed herself appreciatively in the mirror. "Warren, what do you think?"

He was dressed in a dark brown suit, as she had requested, with a soft, gold-hued shirt, and a print silk tie. He stepped back to take in the full view, letting out a weakened version of the classic "wolf whistle." He shook his head in amazement. "Susan," he said appreciatively, "if we weren't already married, I'd probably be chasing you until you agreed to marry me!"

She laughed. She knew she looked good and wanted to be sure he knew it too. She grabbed her oversized purse and slipped her notes inside. "Ready?"

"Never been readier!"

They walked in together and "worked the crowd," as they liked to call it, moving toward separate sides of the room, their name badges pinned to their lapels, greeting old friends and acquaintances and introducing themselves to visitors and prospective new members. They each held a club soda, his with lime, hers with lemon, as they circulated.

The meeting was finally called to order. The "housekeeping" portion was handled—the boring stuff about dues, expenses, updates, and so forth. Susan was seated on one of the chairs in the front row. As a guest speaker, she didn't want to be in the awkward position of tripping her way across people's legs and shoes and looking less than graceful as she made her way up to the speaker's platform.

When her name was called, she rose to considerable applause. These people, above all others, really *understood* what she and Warren were going through. She placed her papers down on the lectern, glad that it was anchored to a thin support that allowed her suit to be mostly visible from the seats below the low stage. She took several slow, deep breaths, just as Dr. Rothman had suggested, to center herself and keep her breathing at a natural, even level.

"As I look out at all of you this evening, I realize how many of you I *already* know. You know," she smiled, "when I started coming to these meetings back in 1976, Warren was on the board. I had the opportunity of listening to some truly wonderful and inspiring speakers." She listed the names for the audience, noticing nods from so many of the members who had been with the group for the past sixteen years. "The discussions were rousing, the arguments vigorous, and sometimes I thought we'd never get out of here before midnight…and we often didn't," she admitted, as many of the long-time members laughed.

"I feel privileged. One of the reasons for this is the fact that I actually *witnessed* the birth of the American Board of Chelation therapy!" There was an enthusiastic round of applause. "The excitement, the furor, the passion of that birth provided those of us present with treasured memories." Her face took on a serious look. "However, we are *still* under attack by the insurance industry, the drug conglomerates, the medical establishment, and the Victor Herberts of this country. We have not yet succeeded in bringing that controversy to a halt."

Susan paused for a long moment, the look on her face regretful. "Let me remind you," she said, softly, her voice a dramatic whisper, "of some of our physicians who have been disciplined, those who fought valiantly to keep their licenses…and those who eventually *lost* their licenses to practice medicine. So many of those who fought the system were left broke…and broken," she intoned, her eyes fixed on Warren, who had taken a seat dead center. Susan listed eighteen names slowly, watching audience members nod in recognition of a familiar name. "I wish I could acknowledge everyone who fought the good fight," she said, her voice stronger. She spread her hands out in a gesture that evoked a feeling of helplessness. "And then there are those of us," she began, nodding her head as she spoke, "who you rarely hear from, who fight behind the scenes, struggling to keep our homes, run our offices, and take care of our children." Her voice was rising in volume with each sentence fragment, invoking the tone of a revival preacher. "It was only *two years ago* that I stood in this room with Jacqueline Deck, as she cried, telling me how her husband Bob was fighting for a stay on the order to revoke his license, and another physician was seeing his patients. She was trying to run their home while dealing with the overwhelming daily stress of the legal battle they were fighting. I identified with it *then*, and I still identify with it *now*, as *our* battle was in force when Jackie and I spoke, and it's *still* raging to this day!" There was a murmur of acknowledgement from the room. "Jackie wasn't even able to tell her little boy, who had outgrown his sneakers, when they would be able to afford to buy him a new pair. Imagine that," she instructed the people, who were shaking their heads in sympathy. "I was moved by her words," she admitted, "just as I am certain all of you are tonight."

Susan shifted her stance, prepared to launch into an update her and Warren's own personal hell. "At that time, we had just renewed *our* fight, which had begun *eleven years earlier*, before there was a break in the action. I remember the families who were forced to relocate to another state and start all over, and their courage is giving me strength. But we have been *mightily* challenged. I'll give you an example." Susan pulled the front page of a *New York Daily News* out from between the pages of her notes and held it up. "Imagine," she said to the audience, "just *imagine* coming into your office one day and seeing these headlines in four-inch type on the front page of the newspaper that was just delivered." Susan was quite sure that the print was visible to most of the people in the room. "'DOCS FROM HELL,' this headline screams in capital letters," she told them, "and listed as one of the potentially most *dangerous* twenty-six doctors in New York State is *my husband*, who is sitting right *there*." She pointed to Warren, who hadn't known what Susan planned to say. He blushed in response to the audience's murmurs of concern. "In *spite* of this," Susan continued, holding up the page with a look of disgust on her face, "I *still* feel strong. I am strengthened by your support and your belief in Warren!" The audience applauded loudly, demonstrating their backing of one of their own.

Susan waited for the room to be silent once again. "So, I realize how important it is to win, because *your* license," she said, pointing to a physician in the front row, "and *your* license," she said, indicating a chiropractor in the rear of the room, "and *your* license," she added, sweeping the back of her hand broadly across her body from left to right, "are in jeopardy if we lose this battle! The diagnostic studies that you use, the vitamins that you prescribe and dispense, the Chelation therapy that you administer, the environmental allergy testing that you perform puts *all of you* at risk."

She chuckled to herself, and then said, almost as an afterthought, "Oh, I know. You're thinking, 'This could *never* happen to *me*,' or 'I'll just keep a low profile,' or 'I've got my hands in enough of the traditional medicine that if they pressure me, I can simply retreat a bit and keep my license.'" She put her hands on her hips dramatically. "Well, let me *tell* you, even as we descended deeper and deeper into this fight, I *never* truly confronted how *we* would make it if Warren lost his license. At this point—and this is the truth," she assured them, placing the palms of her hands on the lectern, "I'm *confronting* it, and so is Warren…big time! We think about it, dream about it, talk about it, consider alternatives to not having the medical office anymore, and we worry and agonize. Then," she said, with renewed energy in her voice, "we come out swinging again, ready to continue the battle. At this point in time, we're looking at all the ways we hope to demonstrate to the Board of Regents of the State of New York what an *outrage* and *affront* this case has been to us. Not only to us, though, to our patients, to all of the physicians who *refuse* to bend to the rules of mainstream medicine and give up the healing practices they have discovered, and to the people of New York, who will no longer have a choice in selecting a physician who practices our kind of medicine if we lose this case."

Susan sighed deeply. "It's no secret, ladies and gentlemen, friends and colleagues. We lost an *important* round in this fight. The Hearing Committee of the OPMC has recommended that Warren's medical license be *revoked!"* She paused as the noise level in the room increased. She heard the word, "revoked," whispered by people throughout the room, like an echo bouncing off the walls and ceiling, horror apparent in the speakers' voices. She noticed several people reach over and pat Warren comfortingly. She saw him smile his thanks.

Once the room got quiet again, she continued her speech. "So that battle is *truly* lost. But it's only *one* battle in a series of battles. We're more than ready to face the next one: the one against the Regents. We believe that our conviction, our integrity, and our commitment to our patients and to you shall prevail."

She bit her bottom lip. She hated saying the next words. "Please ..." she began, and her voice cracked, "please help us so that we do not become just another statistic, another case of a doctor who valiantly lost his license, who will be gone from our midst never to return. Help support us, please, emotionally, as you have been doing, and financially, as many of you already have. We don't want this to be the last ACAM meeting that we attend as members. We want to come back here victorious! We want to return to celebrate, to share our strategies, so that we are able to help those who need our help within these ranks."

Susan smiled a big smile, her winning smile. "And finally," she said, "Warren's greatest hope is that, in this era of public discontent, of soaring medical costs and unaffordable medical insurance, that we can *finally* go before the American people, go into the halls of Congress, and demand," she shook her head forcefully, "not request, but *demand*," she repeated even louder, "a fair assessment of the alternatives that you provide for your patients caringly, thoughtfully, and safely. Thank you."

They stood up and applauded for Susan, long and loud. Levin couldn't take his eyes off her. She came off like a politician running for office. She was a natural, and he was so grateful that her appeal was directed toward his future survival and existence as a physician. He had to fight his way through the crowd to reach

Susan, to tell her how proud he was, how cool and collected she was on the podium, how well she spoke, to thank her, to kiss her. No matter what his future held professionally speaking, he knew that he was still a fortunate man. He had to remember that. No matter what.

CHAPTER 37

"He did what?" Levin asked, the cordless phone pressed to his ear as he stood looking out the window in his private office. "And he wrote it when?"

"Three days ago, on November twenty-second," came the response.

"So he wrote it two days before Thanksgiving," Levin said, "so in case you had a happy holiday, this would be waiting in your office today."

Jimmy Carter chuckled. "Well, you know Victor Herbert: ever the master planner."

When the call ended, Levin sat at his desk thinking about Victor Herbert, the scourge of the medical and legal profession, as far as he was concerned. The guy had written a threatening letter to Carter, who had published a book with another writer and mentioned Herbert's name a number of times, never in a particularly favorable manner, as he recalled from having read it. Now Herbert was demanding *far more* than a simple retraction. In true Victor Herbert style, he had sent Carter a four-page letter, in which he stated unequivocally that he expected to receive a twenty-five thousand dollar check from Carter and his co-author as "token reparations" to avert a ten-million-dollar lawsuit directed at both authors and the publishing company. His demands included removing from the book's Table of Contents the chapter, "Dr. Victor Herbert: A Legend in His Own Mind," a title which immediately brought a smile to Levin's face, as that was always Bob's way of referring to the garrulous doctor as well. Herbert also listed the pages and expressions he wanted removed from the publication. For example, there was the line where Herbert was referred to as "organized med's mouthpiece," who is "paid to say this pseudo-science." There were a number of other unflattering references that he demanded be immediately obliterated.

But Herbert didn't stop there. It seemed as though the very idea of Warren Levin's *existence* was choking the VA physician. He expected Carter to pen a letter of apology, written to Herbert's specifications, and including wording crafted to humiliate Carter and *also* Levin. He included three fat paragraphs from the Hearing Committee's decision against Levin, which was allegedly a confidential document that should *not* have found its way into Herbert's litigious hands. Herbert wanted promotional ads for Carter's book to carry the news, in capital letters, that Carter had paid Herbert $25,000 in "token reparations, obliterated the defamation in all copies of the book within our reach and/or control, and sent out an 'apology letter' with corrective enclosures to all purchasers." He wanted certain documents sent to all requesters and all former buyers of the book. The list incredulously included Herbert's specially prepared, one-page *curriculum vitae;* a flier for the nutrition book authored by Herbert; an article praising Herbert; and a two-column retraction by a particular magazine he had threatened to sue, which also sent him a $10,000 check for 'token reparation'—a photocopy of which was enclosed for inclusion with all of the other documents. Carter was given thirty days to meet these demands and avert the ten-million-dollar lawsuit.

Levin found the whole thing too ridiculous for contemplation, and he truly believed that Herbert had targeted Carter—and probably would *continue* to follow the careers of any and all of Levin's remaining defense witnesses—in an effort to find a niche to crawl into and widen significantly enough to discredit each of them. Herbert had been splattered all over the walls of the OPMC hearing room by Bob Harris. It was not a slight that would soon be forgotten. Levin suspected Herbert wouldn't sleep well until he had made significant progress in his attempts to destroy the credibility of each of Levin's defenders, just as his own reputation was now in such shambles that it was doubtful that Herbert would ever again be called to the stand by New York State as an expert witness.

Levin took a bottle of cold water out of his small refrigerator. He needed to wash the taste of Victor Herbert out of his mouth so he could think about more important things. Although he had no idea when the Regents hearing would take place, Harris had encouraged him and Susan to begin collecting signatures of supporters to impress the reviewers. Levin also wanted to see if he could garner support from an influential agency or two that he figured owed him something; all they had done was harass him over insurance issues for years and years. He decided that it was payback time.

He sat down to write a letter to the Medical Society of the state of New York. He was delighted to inform them that the petitions he and Susan had been circulating since the Hearing Committee's decision came out had already garnered over ten-thousand signatures of support. He reiterated the issues of his case, mentioning that "there was not one allegation of injury to a single patient in the original charges, which were brought after thirteen years of investigation!" He was excited to write that recent issues of the *New York Times* had featured numerous articles recognizing the peer-reviewed literature's support of the use of vitamins and minerals, which he tagged as "the true basis of Victor Herbert's anonymous complaint to OPMC about my practice." He couldn't resist adding, that "the most important paragraph is the last one," in the article he enclosed, where "Victor Herbert (of all people) said he thought it was reasonable to suggest that vitamin E supplements are protective against cardiovascular disease." With glee, he mentioned that Herbert's nutrition textbook did not have *one single positive entry about Vitamin E*, "yet I gave my *first* lecture on vitamin E and antioxidant effect on fatty acids in 1973!"

He closed his letter with his own demand. "I will not accept a *post-facto* apology from MSSNY. *Now* is the time to put your money and your power and energy behind Warren M. Levin, M.D. as a representative of the burgeoning science of nutrition as a basis for health in the Twenty-First Century. I would be *delighted* to appear before a Board of Directors meeting, with counsel, to hopefully assist in what is obviously a difficult decision for an organization weighted down with such inertia as MSSNY." His anger showed through his letter, he realized, but he wasn't willing to soften it one bit.

Several weeks passed before Levin heard back. He realized that his letter had been forwarded to the American Medical Association, as the reply came from their Chicago office. They didn't directly say yes or no to his request but the writer did state that "generally, the AMA cannot participate in licensure actions, due to the large volume of these cases." But the letter did say that, in rare cases, the AMA might intervene, where "issues of importance to the profession as a whole" were at stake. Levin certainly thought that his case was important to the profession as a whole but wasn't sure that the AMA viewed it through quite the same lens.

It wasn't until late April that the Medical Society of the State of New York finally wrote him a direct response. From their letter, he saw that his situation did *not* meet their criteria of "directly affecting physicians as a whole" or "quality medical care." *Well, guys, I kind of knew I couldn't count on you for assistance. All you've ever done is harass me anyway. Whatever made me think that this time would be different?* He pushed the letter away from him with a look of pure disgust, as though the paper itself was viral and carried a deadly infection. *It's a good thing I've got a creative mind. I already have something else up my sleeve.*

Levin had been talking on a regular basis to a number of his colleagues in the field of alternative medicine. Yes, they all agreed, the establishment docs have a monopoly. We've got to do something about it. Monopolies are against the law. It's a violation of the Sherman Antitrust Act, they decided as a group. And they found a law firm willing to consider filing a possible antitrust lawsuit, since it could run into big numbers and yield the firm a large fee for a contingency case. The best part of it was that the doctors wouldn't have to put up too much money to pursue this tactic. The lawyer at the forefront formulated a proposal. Levin sat at the desk in his home office, Susan across from him, and read her what he considered to be a key paragraph from that lawyer's brief proposing a class-action suit.

"By characterizing practitioners of alternate treatments as quacks and prohibiting them from offering services to interested patients, the AMA, hospitals, physicians and insurers limit the availability of desired treatment to consumers. Moreover, by preventing dissemination of information about alternative means to cure diseases, the AMA and its cohorts thwart access to the market, which successfully removes any threat of losing money. This is a violation of the Sherman Act."

He looked over the top of his reading glasses. "So what do you think?" he asked her.

"I think he caught the essence of the whole thing. Are you and the others going to pursue it?"

He shrugged. "I don't think the decision is as much in our hands as it is in the hands of the lawyers," he responded, with honesty.

"I don't understand."

"It's pure, simple economics," he told her. "If this guy brings it to his partners and they talk about it and figure they can get enough money from the whole thing, they'll take the case on contingency. None of us is in a financial position to offer a huge chunk of money. I've said I'll pay something to the lawyer, as well, but not right now. The others plan to collect enough for a retainer up front, but no one can commit to astronomical legal fees. So it's really in their hands." He sighed.

She nodded her understanding. "It always comes down to money."

"That's what makes the world go round."

As he was uttering these words, a number of his fellow physicians, who had united their efforts and approached an attorney under their own steam, had succeeded in paying out of their pockets for yet another lawyer to draw up a brief to mail to the Office of Legal Services of the State Education Department in Albany. This Park Avenue attorney, Michael Kennedy, was just putting the finishing touches on the brief, which he planned to send to three of those doctors to review.

He had his secretary send the copies out by messenger service, and they were in the hands of Levin's colleagues within the hour. Dr. Reich thought that the eighteen-page brief captured the essence of their conversations with the lawyer, to whom they had provided the latest summary of the proceedings Levin had sent after the committee's decision came through. Reich practiced alternative medicine and was familiar with the OPMC battles to be fought. "Every new medical modality is initially 'unaccepted' at first," he read, "but just because the new medical modality is not accepted does not mean that it is bad or non-beneficial or undesirable to patients. Nor does 'unaccepted' mean that the new modality has not enjoyed some positive clinical experience." *It's funny,* Reich thought, *that our type of medicine is still thought of as 'a new modality,' when some of the things we do have been around longer than some of the practices of the establishment physicians. Plus, even the so-called 'newer' stuff involves strategies we've utilized for decades under the guise of 'alternative' care.* He shook his head in consternation and read on.

"Finally the *amici* class believes that the legitimate interests of the medical profession in preventing fraud and minimizing negligence are not well served by substituting the subjective and circumscribed judgments of medical orthodoxy for the deliberate desires of patients, including members of this class, who have the right to choose not only how they live and die but also how and by whom they are treated." *True, true,* thought Reich.

Richard Feiger's last patient of the morning had just left the office when the delivery came. He reviewed the brief, stopping to reread the paragraph that said, "The Constitutional right of privacy—the right to be left alone—includes a patient's right to select alternative, unconventional or unorthodox medical treatment." The lawyer even supported that statement with quotes from Justices Brandeis and Cardozo, which Feiger found interesting and impressive. He liked where the lawyer stated that, "The doctor has a right to deliver the medical treatment chosen by a patient." Feiger's eyebrows went up when he read: "Alternative medicine is much more appreciated by the United States' Congress and millions of American patients than it is by the orthodox medical establishment. In 1992 Congress passed legislation creating and funding an Office of Alternative Medicine at the National Institutes of Health. The task of this office is to study unconventional medical practices." After reading this, Feiger dispensed hot water into his mug, plopped in a packet of green tea, and took it back to his desk to finish reading the brief.

"Dr. Seymour," as the patients who were cared for by Seymour Finkelhammerstein referred to their practitioner of complementary medicine, didn't get to read the brief until the following day. As was his style, he sat at his desk after hours with a red pen in his hand, figuring that the lawyer probably didn't write as well as he did, and moved through the brief at a moderate pace, correcting a grammatical error, a misspelling, a syntactical *faux pas*, or adding an essential fact that had been overlooked. "According to Doctor Joe Jacobs, Director of N.I.H.'s Office of Alternative Medicine," he read, "the popularity of alternative medicine demonstrates a hunger among Americans for a more humane and less intrusive form of treatment than that ordinarily practiced by standard doctors. Dr. Warren M. Levin and other alternative health care providers are filling a serious void that orthodox medicine and conventional practitioners are unwilling or incapable of filling. They are, in fact, healing millions of American patients whose health and medical needs cannot wait for the medical establishment to formally and finally approve, through some imagined 'scientific consensus,' the alternative medicine modalities from which these patients are deriving desperately needed medical benefits." He was pleased with the wording and only added a few things to strengthen the message before getting to the attorney's final section, the conclusion.

Here, Kennedy had written, "The findings of the Hearing Panel are subjective, vindictive, and unfair both to Doctor Levin and to this *amici* class, his actual and prospective patients. The decision of the Hearing Panel should be set aside."

Dr. Seymour's memory was sharp enough to recall that this very same attorney assisted in the defense for the infamous 1969-1970 trial of the Chicago 7. Some characterized that trial as an important battle for the hearts and minds of the American people, whereas Levin's case concerned the health of the American people. Certainly the late sixties was a period in American history where values were questioned by those who fought the tried and true establishment. The seven people on trial were considered radicals whose intent was to start a riot at the 1968 Democratic National Convention in Chicago. The doctor was rather impressed that the same lawyer was interested enough in physicians he probably categorized in his own mind as "radicals," since they fought the "establishment."

Levin had been kept updated by Harris as to the behind-the-scenes occurrences since the hearings ended. For example, when the final deliberations took place in late October, and the panel met in mid-December, they issued their decision nine months later in September of 1992. The decision was sent to the Commissioner of Health, who also received Harris's version of how the decision *should* have been written in the first place. The Commissioner upheld the panel's recommendation, then sent everything to the Regents after another nine months had passed—bringing the never-ending process to June 1993.

However, Harris *already* knew that Levin's case would be sent to the Regents. He had contacted them to learn how much time he would be given during their hearing to make a strong argument on behalf of his client. Harris was aghast when told he would be limited to ten minutes. Harris would still be in the warm-up phase at that point in time, and to make the argument of his life on behalf of his client would require a lot more time, so he decided to think it out with Sandi at his office.

Harris was pacing as he spoke, his volume rising to a fever pitch. "Sandi, those idiots at the Health Department together with the other idiots at the Education Department delayed and delayed and delayed!" He was breathing heavily. "I kept calling and asking them to send the case over to the Regents. 'No,' they said, 'the Respondent has absolutely *no say* in when we send anything over.' I told them repeatedly, 'This is *not* your average case. This has gone on for *years* and the last three years have yielded over five-thousand pages of testimony. Send it over now! Give the Regents sufficient time to read everything!' But no. The idiots waited until the week of June eighth to send it out, and by the time those guys get it, they're only gonna have two weeks until the hearing on June twenty-ninth. This is insane, absolutely insane!"

"So what can you possibly…" began Sandi.

"On top of that," Harris interrupted, "the Regents committee is not about to give me any more than ten minutes to fight for Warren's license!" His face was red and his eyes wild. He swept a pile of papers off the table and they flew haphazardly all around him. As he resumed pacing, the sound of the papers crunching underfoot mobilized Sandi.

"Sit down, Bob!" she ordered. "For God's sake, sit down! Let me clean up this mess so we can figure something out."

He marched over to his desk and buzzed his secretary. "Bring in a couple of diet cokes!"

There was a knock on his office door a moment later, and the secretary had a tray with two cans of soda and two glasses. "Put it on the table," he told her. She walked around him, eyeing him warily and almost tripped over Sandi, who was on her knees picking up papers from the carpet. The young secretary hastily shoved the tray on the table and made a rapid exit, anxious to let the rest of the staff know that Harris was on the rampage.

He sat down and poured out the sodas, taking a big gulp and coughing reflexively. Then they began talking. An hour later, Sandi left his office, wiping her brow with the back of her hand in response to the unasked questions of several lawyers who stood in the immediate vicinity.

Harris, however, had a huge smile on his face. "Come in here!" he said over the intercom, summoning his secretary. He dictated nonstop for the next four hours, as the secretary scrambled to get it all down in shorthand. He offered her double time to stay at the office and type it all up. She made a few phone calls to her family and to a babysitter and agreed. He was still sitting at his desk working when she came in at midnight with the fifty-page document addressed to the Board of Regents: State of New York. It would be mailed first thing in the morning. It summarized *every* important point from Levin's background, to his practice, to Victor Herbert's testimony, to the Kangaroo Court that his client had endured after years of harassment, to the appeal made to the Regents Review Committee for sufficient argument time back in April—which only resulted in their granting an additional five minutes. He referenced the brief from *amici curiae,* he talked about "quackery," about prosecutorial bad faith, informed consent, patient choice, the thirteen-year chase of the OPMC for the prize of Levin's license, the lack of credibility of the state's witnesses and the panel's refusal to accept the defense witnesses as credible. He spoke of the ridicule heaped upon scientists over the ages who were later vindicated and their virtues extolled, he added pertinent quotes from some of the material he found lying around in his office, and he attached ten significant articles that he had carefully described as relating to Levin's case.

He figured that, if the Regents read his fifty-page document and scanned the attachments, they would have the entire essence of the five-thousand plus pages of testimony in their heads in about two hours. Then, if they insisted on laboriously poring through everything else, their mindset would be established, and they would be viewing it all through the eyes of the defense. What could be better?

Harris knew what could be better, actually, so he got behind the wheel of his roomy Cadillac at five o'clock the next morning and headed toward the New York State Thruway. He pulled in at one of the rest stops to use the bathroom then stopped at the concession stand and spent thirty dollars on bags of assorted hard candies. Back in his car, he resumed listening to Levin's PANIC tape—which was now two years old but very thorough in its coverage of significant events in the doctor's battle with the state—to learn if there were any gems he might have overlooked, as he set his sights on the upcoming presentation in front of the Regents.

The traffic on the Thruway was minimal as Harris drove. He had been assisting with a medical defense case for a doctor whose offices were practically in the shadow of the New York State Capitol in Albany. Before he began writing what he hoped would be an influential document for the Regents yesterday, he had done several things. He had contacted Dr. Boodrum's attorney in Albany to schedule an early dinner meeting, asking the other lawyer to select a restaurant with a mouth-watering choice of entrees. He had also called his favorite hotel in the area, the Morgan State House Inn, an amazing, late nineteenth-century structure right on State Street, just a few blocks from the Capitol building. He requested his favorite room, 4B, which they told him would be cleaned and available to him by twelve noon. That suited his purpose just fine.

He completed the one-hundred-and-sixty-two mile trip in a bit over three hours and had the hotel's valet park his car in a nearby lot. He checked in and left his overnight case with the concierge, since it was only eight-thirty in the morning. He freshened up in the guest bathroom off the lobby and, armed with a packed briefcase and his pockets stuffed with individually wrapped hard candies, he set off for the short trek down to the state Capitol, which housed both the Assembly and the Senate. Harris had something special in mind.

It was rare for Harris to walk when he could ride, but today was an exception. He walked out of the hotel, turned right, and headed for where the "big guns hung out," as he had always referred to the heart of New York's lawmaking area. He just stood in front of the magnificent edifice for a moment. *New Yorkers were certainly different from other people*, he reflected. Whereas most of the nation's state capitol buildings copied the domed structure of Washington, D.C.'s Capitol, this wasn't the case in Albany. Its history, however, was strikingly similar to the edifice in the nation's capital. With his interest in historical fact, combined with his law background, Harris was aware that construction had begun on New York's Capitol building in 1867 and continued through 1899 and represented a blended style of four different architects and an expenditure of twenty-five million dollars. Most unfortunately, a fire in 1911 had destroyed 450,000 books and 270,000 manuscripts in the State Library, and Harris recalled that the Capitol in Washington, D.C. had also been hit by destructive fires during its early years of existence. He laughed to himself, because he actually recalled the dimensions of the building. He knew that the five-story Capitol was four-hundred feet long and three-hundred feet wide and had both a full basement and an attic. It had been constructed mainly of gray granite, and Harris remembered that the walls were over sixteen-feet thick at the building's foundation, *literally the width of a decent sized living room in a private home*, he thought. Due to the number of architects involved in the building's design over the years, the exterior sported Italian Renaissance, Romanesque, and French Renaissance influences, the true inspiration provided by the Classical architecture of the Hotel de Ville in Paris, France.

Harris entered the building and stationed himself quite strategically at the foot of the Great Western Staircase, which he knew had taken fourteen years to construct and that its four-hundred and forty-four steps ended at a one-hundred-and-nineteen foot height. There were actually three gorgeous sandstone staircases in the building with a total of seventy-seven faces of famous Americans carved into them. The detailed visages of Washington, Lincoln, Grant, and Susan B. Anthony were recognizable to most people. Harris loved and appreciated the beauty of the Capitol, and he felt happy just being inside the building.

The lawyer was a politically savvy individual and knew the faces of most assemblymen and state senators from either his own lobbying efforts, their photographs in a newspaper, their appearances on television, or from personal meetings. He was about to put all of that knowledge to work on behalf of Warren Levin in his most outrageous scheme to date, as he was aware that most of the lawmakers would be arriving at work just about now.

There would be one-hundred and fifty Assemblymen and sixty-two Senators coming into the building this morning. Harris planned to catch as many of those people as possible. The petition he had on his clipboard, which had a good-quality ballpoint pen attached to its ring by a string, simply read, "We request that adequate argument time be given to complex cases appearing in front of the New York State

Regents Review Committee." Harris hoped to collect enough signatures to change the ridiculous ten-minute rule that currently existed and also ignore the slight increment he had been granted, in favor of a decent amount of time. Greeting each of New York State's political representatives by name as they approached the staircase, Harris said, in a conspiratorial tone, "Senator," or "Assemblyman, I'd like to offer you a *bribe*."

"A bribe?" each one would repeat, the shock value as different as the person mouthing the words.

"Yes, a *bribe*," Harris would say, a note of seriousness in his voice. Harris would then extend his hand and place a piece of wrapped, hard candy in the politician's palm. "I'm greasing your palm," Harris would tell the person, as the individual laughed heartily at the "bribe."

"And what do you want in exchange for this *bribe*?" he'd be asked.

"Just your signature on this piece of paper, nothing else," Harris would say, innocently.

The targeted individual would rapidly scan the short sentence. "Nothing else?" would be the follow-up question.

"Nope."

And they signed, one after the other, then unwrapped the candy, popped it into their mouths, and climbed the massive staircase smiling. No one's smile was any broader than Harris's, though. He planned to present the Regents with a petition to extend the time for his argument at Levin's hearing from the fifteen minutes grudgingly granted to, hopefully, about an hour, which Harris considered to be a reasonable amount of time for a lawyer to make a case after thirteen years and more than five-thousand pages of testimony. He collected one-hundred-and-eighty signatures in record time.

His work at the Capitol completed, Harris headed back to the Morgan State House Inn and went to his room. He had instructed the staff to turn the air-conditioning to the lowest temperature possible. He planned to experience the full benefit of the venerable inn. He walked through the foyer and opened the double doors to the gorgeous bedroom and paused to take in the sight: everything smacked of comfort, comfort, and more comfort. The place was known for its feather mattresses, down comforters, soft cotton sheets, and fabulous amenities.

The comfy king-sized bed had a skylight right above it and was flanked by a red brick wall with a gas fireplace, which Harris immediately turned on. He loved the combination of a chilly, air-conditioned room and a warm, glowing fireplace. It made him think of a hospitable room in an Alpine hotel in Austria in the middle of winter. When he looked out of his window, though, he didn't see skiers descending from a high peak. Instead, his view was of the inn's garden, which surrounded a flagstone patio and glowed with the brilliant colors of late-blooming summer flowers. This hotel billed itself as having, "the most unique accommodations in the Capitol District," and Harris totally agreed. He filled the oversized, six-foot bathtub with hot, but not boiling, water and lowered himself into it with a contented sigh. After luxuriating for a full forty-five minutes, he toweled off, and as the tub drained, he peeled back the comforter and soft sheets and sank into the feather mattress on his bed. He'd take a brief nap, he thought, immediately falling asleep with a smile on his face, lulled by the crackling sounds of the fireplace and relaxed from his bath.

Harris woke spontaneously in an hour, dressed casually, and picked up a snack from the corner vendor. He took a taxi down to the Hudson River and boarded one of the tour boats. He realized that, in all of his trips to Albany for legal reasons, he hadn't done anything that was touristy or really fun. Well, it was a beautiful day. Why not? He thought.

He had plenty of time before tonight's dinner meeting. *Besides,* he thought, *meeting with Dr. Boodrum's lawyer just happened to fit conveniently into my plan for Levin and gave me an excuse for a night in a fabulous inn and what I hope will be a great dinner, if the other guy's got good taste in restaurants. Levin's the reason I drove up here today, and my crazy plan was a resounding success. Can't wait to show that petition to the Regents!*

He clambered out of the taxi, tipping the turbaned driver generously. Harris smiled as he climbed aboard the tour boat.

CHAPTER 38

"Well, Warren, the Regents Review Committee agreed to give me *forty-five minutes* to make my argument!" Harris boasted.

"How did *that* happen?" Levin asked, from the other end of the phone.

"Oh, just a little 'Harris Magic,'" his lawyer told him, modestly.

"Well, however you did it, Bob, I must admit I feel a bit relieved. I just couldn't *bear* to think of my 'final appeal' as a five-minute or a fifteen-minute sound bite."

"Well, it won't be. You can depend on that. Listen, Warren, let me tell you something else. The same way I said that I *expected* we'd lose Round One with the Hearing Committee's decision—and we *did*," he added, unnecessarily, "I'm telling you we have a fighting chance with the Regents. These guys are no dummies. Their objective is to evaluate everything and come to a *fair* decision."

Levin laughed into the mouthpiece of the phone.

"What's so funny?" Harris asked.

"The word 'fair' is what's funny, Bob. I don't think that the state of New York has the word 'fair' in its vocabulary. Why would the Regents Review Committee be any *different* from the Department of Health and its misguided Commissioner, or the OPMC with its hired guns and dogged prosecutor? *Why* should I risk getting my hopes up at all?"

"Warren, you may be the doctor whose defense I've worked on longer than any other doctor's in my entire career, but you're not the *first* guy I've represented in front of the Regents. Unless this group who will be sitting on your case has been drinking from the same poisoned well as the DOH and OPMC guys, I expect fairness from them. I think we have a fighting chance."

Levin laughed again. "All I've been *doing* for endless years is fighting. As Susan told the ACAM members, when she appeared before them last fall, we're ready to take our case to the Regents and prove my innocence." He sighed deeply. "I'm still in the boxing ring, Bob, and the *last* round is finally coming up. I'll manage to stay on my feet until the end. Don't worry."

"That's my man! I'll see you in the hearing room. It should be quite a day!"

Time seemed to be moving at lightning speed for Susan. Before she knew it, June twenty-ninth had arrived. She was standing in front of the full-length mirror in the master bedroom, getting dressed in an outfit that would photograph well. Over *eighty-thousand people* had signed a petition supporting Levin and asking that he be allowed to continue to practice medicine. Susan was elated. She was also excited about what had happened over the past two days. Susan had taken a trip to Albany, alone, on Sunday and had stayed overnight at a hotel. She returned last night.

Zeke Clemens was a patient of Warren's, a black man who had played minor league baseball with Jackie Robinson. He believed in alternative medicine and in Warren Levin, his doctor. He knew things hadn't been going well and Levin's license was tethered by a frail string that could be severed by a strong wind at any moment. He wanted to help. Zeke had called Levin's office and the message had been given to Susan by the staff. After speaking to Zeke for twenty minutes, she knew what she had to do and announced to Warren on Saturday evening, "I'm leaving for Albany in the morning. I'm going to book a hotel room."

"What in the world for?" he had asked her.

"I have a hunch that your patient, Zeke, is going to be a bigger help to our situation than you can imagine. I told him I'd meet him there by lunch time tomorrow."

Levin was puzzled, but he didn't have the energy to explore the situation any further with Susan. She had good instincts. He trusted her completely. She always had his welfare in mind, and her protective stance was a constant. He was sure he'd hear the whole story when she got back.

Zeke had been waiting for her in the hotel lobby when she arrived. She checked in, carried her overnight case to her room, and freshened up. "Okay, Miz Levin, let's go," Zeke said, opening the passenger door of his battered old Chevy. He had insisted that she leave her late model Lexus in the hotel's parking lot.

Susan climbed in. She hoped she was doing the right thing and wasn't wasting the two precious days before Warren's hearing in front of the Regents Review Committee for nothing. "Like I told you on the phone, Miz Levin," the tall, muscular, black man began, "I have a very strong connection with the black caucus. These people will listen to me and do what I ask of them. Just watch." he promised. "You'll see."

Susan laughed, remembering what came next. Zeke literally parked his car at the end of one block after another on the residential streets of Albany, in an area with tightly packed private homes. Then, he would take her on a walking tour up and down each street, ringing the doorbell or knocking instead when bare wires poked out of the doorbell's prior location. If no one responded, he'd simply place a flyer between the storm and main doors, explaining that he'd be back to visit the next day. He'd note the address on his pad. He had equipped himself well for this unusual journey. When a resident opened the door, he'd introduce Susan, because most of the people already knew who he was, although he had to remind some of the folks of his name. He'd tell them the lady's husband was a *wonderful* doctor, *his* doctor, who had kept him in top health for years and years. To the folks who invited them in for a longer chat over a cold drink or a cup of coffee, he would beg off and explain how sorry he was that they were so pressed for time in their mission. There was simply too much work to do. He'd ask them to sign the petition clipped to his board, so that this pretty lady's husband, such a real, fine doctor, wouldn't lose his license. He'd even ask them if they were willing to come down to New York City on Tuesday to be part of an unofficial "parade" to escort Dr. Levin to a special meeting, where a group of 'officials' would be trying to take away his license. Some of the town folks promised to write a letter that Zeke could come by and pick up the next day…and each and every one of them kept their promise, for which Susan was ever so grateful. All of the people they met with were informed that Tuesday, the twenty-ninth of June, was to be a critical day for Dr. Levin.

By the time she got back home to Connecticut on Monday evening, she had several garbage bags full of letters and separately signed petitions from hundreds and hundreds of brand-new supporters, many of whom had given their word to appear at the "parade" on Tuesday. She had told Warren the story over a late dinner last night, and he actually had tears in his eyes. He was especially touched that a patient like Zeke would care so much about him to take two full days working on his behalf, being so convincing that groups of Albany residents would be filling a Greyhound bus headed into Port Authority the following morning to parade on his behalf.

Susan finished getting dressed, the smile on her face winning out over the anxiety that she knew was below the surface. Dr. Rothman had encouraged her to keep positive thoughts in her head, regulate her breathing, and make the confident appearance that would carry her through the tribulations of the day.

Ever the showman, Levin had hosed off the wheelbarrow over the weekend and wiped it down so it looked shiny, red, and new, minus all of the sticky grass and dirt that usually coated it, inside and out. He had packed it into the trunk of the car. That was part of the plan.

They had gotten up a bit after dawn. It promised to be a hot day. Levin and Susan drove into Manhattan and parked very near the building where the Regents Review Committee would be hearing his case. Zeke and his crew had assembled on a street corner nearby, and the Levins had passed them as they drove into the parking garage. Zeke followed them in and took the wheelbarrow out of the trunk after hugging Levin warmly. They grabbed the bags full of petitions and letters and dumped them into the wheelbarrow. Levin's supporters had paid to have signs and banners printed up. Emerging from the parking garage, with Zeke pushing the overflowing wheelbarrow, they saw people everywhere holding up professionally printed signs: "SAVE DR. LEVIN'S MEDICAL LICENSE," and "DON'T TAKE DR. LEVIN'S LICENSE AWAY," and "DR. LEVIN IS A GREAT DOCTOR," and "THANK YOU FOR CURING ME, DR. LEVIN."

Little by little, others joined them, endless rows of medical doctors wearing white coats, as instructed to do during Harris's last appeal on Robert Atkins' radio program. Patients and other non-medical supporters outnumbered the physicians ten to one. With Zeke pushing the wheelbarrow down the sidewalk, since they didn't have a license to hold an official parade, Susan marched proudly beside her husband. He wore a well-tailored, navy blue suit, a white shirt with monogrammed cufflinks, a red silk tie, and brilliantly polished, black oxfords. She wore a fitted, red suit, the hem just skimming her knees, Black pumps, a white, silk blouse, and diamond earrings. They looked like they were heading for the Academy Awards, and the sidewalk was their "Red Carpet."

When the parade reached its destination, the supporters and sign-bearers were instructed to line the inner and outer edges of the sidewalk just outside the building's entrance, so no matter which side the members of the review panel approached from, they would be flanked by this enormous display of support for the accused doctor. The Levins, their lawyer, and a cadre of alternative physicians marched through the ranks and filed into the hearing room. Zeke and the wheelbarrow were positioned to bring up the rear. When he rolled the wheelbarrow into the hearing room, Zeke headed straight for the table, as Harris had instructed, where the five members of the Regents Review Committee were seated. The questioning looks on the faces of the five men were a sight to behold.

Harris walked over to the table. "Gentlemen," he said, with a huge smile on his face, "*behold*!" He pointed to the wheelbarrow and its contents as Sheehan observed the drama in disbelief, shaking his head, his mouth agape, as though poised to ask a question. As the men considered the contents of the overflowing wheelbarrow, Harris announced, "These are a *few*, and I emphasize the word 'few,' of the letters of support Dr. Levin has received from patients, colleagues, and a significant portion of the black caucus in our state's capital," he said, referring to Albany and indicating Zeke Clemmons with one of his signature dramatic gestures. "Would you like me to scoop out a pile for each of you to enjoy with your morning coffee?" he asked, noting the full cups in front of each of them, courtesy of the breakfast table in the corner of the room.

From the corner of his eye, Harris could see that Sheehan had finally closed his mouth, pressed his lips tightly together, and was shaking his head disgustedly. The Regents actually chuckled in amusement while, at the same time, holding out their palms to restrain Harris from following through on his invitation. His point made, Harris told Zeke to "park that wheelbarrow somewhere inside here where none of us will trip over it but in plain sight of these fine gentlemen." He smiled toward the Regents and leaned toward them, saying, "I just don't want you to forget that Warren Levin is loved and respected by so many people." Harris knew that, if he could have, Sheehan would have jumped up at that point and cried, "*Objection*! He's giving testimony again!"

As the proceedings began, Harris glanced at the sea of white coats in the visitors' section of the room, then insisted that each of the physicians present on Levin's behalf stand and announce themselves—name and specialty, for inscription into the record. Sheehan's protest was overruled. The process took an entire forty minutes, since names had to be spelled out for the court reporter.

Eventually, everyone was seated. One of the Regents addressed the group, mentioning that—although they had received the transcripts only two weeks ago—they had *each read every word* of the fifty-one hundred pages, as well as all of the articles and other materials submitted as exhibits. That gentleman turned to the defense lawyer and added, "We've also read your fifty-page summary and the contents of the attached exhibits, Mr. Harris, and we thank you for the succinct presentation." Harris nodded his acknowledgement, obviously pleased.

Sheehan spoke first, using the forty five minutes allotted to him in an efficient way, hoping to put a finish to the endless proceedings that had occupied his life for so many years and achieve the Health Department's objective of separating Warren Levin from his medical license. The spectators in the hearing room numbered over a hundred, unusual but allowable following the submission and acceptance of a special petition to open the hearing to select members of the public—some of Levin's key supporters. Since most of these people were hearing Sheehan's invective for the first time, the 'Greek Chorus' effect—that Sheehan had condemned during one of the sessions held before the Hearing Committee—was in full force. Sheehan would glance their way and give them dirty looks on each occasion, but in trying to stay within his time limit, he was unable to request silence and admonishment as he had done when Storch presided over the OPMC hearings. The crowd sensed his frustration. That only made some of the onlookers bolder.

There was one statement that Sheehan made, however, that proved immensely gratifying to both Levin and his wife, to Harris, and to the gathered supporters, most of whom were physicians practicing alternative medicine. Sheehan complained that Harris had "destroyed the credibility of Victor Herbert," which produced a unanimous and resounding cheer from those assembled and earned them a stern look from the Regents.

When Harris stood up to deliver his 'forty-five-minute summation,' which actually took a full hour, and his plea for Levin to retain his license and continue the good work he had been doing in his medical office for years, the only sounds in the room came from the physician's allies breathing in unison, murmuring supportively, and exhaling noisily while nodding vigorously in agreement with the defense attorney's statements and conclusions. Levin's cheering section earned themselves many an exasperated look from the state's prosecuting lawyer throughout Harris's appeal. Susan also noticed that Sheehan checked his watch periodically and tapped its face significantly, while directing a questioning look at the committee, whose spokesperson merely put up a palm, as if to say, "Don't worry, Mr. Sheehan, everything is just fine." Sheehan's color deepened as every additional group of five minutes passed, until Harris finally wound up his pitch for exoneration after a full sixty minutes. For Harris, who had prepared that fifty-page document for the Regents two weeks ago, every last fact of the past four years seemed to be engraved in the defense attorney's mind, so he spoke extemporaneously and fluidly, skipping nothing and recalling long-forgotten tidbits that would occasionally cause Sheehan's eyebrows to rise in surprise. The Regents asked questions, the attorneys responded, and the entire process—beginning to end—lasted two-and-a-half hours.

As the crowd filed out of the hearing room, one of the Regents caught hold of Bob Harris's sleeve. The man smiled—Harris thought significantly—and nodded his head. Nothing more. Not a word was exchanged. For some reason, that very gesture was what the defense attorney glommed onto, when he said to Levin, "I think it went very well, Warren. I expect us to win this round by a huge margin."

Levin was in a fairly good mood. He was so buoyed by the unprecedented show of support that it set the tone for him. Susan was thrilled at the turnout, as well, and was happy that her trip to Albany had added to the showing so significantly. She was quite pleased that the lawyer she had played such an important role in selecting had performed to her standards. As Bob had said in the very beginning, "Dr. Levin, the important thing is to save your license." Well, there was really nothing more to be done. The final steps had been taken. Warren's fate was now in the hands of a truly impartial party, the Regents Review Board, and no one was pulling *their* strings. While Susan had no idea what their final decision would be, it occurred to her that if this group had heard the case earlier, perhaps their odyssey of the past four years might have been condensed into a four-month ordeal. They wouldn't be in the terrible financial straits they were currently mired in, and she wouldn't be on anti-anxiety medication and in psychotherapy. Warren probably would have used all the time he had already wasted for the purpose of the fight enjoying his family and building wonderful memories, writing articles for publication, and taking an occasional day off just to have fun, something that seemed to have faded from their life as their woes continued unabated.

After expressing sincere thanks to their supporters, one by one, through a handshake, a hug, or a peck on the cheek, Levin and his wife headed to the parking garage with Zeke, who had packed all of the letters and petitions back into garbage bags that he put into the trunk of Levin's car, along with the wheelbarrow. They both embraced the short, friendly man, who had suggested that his fellow Albany residents enjoy the sights of the city for the morning. He had set up a meeting time and place in Times Square, so they could pick up a bite to eat before heading for Port Authority Bus Station to board their Greyhound Bus for the return trip home. Susan set out for Grand Central Station to catch a train home. Levin started walking to his office to see patients. Harris walked into the garage and gave his ticket to the attendant, who retrieved his car. He had an afternoon appointment with a client at his Long Island office. They waved at one another. There was a feeling of optimism that surrounded them that hot afternoon in June.

It was five weeks before they heard from the Regents, which seemed to attest to an efficiency that neither the OPMC nor the Health Department had ever displayed. The attorney for the Regents committee had sent a letter to both Harris and Sheehan requesting that a brief be prepared by each attorney, with five copies mailed to the office of the Regents, and an additional copy to the opposing attorney. The deadline for submission of the briefs was set for September thirtieth, allowing nearly two months. That letter contained guidelines for the briefs, in the form of fourteen, multi-part questions. Those questions were basically appeals for concrete evidence illustrating *standards* regulating a physician's conduct at the time the patients were actually treated by Levin, *evidence* as to why several of the defense witnesses were *not* found to be credible, whether the committee *relied* on Victor Herbert's testimony to find Levin guilty, and if the patients seeking help from Levin had been offered the proper information to truly *give* informed consent.

As soon as he received the letter, Harris wasted no time. He addressed each question and its sub-sections thoroughly, numbering and lettering every portion, in a document that ran fifty-one pages and referenced both the testimony and the exhibits, allowing the Regents to easily review his responses. Sheehan didn't find the exercise necessary or to his liking, so he simply sent the Regents a letter telling them that the answers to *all* of their questions could be found in the one-hundred-and-twenty-nine pages of the committee's report, a figure which also took into account the list of admitted exhibits. In fact, Sheehan had deliberately allowed the September thirtieth deadline to pass and submitted his letter to the Regents by express mail, dated October eighth. Contained in his letter was a section in which Sheehan actually *disparaged* Levin. Sheehan wrote: "It is not Petitioner's burden to prove Respondent knew there was no bona fide professional controversy regarding the fraudulent practices set forth in the statement of charges. Nevertheless, it is clear from the record that he *did* know that the cited practices were *bogus* and not the subject of legitimate scientific debate. One need only look at Respondent's

Chelation therapy consent form to see that he is a *deliberate* con artist." Sheehan called the Hearing Committee's report "one of the most thorough, scholarly reports I have seen during the many years I have worked in this field," and proceeded to refer the Regents to various pages of that report, or sometimes to the *entire* report itself, for answers to their questions. Harris heard this from the Regents' attorney who had written the letter requesting the briefs, and he was delighted by Sheehan's response. Now the Regents would *understand* the attitude of the state very clearly, just from this dismissive piece of action from the prosecutor. *It couldn't be better.* Harris rubbed his hands together gleefully.

Levin had kept the supporters of his Legal Offense Fund informed through a letter he had written several weeks ago, telling them that virtually *all* of the original charges against him had been sustained by the Hearing Committee and his license *revoked*. He even went so far as to admit that the panel concluded that he was *not* practicing up to the minimal standards in New York State, which—in actuality—had *no* published minimal standards. He didn't hesitate to let them know that he was found to be cynical, a consummate actor, glib, and "beyond all hope of rehabilitation." He wrote that he fully expected the Commissioner of Health to "rubberstamp the panel's recommendation," adding that, under the *present* guidelines, he would have had *no* recourse. However, since the hearings had begun over four years ago, his case fell under the *old* law, which charged the Board of Regents with reviewing the decision of both the panel *and* the Commissioner. Levin ended by asking for continuing support: written and financial.

Now that the Regents Review Committee was on the job, Levin wondered exactly what it would mean as far as getting his life back on task. Sure, this final hearing had *seemed* like a positive event, but there was no guarantee. Besides, his income was still down and his hours horribly long in an effort to make up for so much lost time and money. He was barely able to afford the salaries of his large staff, make his office lease payments, and stay current with his monthly office construction loan, keep up his mortgage, and provide for household expenses. Forget about vacations, entertaining, conferences, clothing, or luxuries. Things had not been this financially difficult since he originally went into practice as a family physician, building his reputation and charging low fees for office and home visits.

All he could do now was to sit and wait. Once the Regents rendered their decision, the next task would be to evaluate his circumstances. Thirteen years of his life had been spent living under the black cloud of despair, the last four of which had been pure hell. *It can't possibly get any worse,* he thought, *or can it? I've begun to think that if I didn't have bad luck, I wouldn't have any luck at all!*

CHAPTER 39

Another summer was gone, fall had passed, winter began, and Levin and Susan had snuggled on the couch with Erika to watch television on New Year's Eve, giving their young daughter permission to remain awake for the very first time, so that she could see the ball drop in Times Square and usher in the year 1994. Erika had tried hard but hadn't quite made it to midnight. After her father had tucked his sweet little seven-year-old into bed, he had poured a champagne toast for himself and Susan as the countdown to the New Year began. He had looked long and hard into her eyes and said, "Susan, I feel it in my bones. This is *finally* going to be our year. Things are going to be resolved once and for all. I just know it."

Sipping her champagne, she recalled smiling and nodding, wondering if he really believed what he was saying. She hadn't trusted herself to respond, in case her words weren't the right ones for the moment at hand. Susan knew that they both had the same hopes and dreams for the future, and they were very simple by the day's standards. The holiday sentiment of "Peace on Earth, Good Will to Men," suited them just fine. They had really not experienced a whole lot of peace over the past years, thanks to the Office of Professional Medical Conduct and the Commissioner of Health. She said a silent prayer that the Regents had the wisdom she had granted them in her mind to make a decision consistent with justice and the American way, which would allow her husband to enjoy his career and return wholeheartedly to his personal life once again.

She was thinking of that as she sat in the accounting office at Warren's practice and looked over their financial records. They had already filed their corporate taxes for 1993 last month, and they had just made the April fifteenth deadline with their personal returns last Friday, as Susan had rushed to the post office to get the envelope postmarked before the clerks left their stations for the day. Their finances were an absolute mess, both personal and corporate. They were barely surviving, just managing the necessities.

She was jerked from her reverie when Warren burst in, a look of excitement on his face.

"What is it?" she asked, her mind rapidly scrolling through endless possibilities, including a good word from the Regents, to something positive from the DOH or the OPMC, to an unexpected influx of cash from some unknown source.

"I wrote them a letter!" he announced.

"Who? What?" she asked, thinking, *Oh, God, I hope it's not another appeal letter to the supporters and contributors.*

"Let me read it to you and get your feedback," he responded, settling into the chair across her desk and shoving the door closed with his foot. "It's addressed to Victor Herbert and Michael Victor Herman," he told her.

"Victor Herbert? Michael Victor Herman?" She ran her fingers through her hair agitatedly. "Warren, what for? Let it rest already. It's driving me nuts! What in the world do you have to say to these men? What?" she demanded.

He blinked at her in surprise. "Susan, I thought you were with me in all of this." He was genuinely puzzled.

"With you? *Of course*, I'm with you. I've been going through all of this *with* you for years and years, haven't I? We haven't even heard from the Regents yet, and it's been so long since you've even *seen* these two guys. What could you possibly be so excited about? What kind of letter have you written to them? I just don't understand you sometimes. I really don't." Her speech had accelerated at an alarming pace, along with her level of agitation. She looked exasperated, he noted.

His shoulders rose, as he took a deep breath, and slowly fell as he expelled the air. Still looking at her, he began to gather up the handwritten pages he had laid on her desk. As he started to rise from the chair, she said, "Warren, where are you going now?"

He shrugged. "Back into my office, I guess."

"Why?"

"Why? Because it's obvious that you're not interested in hearing what I wrote."

He looked so sad and dejected, she couldn't stand it. "Oh, for goodness' sake, just sit down. Sit!" she ordered, when he hesitated. "Of course I'll listen to your latest masterpiece. Lay it on me," she said, with exaggerated humor.

Still uncertain, he sank back into the chair, cleared his throat and started to read. "'Drs. Herbert and Herman,'" he began, adding, "by the way, I'm sending this by Certified Mail." 'My long-awaited decision from the Board of Regents is imminent. There are, however, a few weeks left before all of us know the results. I believe it is going to be embarrassing for both of you, to say the least. I am writing this letter to offer each of you a last opportunity to clear the record and avoid the public humiliation that I believe you both deserve on the basis of your sworn testimony."

"Warren," Susan interrupted, "you're writing as though you're sure that the Regents are going to decide in your favor."

"Yes, I *am* writing that way," he responded.

Softening her voice, she said, "I want that as much as you do, but what if that's not the case?" She looked at him pleadingly.

"I'm not even *going* there, Susan," he said, closing the topic. He started reading again. "'Dr. Herbert, you will recall that the gist of Dr. Linus Pauling's testimony about you was that you are *not* a scientist, one reason being that you *refuse* to look at evidence. I am enclosing copies of your sworn testimony in which you indicate that a *single* before-and-after arteriogram study would be *probative*. I enclose herewith copies of such a published study. In addition, to update you both on the chelation literature, I am enclosing a copy of a published meta-analysis reviewing a study on over twenty-two thousand patients, showing *dramatic* positive results by objective findings, and a Danish study showing the remarkable results of Chelation therapy in a cohort of patients given that treatment while waiting for the availability of operating facilities and/or a surgeon for a scheduled coronary artery bypass graft. Only *ten* of ninety-two such patients went for surgery! There were *no* severe side effects or casualties.'"

Susan looked at him in surprise. "Really?" she asked.

"That's right!" he said, triumphantly. "And I want these clowns to know about it. Let me continue. So I wrote, 'It is not too late to send a letter to the Office of

Professional Medical Conduct and to the Board of Regents acknowledging that newer information has been brought to your attention that is sufficiently compelling to warrant some modification of your testimony. Needless to say, I would appreciate receiving a copy of any communication prompted by this letter and its enclosures. Sincerely…'" He looked up at her. "So, what do you think?"

"I think that it sounds just fine. I guess if the Regents were to hear from them, even if they were not considering a favorable verdict for you, letters from either or both of these people—your detractors, who served as the state's witnesses against you—might sway them in your favor. On the other hand, if they *don't* write to the OPMC or the Regents and the decision is a positive one for you, they are going to feel pretty foolish for not swallowing their pride and doing the right thing. Good job, Warren," she conceded.

"Thanks," he said, with a smile, his good humor restored. "I'm just going to get this typed up on my letterhead." He stepped behind the desk and gave her a quick kiss of appreciation before leaving the room.

Three days later, Victor Herbert responded, via a faxed letter to Levin's office. Susan read it the minute it came through, since her husband was in the examining room with a patient. The minute Levin looked at his wife, the color drained from her face, he rushed her into his private office and sat her down. He thought she might be having a panic attack. Then he took the pages she was shoving at him out of her hands.

"Dear Dr. Levin," he read, "I have just received and read your letter dated April nineteenth, and the three articles you enclosed. After reading this material, I telephoned Mr. Sheehan, attorney for the state in the matter of your professional conduct proceedings. I asked Mr. Sheehan what your letter was all about. He told me he would phone your attorney and call me back. He did so. Mr. Sheehan told me that your attorney stated that, despite your letter's implication that you have *advance knowledge* of the decision from the Board of Regents in your matter, you *do not* have such information. Your attorney further told Mr. Sheehan that you did *not* intend to submit the three papers you sent me to the Board of Regents, since such submission would be *totally improper* at this late stage in the proceedings."

Levin blew out a breath. "What is he *talking* about? *Advance knowledge* of the decision? I *never* said I had advance knowledge. That's just the way this jerk twists people's words around." He shook his head and blew out another breath. Susan just sat there, staring at nothing. Levin took up the faxed form again and began reading. "'It is just as well you do not submit those three papers, because they are *scientific garbage*. The first two papers, which you represent as "dramatic positive results by objective findings" show no such thing. The studies are worthless. There is no placebo control, and therefore no way of knowing whether the results are better than those obtained by a placebo. I suggest to you that if those two worthless chelation studies you sent me had been placebo-controlled, they would have shown that the patients who got Chelation therapy did *worse* than those who got a placebo,' he writes. 'Your allegation is pure nonsense that the third study shows widening of narrowed coronary arteries by Chelation therapy. That study is worthless. The arteriograms are *not* before and after a few-week course of Chelation therapy. They are *two years apart*.'"

Levin shook his head in consternation. "'Your letter with its enclosures demonstrates your inability to competently evaluate published data relevant to patient care. A person with such arrogance and ignorance should *not* practice medicine. The arrogance deceives patients that you know what you are talking about, to your patients' health (and financial) detriment.'"

Levin sat down across from Susan and matched her unfocused stare for a moment. "Oh, man," he finally said, "I can't believe this guy is for real. What an absolute idiot!"

Susan finally stirred. "Maybe so," she agreed, "but he really knocked the stuffing out of me with his response."

"Why?" he asked her, ignoring his own original reaction. "This is pure, unadulterated Victor Herbert. Nothing more, nothing less. He is an egotistical jerk who thinks he has all the answers and that nobody else is fit to practice medicine except him."

"Whatever," she responded, noncommittally.

Levin asked his secretary to fax the letter to Bob Harris. At least he could share a little Victor Herbert bashing with his attorney once the document went through.

Levin was too busy at work and at home to waste his time contemplating Victor Herbert's ridiculousness, but the man kept popping up, invited or not. Two months passed since he had received Herbert's communiqué when a friend faxed over a letter he had obtained through channels. It had been sent by Victor Herbert to the Superintendent of the Ellis Island National Monument. Levin read the letter and was totally shocked by its contents. *Once more*, he thought, *this is pure Victor Herbert*. He saw that Herbert, whom he had come to think of as a 'pseudo-scientist' had visited Ellis Island with his family and had seen a scholarly book on alternative medicine in one of the exhibits, and realized that it was also being sold in the bookstore there. His letter lambasted the book and those responsible for allowing it to be viewed by visitors to Ellis Island. He charged fraud and quackery, used words like "questionable," "worthless," and "harmful," since the book was a compendium of alternative medical treatments. He ended his letter by stating the following: "To stop deceiving the American public, please remove this display and issue a press release stating that it has *been* removed, *why* it was removed, and *how* it got put up in the first place."

By August, the book was pulled from the Ellis Island exhibit. The *New York Times* article that reported the results of Herbert's letter was not particularly flattering to Herbert, Harris noted, with satisfaction. He and Levin shared a good laugh at a comment made by a law professor at Harvard regarding Herbert: "I hope he's a better doctor than he is a lawyer." Herbert had not won that round completely, Harris and Levin acknowledged.

Then something had occurred in early July that had Levin jumping for joy. The Assembly and the Senate had passed, in a nearly unanimous vote, the "Alternative Medical Practice Act," a piece of legislation that had been developed and promoted by FAIM, the Foundation for the Advancement of Innovative Medicine, for the past five years. The bill's purpose was to allow patients, through informed consent and under the guidance of a licensed physician, to choose the type of medical care they wished to have. Freedom of choice in the use of alternative therapies was finally approved by law. Besides dedicated lobbyists and political support, the passage was spurred on during hearings by the New York State Assembly Higher Education and Health Committees, where numerous physicians and patients testified on the positive impact of non-traditional medicine. The bill had been rewritten and revised over the two years preceding its approval. The Department of Health, the same organization that had so actively been pursuing and prosecuting Warren Levin for fourteen years, signed the bill on June 27, 1994. Important to Levin and his colleagues were provisions for alternative physicians to be *included* on the OPMC panels for disciplinary hearings.

For the next three weeks, the alternative physicians held their breath then exhaled as a group all over the state of New York on July 26, 1994, when Governor Mario Cuomo signed the bill into law. Levin wondered how this new legislation, coming when it did, might influence the decision of the Regents Review Committee as they deliberated on his case.

With this good news forming the backdrop for the upcoming Regents' decision, Levin and Susan made a decision. The day they received the "envelope"—and they knew it would probably be a big, fat, manila envelope—they would read the document from beginning to end, after dinner, at their home, together with Bob Harris. Susan would call the lawyer to ask him if he would make himself available for this "event," as she referred to it. She hadn't had very much contact with the defense attorney over the years, except for the few hearings she had been present at, but she picked up the phone and issued a verbal invitation after she and Warren had made their decision. No matter what the end result would be, Harris had done his level best over the years and had not taken the typical lawyer's route of charging money for every moment of his time. In fact, he had given of his time so generously and charged so reasonably—and only then for a portion of time spent—that he used to joke with Sandi that he was only getting "pennies per hour from the Levin case." Susan appreciated that. He was trying to help Warren keep his license and had developed some wild and crafty schemes in his perusal of justice for her husband. It was only right for all of them to be together, in a comfortable setting, following a good meal she would cook, served on their best china, eaten with their formal silverware, with a glass of fine wine served in crystal wineglasses, when they finally opened the envelope announcing Warren's fate. It would be comforting for the three of them to be together that evening.

The only problem was that she was planning this wonderful dinner party but couldn't set the date. New York State—which had dictated so much of how their lives were lived over the past fourteen years—would now be informing them when they were allowed to have their special dinner! *How absurd*, she thought. Susan, who always liked to plan ahead, knew that her evening would have to be planned at a moment's notice…at the whim of the state.

CHAPTER 40

The Regents completed their written report on Friday, September 2, 1994, had multiple copies made and brought to the main post office in Albany to be sent out to Levin, Harris, Sheehan, Storch, and each member of the Hearing Committee before the start of the holiday weekend. While the thick envelopes were being weighed and stamped for delivery, the Levins were at the airport about to board their flight to Florida to spend the Labor Day weekend with Susan's parents. Rosh Hashanah began after sundown on Sunday night, so this would be a double holiday for the family, and well-deserved. Erika, who would enter third grade, wasn't due to start school until Wednesday, so it seemed like an ideal time to get away. Harris was already on a plane to California, planning to spend his double holiday with a beloved aunt in Pacific Palisades.

By the time the Levins arrived home on Tuesday and Susan had prepared a bath for Erika and laid her clothes out for the first day of school, it was nearly eight in the evening. Erika was fast asleep within minutes, and her father had only read her four pages from *James and the Giant Peach*, the book that was currently reserved for bedtime only. With the warmth of summer evenings fading rapidly in Connecticut, Levin and Susan grabbed the Afghans off the couches and wrapped themselves cozily to sit outside on the deck and consider their options. They talked about their life together, and realized that most of it had been scarred by the omnipresence of the OPMC. They laughed, wondering if they could ever exist without the constant harassment.

"I could sit out here all night, I think," Levin said. "It's just so beautiful, with a slight chill in the air, and I'm wrapped up like a baby in a blanket."

She tilted her head up. "Look at the stars, Warren."

He looked up. "Should we do something hokey like wish upon a star, you think?"

"What would you wish for?"

He laughed. "You go first."

She laughed too. "Not fame. Fortune? Maybe enough to get out of debt and be comfortable again, but no big fortune. I guess I'd want what we wished for on New Year's Eve: peace. Our lives have been wracked with stress. It's this whole OPMC thing that's killing us." Her face, in the moonlight, took on a look of determination. She folded her hands in a prayerful stance and looked at the array of stars. "I wish," she said, "that the Regents report is a wonderful, uplifting one that blasts the dumb committee's horrible document into oblivion and recognizes you for the devoted, caring physician that your patients and colleagues…and your wife," she added, glancing over at him, "all know you are." She nodded her head with satisfaction. "Your turn."

"First of all, thank you for your unwavering faith and belief in me throughout this entire horrible episode that seems to be following us as a constant companion throughout our marriage." He looked up. "I wish, little star, that you can give my Susan the peace and tranquility that she deserves and, yes, I wish that the Regents Review Committee declares me innocent or exonerates me or whatever it is that they do when a person hasn't done all of the terrible things I'm being accused of doing. I wish that they grant me the right to keep the medical license I worked so hard to get and which means so much to me, so that I can continue to help the patients who believe in my work and often refer others to me for help."

They sat outside, in companionable silence, breathing the fresh air of late summer in New England, warm in their blankets, before finally getting up and going inside for the night. Levin had to be in his office bright and early; a full schedule of patients awaited his attention. Susan would be sending Erika off for the day, a loving note tucked into the nutritious lunch she'd prepare for her daughter's lunchbox in the morning.

Levin's alarm jerked him out of a sound sleep. He had been reading the Regents report in his dream, but the alarm woke him before he got to their final decision at the end. He contemplated laying down again to finish the dream but thought better of it when the smell of fresh coffee wafted into the room as Susan walked in to get something.

After he left the house, Susan stood in the driveway where Erika was dressed in dark blue pants, a white and blue striped shirt, clean white sneakers and a warm sweater. Her hair was in two ponytails, and she was wearing her new backpack that was stuffed with fresh pencils and a notebook and carrying her lunchbox. The little girl was excited to see her friends on the bus and find out who was in her class this year. She had a male teacher for the very first time and was a bit doubtful about whether she would like him or not. Susan was wearing clothing that matched Erika's, color for color, by coincidence, topped by the cardigan her mom had made for her so many years ago. Susan never admitted that she had never worn the sweater in college. It looked homemade and was hardly stylish. But it was great for a chilly morning like today, when the only adult who would see her was Erika's school bus driver.

She ran back into the house after waving until the bus was out of sight and changed into workout clothes for the gym. Susan made a point of eating healthy food and exercising to stay in shape. As she was about to leave the house, after a brief delay for a cup of green tea and a rapid look at the morning paper, the phone rang.

"It came," was all Warren said, and Susan immediately understood.

"The envelope from the Regents?" she asked, just to be sure.

"It's really heavy," was his answer. "Dinner at our house tonight?"

"I'll call Bob. How about seven-thirty?"

"Okay by me," he responded. "Remind Bob not to open the envelope. Unless I hear back from you, I'll assume everything's a go for tonight."

"Fine," she responded, with a slight tremor in her voice. She rushed into her bedroom to change into appropriate clothing for food shopping. As she grabbed her pocketbook and prepared to leave the house with her grocery list, the phone rang again.

"Warren?" she asked, thinking he was calling her back.

"Sorry," a man's voice said, "this *isn't* Warren. It's Warren's defense attorney."

"Bob?"

"One and the same. I called to let you know that I just received the envelope from…"

"The Regents," she said, completing his sentence. "I know. Warren just called me. I was about to call you," she lied, realizing that, in her excitement, she had planned her menu and was going out to get groceries without contacting her intended guest. "Please tell me you're free to come to our home for dinner tonight," she pleaded.

"I'm free to come to your home for dinner tonight," he parroted.

"Wonderful!" she said, and really meant it. "I expect that Erika will be in bed so that we can sit down, uninterrupted, at about seven-thirty. Does that work for you?"

"It works just beautifully," he responded. "Red wine or white wine?"

She was planning on Porterhouse steaks for dinner, which would be a real treat for her and Warren, as they had cut way back on the expensive cuts because of their shrinking nest egg. "Red would be perfect," she said, "thank you."

"You're welcome."

"Oh, and Bob, Warren said to be sure to remind you *not* to open the envelope. And please remember to bring your copy with you. Warren is bringing his."

"It will take every fiber of my being to hold myself back from tearing into this brown package with my teeth, so I can devour every single word the Regents wrote."

"Bob, remember, we planned…"

"Susan, don't worry. I have a *lot* of self-control. You'd be surprised. The envelope will be untouched, in pristine condition when I get there. I promise. See ya!" he said, and hung up.

Susan hated to be hung up on. She put the receiver back on the hook thinking, *self-control, my foot.* She silently vowed to murder him if she noticed that his envelope had been tampered with when he got to the house in the evening.

She returned home with more grocery bags than she could manage to bring in at once. Even with a list, she had added a lot of extras, she realized. *Well, it's my first dinner party in a long time—that is, if I can* call *it a 'dinner party'—and I want it to be a good one.* She put the three Porterhouse steaks into the marinade and put the lid on the glass dish before refrigerating it. She prepared the green bean casserole, so it simply needed to be reheated. Then Susan put together a salad with field greens, baby arugula, tomatoes, seedless cucumbers, and thin slices of radishes. She spread an attractive, cream-colored lace cloth on top of the dark green tablecloth on the large dining room table and put out the Lenox and Waterford, along with her good silver. She stepped back. The table looked good.

The doorbell chimed and she checked her watch. It was a bit early for Erika to be home. She noticed the florist's delivery truck in the driveway and opened the door. Bob had sent a lovely floral centerpiece. She smiled with pleasure. Susan loved fresh flowers and enjoyed gardening. She simply hadn't considered taking the time to run outside and create a bouquet from her own garden.

She checked her watch and hurried down the driveway to meet the school bus. Susan sat with Erika, as her little daughter enjoyed an after-school snack of fruit and milk. Erika had returned home very happy, saying that having a male teacher was suddenly "the coolest thing ever, Mom," and "all my good friends are in my class," and "Michelle's family moved away over the summer," and "I need a few more school supplies for tomorrow." They took a ride down to the Korvette's shopping center and bought everything Erika had on her list and more. After homework and a shower, Erika put on her pajamas, watched one television program, as permitted, and willingly let Susan read her the next chapter of *James and the Giant Peach* at a somewhat earlier than usual hour. Erika had brought home a book from the school library and wanted to keep her reading light on for awhile before she slept, which was fine with Susan.

At twenty minutes after seven, Susan opened the front door so neither Warren nor Bob would ring the bell when they arrived. They came in within minutes of each other, and Warren went to his office in the back of the house to drop off his briefcase and wash his face. He came back into the living room and dropped his thick, manila envelope on the entry table on top of Bob's, which Susan had secretly inspected for evidence of tampering, as she greeted her guest and thanked him for the flowers and wine.

Amid endless compliments over the delicious dinner, the table was quickly cleared and the dishes piled into the sink for Susan to handle in the morning, as she didn't want her fine china and crystal knocking around in the automatic dishwasher.

They brought their wine glasses into the living room. The Levins sat on the couch under the front window, since they were sharing the contents of one envelope, and Harris took the couch to their right.

After they agreed on the "rules" they had earlier established, where they would take turns reading aloud, pausing where necessary to discuss a point or ask a question, promising that the other two would follow the designated reader silently, it was time for them to open their envelopes. They extracted the sixty-nine page document, and as Harris playfully pretended to flip through it to the pages near the end, Susan and her husband lunged toward him in alarm, drawing back when they realized he was only joking. They decided that Levin should be given the honor of commencing with the reading.

He cleared his throat and began. "'In the Matter of the Disciplinary Proceeding against Warren M. Levin, who is currently licensed to practice as a physician in the State of New York.' *Currently*?" he asked. "What's *that* supposed to mean? That by the end of the report it will no longer be the case?" He was only half joking, Harris realized.

"Warren, don't get hung up on the terminology. That's standard."

"You sure?"

"Warren, this is *hardly* my first time through this."

"Well, it's *my* first time with the Regents, so I just…"

"Keep reading, or we'll be here all night, and I've still got to drive home," Harris complained. "Tomorrow's a working day."

"Well, yeah," Levin agreed. He was heading into his office in the morning, as well. "'Report of the Regents Review Committee,'" he read, reviewing the fact that he was the Respondent in the case. "'In this disciplinary proceeding, Respondent has been charged with thirty-three specifications of professional misconduct.'" They annexed the June 20, 1989 statement of charges, which Levin could recall responding to on the train over five years ago with a letter to Sheehan, who initially wasn't allowing an opportunity for Levin to select counsel or prepare a proper defense. He imagined that the others were thinking the same thing, as well.

They threw in the alleged dates of misconduct and the subpoenaed records sought on specific patients. "'A hearing was held on September 27, 1989 and November

13, 1989 before a Hearing Committee of the State Board for Professional Medical Conduct. At these two hearing sessions, Petitioner offered its sole witness, Dr. Victor Herbert, as an expert.'" There was a group groan at the mention of Herbert's name. The entire fiasco over the refusal of Victor Herbert to answer the question of whether or not he was the complainant in the case and his resulting ejection from the hearing room was reviewed in the report. They quoted the phrases Harris used when objecting to the behaviors exhibited by both Herbert and Sheehan at that point, highlighting "chaos," an "affront to the system," not a "lawful process," "contemptuous" and the judge's complaint that Herbert's reluctance to respond made "a mockery of these proceedings."

Levin read that, "'The Hearing Committee issued a report dated November 30, 1989 recommending that the charges against Respondent be *dismissed* in view of the absence of evidence in support of the allegations and that the Commissioner of Health *review* the judge's rulings and decide whether to remand the matter for further proceedings.' Yeah, yeah, we know all that," Levin said, impatiently.

"They've got to go through everything thoroughly, Warren," Harris told him.

So Levin read through the Commissioner's order to reverse the judge's ruling and remand the case back to the hearing room for the completion of the taking of testimony on February 7, 1990. "'The hearing resumed on May 14, 1990, and a total of twenty-eight hearing sessions were held *after* the remand by the Commissioner of Health.'"

"Were there really that many?" Somehow, Susan hadn't recalled that there were twenty-eight more sessions after the initial five.

"To *me*, it felt like hundreds and hundreds of days, dear," he responded. He continued reading, stopping only to say, "I'm boring myself."

"Well, the Regents are very thorough, and they had to review *tons* of stuff, Warren," Harris told him. "That's why they reiterate the charges, how the committee handled them, which were subsequently amended or dropped, and so forth."

"Okay, I'll keep on boring myself and everyone else." He continued to read in a monotone until he got to a paragraph requiring more gravity. "Based on its conclusions, the Hearing Committee recommended that Respondent's license and registration to practice medicine in New York State be *revoked*," he read. "The

Commissioner of Health recommended to the Board of Regents that the findings, conclusions, and recommendation of the Hearing Committee be *accepted*."

He sighed deeply. "I could use some water," he said. "My throat's parched. It's probably from reading this garbage."

Susan called a time-out, made sure both copies of the report were placed on the coffee table before she left the room, and came back with a crystal pitcher filled with water, ice cubes, and thin slices of lemon. She brought three goblets and took away the wine glasses, so they could use the same ceramic coasters as before.

"My turn," she said, picking up their joint copy. "Because the massive record compiled in this matter raises a multitude of issues, we requested that both parties submit, in advance of oral argument, a short statement previewing the issues in dispute before us."

Harris laughed. "Yeah, I sent them a one-pager, to make sure I was in compliance. I had already slipped them a fifty-page 'synopsis' with ten attachments that gave them a *real* preview into the case." He laughed, remembering the typed report his secretary had finally given him at midnight. "Sorry, Susan, go ahead."

"Also, due to the voluminous amount of testimony and exhibits and the "complex" nature of the issues presented, respondent's attorney sought an *extension* of his time for oral argument," she read.

"Oh, yeah!" Harris interrupted, once again. "Their great gift of another five minutes, that is until the Assembly and Senate convinced them otherwise," he joked. They laughed remembering his story of the hard candy bribes that, surprisingly, worked in their favor.

When Susan read the section about the lawyer, Michael Kennedy, who requested permission to submit the "Brief of *Amici Curiae*" he had developed, they were astonished to discover that a total of four-thousand, three-hundred and seventy-five laypersons and medical doctors "who asserted a right to receive and deliver alternative medicine" were behind it.

"I really had *no idea*," Levin mused. "Wow."

"Okay, guys, I'm reading now," Harris stated, without preamble, since they had reached the date of the appearance before the review committee. "'On June 29, 1993, upon Respondent's request and waiver of confidentiality, members of the public attended our meeting. During the two-and-one-half hour oral argument in this matter, we asked questions and listened to the presentations of both parties. Subsequent to our meeting, the parties were requested to answer fourteen enumerated questions. Although we asked the parties to *explain* their answers and cite the *specific evidence* they relied upon as support for their answers, Petitioner's answer to the first question directed us to pages twelve through one-hundred and seventy-three of the Hearing Committee report; its answer to questions three and four directed us to page six of the report; and for questions ten through thirteen, we were directed to the entire Hearing Committee report.'"

They erupted into a round of raucous laughter at that point, remembering how Harris's lengthy written response to the fourteen questions posed carefully addressed *every* question asked and cited pertinent references. Harris knew the nature of these review committees and what he needed to do in order for his defense tactics to be taken seriously. Sheehan had acted in a supercilious and blasé manner, which was probably unhelpful for the prosecution's side of the case. *So much the better,* Harris thought.

Susan jerked her head toward Harris, inviting him to continue reading. "'We have considered the record in this matter as transferred to us by letters, including all briefs, statements, and answers submitted by both parties before and after our meeting.' Good!" he said, "I'm glad, especially since I've given you folks some extras that invite looking into." His remark was addressed to the invisible presence of the Regents. "'Petitioner's written recommendation as to the measure of discipline to be imposed, should Respondent be found guilty, was to *revoke respondent's license to practice medicine*,'" he intoned, then added, "and, of course, we asked for the opposite."

"Read it, Bob," Levin requested.

"I wouldn't dream of *not* reading it. '*Respondent's* written recommendation was *reversal* of the Health Commissioner's decision. In his brief, Respondent sought the *dismissal* of the charges *with prejudice*.'"

Levin snorted. "Yeah, the prejudice introduced by the state's very own star, Victor Herbert."

As the lawyer read, they all learned that deliberations had *twice* been adjourned, due to the illness of one of the committee members, and were finally held and completed on February 22, 1994. "Okay, now we're getting into some interesting stuff," Harris told them. "'Before we review the merits of the Hearing Committee's recommendation, we shall examine the manner in which the record was compiled and the hearing was conducted.' See, I told you these guys took this business seriously," he told the couple. "They're actually starting with Herbert's refusal to answer the question I put to him, so I could find out if he was acting as both judge and jury. 'Respondent has the *right* to cross-examine the witnesses against him. In our unanimous opinion, Respondent was *denied* the right to cross-examine when he was precluded from inquiring of Dr. Victor Herbert whether *he* was the person who had filed a complaint against him. Respondent was prejudiced when he was *not* permitted to attempt to show that Dr. Herbert's *supposed expert opinions* were inaccurate and unworthy of belief because Dr. Herbert had an interest in the outcome of the proceeding, a personal agenda, and a bias against respondent.' How do you like it so far, Warren?"

"Interesting," was all the doctor was about to say at the moment.

"Fine. 'The courts and the Regents have consistently held that Petitioner *may not prevent* appropriate cross-examination of its witness about *relevant* prior statements, *including complaints,* when the credibility of that witness is in issue.' I'd like to call your attention to the fact that the Regents are supporting this with prior cases." The others nodded. They also wrote critically of Sheehan's role in directing the witness, and Harris was glad to see that. "'Consequently, the record in this matter is *not complete* and Respondent has *not received a fair hearing*. We agree with Respondent that, on this issue alone, Respondent has been *denied* due process.'" They cheered.

"Oh, I like the title of this next section: Prejudicial Record. Yes! 'During the hearing, Respondent moved for a mistrial on the ground that Dr. Herbert's conduct as a witness created a prejudicial atmosphere against him and made it *impossible* for Respondent to obtain a fair hearing on the merits of the charges. The record, as hereafter summarized, is replete with continuous *inappropriate* and *unacceptable* behavior which affected the consideration given to the issues in dispute. In our unanimous opinion, Respondent was prejudiced by the record which was developed in this hearing and, therefore, a new hearing should also be granted on this ground.'"

"*A new hearing?* They've got to be kidding. A new hearing? After all these years? After fourteen years of nonsense?" Levin was rapidly becoming furious. "Can they do this, Bob? Can they?"

"Warren, take it easy. We haven't gotten to the end of this thing yet. We're barely a third of the way through. Let's see where this is going. Okay?" Harris was being very gentle with his client, whom he had come to view as a friend over the years. He didn't want to see him unnecessarily upset.

"Yeah, sure," Levin said, grudgingly, sinking deeper into the cushions. "Go on."

Harris looked at him a moment longer, then picked up his packet. "'Dr. Victor Herbert frequently, and in different hearing sessions, called respondent's attorney a 'liar.' Whoa, they actually list twenty different pages where Herbert did that. Boy, were they thorough," Harris said, admiringly. "'Respondent's attorney was also called by Dr. Herbert a 'son of a bitch,' 'scumbag,' 'obnoxious,' 'vicious,' and 'offensive.'" The thought of the reviewers reading the huge piles of transcripts filled with testimony, yet taking the time to note the particular pages where Victor Herbert had hurled a specific insult at Bob Harris, made them all start laughing. Soon, they were wiping their eyes, as the tears ran down their cheeks. Susan, her mascara already forming dark streaks down her face, made them put down the reports while she rushed to the supply closet for a box of tissues, stopping at the bathroom to repair her makeup. She hurried back to them, shushing them, for fear that they would awaken Erika. Levin's mood had brightened considerably, and Harris playfully remarked, "I'm glad you're enjoying yourself at my expense, Warren!" That comment only provoked more raucous laughter.

"Okay, guys, I'm back on the record. 'To no avail, Respondent's attorney sought, during the hearing, adequate protection from such name-calling and from Dr. Herbert acting as both prosecutor and witness.'"

Levin started laughing again. "Sought protection? I love it. It's like Herbert was this monstrous guy, a convicted murderer, and you needed bodyguards to keep him away from you. Actually, he's nothing but a little snake," he spat, disdainfully.

Harris sniffed. "A poisonous snake," he amended. The others nodded their agreement. The report went on to enumerate Herbert's other lapses in proper decorum, the constant value-laden labels he hurled at Levin and his fellow practitioners, calling them "quacks" and "frauds." He criticized Levin's submission of documentary evidence as "quack literature" from the "quackery press." Harris read that, "'Respondent contends that these inflammatory remarks and inappropriate outbursts and characterizations created an emotional atmosphere in which Respondent would be judged by innuendo and improper considerations designed to influence the determination. Respondent also contends that before he could present any defense, he was placed in the 'insurmountable' position of having to overcome both this prejudicial portrayal of his practices and the 'poisoned atmosphere' and tone which had been set for the hearing.'" Here, Harris took a moment to comment to his client. "Remember, Warren, when my behavior seemed 'over the top,' as you occasionally put it, and I told you that I wanted these things put into the record for future reviewers? Well, this is *exactly* what I was talking about. Sheehan would object, calling it testimony on my part, but I would forge through, and this is why. These guys are paying attention to what I said, even if the others didn't."

Levin nodded thoughtfully. He remembered the times he wished he could either disappear altogether or crawl into a hole to hide when Harris's behavior became so questionable, it actually rivaled Victor Herbert's. Now, he could see the wisdom of his attorney's machinations. Susan was thinking similar thoughts, since she had followed most of the proceedings from afar, through her husband's tales of the hearing room.

"Listen to this. It's interesting that the Regents are laying it all on Herbert. 'We cannot say that the Hearing Committee's decision in this matter was not influenced by, or the product of, Dr. Victor Herbert's conduct at the hearing.'" Another big cheer erupted. "Okay, Warren, take over," Harris said.

Levin cleared his throat noisily. "'According to the Hearing Committee chairperson and Administrative Officer, this course of conduct by the parties, 'dramatically' interfered with the record developed herein and created an 'unintelligible' record for this matter to be reviewed.' Ha!"

"What's the 'ha!' Warren?" asked Susan.

"Just 'ha!' plain and simple. Anyway, 'During the hearing the Administrative Officer indicated that there had been a lot of acrimony, inflammatory language, character assassination, and name calling. Victor Herbert was instructed to *cease* characterizing and editorializing about Respondent or about the type of medicine he practiced. He was also directed to cease using 'harangues,' 'innuendos,' 'colloquy,' and 'outbursts.' He was further instructed to desist using 'inflammatory' language and to discontinue volunteering evidence. These instructions and directions, however, were *repeatedly violated and disregarded* by Dr. Herbert.'" The group had consistently broken out into fits of laughter throughout the sentences read by Levin, since the men could recall most of Herbert's antics when those terms had been used and the admonishments that followed. For Susan, who had met the man only once and had heard all of the unflattering stories about him ever since, it was still very amusing. The Regents also severely criticized Storch for not controlling the witness's behavior and not "protecting" Harris.

Truthfully, Harris realized that Storch had done his best to play his role appropriately and to be as fair as possible to all parties within his realm of authority, which was severely limited. So he felt sorry that the reviewers had characterized him so harshly.

"Under all these unique circumstances, we *agree* with Respondent's attorney that Dr. Herbert's pervasive conduct 'tainted' the proceedings and deprived Respondent of a fair hearing on the merits of the charges. Accordingly," Levin read, "the 'cumulative effect' of such prejudicial and outrageous conduct warrants a new hearing. There it is again, Bob! *A new hearing!* What are they thinking? Don't they know what I've already been through?"

"Warren, dear, *please* take it easy." Susan slid a bit closer to her husband and put her hand on his arm. "We don't know the outcome yet. Let's not let it get to us at this point. Please."

He sighed deeply once, then again. He nodded at Harris, passing the reader's mantle back to his attorney.

From what Harris read next, they saw that the group lambasted Sheehan for failure to control his witness, instead facilitating his abominable behavior, even referring to Herbert as "a twenty-four carat witness." Harris laughed. "That's pure gold!" he said. "But Herbert was pure crud! Okay, let me go on. 'Accordingly, a Respondent may attempt to prove on cross-examination that a witness had *motive* to falsify or gave unreliable testimony based upon bias or hostility.'" The Regents interpreted Sheehan's behavior as *encouraging* toward Victor Herbert's improprieties. "'He added the remarks that Respondent's attorney was displaying 'hysterical overreaction,' 'infantile rage,' and 'overt, unjustified emotionalism,' and 'harping' on the issue of the hearing atmosphere. He called Respondent's attorney an 'unguided missile,' 'thin-skinned,' and a 'showboat.' Wow," Harris told them, "they really didn't miss an innuendo or nasty invective in all of those thousands of pages. I'm *really* impressed!"

Levin grunted. "I'm only going to be impressed if they set me free," he said.

"That's an interesting way of putting it," Harris intoned. "Here, listen. They wrote more stuff on Sheehan. 'He responded to the arguments regarding the unfairness of the hearing by claiming that such arguments had 'no meaning' and were 'a waste of everyone's time,' 'bogus,' and 'absolutely ridiculous.' This inappropriate conduct by Petitioner's counsel *compounds the unfairness* resulting from Dr. Victor Herbert's testimony and 'destroys confidence in the fairness' of the hearing procedure and decision.' Good. I'm glad they're seeing those jokers for who they are. Okay, Warren, you're on next. It's Part Three, the Hearing Committee Decision."

Levin took the copy from Susan's hands and held it out so she could see it, as well. "NO!" he said, slamming his fist on the couch. "Oh, man! 'Additional grounds exist for recommending that this matter be remanded for *further proceedings*. Even if it were possible to cure the prejudice which has already occurred in this record and is reflected in the Hearing Committee's report, such report is flawed and should *not* be accepted as adequate for various reasons hereafter set forth. A *remand* would enable the issues raised in this matter to be resolved on a different record after an opportunity was provided for a hearing committee to evaluate and address them in accordance with applicable law and to explain its analysis in a clear and adequate fashion.' Remand again! *Remand*. Another decade of hearings. No!"

Harris ignored the outburst. "Do you know what I'm finding interesting?" he asked no one in particular, nor did he wait for an answer to his question. "Sheehan called the Hearing Committee's report one of the most *thorough* and *scholarly* documents he had seen in his years of work in his current capacity. And, actually, it was a damn good piece and a thorough one, too, as he said. These Regents, though, are looking at the report *after* reading transcripts of the proceedings. In doing so, they *aren't* finding that the whole Kangaroo bunch—the judge, the lawyer, the hired guns, the Commissioner—provided a fair 'trial,' so to speak. So everything in the report is gonna stick in their throats. I already see this, and we've only *started* reading their opinion of the panel's decision."

Levin blinked rapidly, considering Harris's words. He started reading again. The Regents had analyzed and dealt with each of the charges, drawing their own conclusions and supporting them with citations of case law. "'The Hearing Committee has *not* adequately or properly explained its conclusions that Respondent is guilty of practicing fraudulently and negligently. Accordingly, a remand is warranted to obtain a coherent analysis of the issues in dispute and of the elements of the charges. The Hearing Committee misapprehended the elements required to prove fraud pursuant to Education Law. We cannot discern from the Hearing Committee report what Respondent did or did not know regarding the medical value of his alleged tests and treatments. Fraud may *not* be predicated solely upon a licensee's attempt to provide 'new methods' of practice.' Hey, Bob," Levin said, suddenly, "maybe these guys *are* getting it."

He sounded a bit hopeful now, Susan noticed. She was working hard to contain her own anxiety over what a remand for additional hearings might mean for her and for Erika, for the whole family.

Levin continued to read, a bit more enthusiasm in his voice. "They're still talking about fraud," he explained, to get them back on track. "'It also may not be established simply on the basis that many persons do not believe in the efficacy of alternative medicine or in Respondent's philosophy in practicing medicine.' Good going!" he declared. "Keep it up. Nooooo," he said, looking at the next sentence. "'Thus, *a remand is warranted* because the Hearing Committee has not adequately demonstrated that the elements necessary to sustain a charge of fraud were proven. Without deciding or expressing a view as to the issue of whether Respondent's conduct constitutes fraud in the practice of medicine, we recommend that the Hearing Committee's findings and conclusions sustaining the fraud charges *not* be accepted and that a *new hearing be held*.'" The report further stated that the Regents believed that the panel's finding of fraud colored their decisions on the other charges. That was a big plus, they agreed, as they thought about that statement. Levin began to read through the charge of negligence. "'A requirement that a practice must be justified scientifically does not mean that Respondent *must* practice in a conventional manner in accordance with the modalities employed by a majority of practitioners.' That's *exactly* what I've been trying to tell them, Bob, and what you've been trying to say on my behalf. How come these people get it and the others didn't?'" No one had to answer. They had long ago figured out how high the stacked deck was from the very beginning of the hearings. The Regents decided that the panel hadn't met "its burden of proof with the negligence charge," instead complaining about Levin's lack of a hospital affiliation or his style of taking a medical history or his way of examining a patient. "'These conclusions and the findings that Respondent's 'overall care' did not meet the generally accepted minimal standard of patient care were beyond the scope of the negligence charges,'" is how they summed it up. "'In these proceedings to protect the welfare of the general public who deal with state licensed professionals, there is no requirement of any injury being suffered or any foreseeable risk of injury to a specific patient. We note this matter does *not* involve any charge or finding that any patient harm resulted from respondent's conduct.'" They went on to say that, "The Hearing Committee report does not adequately address the issue of the risk of harm to the public from Respondent's continued use of his methods."

The level of enthusiasm in Levin's voice increased as he read. Susan was glad to hear the change. Levin started where he had left off. "'Aside from the inadequacy of its findings of fact, the Hearing Committee did not respond to Respondent's assertion that no risk of harm is created by Respondent prescribing vitamin therapy to patients who seek preventive or alternative measures of treatment. The Hearing Committee *should* have discussed these assertions by Respondent and cited evidence which indicated a lawful basis for prohibiting Respondent from providing vitamin therapy to his patients.' How about that?" Levin asked, with a smile.

"Warren, that's just basic legal procedure," Harris told him. "Something these guys seem to have had no knowledge of, so it makes me wonder *who* guides the decision they finally write…often to the detriment of the doctor 'on trial.'"

Levin nodded his understanding and offered the document to Susan. "Where did you leave off?" she asked him. He pointed to the section. She covered the portion where they wrote about Levin's assertions regarding Chelation therapy and its widespread use in the United States and Europe being disregarded by the panel, because it was not a generally accepted technique in the medical community. "'In our opinion,'" read Susan, "'the Hearing Committee has not shown that it has looked to the *whole* community by which the applicable standard of care would be set.'" The group sat there, impressed because the Regents believed that excluding physicians who practice in a "parallel universe" from assisting in determining the standard of care was yet another error. Again, they spoke of a remand due to the panel's lack of a satisfactory analysis of the charges.

Susan continued into the fourth part of the report, "Evaluation of Evidence. 'Yet another ground exists for remanding this matter. The evidence upon which the Hearing Committee relied *cannot* be ascertained and, in any event, is not all contained within this record.'" The Regents seemed puzzled by the panel's admission of concern regarding Victor Herbert's objectivity, including their acknowledgement that his testimony was biased and inflammatory, yet their willingness to *accept* him as an expert, while refusing to accept *Levin's* experts. The Regents also seemed put off by Sheehan's failure to provide written answers to the fourteen, multi-part questions sent to both attorneys in a letter, since that questionnaire was only designed to assist the reviewers with understanding the Hearing Committee's report. Sheehan was obviously the best person to provide that assistance, yet he hadn't cooperated with their request.

After an animated discussion of the material read so far by Susan, she proceeded with the report. "'Respondent's attorney contended that the Hearing Committee acted improperly and overzealously when it attempted to fill a void in the evidence by resorting to its *own* expertise. Petitioner's attorney has not refuted Respondent's claim that the Hearing Committee obtained corroboration for Dr. Victor Herbert's testimony *by itself serving as an expert witness* for Petitioner.' I didn't know that," Susan said.

"Aha," said Levin. "The truth finally comes out!"

"Well, I knew that," Harris claimed.

"Okay," said Susan, "I actually have the proof, Bob. Listen. 'Respondent's attorney has criticized the Hearing Committee for basing its findings of fact both on Dr. Herbert's testimony, which is contrary to its own report and assessment, and on material *outside* the record, which is in violation of Respondent's right to due process.' Yes, Bob, you did know that," she proclaimed.

"Yes, and I called it 'a fatal flaw in the hearing,'" he told her.

"Now hear this," Susan told them, as she moved into the fifth part, "Fairness of Hearing." "'Petitioner contends that Respondent was afforded a *fair* hearing which was 'as near to a perfect hearing as is possible.' Sheehan's kidding, right?" she asked.

"That's what I always think where Sheehan's concerned. I say to myself, 'that guy's just *got* to be kidding.' Then I answer myself, saying, 'but I *know* he's not," Levin said, throwing his hands out helplessly.

"Oh, but see," Susan said, after she had read a bit further, "the Regents are saying, 'These proceedings were *very* unfair in several respects. The Hearing Committee improperly placed the onus on Respondent to demonstrate that he was *not* a 'quack.' Although Respondent's attorney was not allowed to ask Dr. Herbert certain questions about this subject, Respondent was placed in the position of having to *convince* the Hearing Committee that his 'unconventional' practices did *not* represent 'quackery.'"

Harris intervened at this point. "See, this is what I was trying to tell you from the time we knew that your case would be reviewed by the Regents. These guys are bright and fair-minded people with no agenda. They want to see justice done. The panel, on the other hand, was made up of people determined to do the work that the Commissioner of Health was determined to see done: to run all of the alternative medical practitioners out of New York State. That was why I *consistently* played to the Regents way in advance of them reviewing your case. I figured that, if they missed anything in the testimony itself, my extra-long objections—which Sheehan was probably correct in characterizing as 'testimony,'—would alert them to give extra consideration to your side of the case, Warren. It did the job, I think," Harris said, reaching his right hand over his left shoulder in a blatant attempt to pat himself on the back, causing the others to laughingly agree.

As Susan resumed reading, they understood that the Regents had even set parameters for a remand, stating that the panel should then "evaluate whether a reasonably prudent and diligent physician practicing in good faith would have had a sound scientific basis for using Respondent's methods in caring for patients. The question of the adequacy of Respondent's justification for his practices should *not* be resolved until Respondent obtains a fair hearing." The report went on to say that, "The Hearing Committee should not have required Respondent to prove that his practices had been conclusively established in scholarly recognized peer review literature," and the Regents supported that viewpoint by quoting several decisions by the United States Supreme Court.

"'Thus,'" Susan read, "'it was not sufficient for the Hearing Committee to find Respondent guilty on the basis that he has not proved the efficacy of his practices or has not met optimal rather than minimal standards.'"

Levin chuckled. "You know," he said, "I'm liking these guys more and more. Considering that the panel was made up of only *three* people, two of them physicians, and there were *five* Regents on the review team, I would think it would be *more* difficult for five people to reach unanimous agreement. I'm finding it very interesting that these five see things the same way consistently, and in my favor, no less. Of course, there is the issue of the remand that..."

"Warren, stop while you're ahead," Harris ordered. "Of course the Regents are going to agree. They're actually looking at case law, which is appropriate here. Those others were being more subjective than objective. They were making up the rules as they went along."

"I think Bob's right," Susan added. "Do you guys mind if I continue?"

The men nodded their assent. Susan was pleased as she read that the Regents *disagreed* with the panel's decision to both accept Victor Herbert's so-called expertise on nutrition and reject Linus Pauling's testimony. They were unhappy that the committee didn't allow patients to testify on Levin's behalf and only allowed a small number of testimonials from patients to be admitted into evidence. Due to those reasons, they believed Levin was denied the opportunity of defending himself against both the fraud and moral unfitness charges. Where negligence was concerned, the Regents were appalled that the panel had found Levin's defense to demonstrate "a cynical disregard for standard medical conventions." Also, the Regents seemed confused at the panel's willingness to accept Dr. Majid Ali as a credible witness for Levin yet *ignore the testimony* given by the doctor that there was *value* in the use of Chelation therapy for cardiovascular disease and that he found hair analysis to be a valid test.

As Harris took over from Susan, he read the section on "New Evidence," which referred to the numerous articles, some from peer-reviewed journals that Levin had gathered for Harris to submit on his behalf to the Regents. These articles were helpful in illustrating that Levin's treatment of patients was, as often stated by the defense during the hearings, ahead of its time and certainly tipped the scales in Levin's favor, refuting much of what the prosecution contended. The Regents wanted all of this information submitted to a new Hearing Committee for consideration on remand. "'At this time,'" Harris read, "'we have not evaluated whether the new evidence Respondent has offered us demonstrates the truth or falsity of the parties' positions. We are providing an opportunity on remand so that the record can be completed and technical issues can be understood.'" They went on to say that "hair analysis and DNA testing are examples of diagnostic procedures which have gained recognition in the courts due to the progress made in science in those areas." They even cited a case involving the *Frye* law and the New York Court of Appeals in 1979, where hair analysis met the high *Frye* standard of the scientific technique and had "gained general acceptance." The Regents wrote that, "The Hearing Committee did not analyze the appropriateness of Respondent's tests and treatments at the different times relevant in this matter."

Harris then moved on to a section called, "Unacceptable Findings," and all of them stated the same thing at once: "But they have constantly been talking about 'unacceptable findings' all along!"

"Yeah, but this section even has the name, so it should be pretty good," Harris said. The committee had listed dates and tests that were not included in the official charges, interestingly enough, and the Regents caught that. "Respondent may not be found guilty regarding conduct that he was *not charged* with having committed," they wrote.

"Warren, do you want to read the 'Disposition' section aloud?" Harris asked.

Levin thought it over for a moment. "No," he said somewhat hesitantly, "no. I'd rather you do it, Bob."

"Fine. 'In our unanimous opinion, a dismissal of the charges is *not* warranted. The merits of the charges so vigorously contested by the parties should be determined on remand.'"

"I knew it!" Levin said, under his breath.

"We take no position as to the decision which should be rendered on remand based upon the record that will be compiled at that time. Nevertheless, some of the charges should be dismissed at this time. The remand proceeding must *not* be burdened with any charges that do not have potential merit." The Regents then suggested that, since both the Hearing Committee and the Commissioner of Health had already dismissed a number of charges that those charges should not be brought forth on remand. Then the Regents Review Committee unanimously made its recommendations to the entire Board of Regents regarding which charges should even be *considered* on remand. They then directed that following the new hearing, the Hearing Committee should issue a report of its findings, conclusions, and recommendations—which "would not be inconsistent with the decision and Order remanding this matter as indicated."

"I'm at the final paragraph now," Harris said. "'The Commissioner of Health shall thereafter render his recommendation and this matter shall be reviewed by a Regents Review Committee and subsequently processed to the Board of Regents for final determination.'"

Levin laughed aloud. "Let me tell you something," he said to Harris and his wife. "While I certainly appreciate the fact that these gentlemen took the time to read thousands of pages of testimony, your extensive submission," he said, pointing to Harris, "along with its numerous attachments, and the lengthy answers you wrote to the fourteen questions with sub-sections that they asked you to respond to, and they did all of this in record time, then deliberated and picked pertinent cases and case law to cite when supporting our defense contentions, they're missing one or more *huge* pieces of this puzzle."

"What do you mean, Warren," Susan asked him.

"Susan, I did some figuring. Between salaries for the Hearing Officer and the state's attorney, plus fees and expenses for the committee members, payment to the witnesses they brought, and every other thing they had to pay for, I calculated that the state of New York has already spent in excess of one-million dollars to try to rip my medical license from my hands. God knows, it's cost us a *fortune* in legal expenses, as well. No offense to you, Bob," he added, quickly. "You've been more than fair to us." Harris nodded. "*Why* would they want to spend another fortune to continue this charade?" he asked. "Besides, where are *we* supposed to get the time and money to pay for them to start up from scratch again?"

Harris held his palm out to stop Susan from trying to answer the question. "Warren, look," he said, "you've 'won' this round, loosely speaking. These guys realized that you were dragged through a Kangaroo court that had made up its mind in advance what your penalty would be, and they want to give you a fair shake. I appreciate that. On the other hand, your point is well taken.

"I'll tell you this much, though, you're not finished, and this is not the final word. The *Board of Regents* will make the *final* determination. Who knows what they will decide? But on another note, I think I'll take a short trip to your restroom in preparation for my drive, by the light of the midnight moon, back to New York."

Susan laughed and began to gather up the water pitcher and glasses. Those would be washed in the morning, along with the other dinnerware.

"Thank you for coming here tonight, Bob," Levin said, warmly, as the lawyer prepared to leave. They shook hands.

Harris kissed Susan on the cheek. "I wouldn't have missed it. And, Susan, you outdid yourself with that lovely dinner. I guess I'm willing to go to any lengths for a good meal!" he joked.

"Well, let's hope we won't be having our next big dinner over another thick report on the status of my medical license," Levin said, handing Harris the copy his lawyer had come in with.

"From your mouth to God's ears, Warren," said Harris, as he had many times over the years of defensive argument. He walked down the driveway in the clear night air.

Levin sighed deeply as he closed the door. *If only my prayers could be transmitted by special messenger.*

The next morning, Harris placed a call to Peter Millock, Esq. Millock was chief counsel to the New York State Department of Health, and the man who Harris felt was quite unusual to find in government service. First of all, whenever they met, Harris would refer to Millock as "Harvard, Harvard." This was Harris's way of noting the fact that Millock had attended that university for both his undergraduate and law work. The relationship between the two men transcended humor. Harris felt that Millock was one of the few people he had ever met in government whose word could be trusted absolutely. This was no small thing since Harris had had more than one conversation with Millock, which could not have occurred if Harris could not trust him.

After the usual pleasantries the conversation focused on the fact of the results that Harris had achieved for Warren Levin. Harris was unusually modest and instead of, metaphorically bowing to the applause, he focused on only one thing. " Peter, Warren has suffered enough and I am exhausted. I'm calling because I hope that you are ready to put this matter to bed."

Millock replied that he would get back to Harris fairly soonand that he would see what the department's point of view was.

The next Millock called Harris and during a several minute telephone conversation related to Harris that the saga over the state versus Dr. Warren M Levin was over.

Harris did not call Levin immediately. Instead, he closed his eyes and felt moisture building up within them. Four years ago, this started as a routine case; one of dozens had going at any given time. However, as he began to understand the dimensions of the case and what the state was trying to do to Levin by what Harris perceived as an utter abuse of state authority, it had become a cause celebre for him. He had not only learned to like Levin as a person and as a Doctor, but also as a marvelous teacher. A crazy commissioner elected to abuse his power and authority, and set into motion a years' long series of events which kept Levin sitting on a pin for more than a decade, bankrupted him, and probably contributed to the onset of kidney cancer, stole a lot of joy of raising a young and beautiful and intelligent daughter, and the job of being able to relax with a beautiful and intelligent and absolutely devoted wife. In a strange sense, Harris felt as if the decision to restore Levin's life to sanity was a decision for her too. She had unquestioningly held him up when he was down, and endured one horrific situation after another with a care and grace that not many women would have endured or exhibited.

As for Harris himself, he experienced the unique feeling of having boxed a two-hundred round match and having won. Everything that Harris had experienced in life ideally suited him to defend Levin. His larger than life qualities, his irreverence, his encyclopedic knowledge and ability to retain newly acquired additions to that knowledge, his genuine sense of indignation combined with an absolute and utter commitment to his client almost certainly made him the right guy for the job.

After about a half an hour of rumination, Harris called Levin. "Warren, I have an answer for you as to what the future holds with regard to the health department. I have spoken with Peter Millock today, and he has told me that the department does not intend to prosecute you any further." Levin asked Harris whether he had gotten this in writing and Harris replied that he may or may not get it in writing; he didn't know, but he knew for a fact that Peter Millock's word could be deposited in the bank.

"Warren, don't sweat the details! It's over and you're free!" They failed to make you the

PRIME EXAMPLE.

POSTSCRIPT

This page is being written in March of 2011. Warren Meyer Levin, M.D. is in the practice of integrative medicine in northern Virginia. His wife Susan works with him much of the time.

Victor Herbert was, to the best of my understanding, never used by a disciplinary board again. He died several years ago.

Linus Pauling was 89 years of age when he testified. He died when he was 92 and left the world with the legacy that very few others in history have.

When Harris undertook the representation of Levin he told him that no matter what he did Levin would lose at the hearing level. The judge reported to the Commissioner of Health, the prosecutor reported to the Commissioner of Health and the panel was handpicked by the same commissioner. Harris told Levin that he perceived his job as making a record of such clarity that when the case went to the New York State Board of Regents for review they would reverse any damage sought to be done by the hearing panel. That, of course, is exactly what happened. After 6600 pages of testimony elicited over a three-year period the panel wrote a decision that would have been comical if it wasn't so tragic. They refused to acknowledge the testimony of Dr. Pauling because he was a PhD and not an M.D.. They ignored the fact that being the only person in world history to receive two individual Nobel prizes and having somewhere around 50 honorary doctorates including doctorates in medicine give a person credibility.

The regent's review resulted in the state Department of Health withdrawing the charges. The regents made a specific point of stating that they were ignoring Victor Herbert's testimony in chief.

Tragically, after years of lobbying the NYSDOH successfully appealed to the know very little legislature to remove the Regents from the disciplinary process. Since the Regents were the court of last resort which reversed or modified a large portion of the hearing committee decisions and the only agency to bring integrity to the process of disciplining physicians in NY State. What physicians are left with now is a choice. Appeal to the NYSDOH "review board,' another kangaroo process, or to the Appellate Division, Third Department in Albany. This court literally has a rubber stamp, stating that it will not substitute its opinion to conflict with the "expertise" of the DOH. What a perverse joke. For the past fifteen years there has been virtually no true due process in NY State for a physician accused of wrongdoing!

Perhaps the best way to end this page is to note that many of the things that Warren Levin was prosecuted for (perhaps I should say persecuted) are the standard of medical care in 2011.

BUY A SHARE OF THE FUTURE IN YOUR COMMUNITY

These certificates make great holiday, graduation and birthday gifts that can be personalized with the recipient's name. The cost of one S.H.A.R.E. or one square foot is $54.17. The personalized certificate is suitable for framing and will state the number of shares purchased and the amount of each share, as well as the recipient's name. The home that you participate in "building" will last for many years and will continue to grow in value.

Here is a sample SHARE certificate:

YES, I WOULD LIKE TO HELP!

I support the work that Habitat for Humanity does and I want to be part of the excitement! As a donor, I will receive periodic updates on your construction activities but, more importantly, I know my gift will help a family in our community realize the dream of homeownership. ***I would like to SHARE in your efforts against substandard housing in my community!*** *(Please print below)*

PLEASE SEND ME ___________ SHARES at $54.17 EACH = $ $____________

In Honor Of: ______________________________

Occasion: *(Circle One)* *HOLIDAY* *BIRTHDAY* *ANNIVERSARY*

OTHER: ______________________________

Address of Recipient: ______________________________

Gift From: _______________ ***Donor Address:*** ______________________________

Donor Email: ______________________________

I AM ENCLOSING A CHECK FOR $ $______________ PAYABLE TO HABITAT FOR HUMANITY OR PLEASE CHARGE MY VISA OR MASTERCARD *(CIRCLE ONE)*

Card Number ______________________________ Expiration Date: ____________

Name as it appears on Credit Card ________________ Charge Amount $ ____________

Signature ______________________________

Billing Address ______________________________

Telephone # Day ______________________ Eve ______________________

PLEASE NOTE: Your contribution is tax-deductible to the fullest extent allowed by law.

Habitat for Humanity • P.O. Box 1443 • Newport News, VA 23601 • 757-596-5553

www.HelpHabitatforHumanity.org

CPSIA information can be obtained at www.ICGtesting.com
Printed in the USA
BVOW041314150911

271194BV00003B/3/P